DEATH IN THE
PEACEABLE KINGDOM

DEATH IN THE PEACEABLE KINGDOM

CANADIAN HISTORY SINCE 1867 THROUGH MURDER, EXECUTION, ASSASSINATION, AND SUICIDE

Dimitry Anastakis

UNIVERSITY OF TORONTO PRESS

Library and Archives Canada Cataloguing in Publication

Anastakis, Dimitry, 1970– , author

Death in the peaceable kingdom: Canadian history since 1867 through murder, execution, assassination, and suicide/ Dimitry Anastakis.

Includes bibliographical references and index.

Issued in print and electronic formats.

ISBN 978-1-4426-3455-8 (bound).—ISBN 978-1-4426-0636-4 (pbk.).—ISBN 978-1-4426-0637-1 (pdf). —ISBN 978-1-4426-0638-8 (epub)

1. Canada—History—1867– . 2. Murder—Canada—History. 3. Executions and executioners— Canada—History. 4. Assassins—Canada—History. 5. Suicide victims—Canada—History. I. Title.

FC500.A53 2015   971.05   C2014-907128-0
                              C2014-907129-9

We welcome comments and suggestions regarding any aspect of our publications—please feel free to contact us at news@utphighereducation.com or visit our Internet site at www.utppublishing.com.

North America
5201 Dufferin Street
North York, Ontario, Canada, M3H 5T8

2250 Military Road
Tonawanda, New York, USA, 14150

ORDERS PHONE: 1–800–565–9523
ORDERS FAX: 1–800–221–9985
ORDERS E-MAIL: utpbooks@utpress.utoronto.ca

UK, Ireland, and continental Europe
NBN International
Estover Road, Plymouth, PL6 7PY, UK
ORDERS PHONE: 44 (0) 1752 202301
ORDERS FAX: 44 (0) 1752 202333
ORDERS E-MAIL: enquiries@nbninternational.com

Every effort has been made to contact copyright holders; in the event of an error or omission, please notify the publisher.

This book is printed on paper containing 100% post-consumer fibre.

The University of Toronto Press acknowledges the financial support for its publishing activities of the Government of Canada through the Canada Book Fund.

Printed in the United States of America.

For Jack and William

CONTENTS

ILLUSTRATIONS

ACKNOWLEDGMENTS

I would like to acknowledge and thank Natalie Fingerhut at the University of Toronto Press for approaching me with the idea of turning my second-year Trent University history course of the same name into a book. Thanks also go to the outside reviewers, who provided many very helpful suggestions; Karen Taylor for her detailed editing; Joan Sangster for reading over the manuscript; James Onusko, who fact-checked the entire book; Caroline Durand, Stuart Henderson, and David Wilson, who provided helpful tips; Ms. Colleen Carter and Mr. Glen Carter, who allowed me to tell the story of their uncle, Pte. Harold Carter, in the book; Victoria Yankou, who read many chapters, murderous moments, and tragic tales and provided feedback; Jeff Garner, who also provided feedback; and the Commune gang, who listened to numerous rants about all these deaths.

Most importantly, I would like to thank all the students at Trent University who took the course and provided feedback (whether they realized it or not) on the course and the book itself. This book was inspired by students and is for students and general readers. I hope they enjoy it as much as I enjoyed writing it.

Any errors are my own.

TIMELINE OF CANADIAN HISTORY

1857   Thomas D'Arcy McGee immigrates to Canada from the United States

1854–66   Reciprocity (free trade) Treaty between Canada and the United States

1861–65   United States Civil War

1864   Charlottetown Conference, Prince Edward Island

1866   London Conference, beginning of Fenian Invasions of Canada, Battle of Ridgeway

1867   Confederation: Dominion of Canada created from the Province of Canada (Canada West became Ontario and Canada East became Quebec) and Nova Scotia and New Brunswick; John A. Macdonald was prime minister, 1867–73, 1878–91

1868   D'Arcy McGee assassinated in Ottawa

1869   Patrick James Whelan, McGee's accused assassin, convicted and executed

1869–70   Louis Riel's Red River resistance; Thomas Scott murdered/ executed; Rupert's land sold to Canada; Manitoba and Northwest Territories join Confederation

1871   British Columbia joins Confederation

1873   Prince Edward Island joins Confederation; "Pacific Scandal," John A. Macdonald's government resigns

1876   Indian Act, leading to creation of Indian residential schools (1880s)

1879   National Policy of tariff protectionism implemented

1880   George Brown assassinated

1884–85   North-West Rebellion, Riel executed, as were eight aboriginals

1885   Canadian Pacific Railway completed

1896   Wilfrid Laurier elected prime minister, until 1911; Laurier "boom" period

1898   Yukon joins Confederation

1899–1902   Boer War

1905   Alberta and Saskatchewan join Confederation

1911   Robert Borden elected prime minister, until 1920

1914–18   First World War

1917   Conscription crisis; Private Harold Carter executed in France; Halifax Explosion

1919   Winnipeg General Strike, sympathy strikes across country

1921   William Lyon Mackenzie King elected prime minister, until June 1926, September 1926–30, 1935–48

1929–30   Start of the Great Depression

1931   Estevan strike and "riot"

1935   On-to-Ottawa Trek

1939–45   Second World War

1948   Louis St-Laurent elected prime minister, until 1957

1949   Newfoundland joins Confederation

1950–53   Korean War

1954–59   St. Lawrence Seaway completed

1957   John Diefenbaker elected prime minister, until 1963

1956–57   Suez Crisis, Lester B. Pearson wins Nobel Peace Prize

1961   National Indian Council created

1962   Trans-Canada Highway opened, fully completed in 1971, last executions in Canada, Ronald Turpin and Arthur Lucas

1963   Lester Pearson elected prime minister, until 1968

1965   Maple Leaf flag raised for first time, Canada–US auto pact created, until 2001

1965–66   Canada Pension Plan created

1966–72   Federal medicare program legislated; provinces and territories join in

1967   Expo 67, Canada's centennial

1968   Pierre Trudeau elected prime minster, until 1979, 1980–84; National Indian Brotherhood created

1970   October Crisis, Pierre Laporte assassinated

1973   OPEC oil embargo

1976   René Lévesque elected premier of Quebec, until 1985

1980   First Quebec referendum

1982   Charter of Rights and Freedoms, patriation of British North America Act (renamed the Constitution Act); Assembly of First Nations created

1984   Brian Mulroney elected prime minister, until 1993

1989   Free Trade Agreement with the United States, murder of 14 women at École Polytechnique, Montreal

1990   Meech Lake constitutional accord fails, Oka Crisis in Quebec

1993 Jean Chrétien elected prime minister, until 2003
1995 Death of Dudley George, Ipperwash, Ontario, second Quebec referendum
1999 Nunavut created
2006 Stephen Harper elected prime minister

INTRODUCTION

Canada was and is, despite appearances, sometimes a very violent country. Since Confederation in 1867, where this book starts, there have been innumerable assassinations, murders, executions, and suicides, not to mention invasions, uprisings, and terrorist attacks. This book does not intend in any way to glorify this violence but simply to reflect this reality back to readers and utilize a selection of these violent episodes to illustrate Canadian history.

Death in the Peaceable Kingdom is not a synthesis of Canadian history, however. Using violent death would be a rather distressing way to understand the whole of Canadian history, and an inaccurate one at that. The book, I hope, provides one interesting and provocative way to explore some of the more important themes, events, people, places, and issues in Canada's past and how they have evolved; there are many other approaches to understanding the country's evolution, as the many excellent recent books and studies of Canada's history will attest. At the same time, the book is not solely focused on the "deaths" that provide its inspiration; these episodes act as a helpful entrée into many of the broader themes of Canadian history.

Nor does this book purport to be a complete survey of Canadian history. With this type of approach, such a feat is impossible, and numerous incidents and topics are not included. *Death in the Peaceable Kingdom* is not a traditional textbook of post-Confederation history, nor a counter-narrative that necessarily challenges traditional treatments. The book is focused on telling the story of the social, cultural, political, and economic evolution of the nation-state of Canada. But it does attempt to address many, if not most, of the main currents that have shaped Canada's past since 1867, albeit using a unique approach that sometimes limits the subjects addressed. Canada still has its peaceable moments too, after all.

Though it is focused on various forms of "death," the book also takes some liberties with its main approach and the form of some of these episodes. Along with traditional chapters, the book offers short vignettes, "Murderous Moments" and "Tragic Tales"; these events, some snapshots, but others more extensive, provide illustrative points to broader themes and issues that both complement and often move beyond the main chapters. *Death in the Peaceable Kingdom* also contains a number of "Active History" exercises (a title borrowed from ActiveHistory.ca), including activities, assignments, and primary document analyses that readers (and teachers) may choose to use, emphasize, or ignore as they see fit. As well, it should be stated from the outset that some murders are not literally murders; some "slayings" are more metaphorical, taking licence with the notion of actual death. This is by design and by necessity because the book attempts to cover a vast range of occurrences in Canadian history that explain broader issues.

Indeed, some important issues and events are mentioned only in passing; others are specifically left undetailed, and there are obvious gaps in the book. The book is designed to prompt readers to ask about these events and issues, to go and "look things up," to question and to be curious. For all the murders, executions, assassinations, and suicides in the book, there were so many more cases, both famous and not so famous, that could have been used instead. And although this book is primarily meant as a non-traditional text, it is also intended to be a book that will interest general readers who simply wish to learn more about many of Canada's known and not-so-well-known violent episodes.

As a non-traditional approach to Canadian history, this book clearly builds upon the work of others. Many of the stories, cases, and incidents were taken from books, articles, and biographical entries created by other historians and writers, who have done wonderful work digging, detailing, and bringing to light these fascinating tales. Thanks to all these authors and historians, whose work is a testament to the depth and variety of Canadian writing and scholarship. There is an immense amount of wonderful Canadian history out there (beyond the very brief "Further Readings" provided at the end of each chapter), and I encourage students and readers to seek out these fascinating histories.

Finally, this book begins in 1867, long after contact between First Nations and white settlers. Nonetheless, the book recognizes from the outset that the events described take place upon lands that belonged to aboriginal peoples for thousands of years before North America was colonized.

PART ONE
OUR VIOLENT, BLOODY CONFEDERATION

The tale of Canada's emergence is not for the faint of heart. Creating the nation was a challenging, titanic, often brutish, and thoroughly violent affair—the country itself emerged from a maelstrom of terrorism and invasion, and the early Confederation period witnessed no less than one uprising, one outright rebellion, the assassination of two Fathers of Confederation, and the execution of another.

All of these events are intimately linked, as they form the core elements that help to explain how, when, and why Confederation appeared as it did. Shaping the idea of a new nation-state into a reality in the northern half of North America, albeit a state that was still closely tied to its British mother country, was not solely an act of imagination, nor simply a bloodless legal transaction. To understand the early Canadian political, economic, and social landscape is to recognize that the country's birth and first years were marked by violence and to comprehend the undeniable fragility of the young nation, a fragility seemingly threatened at nearly every turn.

CHAPTER ONE

THOMAS D'ARCY MCGEE, ASSASSINATED, OTTAWA, 1868

TERROR AND INVASION IN CONFEDERATION-ERA CANADA

Let us start by setting the scene: It is Tuesday, April 7, 1868, in Ottawa. The member of Parliament from Montreal, Thomas D'Arcy McGee, is walking down Sparks Street. Ottawa may be Canada's capital, but it is still a rough-and-tumble logging town of around 20,000 people. It's about two in the morning, and the street is deserted. Anyone who has been to Ottawa will know Sparks Street well; today, it is a pedestrian walkway, with quite a few pubs on the street. Sparks Street runs parallel to the beautiful and haunting gothic Parliament Hill government buildings; still under construction in April 1868, the Parliament buildings dominate the city, towering over what is still very much a small town.

McGee has just finished giving a long speech in the House of Commons on persuading Nova Scotians to remain in Confederation. In 1868, Nova Scotia was a major source of anti-Confederation sentiment and home to Canada's first separatist movement. McGee is a great orator, someone who can really pull off a speech, which is not surprising because he is a journalist and author. Born and raised in Ireland, McGee has a thick Irish accent; like so many other immigrants to Canada in the period, he still has strong ties to his homeland. For many of his Irish constituents in Montreal, he is a hero, having spent his life fighting for the Irish in Canada and around the world.

For others, however, McGee is a turncoat and a traitor.

McGee is considered a turncoat and a traitor because, over the last few years, his political views have changed dramatically. And, in North America in the 1850s and 1860s, politics is deadly serious. Indeed, just a few years earlier, the United States had a bloody civil war over politics that cost over 600,000 lives.

Yes, politics is deadly serious, and McGee has tangled with some of the era's most important issues. First, he has been outspoken on "the Irish Question," a phrase used to describe Britain's control of Ireland. Originally an advocate for Irish independence, McGee, since moving to Canada, has changed his tune. Now he argues that Ireland should, like Canada, remain part of the British Empire.

McGee's shifting Irish stance has made him serious enemies, especially the Fenian Brotherhood, an organization dedicated to freeing Ireland. Many Fenians live in the United States and are immigrants like McGee. McGee has called them a "disease" and a form of "political leprosy." Worse for McGee, US-based Fenians have actually launched attacks on Canada in an effort to force the British to give up Ireland, and they would like nothing better than to see him dead.

McGee has also spoken out about religion, another lightning-rod issue. McGee is Catholic, the single largest Christian denomination yet a minority in Canada. In the past, he was no fan of the Catholic Church, blaming it for the failure of Irish independence. This stance also created enemies for McGee, though he has recently made peace with the Church. But memories are long. Many people are unhappy with McGee, over both the Irish Question and religion.

Finally, McGee strongly favours Confederation. He actually is a Father of Confederation, and, although his political fortunes are on the decline in April of 1868, he is still a powerful figure. He is, for instance, a good friend of John A. Macdonald, the Conservative prime minister of Canada. Macdonald and McGee are friends even though one is Conservative, Protestant, and Scottish and the other is Liberal, Catholic, and Irish. They are both in favour of Confederation, both against the Fenians, and both happen to have a fondness for drinking—they imbibe together regularly.

Macdonald has warned McGee that his enemies would like to kill him for changing his views on the Irish Question. In fact, because of the Fenian threat to Canada, Macdonald created a spy network to infiltrate the Fenian organization. Macdonald's spies have reported that the Fenians have offered $1,000 in gold to anyone who will kill McGee. In response, legend has it that, just a few weeks before April 1868, McGee chillingly told a correspondent, "There is no danger of my being converted into a political martyr. If ever I were murdered, it would be by some wretch who would shoot me from behind."[1]

Back on Sparks Street, McGee is about to head upstairs to his rooming house. McGee turns to unlock and open the door. He hears a noise, but, before he can even turn around, a man strides up behind him, puts a gun to the back of his neck, and pulls the trigger. The bullet goes through McGee's neck, out through his mouth, and embeds itself in the wall. McGee crumples to the ground on the open doorstep, blood spurting everywhere, his teeth shattered and sprayed all over the hallway. The assassin disappears into the Ottawa night.

---

1   Though this famous quotation is attributed to McGee by T.P. Slattery, who wrote *The Assassination of D'Arcy McGee* (Toronto: Doubleday, 1968), there is little evidence that he actually said such a thing.

News of the shooting spreads like wildfire across the town. A few blocks over, John A. Macdonald is quickly told. He races to McGee's boarding house and finds his friend lying in the street, covered in blood. John A. cradles McGee's head, checking for vital signs, but he knows that his friend is dead. He has McGee's body taken into the house and then goes to the newspapers to make the announcement.

The next day, in the House of Commons, Macdonald delivers an emotional tribute to McGee before the hushed assembly. It is one of many across the land. In Ottawa, Montreal, and Toronto, flags are lowered. Expressions of grief and anger pour in from all parts of the new nation. People are shocked, disgusted, outraged. Ottawa's mayor offers a $2,000 reward for the capture of McGee's assassin. McGee's Montreal funeral prompts a massive outpouring of grief. *The New York Times* reports that "80,000 people were on the streets" of Montreal, many of them McGee's Irish brethren. "Thousands of people on the sidewalks"

Figure 1.1 *"McGee," by William Kurelek, 1976, Art Gallery of Ontario*

weep as the funeral procession passes.[2] McGee is survived by his wife and two young daughters.

The murder of Thomas D'Arcy McGee is Canada's first political assassination, and a pivotal event for the young country. Yet what does McGee's assassination really represent? What can we learn about the era surrounding the birth of Canada by examining the death of one of its founders?

British North America in the 1860s

When McGee arrived in 1857, just ten years before Confederation, the scattered colonies of British North America (BNA) were small and disconnected. Aside from these colonies, until the 1860s, the Hudson's Bay Company (HBC) controlled the vast majority of the land, called Rupert's Land. The HBC, founded in 1670 and now known as The Bay department store, was originally a fur-trading company. The massive area supposedly overseen by the HBC was populated by First Nations, traders, Métis, and a few white settlers.

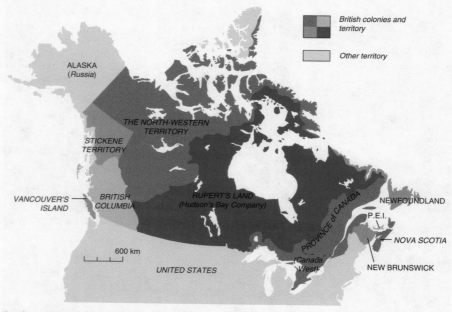

Figure 1.2 *British North America in the 1860s*

Reprinted by permission of *Canadian Geographic*, canadiangeographic.ca

---

2   *The New York Times*, April 14, 1868.

The economy of BNA was largely based on staple resources: furs, fish, farming, and forestry. Probably over 80 per cent of people were involved in this kind of work. Whatever British North Americans didn't consume, they exported. At the same time, however, the colonies were experiencing early industrialization. Some small-scale factories in Montreal and Toronto built horse carriages or farm tools. By the 1860s, railways were also being built in the colonies, and the financial speculation surrounding their success was a growing part of the economy.

British North America was very rural. Of its approximately 3.4 million people, only about 700,000 lived in cities or towns, and only Montreal had a population of around 100,000. About a million citizens of European origin were French, and most of the remainder were British, including approximately 700,000 English, 500,000 Scots, and over 800,000 Irish fellows of McGee's. Beyond that, BNA was very multicultural, a cacophony of different languages and a kaleidoscope of different races: there were over 200,000 Germans, 30,000 blacks, at least 120,000 aboriginals, and thousands of others from all around the globe.

This diversity was fuelled by immigration, mostly from Western Europe. When McGee arrived in Montreal in 1857, he was one of about 22,000 other migrants to the country. In the 11 years after he came to Canada, another 175,000 people had also immigrated. This great immigration boom between the 1840s and the 1860s was largely fuelled by the Irish Potato Famine of the 1840s. The famine wiped out the crops of Ireland, caused widespread starvation, and forced at least one million to flee the island, including McGee.

Religion played a very important role in British North America; its institutions dominated the social and cultural life of ordinary people. In Quebec, the Catholic Church provided social connections to all French and Irish adherents and offered not just religious services but also schools, hospitals, and welfare societies. Outside of Quebec, Protestants were dominant, though there was a distinct hierarchy, with Anglicans usually at the top. In Ontario, the Protestant and strongly anti-Catholic Orange Order was a powerful economic and political society. John A. Macdonald himself was a member.

Religion also dominated education. Indeed, religious schooling was very controversial. As a Father of Confederation, McGee fought to include a protection for Catholic schooling, one that explains why, to this day, Ontario, for example, has a public system (once Protestant schools) and a separate, Catholic system. As to schooling itself, it was difficult to get to school and expensive. In the 1860s, textbooks were almost non-existent, teachers poorly paid, and schooling very basic. University education was for the well-off, and there were only a few universities; Toronto started one in 1827, Queen's opened in 1841, and McGill was established in 1821. Halifax had universities too, as did Catholics in Quebec.

Both religious and educational differences reflected the class divisions within society. There was a small, wealthy, educated elite (often Anglican), but the vast majority of the population was composed of farmers or working-class people.

Because of industrialization, there was an emerging bourgeois class composed of, for example, merchants, doctors, lawyers, small businessmen, and journalists, like McGee. Work and family organization was based on the "family economy": work divided along gendered lines, usually on farms, as most people lived on farms. In cities, an emerging wage economy made gender roles blurrier because both women and men worked for wages; the men worked in factories, but women took in lodgers and boarders, did house cleaning, or sewed, all for pay. Young children worked too.

Thus, emerging industrialization and urbanization, requiring women to work in order to survive, challenged the prevailing notion of "separate spheres," the idea that men should be in the public sphere, working and in politics, while women should be in the private sphere, at home and raising children. This issue becomes far more prevalent in the next few decades as people arguing both for and against the notion of "separate spheres" claim equal rights for women, particularly the right to vote. In 1867, women did not have the right to vote; only men with property did. This is not yet a major political issue; in the 1850s and 1860s, other, sometimes violent, political controversies shaped McGee's world when he arrived in Canada.

Political Problems within the Colonies

Five important events help to explain the politics that McGee found when he came to Canada. First, in 1763 the great imperial battle over North America between the British and the French ended with the Treaty of Paris. With their defeat on the Plains of Abraham, the French ceded all their territory in mainland North America to the British, including Quebec. This meant that, after the 1760s, a few British soldiers and settlers controlled about 70,000 French colonists, whose families had been in Quebec for nearly a century already.

Second, this dynamic changed after the American Revolution. Despite the American defeat of the British in 1783 and the creation of the United States, thousands of British North Americans from the Thirteen Colonies remained loyal to Britain. Over time, about 50,000 settled in Nova Scotia and Quebec. This wave of new immigrants included black and First Nations soldiers who had fought with the British (Thayendanegea, also know as Joseph Brant, a Mohawk after whom the town Brantford is named, is a notable example). This wave saw the creation of Upper Canada (now Ontario) in 1791, where many of the new immigrants settled.

The arrival of so many English speakers eventually caused economic and political conflict, particularly in Quebec (also known as Lower Canada). There, many French speakers were unhappy at being under the rule of the English. Some were unhappy in Upper Canada, too, where there were demands for a more representative form of government; the two colonies were dominated by a tight group of elites, the "Family Compact" in Ontario and the "Château Clique" in Quebec.

Demands for governmental changes were rejected by the British, resulting in the Rebellions of 1837, a third important event. These armed uprisings in Quebec and Upper Canada were eventually violently put down by the British. In Quebec, the situation was far more serious, with casualties in the hundreds, and this uprising was partly based upon French versus English ethnic differences. In Upper Canada, it was an effort to overthrow the British to bring in more representative democracy or republicanism, similar to the political system in the United States.

In the end, the British sent over a representative to study the problems of the colonies. Lord Durham's *Report on the Affairs of British North America* (1839), a fourth important event, suggested that the best way to get rid of colonial problems was to assimilate the French. So, instead of retaining the two provinces created in 1791, namely, Upper and Lower Canada, the British merged the two in 1840. The British North America Act, 1840 (more commonly called the Act of Union) was proclaimed February 10, 1841. It created the new Province of Canada, putting French and English in the same colony and with the same government.

The merger also meant a few other things: there would be equal representation between the two regions; initially, English was made the sole language of the Parliament, though this was challenged by French-speaking representatives and French was eventually recognized; and the new united province would now have responsible government composed of elected representatives instead of an executive appointed by the British.

A final issue was the problem of "political deadlock" that the united Province of Canada faced by the 1850s and 1860s. When the British created the new province in 1840, the French in Quebec (Lower Canada) outnumbered the British in Ontario (Upper Canada). Making the representation of the two regions equal was designed, therefore, to take power away from the French: If each region had 40 representatives, but one region had one million as opposed to 800,000 people, as was the case in Lower and Upper Canada, respectively, the more populous region would be losing out. That was the state of affairs in 1840. However, by the 1860s, immigration growth in Upper Canada had reversed the situation. Now, English speakers were in greater numbers; and they did not like the fact that the minority French had equal power.

The colony was also deadlocked because the two regions argued about how schooling should be funded (Protestants in Ontario did not want to fund Catholic schools in Quebec), paying for the militia (French Canadians did not really want to pay for a militia, which they saw as a reminder of the Conquest), and over infrastructure costs, such as railways and canals. Because the two sides were essentially equal, there was practically an election and a new government every two or three years, and nothing was getting done because no one party or coalition could gain the confidence of Parliament. Consequently, policies were not being pushed forward.

Civil Wars, Fenians, and Discontent

McGee was also keenly aware of the external political pressures facing British North America in this period and of how they also help to explain why the colonies eventually came together to form the new political union of Canada. The first of these is the annexationist movement. Since its creation in 1789, many in the United States believed in "Manifest Destiny," the idea that Canada should eventually be part of the American Republic. In fact, the original US Constitution, the 1781 Articles of Confederation, even called for Canada's eventual absorption. During the 1840s, there was a revived movement to have BNA annexed (i.e., taken over) by the United States. This vibrant movement had a strong Montreal chapter, as many business leaders there thought that their best interests lay in joining the United States.

But many British North Americans were against the annexationist idea. Remember, many people in BNA were loyalist descendants who had left the United States in the first place because they did not want to be part of the American Republic. Moreover, the War of 1812 was still within the living memory of many British North Americans, who bitterly recalled the American invasions of the colonies. Yet the annexationist movement did illustrate an external threat to the country's survival, and that joining the United States was a serious possibility for many.

Another external issue was the US Civil War—an immense, tragic conflict. By 1864, the North (the Union) had defeated the South (the Confederates), after the slave-owning Southern states had tried to break away from the United States to form their own country. The war had a direct impact on BNA in two ways. First was the St. Albans Raid. In 1864, Confederate soldiers operating from Quebec attacked Vermont. This attack caused a strong anti-Canadian reaction in the United States, and it caused the US government to require that all persons from BNA hold a passport. Second, the Civil War affected relations between the United States and Great Britain. During the war, Britain had remained neutral, infuriating many Northerners who believed that British neutrality meant tacit support of the South. At war's end, with the North victorious, the British were in a difficult position. Given that the United States possessed a massive, well-trained, and battle-tested army and that the closest British possessions were the colonies of BNA, there was concern that the United States would invade Canada. After all, they had already done so twice, once during the Revolutionary War and again during the War of 1812.

Consequently, the British wanted to loosen their ties to BNA as much as possible. The British started to suggest to Canadians that they might want to go their own way but retain a strong link to the British Empire. At the same time, the British were happy to cut back on the expense of maintaining military garrisons in BNA. In the 1860s, partly because of the Civil War, the British actively encouraged politicians in BNA to start thinking about forming their own, new country.

The US Civil War had another impact on BNA, which occurred after the war ended. The Fenian Raids are the third external factor to keep in mind. Although the United States itself did not invade Canada, there actually were some invasions from US soil, launched by Irish-American immigrants who had recently served in the Union army. The Fenian supporters of an independent Irish republic were the same people McGee had so upset by switching his view to one against Irish independence. With thousands of trained Irish fighters at the ready, the Fenians now saw their opportunity. They would hit the British in North America and try to force them to grant Irish independence by attacking Canada; their plan was to invade and conquer Canada and force the British to give up Ireland in exchange.

By the mid-1860s, thousands of Fenians had organized along the border, and, over the next few years, they launched attacks into Canada, before and after Confederation. The Fenian Raids, called "the Green Terror" after the green uniforms worn by these Irish supporters, caused fear and distress for thousands of Canadians. In most instances, the invaders were repelled, but the attacks persisted until the early 1870s and included a major skirmish in Niagara in 1866.

The Fenian Raids illustrated a number of important things to the people of BNA. First, the threat of invasion was real, as the US government largely tolerated the Fenians (in part as retribution for the St. Albans Raid). Second, although the British did provide some protection, the home-grown militia had to be counted on to protect the interests of BNA. Third, a feeling of connectedness among the citizens of BNA was starting to emerge as colonists in all regions were being attacked by the Fenians, from Canada West to the Maritime colonies. The Fenian Raids were an external threat that played a large part in bringing the colonies together.

The raids are obviously also important for the story of Thomas D'Arcy McGee. Perhaps more than anything, McGee speaking out against the Fenians and their attacks led to his assassination. Unsurprisingly, given the harsh realities of the volatile politics in this period, the man convicted for McGee's assassination, a tailor by the name of Patrick James Whelan, was a suspected Fenian.

Finally, some economic changes were also important in this period. In 1846, Britain ended mercantilism, its trade system that provided a guaranteed market for colonial goods, particularly wheat, but, in exchange, made the shipping and marketing of colonial goods the monopoly of British merchants and shippers. British North America was thus a market for manufactured products built in the United Kingdom and a supplier of staples, raw materials for British industrial production. Although mercantilism was intended to benefit the British economy, it did provide protection for early economic development in Canada. Its ending caused severe economic hardship in the 1840s and early 1850s, and the politicians and business leaders of the colonies sought out a new solution. In 1854, they signed a trade agreement with the United States called the Reciprocity Treaty (reciprocity means free trade), which led to a boom for the economy of BNA. It allowed for the free exchange of goods, without tariffs (taxes put on goods coming in at the border). Exports of raw materials such as wheat, fish, and other goods, previously sent to Britain, now went to the United States.

The Reciprocity Treaty led to good times, until the Americans cancelled it in 1866, in part because the US government was unhappy with British actions during the Civil War and with the St. Albans Raid. The end of the Reciprocity Treaty was a big blow to the economy of BNA. With no protected outlet for their goods, no reciprocal trade agreement with either Britain or the United States, the politicians and business leaders of BNA started thinking that they might start to trade more among themselves. But to do so would require an agreement among all the provinces of BNA—and perhaps even a new political arrangement.

Confederation

To understand Confederation, we need to look briefly at John A. Macdonald, one of its key players. Like McGee, Macdonald was an immigrant to British North America whose Scottish family settled in Kingston in 1820. At 15, Macdonald was articling as a lawyer, and he quickly made a name for himself in the legal profession. Like McGee, he was one of the emerging bourgeois class of people not born from wealth.

By the 1840s, Macdonald was active in politics and business. He was energetic, witty, and shrewd. Macdonald won election as a Conservative in 1844. Being a Conservative, or Tory, in the nineteenth century was different from being one today: Conservatives were supporters of state religion but also advocates of state intervention in the economy and of a strong centralized state. Compare these Tories with nineteenth-century Liberals, also known as Reformers or Grits, who called for the separation of church and state, thought that the market and the economy should be unregulated, and were determined that government should be small. Today's Conservatives (Tories) and Liberals (Grits) have largely traded viewpoints: Tories are much more individualistic and want to see a reduced state role in the economy; Liberals have a more positive view toward state intervention and collective approaches to governance.

In any event, Macdonald's 1844 election marked the beginning of a long career. In the 1850s and 1860s, he was a key politician in the Province of Canada. Yet the problem of political deadlock kept coming up. Eventually, after much political wrangling, a solution emerged when George Brown, the leader of the Reformers and Macdonald's political enemy, suggested to Macdonald that they put aside their differences and form a "Great Coalition" to propose a grand new idea for the governance of BNA: a new, federal nation.

Macdonald was initially reluctant as he was not in favour of federalism, where two levels of government, provincial and national, coexisted. Provincial demands, he thought, could lead to secession and war, as had happened in the United

States. Macdonald eventually agreed, realizing that there was no way out of the malaise gripping the government. But he also proposed that Canada invite all the British North American colonies to join the scheme. Since the Atlantic colonies were considering their own union, Macdonald and the Canadians were invited to present their plans at a meeting in Charlottetown, PEI, in 1864. This meeting set the colonies on the road to Confederation. Macdonald was a key figure in hammering out an agreement among the colonies of BNA for a new federal state.

There is no need to detail what finally led to Confederation on July 1, 1867. But a few things about the British North America Act are important to keep in mind. Though the government it created was a federal one, the act called for a strong central government, with weaker provinces. It included provisions that reflected the concerns of the various provinces (e.g., Quebec's demand for its own legislature, language protection, and the continuation of its own legal system). The BNA Act also included Section 93, inserted at D'Arcy McGee's insistence, allowing for minority religious education (that is, separate education for Protestants in Quebec and for Catholics outside of Quebec). The provision seemed to solve a major stumbling block on the road to Confederation.

A new nation had been created, and there were celebrations in many towns and cities across the Dominion of Canada, as it was officially named. Many felt the creation of this "new nationality," as McGee himself called it, was a glorious first step in the country's history. But Macdonald, McGee, and the young nation still faced challenges. Some in Quebec were unhappy about the new arrangements, as were many Nova Scotians. Aboriginals had no say in the Confederation agreement. There were also economic challenges. With no more mercantilism and no trade agreement with the United States, Canada had to do something to secure its economic future. There were geographic challenges, too. Clearly, these challenges would shape the new country's next 20 or 30 years.

Fragile Nation: The Meaning of McGee's Assassination

What does McGee's assassination tell us? McGee's murder tells us much about the politics of the period. It clarifies elements of Confederation itself, but also it shows just how profoundly international issues and events shaped the new nation, from the Irish Question and the Irish Potato Famine to the American Civil War. These and other factors all had a hand in explaining why someone killed D'Arcy McGee. McGee was an international figure who had lived in Ireland, the United States, and Canada. He had taken part in the Irish independence movement, had turned his back on it, and had then became a major player in North American politics after first arriving in the United States in the 1840s and then coming to Canada in the 1850s. His attacks on the Fenians and his support for Confederation were directly responsible for his death, but his assassination also provoked an outburst against the Fenian agitation, and McGee himself became a martyr of Confederation, helping to cement the country together. His death became a unifying moment in a country that faced daunting challenges.

The assassination of McGee also tells us much about the people who lived in that period, not just the politicians, but ordinary people. Like so many others in the 1850s and 1860s, McGee was an immigrant to Canada and one who was shaped by his ethnicity, his religion, and his social and economic background. As McGee was a Catholic and a member of the Irish minority in the new country, his life gives us insight into the views of ordinary people.

Finally, the assassination reflects the very real fragility of the young country. Certainly, this is one thing that we can understand: Confederation at the time of McGee's assassination faced serious challenges. His death was symbolic in that it laid out how fragile the country was, faced with threats from the south; with challenges to stitch together a country geographically, politically, and economically; and even with Nova Scotian separatism, which Macdonald was eventually able to quell.

In the speech in Parliament McGee gave on the night he was killed, he addressed the challenge represented by Nova Scotian separatism and defended the idea of a united, federal Canada:

> Our friends [in Nova Scotia], Sir, need have no fear, but that Confederation will ever be administered with serene and even justice. To its whole history, from its earliest inception to its final triumphant consummation, no stigma can be attached, no stain attributed. Its single aim from the beginning has been to consolidate the extent of British North America with the utmost regard to the independent powers and privileges of each Province, and I, Sir, who have been, and who am still, its warm and earnest advocate, speak here not as the representative of any race, or of any Province, but as thoroughly and emphatically a Canadian, ready and bound to recognize the claims, if any, of my Canadian fellow subjects, from the farthest east to the farthest west, equally as those of my nearest neighbour, or of the friend who proposed me on the hustings.[3]

Sadly, McGee would not live to see the country survive all these threats, but his death was not in vain. Like the Fenian Raids, McGee's assassination may have represented the challenges the young country faced, but his murder ironically helped to strengthen the country he had come to love so much.

---

3   Canada, *House of Commons Debates*, 1st Parliament, 1st session, vol. 1 (Monday, April 6, 1868): 471. Available from the Library of Parliament: http://parl.canadiana.ca/view/oop. debates_HOC0101_01/1?r=0&s=1.

Further Reading

Cross, Michael. "The Shiner's War: Social Violence in the Ottawa Valley in the 1830s." *Canadian Historical Review* 54, no. 1 (Spring 1973): 1–26. http://dx.doi.org/10.3138/CHR-054-01-01.

Martin, Ged. "John A. Macdonald and the Bottle." *Journal of Canadian Studies / Revue d'études canadiennes* 40, no. 3 (2006): 162–85.

Shanahan, David. "Young Ireland in a Young Canada: Thomas D'Arcy McGee and the New Nationality." *British Journal of Canadian Studies* 12, no. 1 (1997): 1–8.

Toner, Peter M. "The 'Green Ghost': Canada's Fenians and the Raids." *Éire-Ireland* 16, no. 4 (Winter 1981): 27–47.

Wilson, David. "The Fenians in Montreal, 1862–68: Invasion, Intrigue, and Assassination." *Éire-Ireland* 38, no. 3–4 (Fall/Winter 2003): 109–33.

Wilson, David. *Thomas D'Arcy McGee*, Vol. 1, *Passion, Reason, and Politics, 1825–1857*. Montreal: McGill-Queen's University Press, 2008.

Wilson, David. *Thomas D'Arcy McGee*, Vol. 2, *The Extreme Moderate, 1857–1868*. Montreal: McGill-Queen's University Press, 2012.

ACTIVE HISTORY: QUESTIONS TO CONSIDER

1. What was it like to be of Irish descent in Canada in the period from the 1830s to the 1860s? What were the main influences in Irish life?

2. How did politics from the homeland influence the Irish in Canada, particularly political leaders such as McGee?

3. Why did the Fenian Raids fail? Was it because of political infighting? Poor strategy and preparation? Did the Catholic Church play a role?

4. Why didn't Irish Canadians join the fight? What role did gossip and "news" play in spreading the Fenian fear?

5. How were the Fenian fears used by politicians in Canada, either to influence Confederation or for local purposes such as in PEI?

6. Was McGee a martyr of Confederation or a symbol of Irish failure in North America?

MURDEROUS MOMENT
PATRICK JAMES WHELAN, EXECUTED, OTTAWA, 1869

Justice Delivered or Racial Profiling and Sham Trials in an Earlier Era of Terror?

What happened to D'Arcy McGee's alleged assassin, Patrick James Whelan?

McGee, an enemy of the Fenians, had been killed on Sparks Street after giving a speech in the House of Commons. Unsurprisingly, many people immediately suspected that the assassin was a Fenian. Remember, 1868 was in the midst of the Fenian attacks, and, in this fearful atmosphere, just about anyone sympathetic to the cause of Irish nationalism was suspected of being a potential Fenian.

After McGee's assassination, the Ottawa police embarked on a massive manhunt, fuelled by a $2,000 reward offered by Ottawa Mayor Henry J. Friel for the capture of McGee's killer. Within two days, Patrick James Whelan was arrested for the murder (along with dozens of other suspected Fenians). His name had been given to police by one of John A. Macdonald's spies. The police tracked Whelan to his hotel and found with him a Fenian newspaper and a revolver, which, the police stated, had been fired within the last 48 hours. Whelan himself fit the profile of McGee's suspected killer. Born in Dublin, he was 28 years old, having come to Canada in 1865. He was known as a Fenian sympathizer, and he was in the wrong place at the wrong time.

In September of 1868, Whelan's very unusual and high-profile trial began. Queen's Counsel James O'Reilly, an Irish Catholic, took the lead as chief prosecutor. Halfway through the trial, Prime Minister John A. Macdonald himself showed up. Many observers remarked that Macdonald's appearance was meant to send a message to the jury to bring in a "guilty" verdict. After all, Macdonald was the minister of justice, prime minister, and a friend of McGee's.

The evidence presented at the trial itself was something of a sham. The only eyewitness to the crime, a French Canadian who was walking down Sparks Street around the time of the killing, told the court that McGee was tall and Whelan was short; the opposite was actually true. People speculated that he was either totally confused or a liar after the reward money.

The trial was punctuated by threats of violence against both sides. The police officer who arrested Whelan received death threats, supposedly from the Fenians; on the other hand, anonymous notes left for the authorities stated that if Whelan were not found guilty, he would be lynched by a mob. Some people thought that members of the Protestant Orange Order left these notes. Public pressure was immense to bring someone to justice, and, again, Whelan fit the profile.

Yet there was no direct evidence linking Whelan to the crime; it was all circumstantial. Nevertheless, Whelan was found guilty. When the verdict was read, Whelan declared to the court that,

> I am here standing on the brink of my grave, and I wish to declare to you and to my God that I am innocent, that I never committed this deed . . . I never took that man's blood. I never owed him spite. . . . I am accused of being a Fenian. Every Irish Roman Catholic has to stand just the same imputation. Any man is welcome in England to say what he likes, but if a poor starved Irishman dares to lift his voice in favour of Irish liberty, he is seized, charged with assassination, hanged,

drawn and quartered, or sent in chains to an English goal [jail], to a terrestrial hell—one of the living damned. . . . All that sentence, My Lord, cannot make me Guilty.[4]

When Whelan's lawyers tried to appeal to the Supreme Court of Canada, Macdonald ensured that the execution went ahead before any hearing could be granted. Whelan maintained his innocence and even told his Ottawa jailers that he knew who had shot McGee. But his protestations were too little, too late. In one of the last public executions in Canada, Whelan was hanged in front of 5,000 spectators on the grounds of the Ottawa jail on February 11, 1869. Before being hanged, Whelan declared, "I forgive all parties who have injured me, and ask forgiveness from any one I may have injured. God save Ireland, and God save my soul."[5]

Macdonald ensured that Whelan's body was not given to his family, which Whelan had been promised; instead Macdonald had the body buried in an unmarked grave. Macdonald wanted to make sure that Whelan did not become a martyr and to avoid having Whelan's gravesite become a shrine for Fenianism. Though neither happened, Whelan's declaration of "God save Ireland" became a rallying cry for Fenians in North America.

In the years after the trial and execution, Whelan's family maintained his innocence. For generations, they held that he had been framed for the murder. One of the key pieces of evidence used against Whelan was the gun in his hotel room. But, in 1973, more than a century after the trial, forensic tests done upon the gun proved inconclusive as to whether or not it was the firearm that killed McGee.

Then, in 2002, the family went to Ottawa, dug up Whelan's remains, and had him reburied in Montreal beside his wife—in the same cemetery as D'Arcy McGee. Whelan was finally given proper Catholic burial rites, 133 years after his hanging. Just a few years later, in 2005, the gun that was allegedly used in the assassination was put up for auction and purchased by the Canadian Museum of Civilization in Ottawa for $105,000.

It is a fascinating story. In the end, the assassination of McGee and the Fenian raids proved pivotal to Canada's creation. Whelan was executed, but his guilt or innocence is still not certain. Yet, by reading about McGee and Whelan, we learn much about the atmosphere that existed in the years just after Confederation and we understand the significance of the Fenians, the Irish Question, and the battle between Catholics and Protestants in the formation of Canada.

---

4   From *Trial of Patrick J. Whelan for the murder of the Hon. Thomas d'Arcy McGee: Reported for the* Ottawa Times *by George Spaight, Esq., and revised by a barrister in attendance* (Ottawa: G.E. Desbarats, 1868), 86, 88. Available from https://archive.org/details/cihm_23543.

5   *The British Colonist,* February 13, 1869, p. 3.

CHAPTER TWO

THOMAS SCOTT, EXECUTED OR MURDERED? FORT GARRY, WINNIPEG, 1870

THE RED RIVER RESISTANCE AND THE POLITICS OF WESTWARD EXPANSION

These facts are indisputable: On a snowy March 4, 1870, Thomas Scott was put to death by the provisional government of the Red River Colony outside the walls of Fort Garry, in what is now Winnipeg, Manitoba. The means of execution was firing squad, as a blindfolded Scott was lined up against the Hudson's Bay Company fort wall and shot by at least six riflemen. The charge against Scott? Insubordination.

It is also indisputable that Thomas Scott did not die after the first volley of bullets hit but that a "coup de grace," or a final shot in the head at close range, was required as Scott lay writhing on the ground. This shot was administered by someone, though it is not certain exactly who.

These facts, too, are irrefutable: Thomas Scott was an Orangeman from Ireland, that is, a Protestant born in English-controlled Northern Ireland, in about 1842. Scott was known as a difficult if not unpleasant fellow, a tough man in a tough world. He had come to Canada in 1863, first settling in Canada West (Ontario). But fate took him further west, and, by 1869, he was in Red River, looking for work.

It is undeniable, too, that the Métis provisional government in control of the Red River at the time had court-martialled Scott. The Métis, the mixed European-aboriginal descendants of the fur-trading empires that had battled over the trade for two centuries, had taken control of Fort Garry as part of their resistance to the sale of the vast North-West Territory. During the Métis uprising, Scott had sided with those who saw the provisional government as illegitimate. He had been imprisoned by this government and had escaped. Imprisoned for a second time, he caused such a disturbance that even the other prisoners wanted him controlled. Eventually, his vociferous agitations and his viscious verbal attacks upon the Métis leadership led to the insubordination charge.

But many, many things about this event remain in dispute, including some of the execution's most important details. Written accounts, and even the very images of Scott's death, are still sharply debated. More important, how to categorize Thomas Scott's death remains in dispute. Was it a lawful execution by a legitimate government against an attack on that government's authority? Or was it an illegal act perpetrated by bloodthirsty "half-breeds," as Métis were then sometimes called? Was Scott murdered in cold blood, as many, especially in Protestant Ontario, claimed?

In dispute, too, is the role of the man many claim was ultimately responsible for Scott's death: Louis Riel. Did he make the order? Was it his fault? Did he pull the trigger?

Figure 2.1 *Thomas Scott's Murder or Execution, 1869, from the* Canadian Illustrated News

Courtesy of the Glenbow Museum. Glenbow Museum, NA-1406–71

The execution of Thomas Scott remains controversial not just because of the details of the event but because of its broader meaning: Scott's death provides insight into a singular moment that shaped much of Canadian history. A seemingly insignificant person's death at an isolated fort thousands of miles from (what was then) Canada became one of the burning questions of the late nineteenth century and sparked a chain of events that forever defined the country. If Scott had not been killed, Canada may have developed in a dramatically different way.

At the same time, Scott's death is a microcosm of the conflict that galvanized ordinary people and political leaders in this period. It is a flashpoint for the great effort waged by Prime Minister John A. Macdonald to gain control of the sprawling landmass west of Canada, a fight over the control of land, and the control of government. It also tells us much about the conflicts between aboriginals and whites, French speakers and English speakers, and Catholics and Protestants, conflicts that remained central to Canadians in this period. The execution of Thomas Scott was as much about who would dominate the great expanse of the North West and about Macdonald as it was about Riel. In fact, the conflict over the North West epitomized by the death of Scott reflected a larger battle, a struggle to secure Canada from coast to coast.

Securing Canada

Late nineteenth-century Canada was, in many ways, a fragile country. The brutal assassination of Thomas D'Arcy McGee, the difficulties in forging Confederation, the Fenian attacks, and great social, economic, and political questions all threatened the survival of the young nation. Could the new country survive its early challenges and grow to meet the demands of many people in this "new nationality," as McGee had called it? Could Canada control the whole northern half of North America?

After all, some British colonies in North America had steadfastly refused to join Macdonald's new country, while some new provinces were actually already looking to get *out* of Confederation. Nova Scotia's situation was perhaps most threatening. Many Nova Scotians were unhappy about joining Confederation and felt that tying Nova Scotia to the new Dominion instead of retaining direct United Kingdom connections would weaken the province politically and economically. Newspaperman and politician Joseph Howe, one of Halifax's leading boosters, felt this way, and he challenged the decision to join Canada, even going to Britain in the 1860s to argue against Confederation.

Rebuffed by the British, the energetic Howe created the Anti-Confederation League, Canada's first separatist movement. In the first federal election, in 1867, anti-Confederates took 18 out of Nova Scotia's 19 House of Commons seats. Then, in Nova Scotia's first provincial election, the Anti-Confederation League won 36 of 38 seats. Clearly, Macdonald and the federal government had to quell this Nova Scotian unhappiness before the whole scheme fell apart.

How did Macdonald keep Nova Scotia in Confederation? Ever shrewd, Macdonald effectively bought off the Nova Scotians, including Howe. In 1868, he gave the province "better terms," essentially a bigger grant than their original Confederation agreement. Next, in 1869, Macdonald promised Howe a lucrative federal government position as president of the Privy Council. This largely honorary position was enough to keep Howe, and Nova Scotia, in the fold.

Fenian attacks upon the country, including upon parts of the Maritimes, also convinced ordinary Nova Scotians that Confederation might be their wisest choice. When Howe died in 1873, much Nova Scotian desire to leave Confederation disappeared, and Macdonald turned his attention to yet another Maritime challenge to Canadian union.

Ironically, although Canadians celebrate the famous 1864 Charlottetown Conference that created Confederation, Prince Edward Island did not join Canada until 1873. How did this happen? In the mid-1860s, the Atlantic provinces were considering their own federation; Macdonald and the Canadians essentially crashed their Charlottetown party. But Macdonald's initial offer to PEI did not satisfy Islanders who felt no need to join Canada as the province was relatively prosperous in the mid-1860s and had a good agricultural base. So, like Newfoundland, PEI passed on Confederation.

But, by the early 1870s, PEI was in a bit of trouble, and two issues explain why Islanders changed their minds. First, there was the land question, a recurring theme for Canadians in this period. Since it was first settled in the 1700s, the island was divided into 67 lots owned by English absentee landlords who charged tenants to farm the land. By the 1870s, rents were soaring higher and higher, hurting the colony.

Second, there was the railway issue. Railways were the speculative bubble of their age. Everyone wanted in on them, including PEI, thinking railways would bring prosperity and economic development despite their financial demands. By 1873, the province was in serious debt due to railway construction. Macdonald, always the opportunist, offered to take over all the province's debts, ensure the completion of the railway, and pay for it, too. Ottawa also promised to maintain a ferry to the province (replaced by the 1997 Confederation Bridge). Finally, Macdonald offered PEI an $800,000 fund to buy out the absentee landowners. The British, who did not necessarily want to have to deal with the island's problems, encouraged Islanders to listen to Macdonald. PEI joined Canada on July 1, 1873.

Before returning to Thomas Scott's death, let's look further west, at British Columbia, where Macdonald faced a completely different set of challenges. The colony of British Columbia was created in 1858; it had previously been known as New Caledonia. Vancouver Island (known then as "Vancouver's Island") was also a separate colony. In 1866, the British merged the two colonies; even then, the merged colony was still thinly populated, with less than 50,000 people, including aboriginal peoples. This sparseness of population was a major issue for the British, who felt the colony did not have enough people to protect it against the potential designs of the Americans, as there were many in the United States who wanted control of BC.

This issue became even more important following the 1858 gold rush. The discovery of gold at Fraser River prompted a flood of people to the province, including many Americans. In Ottawa, Macdonald also had his eye on BC. It made sense to get BC into Confederation, as it was a British colony. Yet enticing British Columbia to join the new nation was an immensely difficult task, given BC's distance from Canada, not to mention the fact that a mountain range stood in the way.

Also, there was no real desire, as yet, on the part of the British Columbians to join. Enter Amor De Cosmos ("Lover of the Universe"). Born in Nova Scotia in 1825 as William Smith to loyalist parents, De Cosmos became one of the most important people in getting BC into Confederation. A free spirit during an itinerant age, Smith left Nova Scotia in the 1840s and was drawn to California's gold rush, where he built a lucrative business taking photographs of prospectors on their claims. In 1854, he changed his name to Amor De Cosmos, telling authorities that his new name represented "what I love most, viz: Love of order, beauty, the world, the universe."[1]

In 1858, De Cosmos moved to Vancouver Island, started a newspaper, and became a successful business owner and land speculator. Unlike his fellow native Nova Scotian Howe, in 1870, De Cosmos began to push for Confederation, seeing it as a way to secure the colony's prosperity. He started the Confederation League, which successfully lobbied Ottawa to facilitate British Columbia's inclusion in the new country, and De Cosmos played a key role in negotiations. Amazingly, he managed to secure two important promises from Ottawa as the price of BC's entry into Confederation. First, the new province would be granted its own responsible government, despite its small population. Second, and more astoundingly, De Cosmos successfully demanded that a transcontinental railway linking BC to the rest of the country be started within two years of the colony joining Confederation, and that it be completed within 10 years (by about 1881). Not surprisingly, De Cosmos became known as BC's Father of Confederation, and was its second premier.

Though BC joined Confederation in 1871, there was a vast, virtually impenetrable territory between it, far out on the Pacific Coast, and the original provinces. Not only did Canada not have control of the territory but the idea of building a

---

1   Quoted in Robert A. J. McDonald and H. Keith Ralston, "De Cosmos, Amor," in *Dictionary of Canadian Biography*, vol. 12, University of Toronto/Université Laval, 2003–, accessed November 12, 2014, http://www.biographi.ca/en/bio/de_cosmos_amor_12E.html.

railway across this great expanse seemed impossible. Most important, the aboriginal and Métis peoples who lived in this territory, called Rupert's Land, had their own ideas about what should happen to the land they and their aboriginal ancestors had lived on for thousands of years.

The Métis and the Red River Settlement: Control of the North-West

Even before Confederation, many in Canada wanted to gain control over all of Rupert's Land, the vast continental expanse that stretched north and west from the boundaries of the Province of Canada to the Arctic and the Pacific oceans. According to the British legal system, Rupert's Land was under the exclusive control of the Hudson's Bay Company, but, of course, this control was in name only as the region was huge—one third of Canada's current land mass. Macdonald's political nemesis and erstwhile ally, the newspaper owner George Brown, and many other Ontarians, were particularly keen to establish Canada's claim to Rupert's Land. They thought that the North-West would be good for immigrant farmers from Ontario; in the late nineteenth century, Canada was still very much a rural, farm-driven nation, and land was the easiest and best way to secure oneself economically. Brown and his followers had Rupert's Land in mind when they insisted that the new BNA Act include Section 146, stating that Canada could create new provinces and territories.

Of course, these colonialist designs did not consider the desires of the region's people, not only the extensive aboriginal populations but also the Métis. As descendants of fur traders and aboriginals, their mixed-race heritage certainly placed them in a unique position in the vast territory. How had this Métis "New Nation" emerged as a distinct ethnic, social, and political community? Its roots lay in the epic competition for the fur trade. The Métis were the descendants of employees of two companies: the British-controlled Hudson's Bay Company (HBC), founded in 1670 (to this day "the Bay," North America's oldest company), and the North West Company (NWC) that emerged in 1779 after the demise of the colonial French fur trade following the 1763 British conquest of New France. Both HBC men and the North West Company's *voyageurs* travelled back and forth to Rupert's Land on HBC "York boats" or canoes and lived with and created trade and marriage alliances with the region's First Nations. Indeed, unions between traders and First Nations women, considered "*à la façon du pays*" (after the custom of the country), were essential to traders' success as they cemented alliances with particular aboriginal groups, gained access to kin networks, and had their women or wives act as guides and interpreters. Polygamy, men having more than one wife, was practiced by both NWC and HBC men, though the HBC attempted to end the practice in the 1800s.

For nearly 50 years, the two companies fought a brutal battle over the fur trade, including the 1816 Battle of Seven Oaks, a Métis-led victory by the North West Company over the HBC that left dozens dead. But, after 1821, the two companies were merged into the HBC, given the decline in demand for fur-felt hats in Europe. By the late nineteenth century, there were approximately 10,000 Métis in the North West, mostly spread out but with a concentration along the Red River region in Manitoba, now present-day Winnipeg. Most Métis were French speaking and Catholic because *voyageurs* had initially dominated the trade. Some were Scottish and English or, in many instances, of mixed race, and most had large families and many children.

By the time Thomas Scott arrived in the Red River settlement in 1869, the long-standing rhythms of Métis life were being profoundly disrupted. The fur trade and the buffalo hunt, the central aspects of Métis and aboriginal social, political, and economic organization, declined as demand for furs dried up after beaver-pelt hats fell out of fashion in Europe and the vast herds of bison shrank because of European encroachment and overhunting. In turn, as Métis settled in the Red River to take up farming or paid work, their seasonal hunter-gatherer economy was shifting to a wage-based labour market, one still largely HBC controlled. In addition, by the 1850s and 1860s, older aboriginal conceptions of common property were slowly being replaced by the notion of private property. The ideas that someone could possess the soil and rocks; that one shouldn't trespass on or steal land; and, more important, that those who imposed this system of legal title first could control land—all of these concepts meant a sea change in Métis and aboriginal life.

The world around the Métis was changing, too: Western influences were beginning to be felt in the North-West as technology, European economic patterns, and immigration spread to the Prairies. This Western influence marked an irrevocable change in fur trade society as it challenged the intermingling of peoples, the mixed-marriage arrangements, and the distinctive cultures and customs of the fur trade. Also ending was tolerance of the polygamous marriages occasioned by the fur trade; a new and much harsher attitude toward race and class emerged. Rupert's Land, which became known as the North-West Territories in the 1870s, and the Métis were being integrated into global systems of political and economic exploitation and governance, and Scott's arrival was a very tangible example of this change.

The North West: Land and Politics

In part, Scott's arrival reflected a wave of white immigration to the North-West, which, since the early 1800s, had been seen as North America's "last great frontier," an "unspoiled" landmass despite the presence of thousands of aboriginals and Métis. The territory (see map in Chapter 1, p. 6) became a political issue in the mid-nineteenth century as Canadians and Americans looked at the North West as a prize. The British, who nominally "controlled" the region through the HBC, were aware by the 1850s of Minnesota advocates of Manifest Destiny, Americans who wanted to take control of the area. More prominent were the demands of those in Canada West who wished to annex the territory and saw the North West as the key to creating an industrial, agricultural, and commercial empire spreading from central Canada to the Pacific.

In the 1860s, in his efforts to secure Canada from sea to sea, Macdonald struck a deal with the British government for the sale of the HBC lands to the new Dominion for about £300,000 and one-twentieth of the land. This agreement was a transfer between two parties, the British and the Canadians, who carried it out as one giant real-estate transaction.

But what about the region's people, especially in the one area with a concentrated population, the Red River settlement? By 1870, there were over 10,000 people in the Red River region, 5,700 Métis, 4,100 born in English-speaking countries, 1,500 Canadians, and 550 First Nations people. The Métis had started settling the Red River after 1800, where the Red and Assiniboine rivers meet, carving out their farms in traditional long Quebec lots adjacent to the river, not the square lots favoured by English-speaking whites in Canada West and the United States. The Métis, who in this period faced droughts and economic uncertainty on top of the broader economic and social changes, were aware of both American and Canadian designs on their territory. Ultimately, land and the settlement and future of the North West were at the core of the conflict between Métis and English-speaking settlers, and, more than anything else, these factors help to explain why Scott was killed in March 1870.

Riel and the Red River Resistance

Louis Riel is one of the most fascinating and controversial figures in Canadian history. At the time the Red River resistance took place, Riel was a young man, only 25, yet he exhibited extraordinarily strong leadership and judgment. Riel was born into a prominent Métis family of the Red River settlement in 1844, the eldest of 11 children. An excellent student, Riel was sent to Quebec to be educated. He remained in the East for 10 tumultuous years, fell in love at 21, and then dropped out of school to try a variety of careers only to have his fiancée's family prevent the marriage. In great disappointment, Riel returned to the Red River in 1868.

His timing could have not been more fateful. When he reached home, news of the HBC's sale of Rupert's Land to Canada gripped the Red River. The Métis were determined to have a say in their homeland's fate, and Riel was a natural leader: he was thoughtful, well-spoken, bilingual, and literate, and he had some educational training. Perhaps most important, he was a true son of the Métis.

The Red River resistance, as it has come to be known, emerged because the Métis were fearful of what would happen to them and their rights (both individual and collective) when the Canadians took over following the sale of Rupert's Land to Ottawa. They had questions about their rights to hunt, the ownership of their land, and their place in any new government, including their ability to hold jobs in the civil service. At the same time, they worried about their language and religious rights and about schooling for their children.

These concerns led the Métis, with Riel's leadership, to take an unprecedented and dramatic step. In 1869, they formed a provisional government that took control of the Red River settlement—a direct challenge to the authority of the HBC and the Canadian government, which had made an agreement to purchase the territory. Though dominated by French-speaking Métis, the provisional government also included English speakers. Despite this, a strong "Canadian Party," led by Ontario immigrant John Christian "Doc" Schulz, challenged the legitimacy of the provisional government, especially when Riel prevented the newly appointed governor for Ottawa from entering the settlement and sent three Métis representatives to negotiate with Macdonald. Upon their arrival in Ontario, two of Riel's three delegates spent a brief time in jail, though they did eventually meet with federal officials, arguing that any new province include denominational schools, land guarantees, bilingual political institutions, and a place for the Métis in government.

Back in the Red River, Schulz and a number of his followers, including Thomas Scott, sought to disrupt the efforts of the Métis to negotiate entry into Confederation on their own terms. A number of altercations between Schulz's followers and the provisional government resulted in some violence, including the killing of a young Métis by a number of men, among them Thomas Scott. Feeling as though it had no recourse, Riel's provisional government imprisoned the men. Scott's agitation became ever more violent until he verbally threatened Riel. In response, Riel had Scott court-martialled for insubordination. When he was found guilty, Riel agreed that he should face a firing squad and that making Scott an example might actually prevent more bloodshed: "I take a life to save lives," Riel had reportedly said of the matter.[2]

Despite Scott's execution, negotiations between the Red River representatives and Ottawa were concluded just weeks later. Unable to send troops quickly to the isolated colony to deter the Métis, and fearful that the Americans would take advantage of the situation to press their own claims on the territory, Macdonald was forced to negotiate.

---

2   Quoted in Lionel Groulx, Eucher Forget, Philippe Labelle, and Antonio Dansereau, "Louis Riel: Documents inédits," *Revue d'histoire de l'Amérique française* 3, no. 1 (June 1949): 111–18; see page 113.

Riel had achieved his dream of a province for the Métis, but Manitoba was only a small 100-square-mile area around the settlement, and the rest of Rupert's Land became the federally controlled North-West Territories. Moreover, though the Métis did achieve in the 1870 Manitoba Act some protection for their language and religious rights, the province was not granted control over either public land and natural resources or the 1.4 million acres reserved for the Métis, as much of this territory was still to be determined. Still, the creation of Manitoba was a considerable success for the Métis, and the province officially entered Confederation on July 15, 1870.

But, perhaps most ominously, no written amnesty from Macdonald or the federal government for Riel and the other Métis leaders regarding the events in 1870 was included in the arrangement that created Manitoba. Scott's death would have repercussions far beyond the Red River and the province that Riel had created.

The Consequences of Manitoba's Emergence and Thomas Scott's Death

The events at the Red River held great significance for the new Canadian state. The entry of Manitoba into Confederation and the securing of the North-West Territories from the HBC transferred authority of the region to Canada, not to Minnesota and the Americans. Troublingly for the Métis, when Canadian troops arrived to assert federal authority over the new province, a reign of terror against the Métis ensued, and many, including Riel, were forced to flee in fear of their lives.

Indeed, though Riel and the provisional government had created a new province, theirs was only a temporary victory. As thousands of newcomers moved into Manitoba and the North West, many Métis and aboriginals were pushed further west, and their ancestral rights were challenged by the mostly English-speaking migrants to the region. Yet the issue of the Métis and of Riel, specifically, would reappear, and the Red River resistance would continue to be one of the most significant events in the country's history.

More immediately, reaction to Scott's slaying in Ontario led to outrage among many in the Protestant community. Scott himself became a martyr—and Riel a target for revenge. In the early 1870s, the province witnessed protests, "indignation meetings," and newspapers such as *The Nation*, declaring their hatred for Riel as Scott's "murderer," vowing vengeance. Out of this rage emerged a "Canada First" movement that pushed a white, English, and Protestant form of nationalism, one based on a thinly disguised racism.

Riel, forced to flee the Red River in 1870 as Canadian troops and immigrant farmers overwhelmed his homeland, reappeared on the Canadian scene in 1884, but this time with much more tragic consequences. Scott, buried at Red River, became a lasting symbol of the ongoing conflict between French and English, Catholic and Protestant, and native and white in nineteenth- and twentieth-century Canada.

Further Reading

Brown, Chester. *Louis Riel: A Comic-Strip Biography*. Montreal: Drawn & Quarterly Publications, 2004.

Dick, Lyle. "Nationalism and Visual Media: The Case of Thomas Scott's Execution." *Manitoba History* 48 (Autumn/Winter 2004–2005): 2–18.

Osborne, Brian S. "Corporeal Politics and the Body Politic: The Re-presentation of Louis Riel in Canadian Identity." *International Journal of Heritage Studies* 8, no. 4 (Winter 2002): 303–22. http://dx.doi.org/10.10 80/1352725022000037209.

Siggins, Maggie. *Riel, a Life of Revolution*. Toronto: Harper Collins, 2003.

Stanley, G.F.G. *The Birth of Western Canada: A History of the Riel Rebellions*. Toronto: University of Toronto Press, 1992.

ACTIVE HISTORY: HISTORY AND HISTORIOGRAPHY

Clearly, history is more than "just the facts." Though many people think that history is merely a recitation of events, dates, and places from a long time ago, this is far from the reality of what the study of history is all about. By studying history, you learn that the debates stemming from the historical events you examine are as alive today as they were in the past.

This is because the events, dates, and places from long ago form only one component of history. In fact, most history that is written, including much of the history covered in this book, is actually a debate *about* the events and their causes rather than being a simple recounting of the events themselves. That is to say, the *interpretation* of historical events is sometimes just as important as the events themselves in the writing of history.

Let's look at an example that most people are familiar with and one that you have already read about in this book: the creation of Canada. Now, we know that the nation-state of Canada came together in 1867 under the leadership of John A. Macdonald and a number of other provincial representatives when, following a series of meetings at Quebec, London, and Charlottetown, three British colonies united to become four provinces within the new federal Dominion of Canada: Ontario, Quebec, Nova Scotia, and New Brunswick. These events, dates, and places are irrefutable.

However, the *cause* of these events is far less certain, and the larger question remains: *Why* did Confederation happen? Was it external pressure from the British? The threat of the Fenian Raids? Or was Confederation caused by a genuine patriotic outburst of ordinary British North Americans, idealistically building a "new nationality," as Thomas D'Arcy McGee argued? Was it a "compact" among the colonies or a new arrangement created by a central government? Or was it a political and economic arrangement designed to benefit Canadian and British elites and to maintain the ascendency of these elites? Historians debate which question is more compelling in interpreting Confederation, and provide evidence to support each case.

Debate over which interpretation of a historical event is more convincing is called historiography. You yourself will become part of this historiographical debate as you assess the cases made by different historians and decide which ones you find the most plausible. As you review articles and books by different historians on different events, you, too, will need to make a case as to why you find a particular view more convincing than another.

Along the way (and you might find this surprising), you may realize that the answers to these historiographical questions are important to the events of today. For example, in the debate about

Confederation, Quebec separatists have always maintained that the creation of Canada was indeed a "compact," one between Quebec and the rest of Canada. By making this case, they have hoped to show that Quebec had a special place as an original "maker" of Confederation, so it could "break" Confederation as well. Others have tried to refute this case, arguing that Quebec's role was no more special than that of any other province or player. These historians are trying to convince Quebecers and Canadians of their views, which can have implications in the debate about Quebec's role in Canada. In this case, we see that the debate about a historical event that happened more than a century ago can have implications for current politics.

Remember, then, to keep in mind not only the events, dates, and places of history but also the competing interpretations of the past—the "story" in history. In doing so, you will quickly discover that history is more than "just the facts."

Indeed, in attempting to discern a particular interpretive approach in history, this book offers a good lesson: What is the author's approach, beyond the "murder" format? Is there more of a focus on a particular interpretation or method? Perhaps the author emphasizes political and economic events more than social or cultural ones? Are the stories of political figures highlighted, as opposed to those of ordinary Canadians? Does this approach effectively reflect the perspectives of First Nations peoples or women or workers? Are these approaches a problem? What is *your own* approach? How do you see history and understand it? What are, in your view, the most important elements that shape events in a given episode under examination here?

⤙ MURDEROUS MOMENT ⤚
ELIZABETH WORKMAN, EXECUTED, SARNIA, ONTARIO, 1873

Gender, Race, and the Law in Nineteenth-Century Canada

Sadly, for a woman in Canada in the late nineteenth century, Elizabeth Workman's tale is not atypical, at least, not as her story initially unfolded. Like most Confederation-era women, Elizabeth Workman faced an extraordinarily difficult life. Similar to so many others in this time, Elizabeth was an immigrant, born in Scotland, probably in the late 1830s or early 1840s, as her exact age is not known. Sometime in the early 1850s, she married James Workman, a man who was considerably older than Elizabeth and who had a child, Mary, from a previous marriage. The family migrated to Canada in 1856, and, in 1865, Elizabeth gave birth to a son, Hugh. By 1872, the Workman family was living on the bottom floor of a tiny house in Mooretown, a small farming community just outside Sarnia, Ontario.

During their time in Canada, James and Elizabeth's circumstances had not improved materially, and they faced difficulties. James, a common labourer and occasional butcher, was employed only sporadically and unevenly. This situation was exacerbated by the fact that James was prone to drink and, when drunk, became abusive toward his family. On more than one occasion in the early 1870s, Elizabeth had sought refuge from James's outbursts with neighbours, and daughter Mary left the family home entirely. Typically, women such as Elizabeth had virtually no say in family matters, as wives (and women generally) held a subordinate role owing to men's domination of the legal, political, and economic realms; women could not vote, rarely owned property in their own names, and were denied access to professions and other employment.

This is where Elizabeth's story became tragically atypical. Despite her hardships, in 1873, Elizabeth found employment with Samuel Butler, a newly arrived barber who hired her to do his laundry and help out around his barber shop. Butler struck up a relationship with the Workman family, often visiting with a bottle in hand. Soon, rumours began to circulate around town that Elizabeth and Samuel were romantically involved, a scandal, to be sure, but one that was even more notorious because of one important fact: Butler was black. In nineteenth-century Canada, such relationships were considered completely illicit—and immoral.

On the morning of Thursday, October 24, 1872, Elizabeth was working at Samuel's shop, cleaning. James showed up with eight-year-old Hugh and demanded that Elizabeth immediately come home with him. At first, Elizabeth refused, but, after a brief altercation between Samuel and James, she left with her husband. What happened over the next 48 hours is not entirely clear. James, who apparently had been drinking heavily, retired to his bed. Elizabeth, frustrated by years of James's abusive treatment, finally struck back. She bound James to the bed and allegedly beat him with a mop stick.

That night, with James still confined to bed, Samuel Butler was seen entering the Workman home with clothes for Elizabeth to launder; he left sometime thereafter. According to newspaper accounts and court documents, the next day Elizabeth again allegedly beat James. On Saturday morning, Elizabeth called upon her neighbours to help her with James, who was rapidly deteriorating. But little could be done, and James was dead by the afternoon. When visitors remarked upon the bruises on his body, Elizabeth claimed that he had caused them himself. Following a coroner's examination, both Elizabeth and Samuel were arrested, charged with James's murder, and thrown in jail.

The sensational details of the case—a wife killing a husband was shocking, especially when an affair with a black man was also alleged—made the trial a major news story across Ontario. Though not as notorious as the famous 1880 case of the "Black Donnellys" near London, Ontario, the Workman trial brought reporters from across the province to witness the proceedings. During the two-day trial, Elizabeth's ill-prepared lawyer (who was only assigned the case a day before) did little to demonstrate James's prior terrible treatment of Elizabeth or to use effectively the many character witnesses, mostly neighbours, who called Elizabeth a hard-working mother or who could have testified to James's drinking. In the end, for lack of evidence, Samuel was deemed innocent. Elizabeth, however, was found guilty of the murder, a crime whose punishment was the death penalty, in this case, hanging. Yet, importantly, the jury recommended that she be granted mercy and her sentence be commuted to life in prison, given her circumstances and the abuse she had experienced.

For the next four months, Elizabeth pled her case for mercy from the Sarnia jail. She soon had the support of local officials, including the mayor, backed by a series of petitions signed by community members. The town newspaper also stood on her side, calling James an "intemperate and tyrannical husband and father," while Elizabeth was "a quiet, industrious

and hard-working woman."[3] Federal politician Alexander Mackenzie, who became Canada's first Liberal prime minister a few months after the case, wrote to John A. Macdonald to ask that Elizabeth's sentence be reconsidered.

It was all to no avail. Macdonald, as prime minister and minister of justice, had the final say on whether capital cases could receive clemency (most famously in an 1885 case, as we shall see). He refused the petitions, and, on June 19, 1873, Elizabeth Workman, holding a knot of white flowers, was led to a newly built scaffolding just outside the Sarnia jail. As the noose was placed around her neck, she proclaimed that she had acted in self-defence and was "remarkably grateful" to those who had argued for clemency. In front of a small group of spectators, Workman was hanged. When the act was complete, her body was cut from the gallows and fell into a small pit.

For many involved and for the wider community, the case left a number of lingering questions and issues. Why wasn't Elizabeth granted clemency? Was it because the government wanted to make a statement about women's place in society? Was it because Elizabeth had been rumoured to be involved with a black man, a taboo at the time? And why was Samuel Butler found innocent while she was found guilty?

The Workman execution was the last female execution in Canada until 1899, when Hilda Blake was hanged in Manitoba for killing her employer. The 23-year pause in female executions perhaps suggests that, because of the outcry over Elizabeth's hanging,

---

3   Quoted in Frank Murray Greenwood and Beverley Boissery, *Uncertain Justice: Canadian Women and Capital Punishment 1754–1953* (Toronto: Dundurn Press, 2000), 153.

authorities were somewhat wary of imposing the death penalty upon women, who were, in any event, rarely involved in capital crimes. At the same time, the case foreshadows the great movement toward prohibition of alcohol beginning in the latter part of the nineteenth century and culminating with a ban on the sale of alcohol in many provinces and areas of the country in the twentieth. Perhaps most important, the Workman execution illustrates the economically and legally challenging place of women in nineteenth-century Canada.

CHAPTER THREE

GEORGE BROWN, ASSASSINATED, TORONTO, 1880

DREAMS OF AN EMERGING CANADA

From his own newspaper, the *Globe*, Friday, March 26, 1880:

ATTEMPTED ASSASSINATION

Murderous Attack on the
   Hon. George Brown
   PROMPT ARREST OF THE CRIMINAL.
   Widespread Manifestations of Public Sympathy.

   Yesterday afternoon one of the most audacious and dastardly attempts at murder ever made in this city took place in the private office of the Hon. George Brown, in THE GLOBE building. Fortunately, owing mainly to Mr. Brown's presence of mind and superior physical strength, the attempt was unsuccessful, the only results being a severe flesh wound in the thigh. . . . Had the miscreant who made the murderous assault been a little more prompt in taking his aim, or had the pistol been of a different construction, the attempt could hardly have resulted so favourably, for he persisted in his efforts to effect his bloody purpose until he was overpowered and the weapon was wrenched from his grasp.

George Bennett, a disgruntled former employee of the paper, and according to the *Globe*, "the reputed son of a coloured man and a white woman," had gone to the *Globe* building to demand a letter of reference from Brown. Before arriving at the *Globe*, Bennett had become intoxicated, and was in possession of a handgun. Appearing unannounced in Brown's office, Bennett verbally attacked the publisher, and the argument quickly degenerated. As the two men scuffled,

Figure 3.1 *"Attempted Assassination of Hon. Geo. Brown," Toronto, Illustration by Henri Julien in the* Canadian Illustrated News, *April 10, 1880*

Source: Library and Archives Canada, *Canadian Illustrated News*, 1869–1883, Item Number 38

Bennett pulled out his revolver and attempted to shoot Brown. At the last moment, Brown deflected Bennett's arm downwards, but Bennett still managed to fire a bullet that hit Brown in the leg. Bennett was quickly subdued by *Globe* workers.

Six weeks later, Brown was dead. The bullet wound had caused an infection that had proved fatal. Again, here is a report from his own newspaper, dated May 10, 1880:

He loved his country, and laboured for her good; the objects he set before him were high, the plans he formed vast, and when he failed, it was from no lack of courage or self-sacrifice on his part. The bed of death calls for other consolations than the praise of men, but it may be that his passing spirit was cheered by the thought that in the estimation of his fellow-countrymen he had not lived altogether in vain.[1]

---

1   "Mr. George Brown's Illness and Death," *Globe*, May 10, 1880, p. 4.

Brown, like McGee and Macdonald, was an immigrant. Born and raised in Scotland, he had, also like McGee, initially migrated to the United States and then to Canada. Yet the course of his life, from his arrival in Canada in 1843 until his murder in 1880, intersected with and reflected many of the most important issues that shaped the nation and continued to affect it, even long after his death. Though he was out of public office by the early 1870s, Brown exerted a large influence on politics, the economy, and social issues. Indeed, for such a sometimes dour, straight-laced man, George Brown was quite the dreamer, as the "plans he formed" were undoubtedly vast, and even his failures helped to shape the young nation. Given the events that unfolded in the decades after his death, Brown's vision for those decades warrants assessment.

Brown's Politics of Confederation and the West

More so than that of any other Father of Confederation save perhaps Macdonald himself, Brown's vision shaped Canada as it emerged following the Charlottetown (1864) and London (1866) conferences that hammered out the contours of the new nation. After all, it was Brown who had proposed to his long-standing political enemy Macdonald that Brown's Grits and Macdonald's Tories come together in a Great Coalition to end the political deadlock that had hamstrung the Province of Canada for years.

The price of Brown's cooperation, however, reflected his own vision of how any new political arrangement in British North America should function. In insisting upon that vision, Brown unsurprisingly made proposals that were close to the hearts of his supporters in Ontario, especially his Liberal, "clear Grit," supporters. First, the new state had to be federal. And establishing federalism meant creating a national government in Ottawa controlling major issues such as the economy, defence, and criminal law, but giving Quebec, Ontario, and the other new provinces their own legislatures and thus control over local affairs such as schooling and language. It effectively meant the divorce of the two parties united in the 1841 Province of Canada: Upper Canada, which became Ontario, and Lower Canada, which became Quebec. Brown was keen to achieve this divorce, as he had for years railed against "French domination" in the united legislature.

Second, Brown ensured that the new federal parliament's seats would be apportioned through representation by population, "rep by pop," an indication of Brown's democratic tendencies and of his drive to ensure that populous Ontario had more representation than Quebec. That the two sections of the united Province of Canada were equal in representation had been one of the key features of its dysfunction, and Brown was keen to ensure that such a situation did not arise again. Finally, Brown wanted the new country to take control of the West, allowing for settlement from Ontario, where population growth had put a strain on land resources and farms. At Brown's insistence, the new British North America Act that governed Canada included a clause (Section 146) specifically designed to ensure Canadian expansion. Brown's vision of a West dominated by farmers mainly from Ontario largely came true, eventually. The Canada that emerged after 1880 was as much Brown's as it was Macdonald's.

Dreams of Free Trade, Realities of a National Policy

As a "clear Grit," a Liberal who believed in free trade, Brown was a key advocate of liberalizing the economy, including eradicating as much as possible any tariffs on Canadian trade. In the early 1870s, a few years after the Reciprocity Treaty (1854–66) was revoked by the United States, Brown was sent to Washington to try to resuscitate free trade with the Americans. After many fruitless months, it became clear that the United States was not interested in a renewed trade treaty with the Canadians. Yet the idea of free trade lived on for decades: Wilfrid Laurier, Brown's descendant as Liberal leader, lost two elections on the issue, in 1891 and 1911.

Instead of Brown's free trade, John A. Macdonald's "national policy" became the economic foundation of the country. Macdonald had also favoured free trade, but by the mid-1870s, it was clear that reciprocity was not to be had. In 1879, Macdonald instituted the National Policy tariff of 35 per cent on most finished goods coming into the country. This tariff was applied to any finished goods being imported into Canada that were also manufactured in Canada; the 35 per cent tax was an effort to protect Canadian manufacturers and help create new industries. The tariff was the first element of a three-pronged development policy called the national policy (the term in upper case means the tariff policy itself). The national policy was designed to ensure Canada achieved economic success and secured the northern half of North America as a viable nation.

The second pillar of the national policy called for the construction of a national railway across the country. A transcontinental railroad would ensure that the territories across Canada remained in Canadian hands, and it allowed Canadian farmers who would populate the West to send their products back to the East, thus creating a "wheat economy." Since Canada had abundant land, staples such as wheat were designed to be the backbone of the economy. The federal government contracted with the Canadian Pacific Railway to build a railway across Canada to British Columbia in the 1870s, also as part of the terms of BC's entry into Confederation. The CPR, started in 1873, was not completed until 1885.

Figure 3.2 *John A. Macdonald's Last Campaign Poster, 1891*

Courtesy of the McCord Museum. M965.34.8

The building of the CPR was noteworthy for a number of reasons. First, it was a private company and not government owned. The CPR had shareholders (many of whom were in Britain) and was in the business of making money. As part of its contract, Ottawa gave the CPR $25 million and 25 million acres of land in Western Canada to finish the project. Second, the CPR caught Macdonald in a tremendous political scandal, as he was discovered (in an incriminating telegram) to be accepting funds from the CPR to help the Conservative Party; taxpayers were being fleeced to help Macdonald's re-election. After Macdonald's government fell in 1873 because of the "Pacific Scandal," new prime minister Alexander Mackenzie did not make "Macdonald's railway" a priority, so work did not really get going on the CPR until after 1878, when Macdonald returned to power.

The national policy's third pillar was immigration. John A. hoped to populate the West, providing labour for wheat farms and also a market for the Canadian industrial goods built in Eastern Canada, such as farm equipment. Massey-Ferguson, for instance, built huge factories in Toronto producing farm equipment for sale in the West. Along with building a railway to encourage Canadians from the central provinces to move out west, Ottawa began encouraging immigrants from other countries to settle in Canada to work the land and develop Canadian agriculture.

These three pillars created an east–west economy: the railroad to transport wheat and people; immigration and the railroad to get settlers to the land; and a tariff to protect home-grown products so that settlers would buy Canadian goods transported by the railway. But the national policy generated its own problems, some of which had tragic and long-lasting implications. Most obviously, the policy reflected Brown and Macdonald's commitment to the establishment of a white settler nation at the expense of aboriginal and Métis populations. The treatment of the aboriginal and Métis populations in the pursuit of this goal led to dispossession, disease, and political decline for these groups, and the legacy of colonialism remains central to aboriginal and white relations in contemporary Canada.

Further, as the policy unfolded in the late nineteenth and early twentieth centuries, regional tensions were exacerbated. Although central Canada gained the benefits of industrialization, Canadians in the Maritimes and the West were unhappy about the fact that they were required to pay more for manufactured goods, just because they were made in Canada. Wheat was sold at world market prices, yet manufactured goods, such as farm equipment or eventually cars, were very expensive due to the Canadian tariff; the 35 per cent added to the price of imported goods made American products sold just across the border more expensive than Canadian goods.

Moreover, for most of Macdonald's time as prime minister, the national policy did not really work. The world was caught up in a long depression from about the mid-1870s until the 1890s, and many saw the policy as a failure. However, after Laurier came to power in 1896, immigration increased and the population grew dramatically, as did industrial development. The emergence of the wheat economy finally did occur. In 1891, only approximately 4.8 million people lived in Canada; by 1911, that figure had increased to about 7.2 million, as over 4 million people came to Canada between 1880 and 1914. This period is often referred to as the "Laurier boom." In this sense, Brown's dreams of a West dominated and controlled by Canada and of a place for white farmers to secure their economic prosperity came true, even if free trade was not enacted for another century after his death.

Reformer, Prohibitionist, and Urban Dweller

Brown's dreams weren't limited to national politics or the economy. Brown was a "Reformer," one of the labels attached to nineteenth-century Liberals. And he took his belief in progressive reform very seriously. Brown took passionate stances on many important issues in society. For instance, Brown was one of Canada's leading advocates of the abolition of slavery, and he used his newspaper as a pulpit to argue against the practice. Although the United Kingdom, after abolishing the slave trade in the British Empire in 1807, banned slavery itself in its dominions in 1833 (Canada had its own long history with slavery), in Brown's time, the institution was still a fundamental characteristic of the United States, particularly in the South. Brown championed the abolitionist cause and brought other leading abolitionists to Toronto, often from the United States. The official end of slavery in the United States upon the ratification of the Thirteenth Amendment in 1865, following Abraham Lincoln's Emancipation Proclamation of 1863, was a profoundly gratifying moment for Brown and his abolitionist allies.

Brown was also a leading prohibitionist. In the 1860s and 1870s, alcohol was seen as having a destructive impact upon society. Organizations such as the Women's Christian Temperance Union (1874) sought the prohibition of the production and sale of alcohol, and Brown used his newspaper to advocate for this step. Personally, he rarely touched alcohol; John A. Macdonald's affinity for drink was yet another difference between him and his adversary Brown—for Brown, prohibition was both a political and a personal issue. On more than one occasion, the *Globe* disdainfully hinted at Macdonald's problems with the bottle in its attacks upon the Tory prime minister.

Prohibition was also a reflection of the growing urbanization of Canada. As a proud Torontonian and reformer, Brown could already see by 1880 the changes that were happening to Canadian society as cities and towns grew dramatically in the late nineteenth century. Though it was not until 1921 that more Canadians lived in cities than on farms (and most of Ontario did not get electricity until the early 1900s), Canadians were becoming urbanized: Toronto and Montreal grew dramatically during this period, as waves of migrants from other countries and from Canada's rural areas came to work in the factories that had sprung up in these cities. Rapid urbanization also occurred in the West. In 1901, about 4,000 people lived in Edmonton. By 1921, the city's population was over 58,000.

This massive growth generated serious problems in these urban areas after 1880, problems that Brown, no doubt, would have campaigned against. Along with alcoholism, cities had to deal with poverty, homelessness, and poor sanitation, as municipal governments did not have the capacity to cope with such large populations.

There were responses to the bad conditions and dangers in these newly developing urban areas. In the 1880s and 1890s, upper- and middle-class women and religious groups used organizations such as the Young Men's Christian Association or the Young Women's Christian Association to protect, at least ostensibly, young men and women from the temptations of the city or to keep them out of harm's way. At times, these movements were, however, little more than efforts at social control.

Nonetheless, deficient sewage facilities, polluted water, the consumption of unpasteurized milk, and the lack of effective public health programs contributed to much sickness and death in the cities. For instance, children were particularly vulnerable, as can be seen in their very high mortality rates. In Montreal at the turn of the century, approximately one out of every four infants died before reaching the age of 12 months, and infant mortality was higher in Ontario cities than in the rest of the province. Cities were unhealthy places to live then, and only slowly would an infrastructure be established to provide safe food, water, sewage treatment, and all the other things taken for granted by today's city-dwellers.

The living conditions of the working class in the growing urban centres reflected the fact that workers were severely underpaid by employers. An average family of five typically lived in a one- or two-room apartment that was damp, unventilated, lighted inadequately, furnished sparsely, and heated poorly. Outdoor washrooms—outhouses—were common, as were open sewers. Overcrowding was a constant problem. Toronto's rapid growth led to a housing shortage, and some families lived in hastily constructed shacks, in tents in backyards, or even on the street.

The massive population boom, industrialization, and urbanization put a strain on the Canadian social order, something that Brown would have also recognized. The idea of the traditional family economy, with the male breadwinner at its centre, remained the core of social organization. Yet the traditional family faced many new challenges in the period after Confederation. On the farming homestead, all family members were expected to help ensure the success of the farm. But in the booming cities, economic survival was based on wage labour, such as that paid to Brown's workers at the *Globe*. Wages, work, and unionization in this period were contentious issues, and they took on distinct personal and political tones, especially in the battles between Brown and Macdonald. There was, for instance, the battle over the nine-hour day, one that helps to explain early but limited union recognition. In 1872, Macdonald, infuriated with the *Globe*'s constant attacks, passed the Trade Unions Act. This law allowed those in the typographical trades, newspaper workers primarily, to unionize. Allowing unionized workers in the newspaper trade hurt Brown's profits. The move was also designed to gain working-class support for Macdonald's Conservative Party and its policies (viz., the national policy).

While most men worked in factories for wages, women also contributed through their paid and unpaid labour to support the family. Because families often could not survive on the wages of the father or the mother or even both, children were also in the workforce. Children worked as domestics or as labourers in factories doing the jobs that larger adults could not do, such as cleaning or maintaining machinery. This work could be extremely dangerous, as, before 1914, there were few worker protection laws in place and no real regulation of child labour.

Women took in boarders, sewed from home, or worked as domestics while children also took part in either waged or unwaged work to support the family. In the decades after Brown's death, the idea of the "male breadwinner" supporting his family was increasingly often just that, an idea. Industrialization and urbanization, which required women to work in order to survive, also challenged the notion of "separate spheres for men and women." This issue would come to be far more prevalent after 1880, as the notion of equal rights for women, particularly the right to vote, became a significant political issue. Who knows where Brown would have stood on the question of suffrage.

Provincialism, Imperialism, and Nationalism

Brown's views on some of the other political events after 1880 are likely more easily discerned. One major issue was the growing disconnect in federal–provincial relations that Macdonald faced. Here, Brown would have probably been happy with developments, as he was a strong supporter of provincial rights. Originally, Macdonald had wanted to create very weak provinces with the British North America Act. He argued that strong provinces would eventually cause problems for the country. By the 1880s, his worst fears about growing provincial power were coming true.

In 1886, Honoré Mercier was elected premier of Quebec. One of the first things he did was call the very first interprovincial conference, held in Quebec City in 1887. Twenty years after Confederation, it showed how things had changed. The long depression that gripped the country had begun to really take its toll on Canadians. The premiers called for a host of changes, including new subsidies from Ottawa, control over federal lands in provinces, appointment of half of the Senators to the Senate by provinces, and, perhaps most important, new provincial demands over the shape and evolution of Confederation.

Macdonald totally ignored the premiers. Nonetheless, the conference reflected a longer trend. Although he had wanted a strong central government, the provincial governments were steadily gaining their own power. This change in relative power could be seen in the federal–provincial fights over jurisdiction, over who should control what, which took place especially over issues that did not easily fall into either level's listed jurisdiction. Often times, these disputes were decided by the British Judicial Committee of the Privy Council (JCPC), another reflection of Canada's colonial heritage. (The JCPC had jurisdiction over all colonial courts across the British Empire, including those in the Province of Canada and the Dominion of Canada until 1949.) By the 1890s, thanks in part to JCPC decisions, the provinces had much more economic and political power than Macdonald had originally envisioned. Instead of being a lower or subordinate level of government, provinces became coequal in many ways to the federal government.

In 1891, John A. Macdonald fought his last election. He had been in power for nearly 30 years, and he depended upon the "Old Policy, the Old Party, the Old Leader" to squeeze out one more victory. Although he won, Macdonald did not last long: he died soon after the election. After a series of ineffective Conservative leaders, in 1896, the country turned to a new direction and elected Liberal Quebecer Wilfrid Laurier as prime minister.

Brown and Laurier were contemporaries, of course, Laurier having been elected to the House of Commons in 1874, just as Brown's time in public office was coming to an end. As fellow Liberals, both believed in individual rights, provincial rights, religious tolerance and diversity, and free trade. But Laurier faced a whole series of issues that Brown could never have imagined, especially those related to the growing conflict between imperialism and nationalism in the late nineteenth and early twentieth centuries. Brown might not have liked the direction that Laurier took on these matters, despite his loyalty to liberal ideas.

Canada was a British nation, and many of its traditions and loyalties were toward England and the British Crown. This pro-British orientation conflicted with the ideas of those in Canada more inclined toward an independent route. French Canadians in Quebec, especially, did not have any loyalty to the British Crown and were more nationalistic and Canadian in their outlook. Laurier was among those who wanted to make sure that Canada could go its own way on certain issues, especially on foreign affairs and defence policy. Moreover, some independence for Canada was important for him politically because the base of his support in the Liberal Party was from his home province of Quebec.

Three issues became flashpoints in this tension between imperialism and nationalism. The first was the Boer War. In 1899, not even 20 years after the 1881 Pretoria Convention ended one war between the Transvaal Boers and Britain, another broke out. The Boers in South Africa, descended from Dutch settlers, wanted independence from Britain. The British wanted South Africa for their own imperial ambitions, namely its strategic location and resources. Because Canada was part of the British Empire, many English-speaking Canadians thought that

Canada should send troops to help the British win what was sometimes called the "Second Boer War" and sometimes just the "Boer War."

On the other side were many French Canadians who identified with the Boers. After all, there were many similarities between the Boers and Quebecers; both were conquered minorities fighting for their rights. Quebecers were against Canadians being sent to put down this uprising. Laurier, under intense pressure from both sides, came to a classic Canadian compromise that satisfied no one. Although the Canadian government did not "officially" send troops to the Boer War, it did pay for and supply a completely volunteer force of 1,000 troops. Thus, those agitating for Canadian involvement in Britain's imperial wars were upset because Laurier had not openly declared Canada's support. Those against Canadian involvement were upset because Canada had indeed sent troops, even though Canada's participation in the war was not officially sanctioned. Ultimately, the British did put down the uprising by 1902, and South Africa remained a part of the British Empire.

The 1903 Alaska boundary dispute is a second example of tension between imperialism and nationalism. As part of the British Empire, Canada was still very colonial in its status in 1903. Though the 1867 British North America Act allowed Canadians to make virtually all internal policy decisions, on external matters, Canada remained subservient to British wishes. During the 1903 Alaska boundary dispute between the United States and Canada, the British negotiated for Canada, but largely put British interests ahead of Canadian concerns, upsetting many Canadian nationalists.

A third issue was the "naval question." By 1909, the British were in an arms race with their imperial rival, the Germans, to see who could build the most and the best warships. In Canada, imperialists demanded that the Canadian government contribute by building ships for the British navy. On the other side, nationalists, such as Laurier's fellow French-Canadian Liberal Henri Bourassa, thought that Canada should not take part in such an arms race, arguing that Canadians should formulate their own defence policy, irrespective of British demands. Again, Laurier's decision satisfied neither side. The Canadian government, he said, would build five ships at a cost of $11 million for the Canadian navy, but the British could use these ships in the event of war. All these issues undermined Laurier's support both in English Canada and in Quebec, and they reflected the continuing tensions between these two ethnic groups.

At the turn of the century, Canada was much different than Brown could have imagined in 1880. Yet he would have recognized many of the broader developments that Canadians had experienced—in politics, the economy, and social evolution. In some ways, Canada was as Brown had hoped and fought for; it fulfilled the vision he had. On other matters, however, the nation and its peoples had developed in unexpected and surprising ways—though he may not have agreed with these directions and permutations, Brown no doubt would have been a significant player in their development. Sadly, his relatively early death at the hands of a murderer did not allow him to see his dreams for Canada realized.

Further Reading

Careless, J.M.S. *Brown of the Globe: The Voice of Upper Canada, 1818–59.* Toronto: Dundurn, 1996.

Careless, J.M.S. *Brown of the Globe: Statesman of Confederation, 1860–80.* Toronto: Dundurn, 1996.

CBC. *John A.: Birth of a Country.* http://www.cbc.ca/player/Shows/Shows/ More+Shows/ID/2136716148/.

Dunlop, Joseph. "Politics, Patronage and Scandal at the Provincial Lunatic Asylum, 1848–1857." *Ontario History* 98, no. 2 (Autumn 2006): 183–208.

Moore, Christopher. *1867: How the Fathers Made a Deal.* Toronto: McClelland & Stewart, 1997.

ACTIVE HISTORY: PRIMARY DOCUMENT ANALYSIS

- Visit the *Globe and Mail* archive through your university library. Using the keyword and date utilities, examine dates and events related to the issues discussed above. Examples might include articles on Brown himself; on prohibition, abolition, or various issues related to French–English relations; or on economic and social matters.

- What insights can you gain from using a primary document such as a newspaper like the *Globe*? Does the newspaper provide a particular point of view or bias? How does the language differ from that of today's newspapers? How do the layout and design of the older paper differ? What are the most interesting aspects of reading a newspaper from a century ago?

- In addition, can you use the *Globe* heritage website to determine what happened to George Bennett?

CHAPTER FOUR

LOUIS RIEL, EXECUTED, REGINA, 1885

OPEN REBELLION AND THE FATE OF THE CANADIAN WEST

So, where do you stand?

Should Louis Riel have been executed for treason on November 16, 1885? Hanged from the gallows? Did he deserve his fate? Or was this a crooked trial, meant to get rid of a man who had been a thorn in the side of the Canadian government for nearly two decades? Was Riel an innocent victim or a traitor? A wanted criminal or a statesman? A murderer or Manitoba's Father of Confederation?

Where *do* you stand? This is not an academic question. To this day, Riel and his place in Canadian history are still very much at issue. Over the last two decades, there have been numerous attempts to pardon Riel for his crime and, essentially, to apologize for his execution. These attempts have generated controversy, as many Canadians do not think that a current government should apologize for something that happened more than a century ago.

At the same time, even many Métis are against pardoning Riel. In 2004, Métis leader Clément Chartier stated that the "government should not focus on pardoning or exonerating Riel, or vacating his conviction. That type of gesture will not address the ultimate sacrifice he made. That will not remove the dark cloud hanging over Canada's head. That will not placate the modern citizens of the Métis Nation or lessen our resolve to achieve our rightful place within a Canada based on our fundamental rights and freedoms as a people."[1] In other words,

---

1   For Chartier's full statement, see "Louis Riel Needs No Pardon," *The Métis Nation of Alberta*, May 3, 2004, http://www.albertametis.ca/MNAHome/News-Archive/Louis-Riel-Needs-No-Pardon.aspx.

granting Riel a pardon seemed to Chartier a meaningless symbolic gesture when compared to giving real rights to the Métis, especially over land.

Another example of Riel's legacy and the ongoing controversy surrounding his place in Canadian society can be seen in the 2007 Manitoba government's decision to name its February holiday "Riel Day." Some people thought this name a poor choice and that the day should be called "Family Day" instead, as was done in Alberta and Saskatchewan. Having a holiday named after you: a real turn of events for someone who was basically paid to leave the province and the country and was executed, wouldn't you say?

Indeed, it seems that Riel's ghost continues to haunt Canada. In 2013, nearly a century and a half after Manitoba's creation, the Supreme Court of Canada rendered a verdict that the Métis land agreements that Riel himself had overseen in 1870 had been improperly conducted by the Canadian government and that Métis should receive restitution, potentially worth hundreds of millions of dollars. Long after his execution, Riel still reaches from his grave to shape Canada.

Riel Is Guilty

Let's first make the case against him. There is no question that Riel led an insurrection against the Canadian government. The Métis and their aboriginal allies had battled and killed Canadian troops and mounted police in combat and had, for all intents and purposes, declared war upon the Canadian government. The North-West Rebellion was, in fact, the first and only full-scale, organized, armed uprising in Canadian history (the 1837 rebellions predated Canada's creation). Also, there is no question that, on Riel's orders, blood was shed during the rebellion. Moreover, this insurgency was clearly an attack on Canadian authority because Canada had claimed legal authority over the region since 1870, when the government had purchased the territory from the HBC. (The North-West Rebellion was thus different from the Red River uprising that Riel had led in 1869–70, when the status of Rupert's Land was somewhat up in the air because of the sale of the land.)

And, of course, Riel was wanted, rightly or wrongly, for the murder of Thomas Scott in 1870 and for his role in the Red River uprising; there had been an unclaimed $5,000 reward for his capture since 1872.

Riel's involvement can be traced to the 1884 visit by a group of Métis to Montana in the United States, where Riel had been living for a few years, working as a schoolteacher. The Métis wanted him to return to Canada to lead another insurgency. In part, this delegation approached Riel because he represented the many Métis who had fled Manitoba in the years after 1870. When the Canadian government arrived to establish authority in that year, soldiers from the occupying army instituted a two-year reign of terror, intimidating and assaulting the Métis population. Then, as English-speaking settlers poured into the province and it became obvious that neither the terms of the 1870 Manitoba Act would be upheld nor the land promised to the Métis distributed, thousands of Métis moved further west, into what would become Saskatchewan and Alberta.

Riel, who by 1881 was married and had three children (his youngest son died while Riel awaited execution), was initially reluctant to join the erstwhile rebels. But he had a long-standing grievance against the Canadian government and considered that he had experienced injustice at its hands, and he felt especially aggrieved by John A. Macdonald, whom he considered his political nemesis. The depth of Riel's animosity toward Macdonald can be seen in the 1880 poem he wrote about Macdonald, titled "Sir John A. Shackled by Pride's Endless Chain":

Sir John A. shackled by pride's endless chain
    Governs the Dominion's vast domain,
And through perfidy prolongs my agony
To gain his kind's approval, vain glory.

Disrespecting his commitment,
He does not heed the terms, fair and precise,
    Of our Agreement
    And my stated rights.
Nearly ten years have I endured torment.
A man who reneges on his word is base.
Let my accusing finger state my case (. . .)

Sir John, I do not wish upon you death
Riddled with pain and horror but instead
Days of dull remorse and daily regret,
You, foul vampire, who have left me for dead.
. . .
You will be the seen prevaricator
And on you history will lay the blame.
I pine away in exile but remain
In spite of you my nation's true leader. . . .[2]

Clearly, Riel was determined to get back to Canada—and to get back at John A. Macdonald.

The most damning evidence of Riel's guilt is the reality that the North-West Rebellion was, without question, a full-fledged insurrection. Upon arriving in the

---

2   Quoted in Glen Campbell, ed., *The Selected Poetry of Louis Riel*, translated by Paul Savoie (Toronto: Exile Editions, 2000), 91–93.

North West, Riel went about recruiting to his cause white settlers and aboriginal allies such as Big Bear, a Cree chieftain, and Sitting Bull, a Sioux leader famous for his resistance to the US government. Frustrated by Ottawa's unwillingness to address the grievances of the Métis, settlers, and aboriginal peoples, Riel reprised his Red River tactic in March of 1885 and declared a provisional government in the North West, which he called the Exovedate. He and others seized a supply of munitions, taking several hostages. The North-West Mounted Police (created in 1873) responded by sending 100 armed men to secure provisions at Duck Lake. Gabriel Dumont, Riel's great Métis military leader, met the column and attacked, killing 12 and wounding 11 others.

Dumont's victory at the Battle of Duck Lake on March 26, 1885, was the first in a series of clashes between the Métis, supported by their aboriginal allies, and Canadian government troops. With the near completion of the Canadian Pacific Railway, Ottawa quickly dispatched several thousand soldiers in three columns to face the Métis and First Nations. A series of bitter battles in the spring of 1885 ensued. At Cut Knife, Cree Chief Poundmaker and his warriors defeated Canadian troops armed with Gatling machine guns. The Métis scored an improbable victory over the Canadians at Fish Creek, where 200 Métis stopped the advance of nearly 900 Canadian soldiers. Eventually, in the most pivotal battle of the rebellion, Canadian soldiers laid siege to Batoche, the heartland of the Métis. Nearly a thousand Canadian troops faced 250 Métis fighters. Riel refused to allow Dumont to utilize guerrilla tactics, and after three days, the Métis capital fell. Though the Métis were defeated, Cree warriors continued to fight at Frenchman's Butte and Loon Lake, but with little impact. In the end, a total of 81 Métis and aboriginals went to trial, some charged with treason-felony, some with murder, and one, Riel, with high treason. Along with Riel, eight aboriginals were hanged.

Riel Is Innocent

Let's now state the case in favour of innocence. There is no question that, though he led the North-West Rebellion, Riel never actively fought in the uprising or took up arms against anyone: he was a schoolteacher. Riel was, for all intents and purposes, trying to do the right thing for the Métis, who had been unquestionably treated unfairly both in the Red River and the North West. Moreover, he was undeniably the founder of Manitoba.

Riel's actions were a direct consequence of his treatment at the hands of the federal government. After the Red River resistance, the amnesty that Red River delegates negotiated for Riel and for the rest of the Métis leadership was never put in writing. This happened because Macdonald caved to political pressure from Ontario, whose government offered a $5,000 reward for the arrest of Scott's murderers. In 1870, when Canadian troops arrived in the Red River, Riel's house was ransacked and he was considered a fugitive at large. For a time, he took refuge just south of the border in Dakota Territory. Macdonald, in an effort to rid himself of the Métis leader, paid Riel $1,000 to stay out of the country. But by then Riel was a hero to the Métis.

He ran for federal Parliament as a Conservative (John A.'s party) and won his Manitoba seat in 1873 and then again in 1874. Yet Riel was never able to represent the people of his riding; the furore in Ontario meant that he could never take up his political career. Riel's reputation was ruined, and he was still hated by large swathes of the Canadian population.

Even worse was the Canadian government's treatment of Riel's people, the Métis. Already by the early 1870s, it was clear that the terms of the Manitoba Act were not being met. The new province's government refused to conform to the bilingual provisions created by the Métis; the Lieutenant Governor was not bilingual, and neither the courts nor the legislature really operated in both languages. Though there were denominational schools, this right was slowly being attacked, too, and French-language instruction was effectively ended by the 1890s.

Finally, and most important, was the Canadian government's mistreatment of the Métis when it came to the land they had negotiated as part of their agreement to enter Confederation. The Métis were promised 1.4 million acres of land for their future. Yet implementation of this program was delayed for several years, and, when the Métis did get the land that they were promised, it was in areas that the Métis were not interested in, of poor quality, or broken up into unmanageable pieces. Disillusioned and often pushed to the margins, many Métis sold the land for what little they could get and moved westward.

As they settled in the North West in the 1870s and 1880s, the same problems followed them. The most profound change for them, as for aboriginals of the plains, was the accelerating diminishment of bison. Because of this, Métis began to establish permanent settlements on the Missouri and North Saskatchewan Rivers, in long, rectangular, two-mile-wide river-front lots, in the French-Canadian style. Problems over land title arose because the Métis were settling the lands at time as the Dominion government was surveying it, but government surveyors divided and organized land in a very different fashion from the patterns of Métis traditional use. The government surveyed the lands into regular square blocks, divided into 160-acre quarter sections, following the British and American tradition. Moreover, the question of how to ensure that both Métis and other settlers were granted title to their land remained unclear, and getting title took a frustrating number of years. After more than a decade of petitions, letters, and questions about their land, Métis frustration was boiling over.

Just as legitimate, and perhaps even more so, were the grievances of the aboriginal peoples of the North West. For the First Nations who had lived on the land from time immemorial, the constantly growing intrusion of European settlement had fundamentally changed their circumstances, and not for the better.

For much of the period after contact until the nineteenth century, whites had been dependent upon aboriginals for food, trade, technology, and military alliances. But decades of disease, conflict, and European and Canadian duplicity had left aboriginal groups in significantly reduced circumstances. Aboriginal populations had decreased dramatically, and much of aboriginal territory had been ceded through treaties and white encroachment.

After Confederation, the federal government had taken over the British Crown's responsibility for relations with Canada's aboriginal peoples. Instead of allies, the Canadian government viewed aboriginals in Canada as dependents, and, through the 1876 Indian Act and the Department of Indian Affairs, created in 1880, embarked on a policy of assimilation that fit within a larger state project of colonialism and asserting white, male, liberal control over aboriginal territory. This policy included banning aboriginal cultural practices such as the sun dance and potlatch, creating a reserve system, changing aboriginal governance, and eventually establishing Indian residential schools designed to Canadianize aboriginal children, a policy many scholars have called an attempt at cultural genocide.

By the early 1880s, Cree leader Big Bear was waging a campaign in the North West to reopen treaty negotiations and achieve a better deal, feeling that his people had been forced into poor treaties in order to receive food rations. Throughout 1884 and into 1885, Big Bear launched a political campaign aimed at uniting not only the Cree but also, potentially, their age-old traditional enemies, the Blackfoot.

Given these circumstances, the Canadian government, it could be said, had provoked Riel and his allies into action.

Riel Is Guilty, but Insane, and Should Not Hang

There was another option available to jurors, and to John A. Macdonald, in determining Riel's fate. In fact, much of Riel's trial hinged on the question of his sanity. Riel had delusions of grandeur and a messianic view that he was the "prophet of the new world" and would create a new Rome and Roman Catholic Church in Saskatchewan. There was no doubt that he was delusional, if not at the time of his trial and execution, then at the time of the North-West Rebellion. In March 1876, despite his banishment from Canada, Riel was admitted into a mental asylum in Montreal; because he needed constant attention, he was transferred after a few months to the Beauport asylum outside Quebec City, where he was treated for megalomania and paranoia. Perhaps he was being more hopeful than delusional, but, when Batoche fell to Canadian troops in 1885, Dumont escaped but Riel refused to go, believing he would have a large dramatic trial in Ottawa or Montreal.

Riel's trial is one of the most controversial in Canadian history for a number of reasons. For one, there was the location and jury: Riel did get his trial, but in Regina not in the East. And the trial was criticized by many in French Canada, and by many historians since, as taking place in an unfriendly venue with a jury composed of not one single French Métis. Other historians have suggested that, given the legal framework at the time, the government did obey the law and that, when Riel's trial is compared to other treason trials of the period, he was given a fair hearing.

The trial was controversial, too, because, although Riel was found guilty, the real issue was the defence's attempt to claim that he was insane. The defence was not successful for a couple of reasons. First, in 1885, the rules for insanity were fairly stringent; someone could be medically insane but still legally responsible (this law changed in 1892 to provide more leniency, but it is still not clear that, even under these provisions, Riel would have been found innocent). Moreover, Riel himself protested his innocence.

Figure 4.1 *Louis Riel, 1878*

University of Manitoba, PC 107

Riel had one last chance, and this aspect of his conviction, trial, and hanging is perhaps the most controversial. Once he was convicted, the federal cabinet, as in all capital cases, had the option of granting mercy and staying the execution. Because of the intense public interest in this case, Macdonald sent a committee made up of three doctors, two English speaking and one French speaking, to evaluate Riel's fitness of mind. Riel did not know he was being evaluated. In the committee, there was sharp disagreement: the French-Canadian doctor argued that Riel was insane, but the other two stated that he was of sound mind.

Shockingly, the report to the House of Commons was altered so that it looked as if the committee unanimously agreed that Riel was of sound mind. Although it is not clear what a mixed finding from this committee would have meant, this manipulation of the truth is an example of the willingness of the Macdonald government to alter the situation to see Riel hanged. When representatives from Quebec begged for leniency toward the condemned Métis leader, Macdonald is reported to have remarked that Riel would hang "though every dog in Quebec bark in his favour."[3] With no leniency from the federal government, Riel, who incidentally had become an American citizen in 1883, was hanged from the gallows in the North-West Mounted Police barracks in Regina on November 16, 1885.

The Verdict

Should Riel have been executed? The consequences of his death were tremendous, especially for the Métis and aboriginal peoples of the West, not to mention the political fortunes of the Conservative Party in Quebec and the views of French Canadians toward Confederation.

Riel's execution marked both a symbolic and real end to the domination of the North West by the Métis and First Nations; it signified the assertion of the Canadian government's will over the region. It was more than just the death of one man; it was the death of the dream of a new, Métis nation in the West. Just as symbolically, only a few days before Riel's execution in Regina, further west at Craigellachie, British Columbia, on November 7, the last spike of the Canadian Pacific Railway was driven into the track by Donald Smith, known as Lord Strathcona. Smith, soon to be one of Canada's richest men, was part owner of the railway, the HBC, and the Bank of Montreal. As one dream of Canada's West was executed, another was being birthed.

---

3   Quoted in Maggie Siggins, *Riel: A Life of Revolution* (Toronto: HarperCollins, 1994), 442.

Yet it is important to recognize that this is not just a story of loss and of defeat but one of agency and resistance. Riel, the Métis, and the Aboriginals of Western Canada fought back and challenged the Canadian government and white values. This resistance is something that continued well after 1885. There was a defeat, but it was not the end of the Métis or First Nations societies in Canada, though aboriginals had no choice but to deal with the mechanisms of colonialism going forward.

Further Reading

Groarke, Paul. "The Trial and Execution of Louis Riel: Defending My Country the North West." *Canadian Journal of Native Studies* 33, no. 2 (2013): 1–28.

Mumford, Jeremy Ravi. "Why Was Louis Riel, a United States Citizen, Hanged as a Canadian Traitor in 1885?" *Canadian Historical Review* 88, no. 2 (June 2007): 237–62. http://dx.doi.org/10.3138/chr.88.2.237.

Read, Geoff, and Todd Webb. "'The Catholic Mahdi of the North West': Louis Riel and the Metis Resistance in Transatlantic and Imperial Context." *Canadian Historical Review* 93, no. 1 (June 2012): 171–95.

Reid, Jennifer. *Louis Riel and the Creation of Modern Canada: Mythic Discourse and the Postcolonial State.* Albuquerque: University of New Mexico Press, 2008.

ACTIVE HISTORY: PRIMARY DOCUMENT ANALYSIS, FROM THE FINAL STATEMENT OF LOUIS RIEL AT HIS TRIAL IN REGINA ON FRIDAY, JULY 31, 1885

- Read the following passage: What insights can you gain from Riel's final statement? What were his key concerns? What arguments did he make? Can you make a judgment about Riel's sanity based on his testimony? Why are primary sources such as this useful for understanding historical events?

HIS HONOR: Prisoner, have you any remarks to make to the jury, if so, now is your time to speak?

. . . .

RIEL: Your Honors, gentlemen of the jury: It would be easy for me to-day to play insanity, because the circumstances are such as to excite any man, and under the natural excitement of what is taking place to-day (I cannot speak English very well, but am trying to do so, because most of those here speak English), under the excitement which my trial causes me would justify me not to appear as usual, but with my mind out of its ordinary condition. I hope with the help of God I will maintain calmness and decorum as suits this honorable court, this honorable jury.

You have seen by the papers in the hands of the Crown that I am naturally inclined to think of God at the beginning of my actions. I wish if you—I—do it you won't take it as a mark of insanity, that you won't take it as part of a play of insanity. Oh, my God, help me through Thy grace and the divine influence of Jesus Christ. Oh, my God, bless me, bless this honorable court, bless this honorable jury, bless my good lawyers who have come 700 leagues to try to save my life, bless also the lawyers for the Crown, because they have done, I am sure, what they thought their duty. They have shown me fairness which at first I did not expect from them. Oh, my God, bless all those who are around me through the grace and influence of Jesus Christ our Saviour, change the curiosity of those who are paying attention to me, change that curiosity into sympathy with me. The day of my birth I was helpless and my mother took care of me although she was not able to do it alone, there was someone to help her to take care of me and I lived. Today, although a man I am as helpless before this court, in the Dominion of Canada and in this world, as I was helpless on the knees of my mother the day of my birth.

The North West is also my mother, it is my mother country and although my mother country is sick and confined in a certain way, there are some from Lower Canada who came to help her to take care of me during her sickness and I am sure that my mother country will not kill me more than my mother did forty years ago when I came into the world, because a mother is always a mother, and even if I have my faults if she can see I am true she will be full of love for me.

When I came into the North West in July, the first of July 1884, I found the Indians suffering. I found the half-breeds eating the rotten pork of the Hudson Bay Company and getting sick and weak every day. Although a half breed, and having no pretension to help the whites, I also paid attention to them. I saw they were deprived of responsible government, I saw that they were deprived of their public liberties. I remembered that half-breed meant white and Indian, and while I paid attention to the suffering Indians and the half-breeds I remembered that the greatest part of my heart and blood was white and I have directed my attention to help the Indians, to help the half-breeds and to help the whites to the best of my ability. We have made petitions, I have made petitions with others to the Canadian Government asking to relieve the condition of this country. We have taken time; we have tried to unite all classes, even if I may speak, all parties. Those who have been in close communication with me know I have suffered, that I have waited for months to bring some of the people of the Saskatchewan to an understanding of certain important points in our

petition to the Canadian Government and I have done my duty. I believe I have done my duty. . . .

No one can say that the North-West was not suffering last year, particularly the Saskatchewan, for the other parts of the North-West I cannot say so much; but what I have done, and risked, and to which I have exposed myself, rested certainly on the conviction, I had to do, was called upon to do something for my country.

It is true, gentlemen, I believed for years I had a mission, and when I speak of a mission you will understand me not as trying to play the role of insane before the grand jury so as to have a verdict of acquittal upon that ground. I believe that I have a mission, I believe I had a mission at this very time. What encourages me to speak to you with more confidence in all the imperfections of my English way of speaking, it is that I have yet and still that mission, and with the help of God, who is in this box with me, and He is on the side of my lawyers, even with the honorable court, the Crown and the jury, to help me, and to prove by the extraordinary help that there is a Providence to-day in my trial, as there was a Providence in the battles of the Saskatchewan.

I have not assumed to myself that I had a mission. I was working in Manitoba first, and I did all I could to get free institutions for Manitoba; they have those institutions to-day in Manitoba, and they try to improve them, while myself, who obtained them, I am forgotten as if I was dead. But after I had obtained, with the help of others, a constitution for Manitoba, when the Government at Ottawa was not willing to inaugurate it at the proper time, I have worked till the inauguration should take place, and that is why I have been banished for five years. I had to rest five years, I was willing to do it. I protested, I said: "Oh, my God, I offer You all my existence for that cause, and please to make of my weakness an instrument to help men in my country." And seeing my intentions, the late Archbishop Bourget said: "Riel has no narrow views, he is a man to accomplish great things," and he wrote that letter of which I hope that the Crown has at least a copy. And in another letter, when I became what doctors believed to be insane, Bishop Bourget wrote again and said: "Be ye blessed by God and man and take patience in your evils." Am I not taking patience? Will I be blessed by man as I have been by God?

I say that I have been blessed by God, and I hope that you will not take that as a presumptuous assertion. It has been a great success for me to come through all the dangers I have in that fifteen years. . . .

Even if I was going to be sentenced by you, gentlemen of the jury, I have this satisfaction if I die—that if I die I will not be reputed by all men as insane, as a lunatic. . . .

The agitation in the North-West Territories would have been constitutional, and would certainly be constitutional to-day if, in my opinion, we had not been attacked. Perhaps the Crown has not been able to find out the particulars, that we were attacked, but as we were on the scene it was easy to understand. When we sent petitions to the Government, they used to answer us by sending police, and when the rumors were increasing every day that Riel had been shot here or there, or that Riel was going to be shot by such and such a man, the police would not pay any attention to it. . . .

Your Honors, gentlemen of the jury: If I was a man of today perhaps it would be presumptuous to speak in that way, but the truth is good to say, and it is said in a proper manner, and it is without any presumption, it is not because I have been libeled for fifteen years that I do not believe myself something. I know that through the grace of God I am the founder of Manitoba. I know that though I have no open road for my influence, I have big influence, concentrated as a big amount of vapour in an engine. I believe by what I suffered for fifteen years, by what I have done for Manitoba and the people of the North-West, that my words are worth something. If I give offence, I do not speak to insult. Yes, you are the pioneers of civilization, the whites are the pioneers of civilization, but they bring among the Indians demoralization. Do not be offended, ladies, do not be offended, here are the men who can cure that evil; and if at times I have been strong against my true friends and fathers, the reverend priests of the Saskatchewan, it is because my convictions are strong. There have been witnesses to show that

immediately after great passion I could come back to the great respect I have for them. . . .

I wish you to believe that I am not trying to play insanity, there is in the manner, in the standing of a man, the proof that he is sincere, not playing. You will say, what have you got to say? I have to attend to practical results. Is it practical that you be acknowledged as a prophet? It is practical to say it. I think that if the half-breeds have acknowledged me, as a community, to be a prophet, I have reason to believe that it is beginning to become practical. I do not wish, for my satisfaction, the name of prophet, generally that title is accompanied with such a burden, that if there is satisfaction for your vanity, there is a check to it. . . .

British civilization which rules today the world, and the British constitution has defined such government as this is which rules the North-West Territories as irresponsible government, which plainly means that there is no responsibility, and by all the science which has been shown here yesterday you are compelled to admit if there is no responsibility, it is insane.

Good sense combined with scientific theories lead to the same conclusion. By the testimony laid before you during my trial witnesses on both sides made it certain that petition after petition had been sent to the Federal Government, and so irresponsible is that Government to the North-West that in the course of several years besides doing nothing to satisfy the people of this great land, it has even hardly been able to answer once or to give a single response. That fact would indicate an absolute lack of responsibility, and therefore insanity complicated with paralysis.

The Ministers of an insane and irresponsible Government and its little one—the North-West Council—made up their minds to answer my petitions by surrounding me slyly and by attempting to jump upon me suddenly and upon my people in the Saskatchewan.

Happily when they appeared and showed their teeth to devour, I was ready: that is what is called my crime of high treason, and to which they hold me to-day. Oh, my good jurors, in the name of Jesus Christ, the only one who can save and help me, they have tried to tear me to pieces.

If you take the plea of the defense that I am not responsible for my acts, acquit me completely since I have been quarrelling with an insane and irresponsible Government. If you pronounce in favor of the Crown, which contends that I am responsible, acquit me all the same. You are perfectly justified in declaring that having my reason and sound mind, I have acted reasonably and in self-defense, while the Government, my accuser, being irresponsible, and consequently insane, cannot but have acted wrong, and if high treason there is it must be on its side and not on my part.

HIS HONOR: Are you done?

RIEL: Not yet, if you have the kindness to permit me your attention for a while.

HIS HONOR: Well, proceed.

RIEL: For fifteen years I have been neglecting myself. Even one of the most hard witnesses on me said that with all my vanity, I never was particular to my clothing; yes, because I never had much to buy any clothing. . . . My wife and children are without means, while I am working more than any representative in the North-West. Although I am simply a guest of this country—a guest of the half-breeds of the Saskatchewan—although as a simple guest, I worked to better the condition of the people of the Saskatchewan at the risk of my life, to better the condition of the people of the North-West, I have never had any pay. It has always been my hope to have a fair living one day. It will be for you to pronounce—if you say I was right, you can conscientiously acquit me, as I hope through the help of God you will. You will console those who have been fifteen years around me only partaking in my sufferings. What you will do in justice to me, in justice to my family, in justice to my friends, in justice to the North-West, will be rendered a hundred times to you in this world, and to use a sacred expression, life everlasting in the other.

I thank your Honor for the favor you have granted me in speaking; I thank you for the attention you have given me, gentlemen of the jury, and I thank those who have had the kindness to encourage my imperfect way of speaking the English language by your good attention. I put my speech under the protection of my God, my Saviour, He is the only one who can make it effective. It is possible it should become effective, as it is proposed to good men, to good people, and to good ladies also.[4]

---

4   Transcripts of the trial are available from the University of Missouri-Kansas City (UMKC) School of Law website. See "Final Statement of Louis Riel at His Trial in Regina," http://law2.umkc.edu/faculty/projects/ftrials/riel/rieltrialstatement.html.

TRAGIC TALES
THE FROG LAKE MASSACRE AND THE EXECUTION OF EIGHT FIRST NATIONS WARRIORS, FORT BATTLEFORD, PRESENT-DAY SASKATCHEWAN, 1885

The Violent Coda to Riel's Rebellion

One of Canada's bloodiest days occurred less than two weeks after Riel had been hanged in Regina. In the largest mass execution in Canadian history, on November 27, 1885, eight First Nations warriors, including six Cree and two Assiniboine, were hanged at Fort Battleford, in present-day Saskatchewan. Though the eight aboriginal warriors, including war chief Wandering Spirit (leader of the attack at Frog Lake), were ostensibly hanged for their roles in the uprising, the story is far more complex.

Like that of the Métis, aboriginal groups' involvement in the North-West Rebellion was fuelled by legitimate grievances. By the early 1880s, as the buffalo population dangerously declined and aboriginals faced starvation and marginalization, most of the Plains tribes signed treaties with the Canadian government. Frustrated by years of poor treatment, Big Bear, the Great Plains chief, had steadfastly refused to agree to Treaty 6 (one of the numbered treaties that ceded control of most of the country to whites). Instead, he argued for better terms and sought to build alliances among Plains aboriginals. One such attempt to develop ties to other First Nations involved the Blackfoot, traditional enemies of the Cree. Even after finally agreeing to the treaty in 1882, Big Bear refused to take up land on a reserve. Because of this refusal, his people did not receive rations. By the spring of 1885, matters worsened as his Cree, other aboriginals, and Canadian Indian agents clashed over food and provisions. Longstanding frustrations came to a boil.

When Riel appeared on the scene to make the case for an uprising as a way to drive home the point of the Canadian government's mistreatment of the Métis, aboriginals, and whites in the region (many white settlers felt neglected by the federal government as well), some aboriginals felt they had little choice but to join the Métis leader's insurrection. But, although Big Bear met with Riel in 1884, he was not convinced of Riel's plan.

In April 1885, after Big Bear had gone on a solitary hunt, his tribe's war chief, Wandering Spirit, decided to take action. When Big Bear returned from his hunt, he discovered that Wandering Spirit and a group of warriors (including Big Bear's son Āyimisīs and the warrior Miserable Man), in a desperate effort to obtain food and supplies, had taken hostages at Frog Lake, among them Indian Agent Thomas Quinn, who was despised for his arrogant and unkind treatment of the Cree. Despite Big Bear's pleas for peace, the situation deteriorated, and, when Quinn refused to be moved to an encampment about two kilometres from Frog Lake, Wandering Spirit shot Quinn in the head. In the chaos that followed, Wandering Spirit and his warriors killed eight more men, including two priests, and took more hostages.

The Frog Lake Massacre, as it came to be known in Canada, was a flashpoint of the North-West Rebellion, and it prompted a harsh military response by the Canadian government. More than a thousand Canadian troops were dispatched to subdue the First Nations in the region, as other chiefs such as Poundmaker and One Arrow were drawn into the conflict. Many continued to fight even after Riel's Saskatchewan "capital" at Batoche fell, engaging with Canadian troops at Frenchman's Butte and Loon Lake. Eventually, however, the aboriginal warriors, exhausted and outnumbered, surrendered or were captured.

In the wake of the rebellion, 81 men were put on trial for a range of crimes, from horse stealing to treason, which (as in the case of Riel) was punishable by death. The aboriginals who faced the Canadian justice system were poorly represented, could not understand the English proceedings, and felt the full weight of a government that wanted to send a message. Eventually, although some leaders such as Big Bear, One Arrow, and Poundmaker were sentenced to time in prison (44 aboriginals and 36 Métis were sent to the Manitoba Penitentiary), the eight men condemned to death were subjected to a public execution in Battleford. The executions, as John A. Macdonald coldly told a colleague, "ought to convince the Red Man that the White Man governs."[5]

On the cold morning of November 27, the men climbed the scaffold, which was in the middle of the barracks and had been built with a long beam that held nooses for eight. Hundreds of whites and aboriginals had come to witness the event, including aboriginal children of the Battleford Industrial School, an Indian residential school, who had been made to come to the hanging. All the men were given 10 minutes to speak to the hushed crowd; only Wandering Spirit chose not to. As the ropes were placed around their necks, the men sang aboriginal songs, a last act of defiance. As the trap doors opened, a sudden sharp silence marked the end of the North-West Rebellion.

Frog Lake, the hangings, and the Métis and aboriginal uprising during the rebellion need to be understood in context: the treatment of the aboriginal warriors at the hands of the Canadian state reflected the racist attitudes and colonial approach by Ottawa toward First Nations at the time, one that saw aboriginals as a population to be subdued and assimilated. The Métis and aboriginal peoples of the West (and in the rest of Canada) resisted these attempts, and the events of 1885 remain a testament to their enduring willingness to demand fair treatment.

---

5   Ted McCoy, "Legal Ideology in the Aftermath of Rebellion: The Convicted First Nations Participants, 1885," *Social History* 42, no. 83 (2009): 175–201, see page 186.

MURDEROUS MOMENT
KILLING THE FRENCH FACT OUTSIDE OF QUEBEC—ENDING SEPARATE (FRENCH) SCHOOLING IN NEW BRUNSWICK, MANITOBA, SASKATCHEWAN, ALBERTA, AND ONTARIO, 1871–1912

The French-Canadian Idea of Confederation under Attack

In nineteenth-century Canada, language, religion, and schooling were intimately connected and highly contentious. Minority religious schooling was a flashpoint of conflict in the combined Ontario-Quebec Province of Canada from the time of its creation in 1841 and had been one of the key issues pushing the colony toward political deadlock. English-speaking Protestant Canadians did not want to spend public money on providing Catholic education in Ontario; in Quebec, there was resentment toward the English and Protestant minority that had its own school system. For the predominantly French-speaking Roman Catholic minority in Canada, schooling was not just about religion but about language as well. Eventually, the Confederation agreement included a clause, Section 93, championed by Thomas D'Arcy McGee, meant to solve "the schools question" by ensuring that the federal government protected minority schooling within each province.

But McGee's solution did not hold. Indeed, battles over language instruction only intensified after McGee's assassination in 1868; what resulted was a concerted, decades-long fight over minority schooling that ultimately resulted in the demise or curtailment of French-language instruction in most of Canada outside Quebec. The demise of French schooling outside of Quebec isolated that province and had long-term consequences for the federation. The French-Canadian minority could point to decades of inferior treatment at the hands of the majority and to a cultural and linguistic heritage that, eventually, provided arguments for Quebec nationalism, if not outright separatism.

In the 1870s, the first battle lines over minority schooling occurred in the Maritimes. The French-speaking Acadian population had been expelled from the region during the Seven Years' War (1756–63) between Britain and France, yet the Acadians had returned over time and re-established communities in New Brunswick and Nova Scotia. In 1871, New Brunswick passed a law stating that all schools had to be "common" (i.e., non-denominational) to receive state aid, which effectively prevented support for Catholic and thus French-speaking schooling in the province. This law, the Common Schools Act, greatly upset many Acadians, who demanded their right to Catholic schooling. In Caraquet, an Acadian community on New Brunswick's north shore, protests against the act descended into violence, with two people killed in an 1875 gun battle over the issue. Though amendments were made to the act, no real separate schooling survived in New Brunswick.

Manitoba was another flashpoint of this conflict. The 1870 Manitoba Act, drafted by Louis Riel's provisional government and agreed to by John A. Macdonald, institutionalized the bilingual nature of the province and protected Roman Catholic (and French-language) schools. But by the 1890s, waves of English-speaking settlers, many from Ontario, had completely changed the demographics of the province. In the early 1870s, the province was half French speaking; two decades later, the francophone population was less than one-tenth of the total.

In 1890, Premier Thomas Greenway moved to abolish public funding of Roman Catholic schools in Manitoba entirely, a decision that was sharply contested in court and protested by French Canadians across the country, especially in Quebec.

The Manitoba Schools Question became a major election issue in 1896, and, though the federal Conservative government promised to enact remedial legislation to protect minority religious schooling, Liberal leader Wilfrid Laurier promised that his "sunny ways" could find a way out of the impasse. As a Quebecer and Liberal, Laurier supported provincial rights, and, when he was elected, he made an agreement with Greenway that allowed for limited French instruction in Manitoba: religious instruction could be obtained in a language other than English, but only for half an hour at the end of each school day, and, when 10 pupils in any school district spoke French "or any language other than English," they could get bilingual instruction in that language. This "compromise" reflected Laurier's pragmatic political approach, but it meant, in the long run, that French was put in the same category as any other language that was not English and it offered no protection for the language, religion, or culture of Manitoba's French Canadians. Basically, it wiped out French as a language of instruction in the province.

Laurier also faced the issue of French-language instruction in the North-West Territories. As with Manitoba, these areas had a strong Métis presence but had also experienced a massive influx of English speakers and of immigrants from other countries who spoke neither English nor French. In a period of staunch loyalty to the British imperial idea, many English-speaking Canadians wanted to see English-only education in these new provinces, despite the British North America Act's protection of minority schooling rights. When two new provinces, Alberta and Saskatchewan, were carved out of the North-West Territories

in 1905, Laurier did not enforce minority language rights upon their entry into Confederation. Like Manitoba, these provinces became essentially English, with no French minority schooling rights.

In Ontario, the situation was somewhat different. Thousands of French Canadians had migrated to northern Ontario by the end of the nineteenth century. In the early 1900s, French Canadians constituted nearly one-fifth of the provincial population. Many English-speaking Ontarians saw the growing French-speaking population in Ontario and the idea of French-language instruction as a problem. In 1912, the provincial government passed Regulation 17, which restricted instruction after the first year of school and completely banned the teaching of French after the fourth year.

French Canadians were outraged. Henri Bourassa, one of the leading francophone nationalists of the period, created the newspaper *Le Droit* [The Right] as a pulpit to fight the decision. Eventually, after a long, hard-fought battle, francophones established their own limited separate school system, and bilingual education was re-established in the province in 1927. But, by then, much of the damage to French-language schooling rights had been done. The French minority had lost again.

Across the country, separate schools that taught French had been curtailed dramatically, and, despite the best efforts of French Canadians to retain their language, in the provinces where francophones were in the minority, their assimilation into the English-speaking majority accelerated.

In the end, these cases reflected the willingness of English-speaking Canadians in the late nineteenth and early twentieth centuries to limit French to Quebec, save for a few pockets in New Brunswick, Ontario, and the West. Although this containment might have been seen as a victory for English speakers, eventually, nationalist Quebecers pointed to both the treatment of francophone minorities in other provinces and to their own demographic challenges as reasons to leave Canada.

Ironically, with minority language instruction protected by the 1982 Charter of Rights and Freedoms, a growth of French immersion outside of Quebec, and a boom in English-language instruction inside Quebec since the 1980s, minority language schooling has seen something of a rebirth. Despite this turnaround, it's clear that Canada might have been a dramatically different country if French had been allowed to flourish outside of Quebec, instead of being attacked at every turn.

PART TWO
A NATION FORGED IN BLOOD?

Nations, a great political scientist once argued, are "imagined communities," and nationalism is itself a social construction—an idea that exists and is created by those wishing to build the nation itself.

By the beginning of the First World War, or the Great War, as it was then known, Canada existed as a state that encompassed most of northern North America, but, in many ways, it was not yet a nation. Canadians were no more or less attached to the idea of "Canada" than they were connected to the church, to *le patramonie*, to tribe, to language, or to their local region. And, although it had complete control over its domestic affairs, Canada in its foreign relations remained a colony, and very much an appendage of Britain. Even in its domestic matters, many issues hinged in some way or another upon the fulcrum of imperialism, nationalism or continentalism—in other words, on the central point of identity.

The Great War both exacerbated and changed this state of affairs. The sacrifices and conflict that marked the war were not imagined but real— all too real, in fact. The Great War reshaped the nation and its peoples in innumerable ways; it drastically altered Canadians' views of themselves and of their place in the world. Although this transformation was an ongoing process, the Great War was indeed a significant step along that process, as was the Second World War.

If Canada's evolution was dramatically shaped by the sacrifices of the Great War, then its political and economic evolution was undoubtedly further sped along by the second great global conflagration between 1939 and 1945. Of course, wars were not the sole arbiters of the development of the Canadian peoples. Between these two great wars, Canadians were transformed by a host of events, some of which were symbolized and marked by bloody, tragic, and sometimes mysterious deaths.

MURDEROUS MOMENT

WILLIAM C. HOPKINSON, IMMIGRATION OFFICER AND SECRET AGENT, MURDERED, VANCOUVER, 1914

On the Eve of World War, Immigrants and Spies on the Edge of Empire

On October 21, 1914, Immigration Officer William Charles Hopkinson was dramatically gunned down on the steps of the Vancouver courthouse in broad daylight. While waiting to give evidence in a murder case, Hopkinson was approached by a man who brazenly fired two handguns point blank into Hopkinson's chest. Hopkinson fell to his knees, yet got up and attempted to grab the man. His assailant fired again, putting a bullet through Hopkinson's heart, and then shot Hopkinson three more times. Grabbed by a court janitor, Hopkinson's assailant asked, "Is he dead?" When told that the immigration officer was dead, he replied, "Then I am glad."[1] The murder shocked Vancouver and British Columbia, and more than 2,000 mourners attended Hopkinson's funeral, including immigration officers from Canada and the United States, British officials, and Canadian military units. He left behind a wife and two young children.

Virtually none of Hopkinson's mourners knew that, along with being an immigration officer, Hopkinson was also a spy for the Canadian government, one who often worked closely with British intelligence services. Far from being a simple random murder, Hopkinson's killing in many ways epitomizes Canada's conflicted views on immigration, race, and empire in the late nineteenth and early twentieth centuries.

During the long Laurier immigration boom between 1896 and 1911, over two million people immigrated to Canada. No period before or

since had ever seen such a huge wave of newcomers to the country. Canada's population in 1896 was just over five million; by 1914 it had ballooned to almost eight million. Hopkinson, born in India in 1880 and fluent in Hindi, himself came to Canada in 1907. In 1909, he was hired as a key immigration officer following a similar stint working as a police inspector for the British in India (Britain controlled India until 1947, when Mahatma Ghandi led the country to independence).

By the 1900s, some of the immigrants that had come to Canada during the boom had been non-white, particularly in British Columbia. Situated on the Pacific Rim on the far edge of the British Empire, BC had become a destination for Chinese, Japanese, and other Asian immigrants. The influx of non-whites had raised racial concerns for the mostly British population, even though many of the prospective immigrants, especially those from the Indian subcontinent, were British subjects themselves or came from countries allied with Britain, such as Japan.

For instance, in 1907, white Vancouverites rioted against Chinese and Japanese in the city, destroying property, such as immigrant shops, and physically attacking Asians. A young politician by the name of William Lyon Mackenzie King was dispatched by Ottawa to Vancouver to investigate the riots and convene public sessions for those with claims for damages and losses. Deputy minister of labour in 1907, Mackenzie King eventually became prime minister in 1921. In 1908, King was also dispatched to Britain to investigate immigration to Canada from the Orient. He wrote the following in his

---

1   "Immigration Officer William C. Hopkinson," *The Officer Down Memorial Page*, http://canada.odmp.org/ officer/624-immigration-officer-william-c.-hopkinson.

report: "That Canada should desire to restrict immigration from the Orient is regarded as natural, that Canada should remain a white man's country is believed to be not only desirable for economic and social reasons, but highly necessary on political and national grounds."[2] Of course, this view was challenged in later years, yet it was the attitude of many Canadians in the years before and after 1914.

But back to Hopkinson. In 1914, just before he was murdered, Hopkinson had played a prominent role in the saga of the ship *Komagata Maru*. In 1914, nearly 400 South Asians on a Japanese steamer landed in Vancouver after a two-month trip originating in Hong Kong. All passengers were from India and British subjects—there were 340 Sikhs, 24 Muslims, and 12 Hindus—so they demanded to be allowed entry to Canada. In 1913, Canada, still very much a British colony in its external relations, had accepted over 400,000 immigrants, virtually all white and virtually all from the United Kingdom, the United States, or other areas of Western Europe.

Through months of discussions, Hopkinson, who spoke Hindi and English as first languages, acted as an intermediary between the would-be immigrants and the authorities. As a result of overtly racist Canadian government manoeuvring, the people on board the *Komagata Maru* were refused, and the ship was towed out of Canadian waters by a Canadian vessel. Although 20 passengers were allowed to come ashore, the ship departed with most of its passengers. When it returned to India three months later, authorities, who saw the passengers as dangerous agitators, raided the vessel, and, in an ensuing battle, 19 passengers were killed. It remains, to this day, a black mark on Canadian immigration history.

Hopkinson's murder, connected as it was to the *Komagata Maru* incident, was a consequence of the complications of empire. Being an immigration officer was an ideal position to observe, track, and gather information on potential threats to Britain that might emanate from Canada. In 1914, when Hopkinson was killed, Canada's secret services were, to a large degree, simply reflections of the views and concerns of the mother country. This British orientation had been true for nearly half a century. Originally, the Canadian secret services were created in the 1860s to infiltrate and gather intelligence on supporters of Irish nationalism, such as the Fenians. But, by the time of the First World War, Canada's spies, Hopkinson included, were training their sights on Indian nationalists who were agitating for independence from the British.

Hopkinson, hired on the West Coast to report to Ottawa (and Britain), paid informants, conducted surveillance, and even went undercover to assess the threat of Indians living in Canada. His actions foreshadowed similar ones taken in the 1980s by Canadian security services, whose members infiltrated Sikh communities in BC but were unsuccessful in preventing the 1985 bombing of Air India Flight 182. Infiltrating the nationalist Indian movement in BC and California was a dangerous mission. By the beginning of the First World War, as nationalist Indians saw an opportunity to push the issue given Britain's involvement in the war, Hopkinson's spying activities had made him numerous enemies in the Indian diaspora communities in North America.

Indeed, the man who killed Hopkinson was not simply a stranger but a Sikh whom, after he was arrested, Hopkinson had tried to recruit as an informant. When he was led to his execution, Hopkinson's convicted murderer, Mewa Singh, chillingly told the priest, "I shall gladly have the rope put around my neck, thinking it to be a rosary of god's name."[3]

---

2   William Lyon Mackenzie King, *Report on Mission to England to Confer with the British Authorities on the Subject of Immigration to Canada from the Orient and Immigration from India in Particular* (Ottawa: S.E. Dawson, Printer to the King's Most Excellent Majesty, 1908), 7.

3   As quoted in Reginald Whitaker, Gregory S. Kealey, and Andrew Parnaby, *Secret Service: Political Policing in Canada from the Fenians to Fortress North America* (Toronto: University of Toronto, 2012), 54.

CHAPTER FIVE

PRIVATE HAROLD CARTER, EXECUTED, FRANCE, 1917

THE TRAGEDY AND HEROISM OF THE FIRST WORLD WAR, 1914–18

The glory of war and the sadness of war. We are all familiar with the glory of war. It comes down to us through the generations, venerating, celebrating, holding in highest respect those who fought and those who died.

We know poems such as "In Flanders Fields," and we know what they are supposed to mean to us. We know the heroes such as John McCrae, who wrote the poem and is rightfully famous. McCrae was a doctor from Guelph, Ontario, who served at the front and who died at the front, but whose haunting poetry remains an indelible part of the war and of the memory that is passed down to us of that war. "In Flanders Fields" is recited in Canadian grade schools and during Remembrance Day ceremonies in Canada, the United Kingdom, and Australia. It has even been imprinted on our $10 bill. The poem's presence in our collective memory a century after it was first written is a testament to its haunting words—and to the impact of the Great War on Canadian society.

But there is often another side of the story. The side of war that is not glorious, or triumphant, or celebrated in stories or in poems. There is the forgotten horror of war, as much as there is the glory of it. One such story is that of Private Harold George Carter.

* * *

Little is known of Harold Carter's early life. He was born in Toronto in March of 1896 and his parents were Milly and George Carter, who likely had emigrated from Britain to Canada sometime in the 1880s or 1890s. Harold was, like so many Canadians, of English descent, unsurprising given the massive immigration boom from the United Kingdom that had shaped Toronto in the nineteenth century. Though many Irish had also come to the city, there was no question that Toronto was an English and a Protestant town; the Orange Order, a Protestant organization, reigned supreme in the city. Indeed, the Toronto Harold was born into was very much a city of the British Empire and was often called "the Queen City." It looked and felt and smelled like a British city, from the architecture to the British "bobby-style" helmets worn by police to the stern local laws that virtually shut the city down on Sundays to observe the Sabbath.

By his teens, Harold was working as a teamster, another name for someone who delivered goods using carriages drawn by teams of horses. A slight man, Harold stood about five feet, six inches tall, had brown hair, blue eyes, and belonged to the Anglican Church, also known as the Church of England. In March of 1915, he lived at 143 Cumberland Street, just north of Bloor Street, then practically on the northern edge of the city.

* * *

Figure 5.1 *Pte. Harold Carter, No Date*

Courtesy of the Carter family

In 1914, the empires of Europe were delicately balanced in an alliance system. On one side stood the British Empire, allied with France, Belgium, and Russia. On the other side stood Germany, allied with the Austro-Hungarian Empire and Italy. Each side was connected through a complex series of treaties and family ties. In fact, because of the intermarriage in European royal society, the British royal family was actually closely connected to Germany. Before the royal family changed its name to "Windsor" during the war, it was Saxe-Coburg-Gotha, and Queen Victoria herself had been married to a German prince, Albert; both the German kaiser and the British king were grandchildren of Queen Victoria.

In the decade before 1914, Britain and Germany's imperial competition to gain colonies and control of the seas had caught even Canada in its web. By 1909, the British arms race with Germany revolved around seeing who could build the most and the best warships. In Canada, imperialists demanded that the Canadian government contribute by building ships for the British navy. On the other side, nationalists such as Prime Minister Wilfrid Laurier's fellow French-Canadian Henri Bourassa thought that Canada should not take part in such an arms race, arguing that Canadians should formulate their own defence policy. In the end, Laurier came to a decision that satisfied neither side: the Canadian government would build five ships at a cost of $11 million, which would remain in the Canadian navy, although these could be used by the British in a time of war.

In any event, in 1914, a young Serbian separatist named Gavrilo Princip assassinated the heir to the Austro-Hungarian throne, Archduke Franz Ferdinand. This assassination set off a chain of events that led to the declaration of war between the countries on either side of the system of alliances. Though the assassination was the immediate cause, the imperial rivalry between Germany and Britain, the settling of old scores between France and Germany, and the complex treaty system were driving factors causing the war. The ultimate question was whether or not Europe would be dominated by Germany. With determined forces on both sides, and the lack of a major European war since the Franco-Prussian War of 1870–71 to quell an ardour for battle, in 1914 Germany invaded Belgium and France. The British, allied with those two countries, quickly declared war on Germany and sent troops across the channel.

With the British declaration of war on Germany, Canada, as a colony of Great Britain with no real international standing of its own in external matters, was automatically at war with Germany as well. In fact, when war was declared in August of 1914, Prime Minister Robert Borden was actually on vacation in Muskoka. He did not find out about the fact that Canada was at war until days after the declaration. News, even such world-shaking news, moved a little bit slower back then.

* * *

Harold Carter volunteered to join the Canadian Overseas Expeditionary Force (CEF) on March 10, 1915. For some unknown reason, he enlisted at a recruiting station in Lindsay, Ontario. On his enlistment papers, he wrote his age as nearly 21, when, in fact, he was still only 18 years old. He likely did this to avoid any trouble related to being too young to sign up.

Included on those same attestation papers was an oath: "I . . . do solemnly declare that . . . I will as in duty bound honesty and faithfully defend His Majesty, His Heirs and Successors, in Person, Crown and Dignity, against all enemies, and will observe and obey all orders of His Majesty, His Heirs and Successors, and of all the Generals and Officers set over me. So help me God." Harold signed it, as did his father, George, as a witness. Like Harold, many British-born Canadians who enlisted in the early part of the war were keen to do their duty to their country and their king.

Carter enlisted in the 59th Battalion, and his troubles started pretty soon afterwards. In 1915, during training, he was charged with going AWOL, that is, absent without leave. This was even before his battalion had made it to England. When his battalion finally reached England in early 1916, its troops were used to re-man other units that had taken high casualty rates during the war. Carter was transferred to the 73rd Battalion, part of the 4th Canadian Division of the CEF.

In September 1916, Harold's battalion took part in the heavy fighting north of Flers-Courcelette, France, part of the broader Battle of the Somme. The British were trying to punch a hole through German lines with the help of Canadian and New Zealand troops. At some point during the engagement, Carter again went missing. He was found and charged with desertion, a conviction of which carried the death penalty. Later, his sentence was reduced to 10 years in prison.

* * *

Most Canadians greeted the declaration of war with an outburst of optimism. In Canada, and especially in very British places such as Toronto, there was a heavy dose of romance in the air. Save for the Boer War of 1899–1902, where Canada had played a limited role, Canadians had not seen any large-scale conflict in decades, and war was romanticized as an opportunity for bravery, heroism, and a chance to travel the world. Many Canadians felt that the war would be "over by Christmas" and that the glory and romance of war were far more appealing than the actual notion of fighting.

However, the reality of war was far from the romance being portrayed: the Canadian army, for instance, was no great fighting machine. Prior to 1914, it was tiny, with just over 3,000 permanent soldiers and another approximately 74,000 in the militia. At the time, career soldier Sir Sam Hughes was the minister of the militia and defence; obstinate and resolute, Hughes was determined to build a Canadian army that was thoroughly British.

Instead of sticking with the Canadian army as constituted at the beginning of the war Hughes created a new army from scratch, building a massive new base at Valcartier, Quebec, and calling for volunteers for the new force. Given Canadians' excitement about the prospects of war, more than 30,000 signed up in the first few weeks. There were long lines at recruiting stations, and many young Canadian men (and quite a few Americans who crossed the border to join up for various reasons) were eager to get into uniform. Of course, although they were keen to get to the front, they spent weeks in Quebec waiting for their equipment to arrive and doing basic training. This training included drilling for weeks on end and carrying packs of up to 70 pounds over long distances.

Finally, in October of 1914, the first contingent of the Canadian Expeditionary Force was transported to England, where its soldiers spent a few more months training. When they did arrive at the front, the Canadians were organized along British military lines, and, because no Canadian was considered to have enough experience to assume overall command of the troops, the first contingent served under British command and was included in British war operations.

By the time the CEF got to the front in 1915, the two sides were stalemated. The battlefield across western France was a series of dug-in trenches and barbed wire, and it was virtually impassable. France and Belgium were so devastated by trench warfare, shelling, and heavy rainfall, that the countryside was transformed into a scarred and barren wasteland, devoid of trees, covered by mud, and stunned by the destruction of war.

In the words of one Canadian soldier, Private Donald Fraser, trenches were "small, damp and cold and overrun with rats. . . . For want of sunshine and wind, it is impossible for the ground to dry up and after a while we learn that it is useless trying to keep the trenches passable. The rain loosens the earth and the sides cave in. With additional rain the bottom of the trenches become liquid mud which defies all efforts at drainage."[1] In fact, some men drowned in the mud.

Thus, the old tactics of fast movement dictated by cavalry strikes and rapid marching had been replaced by extensively built trenches and fortifications, a "no man's land" of mud and craters; open charges were now a thing of the past. However, it took commanders on both sides literally years to adapt to the new type of warfare. Committed to the notion of direct frontal attacks, officers were convinced that their enlisted soldiers would break through the lines if they simply rushed harder and were more resolute. This notion flew in the face of the reality of machine guns, which could easily mow down charging men in a few seconds.

---

1   Private Donald Fraser's diary can be read in Reginald H. Roy, ed., *The Journal of Private Fraser, 1914–1918, Canadian Expeditionary Force* (Victoria, BC: Sono Nis Press, 1985) or online at http://www.fordham.edu/halsall/mod/1918Fraser.asp.

The evidence that machine guns could wipe out offensive forces so easily and with so many casualties did not penetrate the officer class's thinking, and the stubbornness of these old-fashioned notions of warfare reflected to a degree the class divisions between officers and ordinary soldiers. Some historians suggest that these divisions meant a failure of communication and empathy that tarnished the reputation of British command, the contention being that brave soldiers were led to the slaughter by indifferent leaders, that the British officers were "donkeys leading lions."[2]

* * *

By 1916, manpower shortages were already stretching the Canadian Expeditionary Force to the breaking point. The initial wave of enthusiastic volunteers had slowed to a trickle, and conscription had not yet been imposed. Because of this, Harold Carter's 10-year sentence for having gone AWOL at Flers-Courcelette was suspended, and he was reattached to his unit in March 1917. This was just a few weeks before the Canadian offensive at Vimy Ridge.

* * *

With the stalemate spread across western France by the spring of 1915, and casualties mounting, commanders on both sides were desperate to break through their enemies' lines. Unable to use traditional techniques, they turned to new technologies. The first of these was the aforementioned machine gun. Though machine guns had existed for many years before the First World War, by 1914 they were nearly perfected as killing machines. The rapid fire of stationary guns could easily kill massed soldiers, and the machine gun profoundly changed the nature of war and led to the creation of trench warfare, though artillery barrages remained the deadliest killer.

A second new technology was gas warfare, an attempt to poison the other side by either releasing clouds of toxic gas so it would be blown over enemy positions or firing shells or entire missiles filled with this gas. Gas attacks caused blindness, suffocation, and disfigurement and were a horrible tactic of war, very far from the ideal of individual bravery that had prompted so many men to enlist.

It so happens that, during the first major Canadian involvement in the war, which was at Ypres, France, in 1915, Canadians faced the brunt of German gas attacks. They were among the first troops in modern warfare to be subjected to chemical weapons designed to kill. Miraculously, the Canadian line held through these attacks, even though the soldiers took thousands of casualties. More than any other tactic, the use of gas indicated that the rules of modern warfare had changed dramatically.

---

2   Quoted in John Keegan, *The First World War* (London: Pimlico, 1999), 337.

One British soldier described what he saw when he arrived to relieve some Canadian troops: "We stopped at a ditch at a first-aid clearing station. There were about 200 to 300 men lying in that ditch. Some were clawing their throats. Their brass buttons were green. Their bodies were swelled. Some of them were still alive. Some were still writhing on the ground, their tongues hanging out."[3]

Now, although gas attacks were obviously deadly, they were not always effective. Crude weapons that were difficult to handle, the cylinders that delivered gas could explode prematurely and could even inflict casualties on the side using them if the wind simply changed direction. The use of poison gas continued throughout the war, though deaths decreased as both sides employed better countermeasures.

Another new technology employed during the Great War was the tank, which allowed soldiers to roll across no man's land protected from the machine guns and barbed wire because of the vehicle's armour. This innovation had a tremendous impact on rendering trenches ineffective and helped to change the course of the war, though tanks were not the determining factor as they did not appear in large numbers until toward the end of the conflict.

A fourth and final new technology, which really emerged during the war as an important aspect of the new tactics being employed, was the airplane. Used for reconnaissance, as a bomber, or in a head-to-head dogfight (and for propaganda purposes), the airplane, and air power, revolutionized war, and created some noteworthy heroes of the conflict.

Despite these technological advances, by 1915, the romantic notion of war had been utterly destroyed by the harsh reality of modern trench warfare. This was warfare on a scale unheard of, and the death and destruction were simply harrowing. During the First Battle of the Somme, for instance, starting in 1916, there were more than one million casualties; on the very first day of battle, almost 20,000 of the British forces were killed.

Indeed, for the first three years of the war, there was little movement, as the Canadians, under British command, took part in a number of engagements with continuously mounting casualties. On top of the terrible conditions and the horror of battle, there were other problems at the front. Many Canadian soldiers suffered from what we would refer to as shell shock as the horror of war incapacitated them. Canadian soldiers were armed with rifles that did not work properly, and the stubborn leader of the army, Sam Hughes, refused to replace them; instead, Canadians picked up the rifles of dead British soldiers. Without antibiotics and with little in the way of front-line medicine, many soldiers were lost to injury and lost limbs, and disease killed thousands of Canadian troops and over three million people on all sides during the war.

It was, in short, a horrible war for these men.

---

3   Quoted from Gordon Reid, ed., *Poor Bloody Murder: Personal Memoirs of the First World War* (Oakville, ON: Mosaic Press, 1980), 82.

* * *

Last known letter from Harold Carter to his mother, Millie:

Pte. Harold G. Carter
454482 C Co.
73rd RH Canadians

France, March 1, 1917

Just a few lines to let you know I am well and hope all at home are the same. I haven't had a letter from you for about 3 or 4 weeks. I was beginning to wonder what was the matter at home.

Well, I had a letter from cousin Florence and she told me Ernie had been there and said all was well at home.

Well I haven't saw Ernie yet or I don't know whether I will be able to. I haven't received the parcel Mrs. Price sent to me yet but hope to soon.

Well mother, how am I to write Mrs. Price as I have not got her address to write. If you have it, send it to me.

We are having nice weather at present but I guess it will rain pretty soon.

Well, I haven't had a letter or parcel for about six weeks and I am beginning to wonder what had happened.

Well all I have to do is cheer up and not be downhearted, one will come soon. I haven't received your comic papers you sent me.

Mother, could you send me a safety razor as it is the only kind I can shave with and we have to shave every day over here.

Well I guess I will close up for to-night and will write a little longer letter next time. Give my Love and Best Wishes to May and Jack, Roy and Dad and also to Will and Tena and tell Will or Tena to write a few lines or send a Post Card. I will say Good Night. Hoping to hear from you all soon.

I remain Your Loving Son;
Harold
PS I wish I was home this year for my birthday but it can't be done.
Ta, Ta, for now. Harold.[4]

* * *

Yet, among all these terrible events, there were instances of incredible bravery and of great Canadian victories and heroes. By 1917, the CEF was a battle-hardened unit and had developed new tactics that relied on heavy bombardment and the

---

4   The text of the letter can be found at http://www.findagrave.com/cgi-bin/fg.cgi?page=gr&G Rid=15930958.

constant replacement of troops. The Canadians now worked as a separate Canadian army commanded by a home-grown hero, Sir Arthur Currie, who helped put these tactics together.

During Easter, in April of 1917, the Canadians scored a major victory when they captured Vimy Ridge, a German-held position that both the French and British had tried to take without success and that had cost both heavy casualties. The victory by the Canadians was a high point in the indecisive struggle raging from April to May known as the Second Battle of Arras, and, thereafter, the Canadians were often considered the "shock troops" of the Allied armies. Taking Vimy Ridge was a significant military accomplishment for Canada, and the haunting memorial constructed at the battle site provides contemporary Canadians with a small sense of how this engagement became a symbol of the country's sacrifice during the war.

There were other heroes, too. Some Canadian soldiers became famous during the war, including Billy Bishop. Bishop, from Owen Sound, Ontario, was the British Empire's greatest First World War flying ace, shooting down 72 planes, though there is historical debate over the accuracy of this count. During and after the war, Bishop became famous in Canada, and there is even a musical written about him, called "Billy Bishop Goes to War," and the island airport in Toronto is named after him. Of course, in such a brutal war, one with so few heroes, even Bishop's accomplishments beg the question of whether his number of "kills" (contested or not) made any military difference, or whether his greatest value was as a propaganda symbol.

Like Billy Bishop, thousands of other Canadian men won medals, including, in a few instances, the Victoria Cross, the highest award given to any of those fighting from England or the British Empire. A Winnipeg street was renamed Valour Road because, amazingly, three men from the same avenue won the Victoria Cross. Women took part in the war as well. Approximately 2,500 women were at the front as nurses and played a pivotal and heroic role in saving thousands of Canadian soldiers. In fact, the Canadian women who served as nurses with the early British and Canadian stationary hospitals were among the ranks awarded the very rare 1914 Star, having made it to the front ahead of most Canadian soldiers.

By the end of the war, approximately 600,000 Canadians had been a part of the CEF, with about 470,000 going overseas. On average, a tour of duty lasted 2 years. Over 60,000 Canadians died during the war: of those, about 40,000 died in action, 7,000 by disease, and another 13,000 in various military accidents. Of course, thousands more were wounded, oftentimes permanently, as battlefield medicine was nowhere near what it is today. Many lost limbs or were blinded or suffered long-lasting psychological damage.

During the Great War, Canada had a population of only 8 million people. With 60,000 killed and hundreds of thousands coming home with both physical and mental injuries, the war touched virtually every city and town in Canada, and almost every family. War's aftermath was particularly difficult for those who were related to or knew university-aged Canadian males, who signed up in great numbers. Anyone in university, then, would have known someone who had been killed, given that so many Canadian university students died in the war.

* * *

Within three weeks of being sent back to his unit, Private Carter once again went AWOL, this time just before Vimy Ridge. It is not known what prompted Harold's decision to desert; it may have been shell shock, a common occurrence during the war. He eluded military police for five days before being recaptured. On April 4, 1917, he was court-martialled and found guilty of desertion. Because the Canadian Forces were under the direction of the British, Carter faced the judgment of British military justice, which was swift and ruthless. As punishment was meant to enforce obedience and discipline, soldiers charged with desertion or cowardice had little opportunity to defend themselves. Such was the harsh nature of war on the Western Front that trials often took only minutes, and the accused were not granted legal counsel or any form of appeal.

Sentenced to death, Carter was executed by firing squad on April 20, 1917, just days following the Canadian success at Vimy. His parents received a photograph of the cross that marked his grave, with the message that he "gave his life for his country." Carter's body was laid to rest in the Villers Station Cemetery, in western France near Arras, and his grave can be found in Plot X. A. 7. Just over 300 British and colonial soldiers were executed for desertion and other military crimes during the First World War, and, of these, 23 Canadians were executed for desertion or cowardice.

* * *

The massive Canadian contribution in people and expenditures meant that Canada's role in the war was significant not only for the Canadian people but for Canada's legal standing within the British Empire. When Canada initially went to war, there was no Canadian input as to the conduct of the war or the placement or use of Canadian troops on the battlefield. The British ran the war effort. They were very happy to use troops from Canada and the other British colonies but were not very interested in hearing what the colonials might have to say about the conduct of the war. Australia, South Africa, India, and New Zealand all contributed to the war as well, though Canada, as the oldest and largest dominion, contributed the most.

Politically, Prime Minister Robert Borden and the other prime ministers were shut out entirely from the decision-making process at first. Obviously, with thousands of Canadian troops dying at the front, this situation was totally unacceptable for Borden. With disastrous campaigns causing massive casualties and providing no victories, Borden demanded that the Canadians be given a say in the conduct of the war. Through his determination, the British finally relented and, in the spring of 1917, created the Imperial War Cabinet, which allowed all of the colonies to have some (though not much) say in the war effort. It marked a clear step in the evolution of the colonies from a subordinate status to one of being on a more equal footing with the United Kingdom.

In 1917, a meeting of the Imperial War Cabinet passed Resolution IX, declaring that imperial foreign relations needed to be adjusted at first opportunity once the war was over. The resolution meant that dominions such as Canada and Australia would be considered autonomous states of the imperial commonwealth and would have a say in imperial foreign policy.

Indeed, when the war finally ended in 1918 and the Treaty of Versailles between the victorious allies and the defeated Germans and Austrians was being negotiated, Borden demanded that Canada, owing to its contribution to the war effort, be allowed to sign the agreement separately. In the end, the treaty was signed by representatives for Canada, Australia, New Zealand, and South Africa, although all signed below and as a subset of the five who signed on behalf of the British Empire. Nevertheless, this event marked a very visible step for Canada in its diplomatic and political relations with Great Britain. The war was not only, as many historians have argued, a turning point when Canadians were jolted out of their colonial isolation and assumed a new attitude toward themselves and their role in the world; it was perhaps the most traumatic event in the country's history.

* * *

The case of Harold Carter, as much as that of John McCrae, tells us much about the tragedy and horror of war, its heroism, the horrible choices men and women made, and the harshness of death that was visited on so many people. Perhaps Harold Carter was not the best soldier, but he enlisted, itself an act of bravery and, despite his service record, he was a casualty of war. The circumstances around his conduct remain unknown. Who is to judge Pte. Harold Carter's actions, given the horror of the war?

In 2001, after a long campaign by family members, the 23 Canadians executed for cowardice and desertion during the First World War were finally included in the Books of Remembrance. The solemn and beautiful Books of Remembrance are housed in the Peace Tower on Parliament Hill and include the names of every Canadian who fought and died for Canada. For nearly a century, given their executions, the names of these 23 men were kept from this record of Canada's war service.

In making this decision to include the 23 men's names, the Canadian minister of veterans affairs stated in the House of Commons that

Those who go to war at the request of their nation do not know the fate that lies in store for them. This was a war of such overwhelming sound, fury and unrelenting horror that few combatants could remain unaffected. While we cannot relive those awful years of a nation at peril in total war, and although the culture of that time is subsequently too distant for us to comprehend fully, we can give these twenty-three soldiers a dignity that is their due, and provide closure to their families.[5]

A few years later, in 2006, the British pardoned more than 300 British and Commonwealth soldiers who had been sentenced to death in the First World War, including the 23 Canadians. Among those Canadians was Pte. Harold Carter.

Further Reading

Cook, Tim. *At the Sharp End: Canadians Fighting the Great War, 1914–1916*. Toronto: Viking Canada, 2007.

Cook, Tim. *Shock Troops: Canadians Fighting the Great War, 1917–1918*. Toronto: Penguin Canada, 2009.

Hayes, Geoffrey, Michael Bechthold, and Andrew Iarocci, eds. *Vimy Ridge: A Canadian Reassessment*. Waterloo, ON: Wilfrid Laurier University Press, 2007.

Iarocci, Andrew. *Shoestring Soldiers: The 1st Canadian Division at War, 1914–1915*. Toronto: University of Toronto Press, 2008.

Morton, Desmond, and Glenn Wright. *Winning the Second Battle: Canadian Veterans and the Return to Civilian Life, 1915–1930*. Toronto: University of Toronto Press, 1987.

Passchendaele. Film. Directed by Paul Gross. Montreal, QC: Alliance Films, 2008.

"World War I." *The Memory Project*. Website. http://www.thememory project.com/.

---

5   Veterans Affairs Minister Ron Duhamel's statement from Tuesday, December 11, 2001, can be seen at http://www.parl.gc.ca/HousePublications/Publication.aspx?Language=E&Mode=1& Parl=37&Ses=1&DocId=1298629.

ACTIVE HISTORY: DISCOVERING THE DIARIES OF GREAT WAR VETERANS

- Visit the "We Were There" archived website of Great War diaries from Library and Archives of Canada at http://www.collectionscanada.gc.ca/firstworldwar/025005-2000-e.html.

- Examine one or two of the diaries, looking at each diary writer's background information and paying particular attention to the personal diary entries.

- What can you learn about these people's experiences? What types of information from the diaries are most important, in your view, in assessing the historical events being discussed?

- What are some of the benefits of using diaries such as these? What are some of the drawbacks?

- How do the range of experiences help to explain the breadth of the war's impact upon ordinary Canadians? What do the diary entries tell us about important events during the war itself, such as the 1917 Battle of Vimy Ridge?

- Can we learn anything about the horror of war that might help to explain Harold Carter's actions, and his execution?

TRAGIC TALES
COLLATERAL DAMAGE—THE BURNING OF PARLIAMENT HILL'S CENTRE BLOCK (1916) AND THE HALIFAX EXPLOSION (1917)

The Violence of War Comes Home to Canada

The years between 1914 and 1919 were horrible for Canadians. The war itself; the brutal election of 1917, dominated by the conscription fight that almost broke the country in two (discussed in the next chapter); an influenza epidemic; and the return of so many wounded and disabled soldiers tested Canadians as never before, and likely not since. In 1917, Canadians had little to celebrate on their country's fiftieth anniversary.

Though the war itself was far from Canadian shores, it did come home to Canada, and wartime-related events killed thousands of Canadians at home. Two incidents, one much less well known and one famous, provide an insight to how Canadians at home were affected by the war, though it was thousands of miles from Canada. These incidents show us the collateral damage inflicted by events in Europe.

On February 3, 1916, at the height of the war and during one of the most challenging periods of Canadian history, tragedy struck Parliament Hill. A fire started in one of the reading rooms near the House of Commons. It quickly spread and soon engulfed much of the Centre Block of the Parliament Buildings. Only quick thinking by a clerk, who slammed shut the iron doors between the Library of Parliament and Centre Block, saved the ornate library from being caught by the flames. In the end, most of Centre Block burned to the ground. Even the bells of the Victoria tower crashed to the ground as firefighting crews battled the blaze late into the frozen February night. Seven people died in the calamity, including one member of Parliament,

for Yarmouth, Nova Scotia's Bowman Brown Law, and two guests of the Speaker who, thinking the fire was not serious, ran to get their fur coats and never made it out.

Immediately, and inevitably, given the wartime fears and paranoia, suspicions were raised that the fire was the work of enemy saboteurs. One man was even arrested in Windsor near the Canada–US border and accused of being a German operative, though he was soon exonerated. Later, it was established that careless smoking had been the cause of the fire, but, in the heated passions of wartime Canada, it is not surprising that sabotage was suspected. The symbolism of Canada's Parliament burning to the ground was profound and reflected the dire situation Canadians faced, and felt, in this moment.

Far more well known is the Halifax Explosion. The scale of the December 6, 1917, explosion was so immense that it almost makes it difficult to understand. A French munitions ship, the SS Mont Blanc, and a Norwegian vessel, the SS Imo, collided in Halifax harbour, a key port and shipping depot in the Allied war effort. A fire broke out on the Mont Blanc, and the blaze rapidly burned uncontrollably. In the meantime, many curious Haligonians went to the shoreline to see the source of the smoke. At shortly after 9 AM, the ship exploded, creating the greatest human-made explosion to that point in history and destroying virtually everything within two square kilometres of the blast.

The explosion killed nearly 2,000 people and injured another 9,000 in a city of about 50,000, as the blast levelled houses, caused fires, and resulted in a tidal wave and sonic boom that levelled much of downtown Halifax and Dartmouth. The explosion was felt nearly 100 kilometres away in towns such as Truro, Nova Scotia. Prime Minister Robert Borden was in Charlottetown, Prince Edward Island, and actually heard the explosion, as did many of his colleagues. A Nova Scotian himself, Borden immediately left for Halifax to oversee the relief and recovery efforts.

As with the Centre Block fire, in the confusion of the destruction, many of the dazed survivors initially thought that the explosion was caused by a German bombing attack. A massive explosion at a New Jersey munitions depot in 1916 that killed at least seven people had been orchestrated by German agents, and German U-Boats prowled the waters of the Atlantic, perhaps just outside of Halifax harbour's antisubmarine defences, so sabotage or an attack was not beyond the realm of possibility.

Surviving troops were put on high alert, and blackout rules were enforced. Eventually, the true cause of the explosion—the accidental collision of the two vessels—overcame these wartime fears of German assault.

Relief efforts were hampered by a snowstorm the day after the explosion, though the downfall helped to quench many of the fires that raged across the city. Within days, rescue efforts had saved hundreds of people from collapsed buildings, and relief began to pour in from across Canada and the United States. Boston, in particular, sent hundreds of rescuers and relief workers, and tons of supplies.

Coming on the heels of the casualties of war, the bitter "khaki" conscription election, and the Parliament Hill fire, the December explosion made 1917 a truly horrific year for Canadians. As thousands of Canadian soldiers were killed or wounded in France, thousands of Canadian civilians died in tragedies at home.

CHAPTER SIX

FOUR RIOTERS KILLED BY THE CANADIAN MILITARY, QUEBEC CITY, EASTER 1918

CONSCRIPTION AND THE POLITICS OF THE GREAT WAR AT HOME

For four days in 1918, Quebec City, far from Europe's Western Front, became a First World War battlefield. The combatants were Canadian soldiers, on the one side, and ordinary Canadians—Quebecers, in this case—on the other. The cause of this battle was the fight over conscription, and the battlefield itself was the narrow, cobblestoned streets and public squares of Canada's oldest city. But the Easter Riots over conscription, which resulted in the deaths of 4 Quebecers, injuries to more than 100, and extensive property damage, were only one aspect of the Canadian government's broader battle to maintain order and impose conscription.

In its efforts to assert its authority over the issue and limit the riots before they exploded into outright rebellion, Ottawa suspended *habeas corpus,* declared martial law, and occupied Quebec City by sending over 6,000 Canadian troops there from Ontario and Western Canada, an occupation that did not end until early the following year. The Easter 1918 fight over conscription was only the most dramatic and bloody fight on the home front over the conduct of the war. Like the devastation wrought upon Canadians on the battlefield, the war at home scarred Canadians for generations to come.

Expanding the Canadian State for War

From the start of the conflict in August 1914, the Canadian government had to expand its reach and authority to control the conduct of the war, both at home

81

and on the Western Front. The demands of war required the Canadian state to develop an apparatus to control its people and to regulate its economy, all to fight the conflict successfully. In 1914, the Conservative government of Robert Borden proposed a new law, the War Measures Act, to help in this task. The War Measures Act gave unprecedented powers to the government to regulate the economy, to control political expression, and to ensure that nothing prevented the government from doing whatever was necessary for the cause of war. In a sign of unity, the Liberal Opposition, led by Wilfrid Laurier, helped the bill pass unanimously in the House of Commons.

In terms of economic control, the act meant that the Canadian state had the authority to extend its power over all transportation, trade, production, and manufacturing on an emergency basis. In this atmosphere, other wartime legislation was passed that gave considerable power to the state. First, Ottawa imposed income taxes with the Income War Tax Act, instituted in 1917 as a temporary measure (but this tax has somehow managed to remain with us to this day). Second, a number of wartime boards were created to control the production of munitions such as artillery shells and rifles, foodstuffs such as wheat, machinery, and a host of other products necessary for the war effort. Third, laws were passed to control Canadians' consumption of a number of items. These laws meant strict rationing for items such as rubber or coal or wood.

In terms of social control, the Canadian state passed a number of laws meant to ensure strict oversight of Canadians' political activities, especially those of "enemy aliens," people from combatant countries. The War Measures Act required any "aliens of enemy nationality" to register with the government. In 1914, there were about 100,000 native-born Germans and Austro-Hungarians living in Canada and another 400,000 people of "enemy alien" extraction from places such as Italy and Eastern Europe. Ottawa viewed these recent immigrants as a potential threat because their sympathies might lie with their former countries.

As a result, the War Measures Act of 1914 required "aliens of enemy nationality" to register with police and make monthly reports about their activities. If government authorities deemed any of these people a threat, they were interned in government camps. During the war, about 8,500 people identified as enemy aliens, including some naturalized Canadian citizens, were interned. Treatment of these so-called enemy aliens became worse as the war continued. In Toronto in 1916, the Anti-German League was founded, and, in many instances, the country became very inhospitable for people from these countries, as verbal and physical assaults were directed at suspected enemy aliens.

The government also controlled the press, especially the foreign-language press. Materials published in German or Austrian, for instance, were monitored much more closely than those published in English and French. In fact, in 1918, the government made it illegal to print, publish, or possess any publication in an "enemy alien" language without government license.

Finally, as part of its social control measures, the government also expanded its use of propaganda to convince Canadians to help the war effort. Posters, literature, flyers, and many types of information were developed to make sure that Canadians did not question the war effort. These posters were plastered across the country, not only as morale boosters but as public information campaigns to encourage rationing, bond buying, or other wartime related activities. The posters were also created to encourage potential soldiers to enlist in the army. This issue, perhaps more than any other, shaped Canadians' home-front experiences during the Great War.

Conscription

Of course, the most dramatic thing a government could do was to conscript its people to fight in the war. In the first year or two of the war, conscription was not an issue. There was great enthusiasm for the war, and thousands of Canadians, such as Private Harold Carter, enlisted voluntarily. Most of these early enlistments in the CEF, however, were, like Harold Carter, recent English immigrants or the children of English immigrants. In fact, until 1917, nearly half of all those who volunteered had been born in the United Kingdom.

By 1916, given the realities of the horror of this war, new recruits for the army were drying up. With the news headlines, images, and stories about no man's land and the scale and carnage of the Western Front, many young Canadian men realized that this war was not as glorious as had been first thought. In January of 1916, there were 30,000 enlistments in the CEF. But by July, that number had decreased to 8,000, and, in December, only 5,300 men signed up to fight. Clearly, manpower was becoming a problem, especially as casualties mounted.

The problem was exacerbated by Sir Sam Hughes, the minister of the militia, who arrogantly used English Protestant recruiters in Quebec to try to sign up a population that was overwhelmingly French and Catholic. Needless to say, these efforts were not effective. Although many French Canadians and their leaders, such as Wilfrid Laurier and Henri Bourassa, had initially supported the war as a noble cause, as the war continued on, many came to see the war as unjust and unnecessary, and they were certainly against conscription. By 1915, the ratio of French Canadians to English Canadians enlisting was about one to eight, and only about 14,000 French Canadians had volunteered by the spring of 1917.

Nor was there uniform enthusiasm from Canadian-born English speakers. Many farm families did not want to see their sons go off to war, and certainly the children of recent immigrants from Eastern Europe were not as keen on fighting for the English as many other Canadians. Furthermore, the demands of industry meant that many men were needed in factories, which further hurt the recruitment effort.

However, as the war went on, Borden determined that the country needed to make an even greater contribution. In 1915, Borden visited Canadian troops in Europe, a trip that eventually convinced him that the only way to fight the war properly was to have an army of 500,000 men, which meant the implementation of conscription.

When Borden announced that he was going to implement conscription in 1917, the French Canadians in his government were adamantly opposed. They knew that people in Quebec would be very much against being forced to fight a war for Britain. Even though the war was being fought in France, few Québécois considered themselves Frenchmen as English Canadians considered themselves British; French Canadians were far more North American in their outlook.

Moreover, French-Canadian rights in Canada had been curtailed significantly in the 30 years prior to the war, making the Québécois question their rights within Canada. French language schooling was curtailed in Manitoba, Ontario, and in the new provinces of Alberta and Saskatchewan, created in 1905. Just as important, the execution of Riel over the protests of Quebec had illustrated that Quebec's minority rights would always be trampled by the majority. The idea of an equal partnership between the French and English in Canada was just that, an idea. Now, Borden was forcing French Canadians (and farmers and workers) who did not want to go to war to do so.

Before making conscription law, in May 1917 Borden, a Conservative, first asked Liberal leader Wilfrid Laurier to join him in a "Union" government representing all parties in an effort to show unity for the war effort. When it became clear that supporting conscription was the price of joining government, Laurier refused, but many English-speaking Liberals did join the new Union government.

Despite Laurier's refusal, Borden and the Conservatives, with the help of the English-speaking Liberals who crossed the floor to support conscription, formed a "Union government" and voted to impose the policy in 1917. The Military Service Act made all men between 20 and 45 years old liable for service; the first to be "called out" would be bachelors and childless widowers between 20 and 34 years old. It did, however, provide exemptions for agricultural workers and some labourers.

In the first month, 20,000 of those on the registered list reported for duty, though another 300,000 men were given exemptions for various reasons, such as being the only son in a family or having a strategically important job in a factory or on a farm. But by April of 1918, with casualties mounting following the CEF's numerous engagements, most exemptions were cancelled. In Quebec, the federal government sent in Dominion Police officers to track down, arrest, and prosecute suspected draft dodgers. In the end, although over 400,000 men registered for the draft, only about 100,000 were actually drafted, and only about 24,000 of those actually made it to France. Though conscription had been passed into law, its actual implementation was still in question.

The Politics of Conscription: The "Khaki Election"

Although the conscription law had been enacted in August 1917, Borden faced a dilemma. The last federal election before the war had been in 1911, when his Conservatives had defeated Laurier's Liberals over issues such as free trade (Laurier had a free trade agreement with the United States that the Tories were against) and the navy (Conservatives wanted more direct support for the British Royal Navy while Liberals advocated building a Canadian navy whose warships could be used by the British). Normally, elections were called every four years or, at most, every five. But since the start of the war, Borden had asked Opposition Leader Laurier to put off elections given the difficulties the country faced. Laurier had agreed and had, in 1916, granted extensions for Parliament to continue for an extra year. But with the conscription issue causing so much turmoil and with Borden's decision to create a Union government, Laurier had no interest in granting him any further extensions. The country was going to have an election over conscription, a wartime "khaki" election, so named for the colour of uniforms that soldiers wore.

But Borden was determined to ensure that conscription remained in place, so, with the help of his minister of justice, Arthur Meighen, Borden used his government's majority to pass two pieces of legislation prior to the election, scheduled for December 17, 1917. Both of these new laws were clearly designed to give the government an electoral advantage so that the incumbent Conservatives could win the campaign and maintain the conscription policy. The first law was the Military Voters Act, which enfranchised all members of the armed forces, no matter how long they had lived in Canada, and allowed their votes to be assigned to any riding an election officer thought was necessary, unless the constituency in which the voter had lived at the time of enlistment was specified. Obviously, soldiers were in favour of conscription, and the fact that many of their votes could be used anywhere in the country gave the government a huge pool of votes to cast in close electoral races.

The second piece of legislation was the Wartime Elections Act. This law gave the vote to women over the age of 21 who were mothers, wives, widows, sisters, or daughters of servicemen. This was the first time that Canadian women could vote federally. The law also denied votes to naturalized Canadians from enemy countries who had settled in Canada after 1902. In one fell swoop, Borden's Union government had found tens of thousands of new voters, who undoubtedly were in support of conscription, and had disenfranchised tens of thousands of others who might vote against the policy.

These laws basically allowed the government to cook the books, and the government used these votes to defeat the Liberals soundly all across the country. This campaign was very bitter; the French and English speakers were at direct odds over the war and the policy of conscription, as well as over the rights of the French-Canadian minority in the face of the English-speaking majority. Unionist advertising stressed that a vote for Laurier was a vote for the German enemy while French Canadians used campaign literature that linked conscription to evil.

In the end, Borden and the pro-conscription Union government won. This was unsurprising, given the extent to which the government had gone to bend the electoral rules in its favour. But the results were telling. Borden and the Unionists

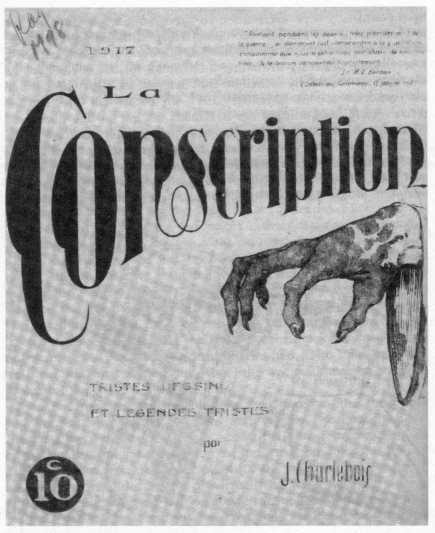

Figure 6.1 *Anti-Conscription Literature, 1917*

won 153 seats to the Laurier Liberals' 82; Unionists won two-thirds of the ridings outside of Quebec and only three predominantly English-speaking ridings in Quebec, the rest going to the Liberals. Over 90 per cent of the soldiers' vote went in favour of Unionist candidates, and these votes were used to shore up ridings with close races. The majority had spoken: conscription would stay, and French Canadians were to be forced to fight a war they did not wish to take a part in.

Quebecers felt betrayed, and many politicians openly questioned the province's place within Confederation. In the Quebec legislature, Joseph-Napoléon Francœur, a Liberal representative from Quebec's Lotbinière district, proposed a motion for the province to secede from Canada, given the severity of the electoral results. This sharp break from the rest of Canada and the isolation of the province because of conscription and the results of the 1917 election were, until the 1980 and 1995 referendums, the closest the country had come to breaking apart.

Civil Disorder and the Easter 1918 Riots

Outrage over the conscription policy, the creation of a Union government, and the wartime election with the government's questionable tactics had raised tensions to the breaking point for many Canadians, especially in Quebec. Publications, speeches, and protests denounced conscription. Following passage of the new law in 1917 and during and after the 1917 election, anti-conscription demonstrations were mounted across the province, resulting in property damages and injuries.

In August of 1917, the home of the publisher of the pro-conscription *Montreal Star* newspaper was bombed by anti-conscription militants who called themselves the *dynamitards*. Following the arrest of more than a dozen men involved in the plot, it was discovered that the *dynamitards* had planned to bomb the Canadian Parliament, kill government officials involved in the conscription policy, and even assassinate Prime Minister Borden. In August 1917, when conscription officially became law, major riots erupted in Montreal, leading to the death of one person and the injury of seven others. Across the province, tensions bubbled just under the surface for the next few months. They would explode during Easter 1918.

As these events often do, the Easter Riots started with one small act. On Thursday, March 28, two Dominion Police constables enforcing the Military Service Act entered a bowling alley in Quebec City. There, they questioned a young man and asked him if he had his exemption papers. Because he did not have these papers with him, the man was immediately taken into custody, following the law's procedure. The arrest of the man sparked outrage among some of the people who had witnessed the incident. They followed the police and the man back to the police station. Though the man was released, by this time, more than 2,000 people had gathered in front of the station. Angered by the arrest and disgusted by months of frustration over conscription and the election, the crowd attacked the police station, ransacking it and assaulting several officers.

In the wake of this attack, tensions continued to mount in the city the next day, Friday, March 29. Quebec City's mayor asked that the local garrison be put on alert in case of further agitation. As evening approached, 3,000 protestors gathered in the working-class district of St. Roch and started moving toward the city centre, where they sacked the offices of two pro-conscription newspapers. By the time they reached the local offices of the Military Service Act registrar, the crowd was approaching 8,000. The mob attacked the building, destroyed all records, and prevented a fire truck from putting out the ensuing blaze.

The events of Friday convinced authorities that an insurrection might be at hand. Given the *dynamitard* plots; the "Red Scares" that had gripped other countries; the Easter Uprising in Dublin, Ireland, the year before; and the tumultuous 1917 Russian Revolution, the events in Quebec City looked to be the beginnings of a full-scale rebellion. In Ottawa, Prime Minister Borden invoked the full weight of the War Measures Act. The federal government took control of the city from local authorities, and, under the act, it could use whatever force necessary to restore order. Martial law was declared for Quebec's capital. Within hours, the order had been given to send thousands of soldiers to Quebec, virtually all of whom were English-speaking troops from outside the province.

The next night, Saturday, March 30, rioters again started to concentrate in districts across the city. Within hours, thousands had surrounded Quebec's military barracks, throwing stones and ice blocks at the troops. Eventually, the cavalry charged the crowd, dispersing it as a series of running battles between rioters and troops spilled onto the adjoining streets, with injuries on both sides. As more troops poured into the city and the rioters regrouped overnight, Quebec City had begun to resemble an urban war zone, with countless buildings damaged and smoke rising from the still-smouldering conscription registrar's office.

On Sunday, March 31, 1918, thousands of troops patrolled the city, awaiting the next clash. When hundreds of rioters attacked a hardware store in an effort to obtain firearms and could not find any, they instead set the building on fire. In front of a crowd of 5,000 people, nationalist leader Armand Lavergne called on the rioters to disperse, which they did. The next day, however, the crowds returned, throwing rocks, bricks, and ice at the soldiers. Some rioters started to fire at troops from rooftops around the city. With Quebec quickly descending into chaos, troops were ordered to fire on the rioters with rifles and machine guns. When the smoke had cleared, at least 4 people were killed and hundreds of others were wounded, including at least 60 soldiers. Order was finally re-established following the fateful Easter Monday clash, though troops would remain in the city for the next six months as Quebec endured martial law.

The Impact of War at Home

The conscription crisis was one of the many transformative moments ushered in by the Great War. The cleavage between French and English Canada represented by the violent reactions to conscription of the Quebec City Easter Riots reflected a broader malaise in the country's national politics. The Union government, and the willingness of many Liberals to abandon their party over conscription and join the Conservatives, disillusioned many Canadians, in Quebec and across the country.

The decline of politics during the Great War led to a birth of alternate, third parties in the 1920s that fundamentally reshaped party politics in Canada. In releasing incredible tensions between French and English and between rural and urban Canadians (especially in the West), the war reordered domestic politics in a way that became very apparent in the 1920s and 1930s. The First World War created a new consciousness among workers and farmers and helped to generate new political parties and demands for change.

The economy of the country was also transformed. Wartime production to maintain an army of hundreds of thousands of men across an ocean meant that industry was galvanized by the war effort. Furthermore, Canada became a major exporter of wheat and industrial products as the country's economic capacity boomed under the wartime demands. For instance, Ford of Canada built thousands of trucks and cars for the war effort, providing employment at home and developing this sector of the economy.

Third, women's status in the country was transformed. In the workplace, though their numbers were not huge, women took on positions in factories that were needed for wartime production. This employment provided a whole new impetus for better working rights for women and gave them an opportunity to earn wages comparable to those earned by men (though still much less). In the political sphere, women earned the right to vote, albeit because the Unionist government wanted to use their votes to ensure that conscription remained a government policy. But the passage of the Wartime Elections Act meant that women, who had been fighting for these rights for decades, now demanded suffrage (the vote) for all women.

Finally, even with all the fissures and fragmentation that the conscription crisis and the challenges that war created, within a few years, Canada's wartime experience had also created a newfound sense of Canadianness, which exploded in a burst of artistic and nationalistic creativity, especially during the 1920s. Canadians, despite the trials and tribulations of wartime, realized that they had accomplished something special during the war. The new nationalism and confidence could be seen most astonishingly in the colourful works of emerging artists such as Tom Thomson, whose vibrant and colourful brush strokes, as we shall see, contrasted so stunningly with the dire greyness and hopelessness of the war.

Further Reading

Auger, Martin F. "On the Brink of Civil War: The Canadian Government and the Suppression of the 1918 Quebec Easter Riots." *Canadian Historical Review* 89, no. 4 (December 2008): 503–40. http://dx.doi.org/10.3138/chr.89.4.503.

Granatstein, J.L., and J.M. Hitsman. *Broken Promises: A History of Conscription in Canada.* Toronto: Oxford University Press, 1977.

Keshen, Jeffrey A. *Propaganda and Censorship Behind Canada's Great War.* Edmonton: University of Alberta Press, 1996.

Kordan, Bohdan S. *Enemy Aliens, Prisoners of War: Internment in Canada during the Great War.* Montreal: McGill-Queen's University Press, 2002.

Moogk, Peter. "Uncovering the Enemy Within: British Columbians and the German Menace." *BC Studies* 182 (Summer 2014): 45–72, 251.

Walker, James W. St. G. "Race and Recruitment in World War I." *Canadian Historical Review* 70, no. 1 (March 1989): 1–26.

ACTIVE HISTORY: QUESTIONS FOR CONSIDERATION

Examine the article by Walker, "Race and Recruitment," and consider the following questions:

1. What is the main argument or thesis of the article? Is the argument easily identifiable? Can you make any comment on the writing style of the author?

2. How does the author address the question of historiography, if he does so at all?

3. According to Walker, how did minorities respond to the challenges of recruitment in the First World War? Was there a difference in approach among different minorities? How did the state help or hinder this recruitment? What does this article tell us about the attitudes of Canadians toward race in this period?

5. What are the main sources employed by the author? Are they effective? What other sources could have been used? What can the sources used tell us about the author's methodological approach?

6. Overall, is this article effective and persuasive? If so, why? If not, why not?

CHAPTER SEVEN

MICHAEL SOKOLOWISKI AND STEVEN SKEZERBANOVICZ, MURDERED, WINNIPEG, 1919

CAPITAL AND LABOUR COLLIDE IN INDUSTRIALIZING CANADA

By 1918, the war was over. The country was licking its wounds. More than 60,000 Canadians were dead, and hundreds of thousands were returning home wounded and broken. Conscription had been imposed by the Union government (really the Conservatives) after its 1917 election victory; party politics was in disarray following the fracturing of the Liberal Party, many of whose members had joined the Conservatives to form the Unionist Party. Tensions were high between French and English Canadians, and there was even talk of Quebec leaving Canada after the 1917 election; few French Canadians had supported the Union government, most opting to stay with Laurier's anti-conscription Liberal Party.

The war in Europe was over, but, in June of 1919, Winnipeg was at the centre of its own war. This was a war between capital and labour, between the East and the West, and between ordinary working people and bosses. About 30,000 people were on strike, and virtually the whole city was shut down. Some people were thinking it was a revolution not unlike what had just happened in Russia in 1917, when Communists had taken control of that country.

This strike was, for many people, truly a war. The bloodiest battle of this war occurred on June 21, 1919, when mounted RCMP officers charged into a mass of strikers in downtown Winnipeg. After the dust had cleared, hundreds had been hurt, and two had been killed. The two men's names were Michael Sokolowiski and Steven Skezerbanovicz. Not much is known about them: Both were immigrants. One was Jewish, the other was Ukrainian. Both were workers.

Sokolowiski died instantly, a bullet through his heart. Skezerbanovicz died a few days later, after infection from his bullet wounds became too severe.

Like Private Harold Carter, the soldier whose execution was described in Chapter 5, these men were not famous. They are not like D'Arcy McGee or Louis Riel. They were ordinary people caught up in extraordinary times. But, to this day, their deaths are still memorialized in Winnipeg.

The incident would become known as Bloody Saturday. It seemed as though Canada was on the verge of outright class warfare and political revolution. At the very least, the strike marked a pivotal moment in the awakening of labour groups in Canada, groups that challenged the prevailing economic system.

Thus, the confrontation in Winnipeg symbolized another sort of Canadian awakening after the war. It reflected the harsh realities of an industrialized, urbanized, and regional country coming to terms with the realities of modern capitalism that had emerged with the national policy and with the changes to the Canadian economy created by the Laurier boom. The Winnipeg General Strike also demonstrated the growing class conflict between workers and capital in the new industrialized Canada, and it provided an opportunity for elites to reinforce the prevailing liberal, capitalist ethos in the country through repression of this movement.

But to understand why these two men died in Winnipeg in 1919, and why the city became the centre of a larger battle between capital and labour in Canada, we need to understand the emergence of industrialization, the growth of the labour movement, and Winnipeg itself.

The Industrial Revolution

Between the 1700s and the early 1900s, there were dramatic changes in the nature of work. In fact, over the course of the nineteenth century, there were really two industrial revolutions; the first began in the late 1700s and was an early industrialization marked by the advent of steam power, railroads, and machinery. In the early years of the 1800s, small factories employed only a few people to create industrial products; manufacturers began to use new techniques for limited mass production, as happened in the textile mills of New England; and early iron and steel production developed for the building of railways.

The end of the nineteenth century saw a second industrial revolution resulting in five major developments that fundamentally changed the nature of work. First, mechanization accelerated: machinery now controlled the actions of workers, as opposed to the other way around. At the Ford Motor Company of Canada plant in Windsor, Ontario, the moving assembly line dictated the speed of work and the work process. Mechanization created a new class of unskilled labourers working at repetitive industrial tasks, as opposed to the skilled tradesmen who dominated small-scale industry in the earlier years of the century.

Second, because of mechanization and mass production techniques, the scale of the workplace grew dramatically. Instead of small artisan shops employing a few dozen workers, factories now were massive structures employing thousands of people. By the end of the First World War, Ford's Windsor plant employed over 3,000 people. As the war itself continued, many large-scale factories were built to feed the wartime demand for munitions and material; these factories required many workers. Fordism, as it came to be known, was the mass production of goods on such a huge scale as to make that production profitable.

Third, this mechanization and large-scale industrialization required the development of new management systems. These larger industrial corporate structures became highly regimented, hierarchical, and bureaucratized. New management systems were designed to coordinate work, control costs, and integrate work processes. "Time-management" studies from new management experts such as Frederick Winslow (F.W.) Taylor pioneered "scientific management" of the workplace. Taylorism, the science of managing a large industrial workforce for full efficiency so that the clock became the most important aspect of a worker's day, went hand in hand with Fordism.

Fourth, the number of workers needed in these new factories required new pools of labour. Now women, children, immigrants, and non-whites (in some cases) joined the industrial labour force. Usually, these people took the worst jobs in the factory, but their presence did change the dynamic of the workplace.

Finally, these large-scale entities meant the creation of "corporate welfare," the paternalistic, company-based approach to employee relations that was designed to keep workers happy and healthy (at least happy and healthy enough to work efficiently). These gestures included small-scale welfare and benefits programs, picnics, life-insurance policies, company magazines, and the like, all designed to keep workers content—and to keep unions out of a company.

Labour in Canada in the Late Nineteenth and Early Twentieth Centuries

For much of the nineteenth and early twentieth centuries, Canadian workers struggled to gain recognition, rights, and better working conditions and wages. Most of the workers who began the organized labour movement in this period were skilled; they were tradespeople, for example, as opposed to unskilled workers who toiled in factories doing repetitive tasks. One of the first successful unions in Canada was in the newspaper industry. The Toronto Typographical Union, started in 1832, was made of men (and they were always men, exclusively) who were skilled printing-press setters and workers.

But the nineteenth-century union movement was not widespread and faced a number of challenges. Technological changes made some skilled trades jobs obsolete, weakening some early unions. For example, the coopers union, whose members repaired wooden casks and tubs, was hurt by technological changes (the advent of metal containers) that made these items unlikely to require repair. There was also an inhospitable legal climate, as many court rulings found unions a "restraint of trade" and therefore illegal. The movement was very narrow, too, with few women or minorities in unions and the vast majority of male workers excluded as well.

Yet, from the 1870s and 1880s onwards, workers and unions were starting to agitate. Unionized men fought for better wages and safer working conditions. Many Canadian workplaces were extremely dangerous. An example from a later date provides evidence of this danger: in a single month in 1911, 92 Canadian workers were killed on the job. Many others were maimed or left blind by industrial accidents. There was no worker's compensation legislation until 1915, and the laws designed to ensure that employers provided compensation were ineffective. Workers also became mobilized over the battle for the 9 hour day. Before the 1870s, most workers worked a 12- or 14-hour day, a considerable hardship.

The 1872 Trade Unions Act, passed by John A. Macdonald to spite his newspaper-owning rival George Brown, also gave the union movement impetus. However, the rights granted by these new laws were very limited: employers were not required to recognize or bargain with unions, so bosses could hire scabs (or replacement workers). Also, some employers required workers to pledge not to join a union before being hired.

Nonetheless, after 1872, when forming a union was no longer considered an offence under the laws forbidding "restraint of trade," there was a considerable growth in the Canadian union movement. On the one hand, new labour organizations were founded. The Trades and Labor Congress of Canada, created in 1883, provided an umbrella group for many unions in the era. In Quebec, different from English-speaking Canada, there was the development of Catholic-based unions. These unions remained very conservative, and reflected the more conservative and Catholic background of the province.

On the other hand, the Canadian union movement imported ideas and organizations from the United States. For example, in the 1880s, the Knights of Labor expanded into Canada. The Knights were far more inclusive than most Canadian unions and granted membership to women and unskilled workers. Another American import was the American Federation of Labor (AFL), arriving in 1886. This gigantic union group was led by Samuel Gompers, who dominated the labour movement in North America for the next 30 years.

The AFL remained committed to craft unions with skilled male membership, focused on workplace issues, and wanted to stay out of politics. It also used hardball tactics when organizing, expelling unions or groups with which it did not agree, such as the Knights of Labor. Gompers also saw to it that his American union came to dominate Canadian unions, causing friction between Canadian and American union leaders.

In response to the union movement's growth and the agitation over issues such as the nine-hour day, the government established the 1889 Royal Commission on the Relations of Labour and Capital, which spent a number of years studying issues such as working conditions, child labour, sanitation laws, the extension of education, and workplace safety. However, the report was largely ineffective. The government acted on only one of the commission's recommendations: in 1894, it created Labour Day, the minimum that government could do to advance the interests of the working class. Indeed, the state remained predisposed against collective workers' rights. Between 1867 and 1914, the militia was called out during labour conflicts on at least 33 occasions, including during bloody battles in Cape Breton, Springhill, Nova Scotia, and Vancouver Island. Yet unions continued to grow rapidly, from just over 130,000 people in 1911 to just over 375,000 by 1919.

Post—First World War Issues

Along with these dramatic workplace changes were other postwar factors that led to the confrontation at Winnipeg. The war was a period of severe disruption and had a significant impact upon the psyche of Canadians: the war itself, the mobilization for the war effort, conscription, and the very difficult period surrounding the 1917 election put an incredible strain on Canadians, on both an individual and collective basis, in this period.

Adding to this wartime disruption were the effects of a widespread influenza epidemic. This worldwide pandemic ravaged Canada in 1918 and 1919, most likely having been brought back to the country by returning soldiers. Many cities ordered people to wear gauze masks in public, which were actually useless against the virus. Theatres and schools were closed, public meetings banned, and church services cancelled in an effort to check the deadly disease. An estimated 50,000 Canadians died from this "silent enemy," about 11,000 shy of the number of lives lost in the war.

The return of thousands of soldiers from the front further added to the strain on Canadian life. By the time they returned home, many of these men were militant, radicalized, or at least politically awakened. Soldiers were disillusioned by war and critical of the government that had sent them to the front. Many experienced the development of a working-class consciousness: they felt that they did not receive proper recognition for their efforts, and many working men and veterans were upset that, although manpower was conscripted during the war, there was no similar conscription of wealth.

Canada faced an economic slowdown after the war, too. Unemployment increased as veterans returned. Industries geared for wartime production were no longer building for the war effort. Along with high unemployment, money was scarce, causing the cost of goods to increase. At the same time, real wages declined. Thus, the cost of goods increased, but workers' wages were not keeping pace, causing widespread economic hardship.

There was also a growing division between the West and the rest of Canada in the labour movement. In the western provinces, militancy grew, as unionists tried to get the attention of the eastern and central workers and bosses. Western labour leaders also felt that Canadian unions in the rest of English-speaking Canada were dominated by the AFL, were not radical enough, and catered to skilled craft workers as opposed to the wider working class. For labour leaders in the West, the struggle for workers' rights was not just a class issue but also a regional issue in Canada.

J.S. Woodsworth, leader of the western labour movement and, eventually, of the Co-operative Commonwealth Federation (or CCF, which became the New Democratic Party) described these regional differences: "For years among labour men, as among farmers and business men, the Western outlook and spirit have differed somewhat from that of the East. . . .There had been [before 1919] a growing feeling that policies were too much under the control of the headquarters of unions situated in Eastern American cities."[1]

For instance, during the 1918 meeting of the Trades and Labor Congress of Canada, delegates disagreed over the level of militancy needed to achieve their goals. Western delegates wanted stronger unions and general strikes, and they called for greater social reform, but these ideas were rejected by eastern delegates. Instead, western delegates met at Calgary in 1919 and called for the creation of the OBU, the One Big Union, aimed not just at labour reform but at wider social reform.

Finally, worldwide events played a role in the build-up to the confrontation at Winnipeg. Labour leaders were inspired to a degree by the events in Russia, where the Bolsheviks (the name of Vladimir Lenin's Communists) had taken control of the government in a workers' revolution in 1917. Many Canadians saw this change as a positive development, and were inspired by the rhetoric and images of the revolution in Russia. Other Canadians saw these Russian developments as a terrifying sign of what might be coming in Canada if the labour movement was not stopped.

Winnipeg and the Strike, 1919

Winnipeg became the centre of confrontation. But why Winnipeg? There are a number of reasons. Winnipeg was starkly divided by geography and class; the

---

1   J.S. Woodsworth, "The Labour Movement in the West," *The Canadian Forum* 2, no. 19 (April 1922), 585–87, see 586.

south was wealthy, the north was poor. Winnipeg was also heavily urbanized, and urbanization had been rapid. By 1919, it was the third largest city in Canada, after Montreal and Toronto. The population boom had seen immense construction and industrial growth, and people saw Winnipeg as Canada's Chicago. Postwar Winnipeg was very different from Louis Riel's small Red River settlement.

Winnipeg was also ethnically diverse, and ethnic categories reflected class divisions. New immigrant communities made up much of the working class while employers were mostly middle- and upper-class, white, and British- or Canadian-born residents. In 1901, Winnipeg had about 3,000 central Europeans, growing to nearly 25,000 by 1911 and representing about 15 per cent of the population. Among the wave of new immigrants were many people with differing political views, including socialists from places such as Finland. Winnipeg also had a critical mass of middle-class intellectuals attached to labour and social reform issues, such as J.S. Woodsworth.

Winnipeg was a large manufacturing centre with many unions and was a centre for the Canadian Pacific and Canadian National rail yards whose trains crossed the country, making the city a gateway to the West and the main terminus for the wheat economy. There was tremendous growth before the war in construction, railway activity, migration, and the transport of goods across Canada. But, in 1919, Winnipeg was in the midst of a bust. After the war, a serious economic downturn caused high unemployment and a feeling among workers that they were being exploited because they endured low wages, high accident rates, and little security.

All of these issues came to a head in May 1919. That month, the city's building trades union demanded higher wages. The metal trades also wanted to get all the metalworkers to bargain as one collective unit. The Employers' Association and the Winnipeg Board of Trade, representing the largely British and white middle and upper classes, rejected these demands. In response, the unions went on strike.

Other unions quickly joined in sympathy strikes. Before long, all the unions in the city called for a general strike. On May 15, 1919, 22,000 unionized workers struck and many non-union workers joined them. This was the most widespread and complete general strike in Canadian history: there was no mail, no public transportation, no firefighters, no water pressure, no delivery of food or bread. Even the police voted to strike, but they did not do so on the advice of strike leaders. Rail yard employees, however, did not strike. Because of this widespread disruption, a Central Strike Committee was formed to provide basic services and to bargain with employers. After a few days, the committee allowed the delivery of food and a few other necessities. Workers had effectively taken control of Canada's third largest city.

In response, the middle and upper classes formed the "Citizens' Committee of 1,000," which really represented the interests of the employers; it aimed to recapture civil control of the city and demanded government intervention in the strike. Although both the city and the province remained on the sidelines, the

Citizens' Committee of 1,000 found a sympathetic ear in Ottawa, where the Union government of Conservative Robert Borden was still in power.

The Union government and many upper- and middle-class people in Winnipeg and across the country saw the events in Winnipeg as the beginning of a revolution, as had occurred in Russia. They responded to the situation with outright repression. Right away, the Union government sent Minister of the Interior Arthur Meighen to Winnipeg. Meighen was already famous for having orchestrated the electoral changes during the 1917 election, and he worked with the Citizens' Committee of 1,000 in opposition to the strike. As an MP from Winnipeg and one of the city's financial and political elite, Meighen was completely unsympathetic to the strikers. He recommended a hard line to Ottawa, which immediately told postal workers that they would be fired if they didn't return to work by May 26. Meighen thought this response might break the will of the strikers, though it did not work.

In May and June, as the situation became increasingly tense, the two sides settled in for a hot summer. Both tried to win the support of veterans; returned soldiers were on either side, but many were unemployed, and quite a few were sympathetic to the strikers. Worrying about the veterans, on June 6, Mayor Charles Gray of Winnipeg banned parades and public demonstrations for fear of violence.

Next, the federal government changed laws to repress the strike. This change echoed Meighen's legislative moves during the 1917 election. Specifically, Section 41 of the Immigration Act was changed to allow the deportation of people deemed to be attempting to overthrow the government. Section 98 of the Criminal Code was also changed, although this change did not come into effect until after the strike was over. Under this section, it was an offence to belong to any organization trying to bring about governmental, industrial, or economic change by force or violence or advocating the use of force or violence. This was a reverse onus law; those charged had to prove their innocence, as opposed to the prosecution proving their guilt.

The government also built up the militia and the North-West Mounted Police (which changed its name to the Royal Canadian Mounted Police in 1920). On June 9, all but 16 members of the city's regular police force of about 240 men were fired for refusing to sign a loyalty oath; they were replaced by approximately 1,800 "special constables" recruited by the Citizens' Committee of 1,000. The meetings of this committee were held in secret, and no list of its members was ever published. Some of the constables were recently demobilized servicemen.

With all this build-up, things started to get nasty. There was an increasing backlash against any "ethnics" who supported the strike. As newspaper editor John Dafoe of the *Winnipeg Free Press* put it, the best way to end the strike is "to clean the aliens out of this community and ship them back to their happy homes in Europe which vomited them forth a decade ago."[2] The first incident of open violence erupted on June 10, when special constables clashed with demonstrators.

When this incident was reported, Prime Minister Borden became convinced that revolution was under way. He wrote to one associate: "A dispatch informs us of the intention to arrest several strike leaders. These leaders have plotted to overthrow the government of the country and to establish a Soviet government."[3] Three days later, 10 strike leaders (6 of British background and 4 "foreigners") were arrested, and union offices were searched.

Finally, the conflict broke into an open confrontation on June 21, known as Bloody Saturday. The initial incident started with a streetcar. Winnipeg street railways had attempted to start up service using replacement workers, called scabs. This move sparked a riot as the strikers attempted to stop the scabs from operating the streetcar. Because parades and public demonstrations had been deemed illegal, the mayor read the Riot Act and the Mounties, on horseback, charged the protestors. In the ensuing clash, many were injured, and two marchers were killed. When the charge was finished, the militia had cleared the streets. The same day, the government arrested a number of "foreign rioters," closed the newspaper the *Western Labour News*, and also arrested its editor, J.S. Woodsworth.

Figure 7.1 *Mounted Police Charge during the Winnipeg General Strike, June 1919*

University of Manitoba Archives, PC 18/7188/18–6233a-019

2   As quoted in Donald Avery, *"Dangerous Foreigners": European Immigrant Workers and Labour Radicalism in Canada, 1896–1932* (Toronto: McClelland and Stewart, 1979), 84.

3   As quoted in Robert Craig Brown, and Ramsay Cook, *Canada 1896–1921: A Nation Transformed* (Toronto: McClelland and Stewart, 1974), 313.

These events effectively broke the back of the strike. Two days later, what was left of the Central Strike Committee offered to end the strike if a royal commission would investigate the underlying causes. The government had made it clear that it would call in military (or, in this case, paramilitary) forces to put an end to labour conflict and that it would give little thought to the rights of workers to organize and protest—these rights were to be severely curtailed. By June 25, the strike was officially called off. It seemed that labour had lost.

The Impact of the Strike

The strike had both immediate and long-term consequences. In the short term, workers saw few tangible benefits: many were laid off, and most workers did not make the gains they had hoped to. At the same time, across Canada at least nine major sympathy strikes occurred. These included general strikes in Nova Scotia and Toronto and in Alberta's coalfields. In fact, there were strikes all across the country, which had a galvanizing impact on the Canadian labour movement.

In reaction, the widespread labour agitation provoked repressive government responses across the country. Just as in Winnipeg, many groups like the Citizens' Committee of 1,000 were created to challenge workers. The government's repressive attitude was further fuelled by the period's Red Scare. With the fall of Russia to Lenin's Bolsheviks, many in the Western world feared that a worldwide revolution was upon them. There was a crackdown against any "communistic agitation" in the United States, the United Kingdom, and Canada. Though many Canadian political elites saw the end of the strike as Canada having averted a revolution, most Canadians saw it as just another strike.

Finally, a significant impact was an increase in the incidents of ethnic discrimination generated by the strike. Many Canadians blamed the strike upon "dangerous foreigners," and legal changes allowing for the deportation of immigrants reflected a wider view that the immigrant influence in Winnipeg was the root of a foreign plot. Although the main leaders of the strike were Canadian-born or British, people blamed "foreigners" from other ethnic groups for the confrontation. This finger-pointing further widened the gap between visible minorities and Canadians of English ancestry and proved, yet again, that Canada was not the multicultural haven many have said it was.

The long-term impact of the strike included a number of developments. Government repression toward labour movements was codified. Section 98 of the Criminal Code stayed on the books until the late 1930s, and its violation carried the maximum penalty of a 20-year jail term. This law had a significant impact on the mobilization and organization of workers in the period.

The strike also caused a radicalization and political fragmentation of the Left and the working-class movement. Radicalization was strongest in the West, which spawned a host of labour movements and workers' parties that eventually took the form of the Co-operative Commonwealth Federation (CCF) and gained power in places such as Saskatchewan. As part of this radicalization, labour groups fragmented. Instead of the effort to have One Big Union all working together, as in Winnipeg, a host of groups emerged. The Communist Party of Canada formed in Guelph in 1921, but there were also syndicalists, Marxists, socialists, and various other groups. These labour leaders were conflicted over the Winnipeg General Strike and whether it had required more militancy or less. Finally, a growing farmer's movement developed in response to and as a part of the largely urban labour movement.

One other legacy of the Winnipeg General Strike is, of course, the continued commemoration of the two men who lost their lives as a consequence of the violence of that confrontation, a commemoration that continues to this day, a century after "Bloody Saturday."

Further Reading

Heron, Craig, ed. *The Workers' Revolt in Canada, 1917–1925*. Toronto: University of Toronto Press, 1998.

Isitt, Benjamin. "Searching for Workers' Solidarity: The One Big Union and the Victoria General Strike of 1919." *Labour / Le Travail* 60 (Fall 2007): 9–42.

Kealey, Greg. "1919: The Canadian Labour Revolt." *Labour / Le Travail* 13 (Spring 1984): 11–44. http://dx.doi.org/10.2307/25140399.

Korneski, Kurt. "Prairie Fire: The Winnipeg General Strike." *Labour / Le Travail* 45 (Spring 2000): 59–66.

Kramer, Reinhold, and Tom Mitchell. *When the State Trembled: How A.J. Andrews and the Citizens' Committee Broke the Winnipeg General Strike*. Toronto: University of Toronto Press, 2010.

ACTIVE HISTORY: THE HISTORIOGRAPHY OF THE WINNIPEG GENERAL STRIKE

- In the words of one Canadian historian, Greg Kealey, the idea that the West and particularly Winnipeg were exceptional in the great labour uprising of 1919 is a "sorry shibboleth." Instead, he sees Winnipeg as but one important battle in a national and international labour uprising. From his perspective, the focus on Winnipeg has obscured the wave of strikes in the period before 1919, as well as the sympathy strikes across the country during and after the events at Winnipeg.

- What is your view? Examine the readings and the chapter and assess the evidence and arguments in this historiographical debate. Which interpretation is more convincing and why?

- How does the Winnipeg General Strike fit within the national and international context of the time?

🔫 MURDEROUS MOMENT 🔫
THEATRE IMPRESARIO AMBROSE SMALL, MURDERED? TORONTO, 1919

An Early Twentieth-Century "E! True" Story of Murder, Money, and Mystery

At the time, it was the scandal of the century: Ambrose Small's story is truly a tale of murder, money, and mystery.

Ambrose Small was born in Bradford, Ontario, in 1866. When Ambrose was nine, his father moved the Small family to the growing city of Toronto to run a hotel and saloon, and, by 1880, Small's father had taken over the city's Grand Hotel, right next door to the marquee Grand Opera House in the heart of bustling downtown Toronto.

From a young age, Ambrose was industrious and entrepreneurial, and a bit of showman, something he picked up from his father. By the 1890s, he was running a number of theatres across Ontario, booking some of the biggest acts from America and Europe for his audiences. Known as a gambler who liked to bet on horse races, Small was nonetheless a shrewd businessman who capitalized on the booming growth of cities in this period, and on urban dwellers' desire for entertainment. In 1902, he took control of a live theatre chain that, by 1906, boasted 34 venues in Ontario and the United States. His ventures soon expanded into vaudeville and moving pictures. In the process, Small became a very wealthy man.

Dynamic and driven, Small, called "Ambie" by his intimates, was also something of a ladies' man. Rich, ambitious, and charming, he attracted women, many of them show girls that he showered with gifts. By 1902, he had seemingly settled down by marrying Theresa Kormann, his stepmother's younger sister. Lively, artistic, and deeply religious, Theresa and Ambrose were something of a celebrity couple, and they settled in posh Rosedale as Small's theatre empire company grew. In 1903, he purchased the Grand Opera House, along with its sister theatre in London, Ontario.

Purchasing the Grand, a leading light in Toronto's entertainment district, had been a long-time goal of Small's, and, once it was in his possession, Small outfitted the theatre with a secret chamber while Theresa was in Europe. The secret chamber held a bar, a portrait of a nude woman, and an opulent bed, where Small consorted with his many lovers. Though Theresa knew of these affairs, she turned a blind eye.

In 1919, the theatre business, though still lucrative, was in decline as costs increased and motion pictures started to attract huge audiences. The Smalls decided to sell their huge holdings for the astounding sum of $1.7 million (equal to $22 million in 2015) to a Canadian theatre conglomerate. The day of the sale, Small went on a spending spree, buying fur coats and jewellery and ordering a Cadillac. That evening, Small disappeared without a trace.

Initially, Theresa held that Small was probably cavorting with one of his mistresses and would turn up soon. But the timing of the disappearance—the same day a $1 million cheque had been deposited into the couple's account following the sale of the theatre chain—raised suspicions. Within weeks, it was clear that Small was not simply in the company of another woman. Soon, an international manhunt commenced, with Theresa offering a substantial reward for information on "Ambie's" whereabouts. Although a former Grand employee was convicted of stealing bonds from Small's safe in that theatre, kidnapping charges were never laid, and Small remained nowhere to be found.

Small's disappearance sparked a media frenzy of accusation and suspicion. Had Theresa played a role in his vanishing? Did Small's enemies in the theatre world have something to do with the disappearance? A worker at Small's Grand Theatre in London, who reported having smelled unusual fumes coming from the furnace, claimed that Theresa and a lover had burned Small's body. The police were certain that foul play had indeed been committed but could not crack the case. When Theresa announced that the Small fortune would be left to the Catholic Church *after* she passed away, Small's sisters hired a private detective to find Small, or at least find out what had happened to him.

By 1923, despite the manhunts, the police and private investigations, and the rewards, the mystery remained unsolved. Small was declared dead for legal purposes, and his 1903 will left everything to his wife. Though his sisters challenged the validity of the will, Theresa, who had now become a recluse, won. When she died in 1935, she kept to her word and left more than a $1 million to the Catholic Church.

Though the mystery of Small's disappearance was never solved, the story reflects the growth of urban Canada, the development of the entertainment industry, the increasing prosperity of Canadians, and their willingness to spend their hard-earned money on leisure pursuits. Since Small vanished in 1919, his case has only grown in stature; it has become the subject of books, articles, plays, paintings, and even a radio play. Author Michael Ondaatje includes the Small story in his internationally renowned novel *In the Skin of a Lion*.

It seems Ambrose Small remains almost as famous in death as he was during his scandalous, tabloid-worthy, soap-opera life.

CHAPTER EIGHT

TOM THOMSON, MURDERED? CANOE LAKE, ONTARIO, 1917

ART, NATIONALISM, AND AMERICANIZATION IN THE INTERWAR PERIOD

The man was, and remains, an icon. He was so young, so good looking. He was a painter and an outdoorsman. He epitomizes in so many ways the romantic notions of the North.

Tom Thomson is famous because his paintings captured the imagination of generations of Canadians. Not only did he inspire those who would form the famous Group of Seven, but his and the Group of Seven's successes signified the beginnings of an outburst of cultural nationalism.

Thomson was born in 1877 near Claremont, Ontario. As a young man, he moved to Seattle, Washington, where he worked as a photo-engraver, which got him interested in art and painting. Thomson seemed to have a natural talent for art. He moved to Toronto in 1905, where he got a job at Grip Limited, a design firm. That's where he met J.E.H. MacDonald, with whom he started going on weekend sketching trips to nearby lakes. He made his first trip to Algonquin Park, Ontario, in the summer of 1912, over a century ago.

Tom Thomson

Thomson fell in love with the North. He spent the summers from 1913 to 1917 as an Algonquin Park ranger, making numerous sketches of the rugged northern landscapes. Although he painted for only about four years, he produced quite a bit of work. He went into the wilderness during the summer months and used the sketches he made there as models for the canvases that he painted during the winter. His work broke with the conventional landscape style; his art was vividly realistic yet almost abstract in its use of bright colours and its manipulation of texture.

But Thomson is also famous because of the mystery surrounding his death. Because he was an experienced canoeist, the curious circumstances of his apparent drowning at Canoe Lake in 1917 have been scrutinized for decades. Did he really die by accident, or was there something more sinister at hand? Was he murdered? There have been so many questions, so many investigations. In fact, the evidence suggests that something strange surrounded not only Thomson's death but also his burial and the removal of his body.

Thomson's mysterious death has helped make him famous, and his paintings very valuable. At the same time, Thomson's death, though a sad end to his life, marks a symbolic beginning of something new in Canada in the postwar period. This is especially ironic, given that he died even before the war was over. Yet his death, and the war itself, unleashed a newfound confidence of Canadians in themselves and in their standing in the world. The end of the war released a new nationalism, which seemed to explode from Canadians' paintbrushes. Along with art, other areas of Canadian cultural life experienced intensive growth at this time.

Yet, paradoxically, the decade also signified the growth of a common North American culture, one dominated by the immense cultural and political presence of the United States of America. Indeed, the 1920s was the "roaring" decade of flappers, speakeasies, talkies, and Al Capone. This cross-border culture was fuelled by magazines, movies, and radio, all of which exposed Canadians to American mass media in a way they had never experienced before. Despite the growth of nationalism, Canadians embraced American cultural influences more than those from any other country. In response, Canadians and their government developed new ways to protect Canadian culture, from the creation of the Canadian Broadcasting Corporation (CBC) to tariffs on magazines. Though some of these efforts provided a measure of Canadianness on a continent engulfed by American culture, others were less successful.

Tom Thomson's Mysterious Death

As he had done every year since 1913, Tom Thomson went north to Algonquin Park from Toronto in the spring of 1917. Over his years of sketching in the park, Thomson had become familiar with the area, and with Canoe Lake, which he used as a base of operations for his painting expeditions. By 1917, Thomson was considered an expert canoeist and fisherman, and a good swimmer, and he knew the terrain around Canoe Lake well.

He was last seen on July 8, 1917. Within a few days, his absence started to generate news, curiosity, and then, suspicion. Here is an initial news report about his disappearance from the July 13 Toronto *Globe*:

Figure 8.1 *Tom Thomson on Canoe Lake, 1916*

Archives of Ontario, 10001309 –F-1066–6

TORONTO ARTIST MISSING IN NORTH

Tom Thomson Missing From Canoe Lake since Sunday—A Talented Landscapist

Toronto art circles were shocked yesterday at the news received from Algonquin Park that Tom Thomson, one of the most talented of the younger artists of the city, had been missing since Sunday and was thought to have been drowned or the victim of foul play. Mr. Thomson was last seen at Canoe Lake at noon on Sunday, and at 3:30 in the afternoon his canoe was found adrift in the lake, upside down. There was no storm, only a light wind prevailing, and the fact that both paddles were in place in the canoe as if for a portage, adds to the mystery. Mr. Thomson carried a light fishing rod and this and his dunnage bag were missing.

A Lover of the Wilderness

Mr. Thomson, who made his home in the city at the Studio building in Severn street, was especially fond of the woods, and spent more than half of each year in the northern wilderness. He has risen rapidly in esteem as a landscape painter, his interpretation of the north country having an indefinable charm and feeling that could only come from a deep love of nature. One of his paintings, "Northern River," attracted much attention at the Ontario Society of Artists Exhibition a year or so ago, and was subsequently bought by the National Gallery at Ottawa.

Once Lived in B.C.

Mr. Thomson came from Owen Sound, where his father still lives. Part of his forty-two years of life were spent in British Columbia. After coming to Toronto a few years ago he was engaged for a time in commercial art. There is still a chance that Mr. Thomson may be alive, but this is considered doubtful as four days' search has failed to find a trace of him.[1]

As the article indicates, rumours swirled around Thomson's disappearance. Weather could not have played a factor, and there was no indication that Thomson wanted to take his own life. If his death was an accident, it must have been a very curious set of circumstances leading to such an incident. Otherwise, there was always the possibility of foul play, as the *Globe* report hints.

Before he disappeared, Thomson had been involved with a woman, Winnifred Trainor, which led some to suspect a lover's quarrel or some sort of altercation over a woman. There were also rumours of German spies hiding in the park,

---

1 *Globe*, Friday, July 13, 1917, p. 7.

given the wartime paranoia that gripped much of the country. More prosaic explanations for his death, such as Thomson having a run-in with illegal poachers who stalked Algonquin Park for game, were also presented. None seemed to satisfy, and the most logical, and the one reported by the coroner, that Thomson had died of an accidental drowning, seemed implausible given the artist's natural ability and affinity for canoes and lakes.

Following the discovery of Thomson's body on July 16, matters became even more curious. One of the men who discovered the body, Dr. G.W. Howland, swore out an affidavit on July 17, which stated the following:

Canoe Lake
July 17-17.

Dr. G.W. Howland qualified medical practitioner of Toronto, Ont., Sworn, Said:

I saw body of man floating in Canoe Lake Monday, July 16th, at about 10 A.M. and notified Mr. George Rowe a resident who removed body to shore. On 17th Tuesday, I examined body and found it to be that of a man aged about 40 years in advanced stage of decomposition, face abdomen and limbs swollen, blisters on limbs, was a bruise on right temple size of 4" long, no other sign of external marks visible on body, air issuing from mouth, some bleeding from right ear, cause of death drowning.

(Sgd.) Gordon W. Howland,
M.R. N.A.C.P.[2]

Mark Robinson, the park ranger who was also present when the body was pulled out of the lake, wrote in his own journal that the bruise was "Evidently caused by falling on a Rock otherwise no marks of Violence on Body," yet questions remained. Why did it take so long to find the body? Was it as simple as a slip? Or was the bruise caused by more nefarious means? If air was found in the lungs, was Thomson still alive when he allegedly struck his head and then fell into the lake? Perhaps most mysterious, fishing line seemed to have been wrapped around his ankle. Then, reports started to circulate that Thomson's body, initially buried at Canoe Lake following his death, had been removed and reburied.

These questions and the uncertain circumstances surrounding his burial led to a host of investigations, starting in the 1920s and lasting until the

---

2   This and other documents in the chapter can be found at the *Death on a Painted Lake* website, http://www.canadianmysteries.ca/sites/thomson/home/indexen.html.

1990s, over the truth about the great artist's mysterious death. So much speculation existed that, in the 1950s, the body was supposedly exhumed from the Canoe Lake grave and inspected to discover whether the remains were Thomson's, prompting a sharp 1956 letter to the *Toronto Star* from one M.R. Dixon, who had been present when Thomson was buried nearly four decades earlier:

M.R. Dixon, "I Buried Tom Thomson, No Foul Play," *Toronto Daily Star*, October 12, 1956

Thomson Drowned

Sir: I was the undertaker who embalmed and interred the remains of Tom Thomson at Canoe Lake in 1917, and have a very distinct recollection of all the official proceedings at that time. I beg to take issue with reports that appeared last week suggesting death by foul play.

I was called from Algonquin park headquarters to remove the body from the water and prepare it for shipment. When I arrived at Joe Lake Station I was met by Mark Robinson, ranger. His first question was, "Is the coroner from North Bay on the train?" He was not and I informed him I could do nothing without a death certificate. He got in touch with Mr. Bartlett, the superintendent of the park, and he sent over a certificate of accidental death by drowning.

As superintendent, he said, he was ex-officio a coroner. We brought the body to the island and proceeded to embalm it.

There was certainly no blood on the face or any indication of foul play, just the usual post-mortem staining that is on the body of any person that is in the water of a small lake for 10 days in the heat of the summer.

No one else assisted us. The relatives of friends did not arrive on the next train, so Mr. Bartlett gave me a burial permit to inter the remains in the burial ground there. A tourist who was a minister conducted the service. The casket was not a cedar coffin but a good hardwood one.

I cannot believe Mark Robinson said, as reported by Mr. Little, that the body was never removed. He told me they removed the body some time later and that it was in a remarkable state of preservation and must have been well embalmed. If these people wanted to make sure of these "old wives tales" why didn't they get an exhumation order and examine the casket that was alleged to be empty instead of desecrating the cemetery at Canoe Lake? In British Columbia they put them in jail for that kind of thing.[3]

M.R. Dixon
Parry Sound

---

3   *Toronto Daily Star*, October 16, 1956, p. 6.

Already famous at his death in 1917, Thomson gained stature, and his legend and interest in his work grew immensely over the next century as investigative reports, books, stories, songs, novels, and even documentary films explored his life, his art, and his death.

Cultural Nationalism in the 1920s

Thomson's death sparked a flourishing of Canadian cultural nationalism, one also fuelled by the sacrifice of the war. The war had given many Canadians a new sense of identity and national consciousness. The impact of the war on Canadian cultural producers, especially artists and writers, was immense. The victories at Ypres and Vimy Ridge had shown Canadians that they could perform on the world stage, and perform exceedingly well. Now, in peace, they hoped to show that they also had what it took in the cultural realm.

The new nationalism of the 1920s probably found its most eloquent expression in art. Canadian artists, many of them inspired by the nationalism evoked by the war, set out to create a distinctive Canadian style that not only broke the shackles of Victorian taste, as poets and other artists wished to do, but also was uniquely Canadian. Most notable in their efforts during this period were, of course, the artists of the famous Group of Seven, who consciously set out to create an original Canadian artistic style. The group formed in Toronto just after the war and, originally, included J.E.H. MacDonald, Lawren Harris, A.Y. Jackson, Fred Varley, Frank Carmichael, Arthur Lismer, and Frank (or Franz) Johnston. (After Johnston's resignation from the group, A.J. Casson replaced him in 1926, and Edwin Holgate and Lemoine Fitzgerald joined in 1930 and 1932, respectively.) Four of the group (Lismer, Johnston, Varley, and Jackson) had served as war artists, which contributed to their sense of nationalism and their search for a distinctive Canadian style.

Group of Seven artists wanted to replace European paintings in Canadian salons, and they did so very successfully, through self-promotion and a blinding style mixed with a bit of myth making. Indeed, they were not the first to embrace a nationalistic Canadian style or the first to paint the North; nor were they as ill received by Canadian patrons as they claimed. Mostly painting Canadian landscapes in a new, modern style, they used many bold, bright colours and heavy brush strokes, and lots of paint, which, at the time, was not a radical departure from international trends. Lawren Harris, the group's leader, explained their motives in 1920:

A group of young Canadian painters came together drawn by an irresistible urge to replace this "foreign-begotten technique" by a way of painting dictated by Canada itself, to concentrate all their energies on making a Canadian statement in art in Canadian terms . . . it meant that these young painters would be obliged to free themselves from every influence which might come between them and Canada as a new world for creative adventure in art. This, broadly speaking, was the motive force behind the "Group of Seven."[4]

The group's success was in the promotional ability and flair of its members and in the subjects they chose to paint. They held their first exhibition in Toronto in 1920 and, thereafter, at the National Gallery in Ottawa, which actively promoted their work, and at a British Empire Exhibition in Wembley in 1924–25. All of these exhibitions helped to speed them to fame, and their favourable reviews played well in the nationalistic mood of the period.

What they chose to focus their painting upon was a uniquely Canadian theme: the North. The group's paintings stressed the nature, ruggedness, and vastness of Canada. Many Group of Seven artists took northern excursions and spent long periods in the bush. They wanted to emphasize the strength, space, and beauty of the Canadian North in an effort to foster a sense of pride in the land. Some would say that they were so successful in developing these images that they created a Canadian style and cultural presence that was rarely challenged in the period. Their successes still reverberate today, as many of the images that first come to mind when one mentions the words "Canadian art" have sprung from their brush strokes.

Yet the Group of Seven has not been without its critics, as well. In the 1920s, the group claimed a national status, though its artists really were based almost exclusively in Toronto. Much of their work was of landscapes of Ontario: the West and the Maritimes were subjects for the group, but not a focus. In this aspect, Thomson's art is similar; virtually all of his work was done in or inspired by Algonquin Park. Though Group of Seven artists claimed national status, their work was not really national at all but rather central Canadian.

At the same time, the group's emphasis on landscape painting left members open to the charge that they were much too narrow in their subject material.

---

4 As quoted in Harry Hunkin, *A Story of the Group of Seven* (Toronto: McGraw-Hill Ryerson, 1979), 36.

Their paintings exhibited little introspection related to the character of the culture of Canada beyond the natural world, and little of their work reflected upon the postwar economic and social malaise, the negative economic effects of the Great War, or the social problems affecting so many Canadians, who were being forced to work long hours for menial wages and live in urban slums. Though the Group of Seven and other Canadian artists of the period, such as Emily Carr, expressed a distinct image of Canada, they left little impression of the radical changes that had dramatically remade the face of the nation.

In fact, the Group of Seven became famous painting the wilderness at a time when Canada was becoming increasingly urbanized and industrialized. All of the members of the group were actually city-dwellers, though they did spend considerable time in the North painting. They were also very well funded, with Harris himself being an heir to the tractor-making Massey-Ferguson company. Critics have argued that the group's artists simply were very good salesmen and that, in fact, they were not really painting in a new style: they were just good at creating a myth around their work, a myth lying far more in the realm of fancy than reality. For instance, many have said that their work really was inspired by Scandinavian artists who were doing similar paintings in the same period.

Clearly, the postwar period marked a spectacular, colourful growth in the Canadian art scene, one undoubtedly spurred in part by postwar nationalism and by the new sense of maturity that Canadians felt in the period. All across the country, this newfound patriotism could be seen, not just in art but in the dizzying growth of cultural production. Writers such as Lucy Maud Montgomery, author of *Anne of Green Gables*, first became popular in the period, as did Morley Callaghan, whose 1928 novel *Strange Fugitive* gained a widespread following. Callaghan, a contemporary of F. Scott Fitzgerald and Ernest Hemingway (he and Hemingway worked together at the *Toronto Daily Star*), had a very long career after the 1920s. Of course, many Canadians said that Callaghan's was not a distinctive Canadian style and that his work did not really add to a particular understanding of Canada.

Canadian poets also were striving for a new style, one that broke from the traditions of English Victorian poetry, which still prevailed in the popular Canadian poetry of the period. This struggle toward modernism was more forceful among poets than among novelists. Poets at McGill University, referred to as the Montreal Group, led the charge. In a sense, by challenging Canadians' usual style of versification, poets such as F.R. Scott were embarking on a path that laid the seeds for an original poetic culture, which came of age in the poetic forms of Leonard Cohen and others after the Second World War.

The growth in national culture was also evident in the creation of new publishing ventures and academic organizations. For example, the *Canadian Forum*, a magazine promoting Canadian ideas, art, and literature appeared in 1920. *The Dalhousie Review* (1921–), *The Canadian Bookman* (1914–15, 1919–41), and

The Canadian Magazine (1893–1937) were journals committed to promoting Canadian topics, authors, and works. Many of the academics, authors, and journalists who worked on these publications were also actively involved in the Canadian booster clubs that proliferated after the war. Patriotic associations such as the Canadian Club reached 115 chapters by 1928.

Courses in Canadian history and, more generally, the study of Canada started to emerge; the Canadian Historical Association was founded in 1922. Historians such as Frank Underhill, A.R.M. Lower, and Harold Innis were veterans, so it was no surprise that, in the 1920s, they advocated a distinctly Canadian historical and political economic scholarship. The *Canadian Historical Review* began to publish in 1920, and its second issue hailed "The Growth of Canadian National Feeling."

Mass American Culture

But the 1920s were just as noteworthy for the growth in mass consumer culture. Much of this mass consumer culture was encouraged through new forms of American-dominated technology, and many Canadian nationalists in the period (especially those from the elite) thought the wave of American culture crashing in upon Canada was destructive for the nation. In their view, it was crass, of low quality, and epitomized American ideals, which they saw as rough, overly individualistic, loud, and sometimes crude. But most ordinary Canadians, nonetheless, embraced aspects of the great American cultural tidal wave that swept the country in the postwar period.

American mass consumer culture came to Canada in a number of forms. First, there were magazines. Technology such as printing presses, conveyor belts, and delivery trucks allowed the production and delivery of massive numbers of periodicals. By the 1920s, American magazines such as the *Ladies' Home Journal* or the *Saturday Evening Post* each had a weekly circulation of over 100,000 in Canada. The most popular Canadian magazine in the period, *Maclean's*, had a circulation of just over 82,000. In fact, the top five US magazines in Canada were more popular than the top five Canadian magazines, and historians have estimated that, in 1926, Canadians consumed over 50 million US magazines. Many of these magazines were part of the US "star system," which publicized and popularized US movies stars from Hollywood, not unlike today.

Motion pictures were a second type of hugely successful American mass cultural import. Watching silent films and then "talkies" became one of the most prominent leisure and entertainment activities of Canadians, and virtually all of these films were American. One reason for the Canadian "consumption" of American films was that Canadian movie house companies were dominated by US-owned firms. The giant Famous Players chain was part of the US studio system, which meant that whatever Canadian films were made were very rarely shown on Canadian screens.

The proximity of Hollywood also had an impact upon the development of a Canadian film industry. Many Canadians headed south to work in the well-paying Hollywood studios. Also, because of Hollywood's better climate, movies could be shot there year round. Famous Canadians in Hollywood included Jack Warner (Warner Brothers), Louis B. Mayer (MGM), Mack Sennett, (creator of the Keystone Kops and the director who recruited Charlie Chaplin), and actors Mary Pickford and Norma Shearer (both of whom won early Academy Awards). This is not to say that Canada was not on the screens. In the 1930s, Hollywood created an image of Canada that remains to this day: Mounties, mountains, and maple trees.

Another significant American cultural product, encouraged by technological change, affected Canadian culture in the period: radio. By the 1920s, radio had swept North America, as thousands of Canadians purchased receivers for the first time. Canadian airwaves were dominated by US programming for two reasons. First, with so much of the Canadian population close to the US border, Canadians listened in as US stations began broadcasting—before Canadian stations existed. Many Canadians soon became familiar with and appreciative of American programming. Comedy and sports programs, especially American baseball, became very popular in Canada. Second, much of the programming on Canadian radio in the 1920s was imported from the United States, as it was cheaper just to buy popular US productions rather than to pay for creating original Canadian programming (a dynamic that continues to this day).

Fourth and finally, mass spectator sports were another cultural import. Not a technological change, mass sports, nevertheless, were made possible by technological developments that enabled better information dispersal through the radio and newspapers. Although Canadians had developed their own unique and popular games, such as Canadian football and, most important, hockey, Canadian spectator sports remained dominated by the US market. For example, the National Hockey League (NHL), founded in 1917, soon came largely under the control of US interests, as Americans owned more than half the teams by 1926.

Even the Stanley Cup, meant to be the trophy recognizing excellence in Canadian hockey, became the permanent possession of the NHL in the mid-1920s and was regularly awarded to American professional teams. Hockey represented a particular mix of mass culture. Radio personalities such as Foster Hewitt became famous as the first hockey matches were broadcast across the country on the growing Canadian radio networks in the period.

Yet, for all the success of hockey, baseball, the quintessential American pastime, remained as popular in Canada as hockey, if not more so. Most Canadians followed American teams, and minor league teams established in cities such as Montreal and Toronto had huge followings. Canadian newspapers and radio reported the pennant races of the famous New York Yankees of the 1920s; Babe Ruth, the star of that team, was one of the most famous people in North America.

Ruth hit his first professional home run in Toronto, while playing against the Maple Leafs *baseball* team.

In response to the wave of American popular mass culture in the period, many Canadian nationalists sought protectionist measures to support Canadian cultural industries. For instance, in broadcasting, cultural nationalists complained that the domination of airwaves by US broadcasters and programming led to a debasement of Canadian culture. Many of these critics saw US culture as lowbrow and immoral and argued that Canadians should have their own cultural outlet. The best way to achieve this, they argued, was to get the state to take a role in broadcasting, to create a public broadcaster as had been done in the United Kingdom.

Graham Spry, one of the first defenders of Canadian public radio and the founder of the Canadian Radio League in 1930, argued that the issue was whether Canadian airwaves would be dominated by "the State" or "the United States." In response to these pressures, Prime Minister William Lyon Mackenzie King created a royal commission in 1928 to look into the issue of radio. The commission recommended that government take a more active role in radio, leading to the creation in 1932 of the Canadian Radio Broadcasting Commission, which eventually became the Canadian Broadcasting Corporation (CBC) in 1936.

As a result, Canada developed a "mixed market" in broadcasting. While private stations continued, government funded and supported a network of publicly owned stations, in French and English. These stations stretched across the country and provided Canadians (especially rural Canadians) with radio service that was Canadian, as opposed to the American stations and content they had been receiving.

In the magazine industry, Canadian cultural nationalism took the form of the protectionist National Policy. Magazine owners in Canada demanded and received tariffs upon US magazines, which made imports more costly and hurt their circulations. The tariff enacted by Conservative Prime Minister Richard Bedford Bennett, who came to power in 1930, resulted in a decline of US magazine sales of 62 per cent, while Canadian sales improved 64 per cent. In the 1930s, American magazines were still tremendously popular in Canada, but Canadian magazines had gained due to the protectionist measures imposed by the government.

Of course, some of these measures were designed to protect not only culture but the industries that produced this culture. For example, in the magazine industry, many of the advocates of tariffs on US magazines were simply trying to advance their business interests and were not necessarily concerned with the plight of Canadian culture. They viewed magazines and other cultural pursuits as products or services, like those provided by any other industry, and these required protection under the National Policy. After the Second World War, Canadian cultural nationalists continued to advocate for cultural protectionism and support. Although they would not always be successful, they did leave a legacy.

In the end, Thomson's mysterious death became an important signpost and symbol for Canadian cultural production in the twentieth century. The sad end of an emerging artist's life marked the flourishing beginning of an art movement, one that was challenged by the great cultural colossus from the south but that seemed to thrive, beyond all expectation.

Further Reading

Edwardson, Ryan. *Canadian Content: Culture and the Quest for Nationhood.* Toronto: University of Toronto Press, 2008.

Great Unsolved Mysteries in Canadian History Project. *Death on a Painted Lake: The Tom Thomson Tragedy.* 2008. http://www.canadianmysteries.ca/sites/thomson/home/indexen.html.

King, Ross. *Defiant Spirits: The Modernist Revolution of the Group of Seven.* Vancouver: Douglas & McIntyre, 2011.

McGregor, Roy. *Northern Light: The Enduring Mystery of Tom Thomson and the Woman Who Loved Him.* Toronto: Vintage Canada, 2011.

Vipond, Mary. "Canadian Nationalism and the Plight of Canadian Magazines in the 1920s." *Canadian Historical Review* 58, no. 1 (March 1977): 43–65. http://dx.doi.org/10.3138/CHR-058-01-04.

ACTIVE HISTORY: THE MYSTERY OF TOM THOMSON'S DEATH

- Explore the website *Death on a Painted Lake: The Tom Thomson Tragedy*, which is part of the Great Unsolved Mysteries in Canadian History project (http://www.canadianmysteries.ca/sites/thomson/home/indexen.html). Once you have done so, consider the evidence presented and develop your own interpretation of the mystery of Tom Thomson's death and its aftermath.

- What do you think happened in July of 1917? Which of the various theories that emerged in subsequent years about Thomson's death make sense to you? What evidence can you cite for your interpretation? How do the different sources and primary documents help or hinder your case? What is the most interesting thing about this mystery, in your view?

- Is Tom Thomson's work more famous because of his mysterious death?

MURDEROUS MOMENT
WILLIAM LYON MACKENZIE KING COMMITS REGICIDE BY (MOSTLY) KILLING THE BRITISH CONSTITUTIONAL CONNECTION TO CANADA, 1920S

Imperialism and Nationalism: From British Subjects to Canadian Citizens

Much has been written about Canada's longest-serving prime minister, William Lyon Mackenzie King. Books, biographies, collections, poems, and plays abound. And then, of course, there is King's own writing, the crowning achievement of which is his diary, an incredible 50-year, 50,000 page magnum opus that ranks among the most interesting works in the English language.

After considering all that writing, scholars have described King in many ways—shrewd, creepy, studious, tedious, dedicated, strange, traditional, a racist, a mamma's boy, and as both an Anglophile and an Anglophobe. On this last point, King would probably agree. Though he loved many aspects of the British and the royal family, he would probably consider as one of his greatest achievements his key role in the ongoing task of severing constitutional connections between Canada and the United Kingdom. When it came to Canada's external policies, killing this link consumed Mackenzie King in the 1920s.

Despite his weeble-wobble approach to so many questions of politics and policy (there is a famous cartoon in the 1920s depicting him as a roly-poly toy, the contemporary equivalent of a Weeble), King was, in many ways, a nationalist. This was particularly true when it came to foreign relations. King's (and the country's) experience during the First World War with conscription meant that his guiding principle was to stay out of Europe's affairs and chart Canada on a more independent course. This policy was, to a large degree, a continuation of what had already happened in Canada.

By the end of the war, Prime Minister Robert Borden had already made great strides in reshaping Canada's relations with the British Empire. Borden was keen to ensure that Canada was granted a new standing internationally because of the country's sacrifices during the war. At Borden's insistence, in 1917, the Imperial War Cabinet (composed of Britain and its dominions, such as Canada, Australia, New Zealand, and South Africa) passed Resolution IX; after the war, the dominions would be considered autonomous states, although still under the umbrella of the British Empire, and have a say in imperial foreign policy. Also at Borden's insistence, Canada signed the Treaty of Versailles and was included in the League of Nations, giving it a new status internationally.

King, prime minister after 1921, was keen to continue in this more independent manner. This strategy was tested at the Imperial Conference of 1923. When King met the British prime minister and the other prime ministers, he expanded upon Borden's previous independent policy. Keeping in mind the fact that his power was centred in Quebec, King made sure that Canada would not be subject to any imperial entanglements, such as had happened in the First World War. The conscription crisis had made King determined that such an occurrence would not happen again.

King's determination to stay out of foreign entanglements and chart an independent course had become apparent in 1922. The Chanak affair was an uprising against the British in a part of Turkey they controlled. The British expected the Canadians to send troops, just as they had done during the Boer War and the First World War. But this time, King flatly refused. Few in Canada really protested this move, as most had had enough of far-off British wars.

Another incident that shows King's willingness to create an independent foreign policy can be seen in the signing of the 1923 Halibut Treaty. For the first time in history, the Canadian government negotiated and signed a treaty with the United States on its own and without any countersignature of a British representative. The British were not too happy about this, but that did not stop King.

Canada also began to set up an independent foreign service that dealt directly with other countries. For the first time, Canada had its own representatives in places such as Washington and Paris. Canada's foreign service, led by Queen's University scholar O.D. Skelton, eventually included an incredibly competent group of men (and they were largely men) such as Lester B. Pearson who would shape Canadian foreign and domestic policy for years to come.

Then, of course, there was the King-Byng affair. Without getting into the complicated details, the issue hinged on whether or not King as prime minister, or the Governor General (at the time, British general Lord Byng of Vimy) had final say on certain aspects of parliamentary practice, which was a bit of a constitutional grey area. In contrast to the gentlemanly Byng, King did not distinguish himself in the episode, but he did succeed in making the incident an election issue; he subsequently won the election. After 1926,

British-appointed governors general shed their duties as imperial representatives, and, in due course, Canadians held the position.

Eventually, King's determination to distance Canada from Britain paid off. In 1926, the British issued the Balfour Declaration, stating that all former British Colonies were equal to each other and independent in their external affairs. Instead of an empire of subordinates, Britain now had a commonwealth of more or less equal nations. Finally, the 1931 Statute of Westminster made all dominion legislatures equal to the British Parliament and granted the right to all former colonies to patriate (bring home) and amend their constitutions as they saw fit. Up to that point, these colonial constitutions were kept in the United Kingdom, as acts of the British Parliament. Now they could be taken "home" and changed without any British input. The problem for Canada, however, was that, because of squabbling between the provinces and the federal government, Canadians could not decide how to amend their Constitution, so the 1867 British North America Act sat at Westminster until 1982(!), when Pierre Trudeau finally patriated it.

In 1947, just a year before he ended his almost 22 years as prime minister, King took part in Canada's first citizenship ceremony. Prior to this, Canadians had been British subjects living in Canada. As Canada's first official citizen, King no doubt took great pleasure in celebrating Canada's, and his own, independence from Great Britain.

CHAPTER NINE

FILUMENA LASSANDRO, EXECUTED, EDMONTON, 1923
WOMEN, THE ROARING TWENTIES, AND THE LAW

This is the story of Filumena Lassandro. A fascinating tale of interwar Canada, Lassandro's story personifies the Roaring Twenties—fast cars, crime, booze, and, of course, an execution. Filumena was only 22 when she was executed, and her controversial story ignited a national debate about women's place in modern society. Such was her fame, and tragedy, that, in 2003, 80 years after her death, an opera, *Filumena*, was created to tell her tale.

Young Canada

Filumena Lassandro was born in Italy in about 1900. She immigrated to Canada with her parents, sister, and brother in 1909. The family settled in Fernie, BC, in the Crowsnest Pass area, where her father was employed as a coalminer. Filumena's story was like that of so many new Canadians in this period: a story of immigration, of hard work, and of coming to Canada to start a new life. In 1909, when Filumena's family came to Canada, she was joined by about 175,000 other migrants from around the world, and Canada was in the midst of the largest immigration boom in its history. There were Italians, like Filumena, but also tens of thousands of Germans, Austrians, Hungarians, Greeks, Russians, Chinese, Romanians, and people from a host of other countries. In 1901, while most new Canadians were still from the British Isles, Canada was very much a magnet for young people and young families from all around the world looking to make better lives for themselves.

In 1915, at the age of 14, Filumena married 23-year-old Carlo Sanfidele. As was then common, her father arranged the marriage. The young couple settled in Blairmore, Alberta. By 1916, Filumena's husband, was employed as a chauffeur to local businessman Emilio Picariello, whose interests included the local hotel. Emilio was known as a showman and a real entrepreneur. Emilio's nickname in Blairmore was "Emperor Pic."

It was a good time to be in Blairmore. The "Laurier Boom," as the prosperity of that period is known, was particularly good in the West, and the region was thriving. After fits and starts in the 1880s and 1890s, the wheat economy had finally started to function as Macdonald had envisioned in his national policy, and times were good. In the little frontier town of Blairmore, coalmining, lumber, and the railway meant prosperity, while, across the rest of the province (Alberta was created, along with Saskatchewan, out of the North-West Territories in 1905), farming, ranching, and mining were all doing well.

After 1916, another business was booming, as well. When Alberta decided to go "dry," to prohibit the sale of alcohol, Emperor Pic saw an opening: bootlegging (the illegal making, transporting, or selling of alcohol). Little did he know it, but Emperor Pic's quickly growing illegal empire would have catastrophic consequences for both himself and for young Filumena.

Booze and Fast Cars

Though the 1920s are often remembered as the decade of prohibition, Alberta's decision to prohibit the sale of booze had actually been a long time coming. In the half-century before the First World War, one of the longest and most important political campaigns fought by upper- and middle-class women and their allies was the battle against alcohol. Organizations such as the Women's Christian Temperance Union (WCTU), founded in 1874, were committed to the essentially conservative ideology of maternal feminism. Their view was that the superior qualities of womanhood rendered women, as the mothers of the world, more fit than men to direct society. In the case of the WCTU, advancing the aims of maternal feminism was to be done primarily through the prohibition of the sale of alcohol, which they saw as causing addiction, sickness, moral decay, poverty, prostitution, and abuse. And it was undoubtedly true that (largely male) alcohol consumption had led to a myriad of problems in Canadian society. As one WCTU song went,

We women pray for better times,
And work right hard to make 'em;

You men vote liquor with its crimes,
And we just have to take 'em.[1]

Notwithstanding that pessimistic song, by the 1910s most provinces in Canada had voted to "go dry," including Alberta. With prohibition in place, people looking for a drink found ways to get around the rules. Alcohol was imported from British Columbia (until its prohibition in 1918), from Quebec (where only hard liquor was prohibited), or from other "wet" provinces or states, and there was always the possibility of getting a prescription from your doctor or your druggist. In 1924, Ontario's doctors issued more than 800,000 prescriptions for alcohol, undoubtedly for medical use.

Then, of course, there was always moonshining (or the production of illegal alcohol), which became a huge business in Canada. In fact, because some Canadian provinces had not prohibited the production of alcohol, illegal Canadian exports to the United States (where prohibition was also in force), boomed. Rum-running became the stuff of Hollywood legends and family fortunes. As gangsters such as Al Capone smuggled Canadian alcohol south to quench thirsty Americans, Canadians such as Samuel Bronfman of Montreal got rich in the process. There were hundreds of tales in the news of rum-runners trying to make it across the Detroit River, and almost constant announcements of the raids on speakeasies on both sides of the border.

Emperor Pic was one of these bootleggers. In 1916, soon after prohibition came into force in Alberta, Emilio's chauffeur Carlo Sanfidele was taking Emperor Pic's speedy McLaughlin Six motor car on bootlegging runs. Emilio's operation was extensive, stretching from British Columbia to Saskatchewan, and sometimes even into the United States. His son Stefano (Steve) was also a driver. Emilio soon realized that, because Filumena and his son were close in age, he could get them to pretend to be a young couple seemingly out for an afternoon picnic, the perfect cover for bootlegging runs. As a result, the two rode together on numerous runs; but sometimes Filumena went alone on bootlegging runs in the powerful car.

In the prohibition era, booze and fast cars went hand in hand, and the McLaughlin car personified the Roaring Twenties in Canada and North America. The McLaughlin, made in Oshawa, Ontario, was one of hundreds of thousands of cars built in Canada in the 1910s and 1920s as the automobile completely remade the Canadian landscape and reordered Canadian society. Led by Henry Ford's ubiquitous Model-T (nicknamed the Tin Lizzie), cars transformed Canadians' way of life. Farmers loved the car for its sturdiness and its ability to take them to market and to town; doctors used cars to make house calls. The car completely changed policing; cities and towns had to rebuild themselves to accommodate the mass influx of vehicles. Time and distance became quickly

---

1   As quoted in Craig Heron, *Booze: A Distilled History* (Toronto: Between the Lines, 2003), 154.

surmounted, as millions of North Americans took up driving. Owing to Canada's proximity to the United States (and the willingness of American car manufacturers to set up branch plants in Canada to avoid the costs of the National Policy tariff), by the end of the decade, Canada soon had a booming car industry and Canadians were the second greatest users of cars on the planet, after Americans. The car's arrival meant a newfound modernity in so many ways.

In a place like Blairmore, the car meant freedom. For a young woman like Filumena, and for so many women of her generation, driving the powerful McLaughlin Six meant nothing less than a form of liberation, if not equality.

Equality?

Indeed, that Filumena would drive often by herself on these bootlegging runs was a reflection of the profound changes for women in Canada in this period. In the 1920s, driving a car was just one of the myriad ways that women were breaking down political, social, and economic barriers; Filumena's willingness to do so would have been no surprise to many people at this time.

But it had not always been this way. Prior to the First World War, women had the status of second-class citizens. In fact, until the mid-nineteenth century, women were essentially non-existent under the law when it came to property and rights. Culturally and economically, women were essentially restricted to the "private sphere"; much of their political and social roles were as mothers and wives, and little else. But things began to change in the late nineteenth and early twentieth centuries.

This transformation is most apparent when one considers the issue of women's right to vote, also known as suffrage. Canadian women had been fighting for the right to vote for decades. Indeed, Canadian women's fight for suffrage was just one such struggle taking place around the world in that period. In the United States, the United Kingdom, Australia, New Zealand, and many other countries, a network of largely upper- and middle-class women had been arguing for the vote. This movement, along with women's efforts to implement prohibition and to gain access for women into jobs and professions, was part of a broader effort often referred to as "first-wave feminism."

In Canada, the leaders of this movement included people such as Nellie McClung. McClung was the Prairie suffrage movement's dominant figure. She forced male politicians to listen to women, led protests, and demanded action. Eventually, in 1916 Manitoba women became the first in Canada to win the right to vote and to hold provincial office, followed that year by Saskatchewan and Alberta. In 1917, just around the time that Filumena first started driving and getting involved in bootlegging, British Columbia approved women's suffrage, as did Ontario.

It was also around the time that women were first gaining the right to vote federally, too. This fight had been going on for some time. National efforts for the vote included the Dominion Women's Enfranchisement Association, one of many organizations promoting women's right to vote. Initiated in 1894, this tiny group of 18 prominent suffragists faced indifference and hostility in its drive for women's suffrage, as did much of the movement.

But then the war came, and it changed the dynamic of the fight for female suffrage. During the war, the Unionist government of Robert Borden had granted some women the right to vote in an effort to ensure that the 1917 election outcome was in favour of conscription. This move had opened the floodgates, and many suffrage leaders demanded that all women be granted the franchise. It simply did not make sense to extend the franchise to some women and not others. So, after years of political pressure, their efforts finally paid off.

In 1918, the Women's Franchise Act gave all women who were British subjects age 21 or over the right to vote in federal elections (aboriginal women were still denied the federal franchise). In 1919, women became eligible to stand for the House of Commons. By 1922, all the provinces had also given women the right to vote, save for Quebec, which held out until 1940. This delay was a reflection of the much more conservative and Catholic attitude of the province. At the same time, not all men were convinced that women getting the vote was a good thing. As one male political observer stated in 1921,

> Few mature women really desired the franchise. What good, then, has been done by this fine and radical extension of the franchise? It has simply doubled the electorate, without making it wiser or better or more discriminating. It has greatly complicated the election preparations. It has opened the door to far wider and more demoralizing corruption. . . . It has wrought prospective evil in this; while many of the better class of women will not vote, no such abstention is to be expected from a less desirable class. . . . The thing does not look pleasant or commendable just now, but it may improve on acquaintance. Let us hope so. Everyone, however, may as well awake from the dream that women are going to "elevate politics" by their votes or otherwise.[2]

In any event, Filumena probably did not vote in the federal election of 1921, as the women's rights issue was still largely a concern for middle- and upper-class women. But the 1921 election did see the very first woman, Agnes Macphail, elected to Parliament.

---

2   As quoted in Catherine Cleverdon, *The Woman Suffrage Movement in Canada* (Toronto: University of Toronto Press, 1974), 139.

Of course, political liberation also meant greater social liberation. As Filumena's case shows, women took on new roles in society. By the 1920s, women had dramatically broken with the notion that they should be confined to a "private sphere," that they were only supposed to be mothers or wives. How do we know?

First, women were increasingly seen in the "public sphere" in this period. Not only were they voting, but they were going to university in greater numbers. Women had been fighting for the right to go to university since the middle of the nineteenth century, with some success. Although not all universities (or all university programs) allowed women, by the 1920s, most did. Again, this achievement was significant, although it was largely an upper-class success.

Second, women were taking a growing role in the workforce. As industrialization spread in the nineteenth century, women had taken on all kinds of paid work such as boarding, sewing, and cleaning. But, by the 1920s, women had also become very prominent in domestic service, clerical, and professional jobs, as office staff, secretaries, nurses, and teachers. A third of all office employees in Canada were women. There was a "feminization" of the clerical field, which provided an opportunity for many women, especially middle-class women, to be in the workforce. Of course, women were paid far less than men, and, although they did have more opportunities than previously, they were still greatly constricted in their employment choices.

Third, as part of their liberation, women were also taking part in the newfound emphasis on leisure and entertainment in the period. During the Roaring Twenties, the "flapper" became a common sight for Canadians. These were liberated women who were partaking in the new social ethos of the decade by dressing and acting in a way that represented the "new" liberated single woman. They were going to clubs and dances; they were single women, without chaperones, meeting men; they were doing the Charleston, a gender-neutral dance done with equal enthusiasm by both sexes, one of the great fads of the decade, and a symbol of the happy-go-lucky nature of the time.

Fourth, women also became consumers in a new way in this postwar period. The proliferation of mass consumer products meant that women took on an increasingly important role in the determination of household purchases: the creation of household products such as kitchenware, or personal products such as deodorant or various cosmetics, meant that women took on a particular role in the mass consumer culture and society, one still evident today. For instance, much advertising for household consumer goods was pitched at women, which is why daytime radio (and later television) dramas came to be called "soap operas." But car ads were directed at women too, cars being a prominent aspect of women's consumption.

Finally, along with all of these new roles, women were taking part in activities considered to be the domain of men: organized sports. For instance, women athletics became very popular in the 1920s. One of Canada's most famous teams was the Edmonton Grads women's basketball team, which had a stunning record of success against virtually all other women's teams in North America, and not a few men's teams. Women were playing in all kinds of different sports in an organized way, and they participated in increasing numbers at the Olympics in the 1920s and 1930s.

Of course, this is just a small sampling of the many different ways that women entered the public sphere in the 1920s. Women became more prominent than ever before in the life of the country. There were artists such as Emily Carr, journalists such as Emily Murphy, politicians such as Louise McKinney, and lawyers, poets, writers, and a host of other well-known women. Clearly, the point is that women had made many advances, though they still faced challenges, too.

Women and the Law

By the early 1920s, Emperor Pic's rum-running crew of Filumena, Carlo, and Stefano had become fairly successful. But the cops were catching on. In the fall of 1922, police noticed a pattern wherein one particular vehicle, a speedy McLaughlin Six, was often travelling along certain roads at certain times. In September of that year, suspecting foul play, police constable Stephen Lawson attempted to pull over the car, then being driven by Stefano. When Stefano refused to comply and made a run for it, Lawson fired at the car, hitting Stefano in the hand. Despite this, Stefano refused to surrender and drove off, easily outdistancing the slower police vehicles.

When news of the shooting and car chase reached Emilio, he became convinced that Stefano was either injured or killed. Arming himself, Emilio, with Filumena, drove to the police barracks to confront Constable Lawson. The two men exchanged heated words as Lawson stood in the doorway of the barracks; his wife and daughter witnessed the confrontation. During the altercation, shots were fired, apparently from Emilio's car where he and Filumena were seated. One bullet fatally struck Lawson in the back as he turned away to retrieve his own firearm. Emilo and Filumena fled the scene and sparked a massive police manhunt across Alberta that lasted two days and generated national attention. Eventually, the pair were captured and charged with the murder of a police officer, a crime that brought the death penalty.

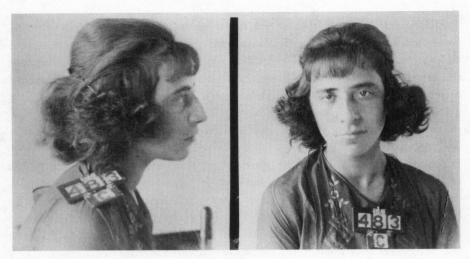

Figure 9.1 *Filumena Lassandro's Mug Shot, 1922*

Courtesy of the Glenbow Museum, NA-3282–2

At trial, Filumena's lawyer argued that any evidence linking her directly to the fatal shot that killed Constable Lawson was purely circumstantial. In the defence's view, Lassandro was only in the wrong place at the wrong time and was in the car only because Picariello had forced her into the vehicle. Indeed, Lassandro may have been involved in rum-running (so many Canadians were during the Roaring Twenties), but she was no cold-blooded killer. Moreover, because she was a woman, her lawyer argued, Lassandro did not deserve the same punishment as a man. After all, in the 1920s, women were not equal to men under the law, which treated the two genders very differently.

The arguments Lassandro's lawyer used showed that, although women had achieved the vote in Canada, had experienced much social liberation, and had such tremendous influence in pushing the prohibition movement to success, they were still unequal under the law. Even though women had been granted the right to vote, they still lacked many rights granted to men, and were in many ways still subservient.

Indeed, Canadian law stated that women were not "persons" under the law: they may have been "persons in matters of pain and penalties but not persons in the matter of rights and privileges."[3] One of the ways women were not considered "persons" was that they didn't have the right to be appointed to the Senate. In the 1920s, a group of women led by Nellie McClung challenged this idea. McClung and her group, called the "Famous Five," fought the "Persons" case, as it became known, all the way to the Supreme Court in Ottawa. Along

---

3   Audrey D. Doerr, and Micheline Carrier, *Women and the Constitution in Canada* (Ottawa: Canadian Advisory Council of the Status of Women, 1981), 8.

with McClung, the women involved included Emily Murphy, Louise McKinney, Henrietta Muir Edwards, and Irene Parlby.

In 1928, the Supreme Court decided that women were not, in fact, persons under the law. McClung and her group, however, were not to be denied. They took the case to the JCPC in Britain, which was, at the time, still Canada's final court of appeal. In 1929, the committee decided that women were indeed persons under the law. In a victory for women's rights in this country, the first woman Senator, Cairine Wilson, was appointed in 1930.

Filumena Lassandro did not live to see these changes. Despite her protestations of innocence and her lawyer's argument that she be treated differently because of her sex, the jury was not convinced, and the trial resulted in convictions for both the accused. In passing the obligatory sentence of death, the judge did acknowledge that some leniency might be extended to Lassandro because she was a woman—but that she should nevertheless prepare to meet her end.

Imprisoned in Fort Saskatchewan, Filumena maintained her innocence as her lawyer made attempts to have her sentence reduced or commuted. Despite her pleas and her lawyer's efforts, no reprieve was granted and Lassandro was resigned to her fate. On May 2, 1923, Emilio Picariello and Filumena Lassandro were both led to the scaffolding. Emperor Pic was hung first, and, a few minutes later, Lassandro herself climbed the steps to face execution. Before the noose was wrapped around her neck, she declared that she forgave "everyone." After the hangings, both Lassandro and Picariello were laid to rest in an unmarked grave in a cemetery in Edmonton.

It was a tragic end to a young life. Filumena Lassandro's execution in 1923 set off a firestorm of interest and debate over a number of issues in the period: the role of women, prohibition, fast cars, and, of course, capital punishment. The case became famous across the country, as many Italian Canadians were outraged at her execution; others thought she deserved what she got. Filumena goes down in history as the only woman ever executed in Alberta. Did she deserve to be executed?

The story of Filumena Lassandro helps us to understand the changing role of women in the 1920s. Lassandro's execution shows us that the legal status of women was still ambiguous in the period, notwithstanding the many advances toward "personhood" that did occur. Second, it also shows us that, far from being relegated to the private sphere, women could and did partake in very public, and even criminal activities, just like everyone else. Finally, it gives us an insight into the many diverse political and social activities that women tackled in the period.

Further Reading

Pedersen, Diana. "The Photographic Record of the Canadian YWCA, 1890–1930: A Visual Source for Women's History." *Archivaria* 24 (Summer 1987): 10–35.

Sangster, Joan. "'Pardon Tales' from Magistrate's Court: Women in Peterborough, 1920–1950." *Canadian Historical Review* 74, no. 2 (June 1993): 161–97.

Sharpe, Robert J., and Patricia I. McMahon. *The Persons Case: The Origins and Legacy of the Fight for Legal Personhood*. Toronto: University of Toronto Press, 2007.

Strong-Boag, Veronica. "The Girl of the New Day: Canadian Women Working in the 1920s." *Labour / Le Travail* 4 (1979): 131–64.

Warner, Anne. "'The Coming of the Skirts': Women's Intercollegiate Basketball at Queen's University in the 1920s." *Sport History Review* 41, no. 1 (May 2010): 33–49.

ACTIVE HISTORY: THE MACKENZIE KING DIARY

- Examine the diaries of William Lyon Mackenzie King, Canada's longest-serving prime minister (1921–25, 1926–30, 1935–48). These diaries are available online at Library and Archives Canada's website, as a searchable database (http://www.bac-lac.gc.ca/eng/discover/politics-government/prime-ministers/william-lyon-mackenzie-king/Pages/diaries-william-lyon-mackenzie-king.aspx). Also available from this site is a virtual exhibition entitled *A Real Companion and Friend: The Diary of William Lyon Mackenzie King, 1893–1950*.

- Approximately 50,000 pages of King's diaries can be viewed and searched, and these cover virtually every event in the first half of the twentieth century in Canada, including the 1920s, when King was prime minister. Taken together, the diaries form an amazing document.

- Using keyword and date searches, examine various days that King addresses the question of women's role in society, the Roaring Twenties, and the "Persons" case, including King's appointment of the first female Senator. What can the diary tell us about Mackenzie King? What can it tell us about the context of the period he is writing about? What are the challenges posed by such a first-hand document? What are the benefits of being able to examine this type of resource?

☜ MURDEROUS MOMENT ☞
QALLANAAQ (WHITE MAN)
RICHARD JANES, KILLED BY INUIT
HUNTERS, BAFFIN ISLAND, 1920

Race, Culture, Death, and Sadness in Canada's High North

Richard Janes was a fur trader from Newfoundland who had been operating in the North for at least four years by 1920, trading with the Inuk of Baffin Island. In March of 1920, during one of his routine dealings with the Inuit of Admiralty Inlet, he claimed that a number of fox pelts were owed to him by Inuit hunters and that, if he did not receive them, he would kill the hunter's dogs and perhaps one of the Inuit hunters themselves. The Inuit took these threats seriously, so, after consulting an elder, they decided that Janes should be killed before he killed any dogs, which would threaten the very existence of the group. Three Inuit hunters discussed the plan, and one, a man in his forties named Nuqallaq, who had already been threatened by this *qallanaaq* ("white man" in Inuktitut), was chosen to commit the deed of killing Janes.

On the night of March 15, 1920, Nuqallaq and the two other Inuit hunters stalked Janes through the snow and eventually shot him twice. Yet this was not a cold-blooded murder or a crime of passion: it was a response to a legitimate threat to the community's survival. As was the custom of the Inuit, Janes's body was wrapped in caribou skins, and mitts were put on the dead man's feet and hands; the Inuit stayed in camp for three days as a gesture of respect for the spirit of the dead trader; and a few Inuit hunters presented furs to Nuqallaq as a gift for ending this danger to their community.

Initially, the incident garnered little attention. After all, the Inuit were acting in accordance with their centuries-old customs. The trader at Igarjuaq, for example, to whom those responsible for the shooting entrusted Janes's furs and other possessions, did not raise an issue.

Yet 18 months later, a police officer arrived to conduct an investigation into the death. The police determined that the act had been premeditated murder, charged the three men, and put them under house arrest in Pond Inlet for the next year, until a court could be convened in the Far North.

The trial took place in 1923 in Pond Inlet; the three men did not face a jury of their peers but of white men versed not in the customs of the North but in Canadian and British legal traditions. Eventually, Nuqallaq's charge was reduced to manslaughter; he was convicted and sentenced to 10 years hard labour at the Stony Mountain Penitentiary in Manitoba, the same institution where Chief Poundmaker and other aboriginal and Métis had been incarcerated following the 1885 North-West Rebellion. Of the two other Inuit initially charged in the killing, one was sentenced to two years of hard labour at Pond Inlet, and the other was acquitted for lack of evidence.

Nuqallaq had served less than one and a half years of his sentence in Manitoba before he contracted tuberculosis, an often-fatal bacterial infection that attacks the lungs. At the request of senior prison officials and with the agreement of the RCMP commissioner, Nuqallaq was released and returned to Pond Inlet to spend time with his wife, in the hopes that the North's cold air would stem the disease's spread. Sadly, within a few months, Nuqallaq was dead. Even more tragically, his return caused a tuberculosis outbreak among the Inuit communities of Baffin Island, bringing more death and sorrow to the people.

Nuqallaq's tale reflects the clash between the customs of the North and white man's law; ultimately, whites were asserting Canadian legal and governmental authority over the Inuit of the North, in an attempt both to exert their rule over aboriginal peoples (as had been done in southern Canada) and to assert Canadian sovereignty over these sparsely populated northern regions that Canada had claimed. This clash between two very different cultures and worldviews played out throughout the twentieth century, often with horrible results for the Inuit of the North.

This was especially true after 1945, during the Cold War, when the North became strategically important. As the Soviet Union and the United States squared off in global-nuclear brinkmanship, the North, over which the two countries' bombers and ballistic missiles would fly in the event of a full-scale nuclear war, soon became a site of contention and militarization. As America's ally, Canada helped the United States build a string of radar stations in the 1950s, designed to warn of any impending Soviet bomber or missile attack across the Arctic. These included the DEW (Distant Early Warning) line and the Mid-Canada and Pinetree lines. These installations not only established Canadian claims to the North but profoundly reshaped the region.

Just as damaging was the Canadian government's willingness to move Inuit families as part of a Cold War tactic to assert Canadian sovereignty over the region. In 1953, a number of families from northern Quebec and from Pond Inlet, where Nuqallaq's trial had been held, were relocated to Resolute Bay and Grise Fiord in the High Arctic. This relocation had a devastating impact upon these communities, which were forced to move nearly 2,000 miles from their age-old communities to completely different geographic and environmental locales. In 2010, after decades of refusing to acknowledge the impact of the relocation, the Canadian government apologized for the policy.

More recently, there has been a move toward greater accommodation of Inuit society in the North, most obviously with the creation of Nunavut on April 1, 1999, out of the Northwest Territories. This aboriginally governed territory, with a capital at Iqaluit (formerly called Frobisher Bay) on Baffin Island, marks an important step forward on the path toward self-government for Inuit of the North, and for aboriginal communities in Canada.

Despite these changes, the challenge that Inuit communities faced in Nuqallaq's time—the clash between Inuit and white culture and society, and the struggle for the decolonization of aboriginal peoples in Canada—continues.

🔫 MURDEROUS MOMENT 🔫
COALMINER WILLIAM DAVIS, KILLED BY COMPANY POLICE, CAPE BRETON, NOVA SCOTIA, 1925

Miners, Murder, and Maritime Rights in the Tumultuous 1920s

In the late nineteenth and early twentieth centuries, Cape Breton's coalmining industry, largely controlled by a few foreign companies, boomed as coal became the main fuel of the North American industrial revolution. A region that had prospered during the age of "wood, wind, and water" found new fortune in an era of "coal, steam, and iron." Towns such as Sydney, Glace Bay, and New Waterford grew tremendously as mining interests sought to exploit the estimated one billion tons of reserves in the island's mines, and to exploit the workers who toiled in these mines. Ample coal soon begat steel factories, and, by the 1910s, Nova Scotia, and Cape Breton in particular, was dotted with company towns where firms such as the Dominion Coal Company Limited or the British Empire Steel Company (BESCO) controlled virtually every aspect of workers' lives.

William Davis was born into this life in 1887. His father had been a coalminer, as had an older brother who had died in the horrible 1891 explosion and fire in the coalmines of Springhill, Nova Scotia, when over 100 workers, some as young as 13 years old, had been killed. Starting in 1905, Davis worked at Nos. 1, 6, 12, and 16 collieries of the Dominion Coal Company Limited. During this period, the industry was wracked by labour conflict, as the companies pushed their workers to the limits of endurance. As the cost of living increased and wages failed to keep up, nearly 60 brutal strikes occurred between 1920 and 1925.

By the spring of 1925, Davis was a road maker for Dominion when a titanic struggle between the United Mine Workers of America and BESCO over wages and working conditions led to approximately 12,000 workers in Cape Breton going on strike. The company was determined to break the union and cruelly cut off credit at the company-owned stores, often the only place where miners and their families could buy food. Four days later, on March 6, the miners went on strike. Davis, who had nine children to feed when the strike broke out, joined thousands of workers who marched on June 11 to New Waterford to try to convince the replacement workers to quit. Whole towns across Cape Breton faced destitution and starvation if they did not.

The marchers were met with violence. BESCO sent company policemen into the peaceful demonstration. Before the workers could make their request to the strikebreakers, the armed and mounted company men charged. During the melee that ensued, over 300 shots were fired at the strikers, and Davis, a slight man of 5 feet 3 inches and only 150 pounds, was shot through the heart by one of BESCO's hired security men.

Davis quickly became a symbol of the striker's fight for fair wages and treatment. His funeral, three days after the shooting, attracted nearly 5,000 people and steeled the workers' resolve; they launched raids on company stores and property in response. By the end of the strike, the government had called in the provincial police and nearly 2,000 Canadian troops. Eventually, the strike was settled, but June 11 became William Davis Day in Nova Scotia and it is still a provincial day of remembrance that recognizes the importance of Nova Scotia's industrial past and the sacrifices of its working people.

Davis's death was also a symbol of the challenges and changes the region faced in this period. Despite the boom in the Cape Breton coal industry, much of the Maritimes was falling on hard times. When the Maritime provinces joined Confederation, the region was very successful economically and politically. By the 1920s, the great economic and population boom that had transformed Canada had largely left the Maritime provinces behind, and they had lost economic and political power, especially as the National Policy seemed to benefit industrialists in central Canada or favour Western farmers. Many in the Atlantic region felt that they were simply not keeping up with the rest of the country, or being treated fairly by Ottawa.

Maritimers also had specific grievances during this period. One of these grievances was the setting of railway rates. By the 1920s, virtually all of Canada's railways were dominated by railway companies based in central Canada. These companies set the rates for freight for all the regions, including the Maritimes. Many Maritimers felt that these rates were far too expensive for them, and unfair, because rates reflected the needs of the "wheat economy" rather than those of Atlantic Canada. Another grievance stemmed from the fact that, by the 1920s, the products of the industries in the Maritimes, such as the lumber industry and the fisheries, were no longer in demand, causing great economic hardship and unemployment for many Maritime families. Further, as population shifted westward, Maritime representation in the House of Commons, and within the Canadian political system in general, became less and less influential. Nova Scotian Robert Borden, who stepped down in 1920, was the last prime minister from Atlantic Canada.

As a result, in the early 1920s, a "Maritime Rights" movement developed that reflected this unhappiness with the state of the country. Maritimers demanded that Ottawa listen to their problems and address their economic and political demands. But, instead of starting a new party, as the Progressives in Ontario and the West had done, Maritimers threatened to switch their votes from the Liberals to the Tories as a way of forcing then Prime Minister Mackenzie King to listen to them.

King, who was more concerned with the emerging Progressive Party in the West, did not pay too much attention to the Maritimes. Typically, in 1926, he did order a royal commission to look into the freight rates: the Duncan Commission, as it was called. But this move was unsatisfactory to those agitating for Maritime rights, and many Maritime votes switched to the Conservatives to punish King. Despite helping to cause King's downfall in the 1925 election, the Maritime Rights movement had largely petered out by the end of the decade.

As, eventually, did the coalmines. By the 1930s, the Great Depression hit Cape Breton's and Nova Scotia's coalmines hard, and there was widespread unemployment in the region, as in the rest of the country. In the postwar period, coalmining continued, but, by the 1980s, Cape Breton's mines slowly started closing, the victims of cheaper sources of other fuels and of the more general move away from coal. The last coalmine in Cape Breton closed in 2001, but William Davis Day is still commemorated, decades after his tragic death.

CHAPTER TEN

PETER MARKUNAS, NICK NARGAN, AND JULIAN GRYSHKO, MURDERED, SASKATCHEWAN, 1931

LABOUR, THE GREAT DEPRESSION, REGIONAL ALIENATION, AND STATE RESPONSE

The Estevan "Riots" 1931

Twelve years later, it was much like 1919 in Winnipeg, all over again—a battle between labour and capital, between striking workers and bosses. And, of course, the RCMP made an appearance. Here was the situation: in the summer of 1931, coalminers in southern Saskatchewan faced wage cuts, unsafe working conditions, and squalid company housing.

The men who worked the coalmines near Estevan approached the Workers' Unity League and its affiliate, the Mine Workers' Union of Canada (MWUC), to help them organize. The MWUC organized the miners and tried to bargain with the South Saskatchewan Coal Operators Association, which refused to negotiate or recognize the union, forcing a strike in the first week of September. The strike gained publicity and had sympathy from the towns around the coalmines. Three weeks into the strike, the miners decided to head from Bienfait to one of the bigger towns, Estevan, to try to gain support for the strike.

During their peaceful procession through Estevan, the miners came upon an RCMP cordon across the street; the police were determined to stop the protest and provoked a confrontation with the strikers. A long-running battle between the police and the miners ensued, and, during the battle, the RCMP shot three of the picketing miners dead. Their names were Peter Markunas, Nick Nargan, and Julian Gryshko. They were ordinary men, ordinary workers, just looking to improve their lives in the face of some pretty harsh conditions.

Just as in Winnipeg, the mayor had banned public demonstrations; just as in Winnipeg, the RCMP had been called in; just as in Winnipeg, the strike was essentially broken. But there were some very important differences, too, between Estevan and Winnipeg.

First, unlike in the Winnipeg General Strike of 1919, women played a significant role, as they had since the 1920s in the political and social affairs of the country. That women were in the public eye was true in Estevan as well, where one person is particularly noteworthy: Annie Buller. Buller, a founding member of the Canadian Communist Party, had been involved in labour fights since 1919.

The union asked Winnipegger Buller to go to Saskatchewan and offer support and encouragement to the miners' wives and families. She ended up becoming one of the leaders of the strike. During the Estevan strike, Buller was arrested for inciting a riot, unlawful assembly, and rioting. She was tried in 1932 in the Estevan courthouse, convicted, and sentenced to one year of hard labour in jail and a $500 fine. Shockingly, she served the sentence in solitary confinement.

Here is the police report on Annie Buller following her 1931 arrest:

Age: 36;
Height: 5'10";
Weight: 140 lbs;
Build: medium;
Hair: dark brown;
Eyes: brown; wears heavy dark-rimmed spectacles;
Religion: loyalty to the working class. Is a very powerful speaker; very well liked. Dangerous agitator.[1]

Clearly, women like Annie Buller took a leading role in this incident.

Second, the RCMP's actions provoked serious criticism. Few challenged the RCMP or its tactics after the Winnipeg uprising, especially given the Red Scare at the time. But, after Estevan, the RCMP came under severe scrutiny. People asked if this was the right thing to do. In fact, to this day, the RCMP's role is still argued over in a very public way. The argument takes place on the very gravestones of the three men killed, whose combined tombstone states that they were "MURDERED IN ESTEVAN SEP. 29 1931 BY RCMP." Every so often, unknown parties paint over this inscription, hiding the condemning words, especially the "RCMP." Every so often, unknown parties restore it, so the incriminating statement can be read clearly by anyone visiting the cemetery.

---

1   As quoted in Stephen Lyon Endicot, *Bienfait: The Saskatchewan Miners' Struggle of '31* (Toronto: University of Toronto Press, 2002), 119.

Figure 10.1 *Estevan Gravesite, Saskatchewan*

Courtesy of the Glenbow Museum, NA-5211–17

Another difference between the strikes of 1919 and 1931 was that there was much more sympathy and understanding toward the strikers during the latter strike because most Canadians understood what they were going through. Estevan happened at one of the low points of the Great Depression. Though the Estevan strike might have ended in defeat, it shows that Canadians were reacting to the economic problems of the period very differently than they had after the Winnipeg General Strike.

To really understand Estevan and the reaction to it, one needs to understand the period between 1929 and 1939, the "Dirty Thirties." It was a low-down decade when people, such as those miners in Estevan and their families, suffered incredibly difficult times. The harshness of the Great Depression and the Dirty Thirties contrasted sharply with the happy-go-lucky Roaring Twenties.

Because of the Great Depression, Canadians suffered widespread unemployment and poverty, and hunger was a problem for many. Just as devastating was the feeling of hopelessness that permeated the land; Canadians despaired that nothing could be done to alleviate their problems. As the economic system broke down and the old ways of survival were no longer helpful, people looked to government to help them out. But they found little support in Ottawa, and the provinces were fiscally and constitutionally incapable of doing anything much to counter the devastating effects of this economic downturn.

Eventually, however, the crisis in capitalism that the Great Depression created provoked new ways of thinking about the state and its relationship to the citizens of Canada. This reconsideration eventually led to the development of the welfare state; but it also led to the criticism that the social welfare measures taken were really designed not to make society a better place for all people but to save capitalism for capitalists. In that sense, the deaths of Peter Markunas, Nick Nargan, and Julian Gryshko, far from being in vain, marked a moment that symbolized very real change to the way Canadians treated one another.

Causes of the Great Depression

One key cause of the Great Depression was the international instability in the world economy. Although there was prosperity after the war, the 1920s also witnessed a massive shift in the international order. Britain, the preeminent economic and military power for most of the nineteenth century, faced increasing economic difficulties in this period, after borrowing billions to pay for the cost of the Great War.

The First World War also had a tremendously destabilizing impact on Germany, Europe's largest economy. At the war's end, the victorious Allies decided that Germany should pay reparations, economic and financial penalties, to the winners. This expectation was somewhat unrealistic, as Germany also suffered because of the high cost of the war. One reparation, giving up the country's industrial heartland, the Ruhr Valley, was particularly harmful to Germany's economic recovery. With reparations and the loss of the Ruhr, Germany was soon in a vicious cycle of hyperinflation and political radicalism. Thus, by the late 1920s, Europe's two most important economies were in grave difficulties. And the United States, by then the world's leading economy, had become largely isolationist and did not fill the power gap created by the decline of Britain and Germany.

Another major factor that caused the Depression was protectionism; the shielding of domestic industries from the competition of foreign goods, which was practiced by the United States, Canada, and other countries, effectively cut off world trade through high tariffs in the interwar period. High tariffs reduced world trade, reduced production, reduced employment, and caused economic hardship for average workers. Countries such as Canada—whose economies depend on trade (in Canada's case on the export of wheat, pulp and paper, and other commodities)—were hurt by this rampant protectionism. Even though Canada had its own tariffs, when world trade stopped, so did the Canadian economy.

At the same time, although Canada and the United States had done relatively well during the 1920s, it was only a matter of time before these expanding economies faced an inevitable slowdown. This slowdown was caused, in part, by industrial overcapacity, which occurs when technological advances in mass production techniques make industry increasingly efficient. In some Canadian industries at that time, capacity outstripped supply. For instance, in the 1920s, Windsor and Oshawa's car factories could produce 400,000 cars a year. But the highest Canadian demand in the decade was only 260,000 cars.

The economic downturn was exacerbated by the plight of the urban working-class population, which was dependent on waged labour in this new industrial economy. By 1921, the majority of Canadians lived in urban areas. A large proportion of people in the cities worked in factories, which caused grave difficulties during the downturn; when factories closed, unemployed people had nowhere to go, no way to survive. Previously, most people had farms or homesteads they could depend on for food; without wages, and without a farm, there was no way to get food.

Of course, being on farms during this period wasn't much better than working in factories. During the late 1920s and early 1930s, Canadian farmers faced a crisis. On the one hand, overfarming and poor weather created a "dustbowl" on the Canadian Prairies. Whole acres of farmland were swept away by the wind or produced little because of soil degradation; one couldn't drive for more than a short while without having to stop and clean out all the dead grasshoppers from the engine.

On the other hand, the Canadian wheat economy had been almost too successful: so many farms meant a glut on the wheat market. By the end of the decade, tons of wheat sat rotting in storehouses, unsold because of overproduction and low prices. Farmers, unable to grow or sell crops, faced massive debts, and were forced to foreclose on their farms. The bank took over these farms and often sold them at bargain prices on the open market because farmers could not afford their mortgages or debts.

Finally, the Depression's immediate cause, and its most visible image, was the stock market crash. Stock markets had funded the massive new corporations that had built up industrial capacity. Many ordinary Americans and Canadians had "gotten into" the market, but weak securities regulation meant that one could buy stocks "on margin" with only 10 per cent down while borrowing the rest of the value of the stock. Buying stocks this way was no problem if a stock's value was increasing, because one could resell later and recoup one's original investment. But, if the stock declined and lenders called in their loans, bankruptcy and panic could result, which happened when the stock market frenzy of the Roaring Twenties finally came to an end with the crash of October 1929. It marked the beginning of the sharpest downturn in world economic history.

Impact upon Canada

Between 1929 and 1932, the value of world trade declined by at least a third; in Canada, external trade declined from $1.15 billion in 1928 to $530 million in 1933. Wheat, flour, and pulp and paper were hurt particularly hard. For example, wheat sold at $1.35 a bushel in the early 1920s; by the early 1930s, wheat prices dropped to $0.35 cents a bushel. As a result, in 1928, total farm income for the Prairies was $120 million; in 1931, it was *negative* $8.9 million.

In other words, thousands of farmers were losing money, declaring bankruptcy, and being driven off their land, their homesteads taken over by the bank. Here is how one Prairie farmer described the Depression and the conditions:

> The terrible winters. The 'hoppers. People at the door begging, for a sandwich, a meal, a cement patch for their tire, a glass of water, the school teacher who boarded with us crying because the board couldn't pay her any more and were closing down the school and she had to go away and she was in love with a local lad. . . . People getting caught on the roads and some freezing to death. Yes, that happened. Good friends leaving for the coast, and then writing back and asking how things were, were they getting any better, was there any point in coming back home again?[2]

Overall, the economic impact was devastating: Canada's gross national product fell from almost $6.1 billion in 1928 to just under $3.5 billion in 1933, and industrial production decreased by half.

With all of these economic problems, Canadians themselves were poorly prepared for the downturn, with no welfare system or unemployment insurance in place to help. As a result of all these events, unemployment increased dramatically after 1930. By 1933, 20 per cent of the labour force was unemployed, amazingly, one worker out of every five. Thus, while many farming communities faced hardships, those in industrial areas such as Windsor and Oshawa and Montreal did so as well.

The large-scale economic hardship provoked a racist backlash in various areas of the country as many who suffered looked to find easy scapegoats to blame. By the early 1930s, the Ku Klux Klan (a racist group originally from the American South) had grown popular in Saskatchewan and Ontario. The KKK and other racist groups targeted visible and religious minorities as the cause of their difficulties. In Quebec, where there was also widespread unemployment, anti-Jewish sentiment rose.

With people out of work, many turned to emergency relief, usually provided for by municipal and provincial governments or charity or religious groups. Between 1933 and 1936, on average, 12 per cent of the population sought emergency relief. But in the worst year of the Depression, 1933, about one in five Canadians, or about two million people, were dependent on public hand-outs to survive. However, these public relief systems were strained to the point of breaking, and most did not meet

---

2   Barry Broadfoot, *Ten Lost Years, 1929–1939: Memories of the Canadians Who Survived the Depression* (Toronto: McClelland & Stewart, 1997), 45–46.

the needs of those who were looking for help. For example, although historians have calculated that an average family required $8 a week to survive, many local agencies provided less than $5. Even those meagre hand-outs were too much for some provinces: by the mid-1930s, Alberta and Saskatchewan teetered on the edge of bankruptcy, no longer able to support all their relief agencies.

In the face of all of this tragedy, people started to question the economic system that had caused the Great Depression: capitalism.

Federal Government Responses

William Lyon Mackenzie King was a very cautious man politically. As prime minister for most of the 1920s, he wanted to do as little as possible in domestic affairs so as to ruffle as few feathers as possible. Leading poet and constitutional scholar F.R. Scott wrote a 1957 poem, "W.L.M.K." (King died in 1950), describing his governing style:

> How shall we speak of Canada,
> Mackenzie King dead?
> The Mother's boy in the lonely room
> With his dog, his medium and his ruins?
>
> He blunted us.
>
> We had no shape
> Because he never took sides,
> And no sides
> Because he never allowed them to take shape.
>
> He skillfully avoided what was wrong
> Without saying what was right,
> And never let his on the one hand
> Know what his on the other hand was doing.
>
> The height of his ambition
>   Was to pile a Parliamentary Committee on a Royal Commission,
> To have "conscription if necessary
> But not necessarily conscription,"
> To let Parliament decide—
> Later.
>
> Postpone, postpone, abstain.

Only one thread was certain:
   After World War I
   Business as usual,

   After World War II
   Orderly decontrol.
   Always he led us back to where we were before.

   He seemed to be in the centre
   Because we had no centre,
   No vision
   To pierce the smoke-screen of his politics.

   Truly he will be remembered
   Wherever men honour ingenuity,
   Ambiguity, inactivity, and political longevity.

   Let us raise up a temple
   To the cult of mediocrity,
   Do nothing by halves
   Which can be done by quarters.[3]

During the Depression, King's approach was not the best to have in such a crisis situation. In fact, initially King did not see the crisis as anything more than a regular downturn in the economy. Thinking it was just a matter of time before things returned to normal, King felt that no special measures by government were necessary to alleviate the problems faced by Canadians. His main policy was to balance the budget, which actually meant cutting back on government support for programs such as welfare and relief, not to mention public works projects.

   Thus, as provinces begged for funds for their strained relief systems, King's attitude was dismissive. Famously, he declared that he would "not give . . . a five-cent piece" to any province asking for financial support.[4] Part of King's response was political: by the late 1920s, nearly all of the provincial governments were Conservative, and King's Liberal saw their pleas as a partisan effort to put him in a bad light and grab power and money from the federal government.

   Part of his response was owing to King's personality, too. King's attitude reflected a nineteenth-century view of the state that believed government should

---

3   The poem can be seen at Canadian Poetry Online, at http://www.library.utoronto.ca/canpoetry/scott_fr/poem5.htm. Reprinted by permission of William Toye, on behalf of the estate of F.R. Scott.
4   Canada, House of Commons, *Debates*, April 3, 1930.

have as little as possible to do with the economy, that it was up to individuals to help themselves, regardless of their circumstances. The notion of the state intervening to change economic outcomes was not really developed yet. In fact, it took the Great Depression to make such an idea acceptable.

In any event, "do nothing" King lost the 1930 election. With times so difficult, people mocked him for being miserly and called him "five-cent" King. He was defeated by Conservative R.B. Bennett. In one way, King was incredibly lucky in losing this election. By not being in government during the worst years of the Depression, King was able to win again in 1935.

Richard Bedford Bennett became Conservative leader in 1927, taking over from Arthur Meighen. Born in New Brunswick, Bennett was the first millionaire prime minister, having made his fortune as a very successful lawyer in Calgary, a riding he had represented since 1911. The Calgary law firm he founded still exists today and is one of Canada's largest. Like King, Bennett was a bachelor. He was also an Anglophile and ended up being buried in England, where he went to live following his time as prime minister.

Initially, Bennett took a traditionally Conservative approach to the Depression, increasing the National Policy tariff, to "blast a way" to markets. At the same time, he also initiated trade deals with the British in 1932 to get some trade moving within the British Commonwealth. Thus, Bennett had a rather curious approach to boosting Canadian trade: at the same time he increased tariffs generally, he lowered tariffs among the British Commonwealth countries. This confusing strategy did not work, as Canada's trade was increasingly with the United States.

Bennett also began a few minor public works projects and started to set up some relief camps. These were designed to keep unemployed men out of cities where they could cause trouble. Fundamentally, however, Bennett's approach differed little from King's. Bennett sought budget balances, just as King had. Bennett also saw provincial demands for change as unconstitutional: the British North America Act, in other words, became an excuse for both King and Bennett to avoid taking action. Because welfare was a provincial jurisdiction, neither thought that Ottawa should provide relief to the provinces.

However, as unemployment grew and Bennett's trade measures failed, he became the target of derision and hatred. Many Canadians saw him as overly controlling and unwilling to consider others' views. Because he was a millionaire, he symbolized everything wrong with capitalism. One group, the "Sudbury Starving Unemployed," wrote him in 1931: "Since you have been elected, work has been impossible to get. We have decided that in a month from this date, if thing's [sic] are the same, We'll skin you alive, the first chance we get."[5] And there were other

---

5 Quoted in Michael Bliss and L.M. Grayson, eds., *The Wretched of Canada: Letters to R.B. Bennett, 1930–1935* (Toronto: University of Toronto Press, 1971), 13.

signs of dissatisfaction: "Bennett Buggies" were cars whose owners couldn't pay for gas or repairs, so the automobiles were drawn by horses; a "Bennett Blanket" was a newspaper to cover a homeless person; and "Eggs Bennett" were broiled chestnuts.

Clearly, by 1933 and 1934, when things were at their worst, many Canadians realized that something had to be done.

Provincial Political Responses to the Depression

Ottawa's unwillingness to do anything in the face of this massive dislocation and hardship provoked a number of new provincial political responses in the 1930s. Underlying all these responses were innovative efforts to get the state more involved by boosting government expenditures in an effort to kick-start the economy. These ideas were embraced primarily in western Canada, already a hotbed of third parties and new ideas. The West had spawned the 1920s Progressive Party of Canada (a third federal party that challenged the two main parties), the United Farmers of Alberta, and, of course, the Winnipeg General Strike. But the Great Depression created even more new ideas, two examples of which tell us much about provincial efforts to fight the Depression.

The first example is Alberta's William "Bible Bill" Aberhart and the Social Credit (SC) Party. Social Credit, as an economic doctrine, was based on the ideas of Scottish engineer Major Douglas, who argued that, though technology allowed for high productivity, it did not allow for high consumption. This result occurred because bankers and financiers, who had all the money, did not put it into circulation. Douglas argued that, with wages too low, governments needed to boost purchasing power. To solve the problem, his idea was to give people a new type of money, "scrip," making the capitalist system run more smoothly.

Social Credit's leading Alberta proponent, "Bible Bill" Aberhart, a preacher and high school teacher, ran the Calgary Prophetic Bible Institute. Aberhart also had an immensely popular radio show, which he used to spread SC ideas. Aberhart's rhetoric could be very convincing, as a 1934 speech illustrates:

> Let us remember that our province is potentially a land of plenty. None of our citizens should be suffering from want or privation. The granaries are full and goods are piled high in the storehouses. We have an abundance of foodstuffs that are being wasted, or wantonly destroyed. Why then should many of our people be in dire need, in suffering from worry, from privation, from hopelessness?[6]

---

6   Alberta, Legislative Assembly, Agricultural Committee, *The Douglas System of Social Credit: Evidence Taken by the Agricultural Committee of the Alberta Legislature, Session 1934* (Edmonton: King's Printer, 1934), 11.

By 1935, with the Depression at its height, Aberhart condemned banks and big business, ran for office, and swept into power: SC won 56 of 63 provincial seats.

However, once in power, Aberhart could not fulfill his promise to use scrip money to fuel the economy. The "funny money legislation" was deemed unconstitutional, since provinces cannot print their own money. Aberhart instead concentrated on eliminating waste in government. By the Second World War's start in 1939, the SC ideas were largely replaced by a staunch fiscal conservatism, a shift that was further accelerated when Ernest Manning took over from Aberhart following the latter's death in 1943. This change was sped further after oil was discovered in the province in 1947 at Leduc.

Another example of efforts to involve the state more actively in the economy comes from BC. There, Duff Pattullo's Liberal government won election in 1933 on a slogan of "Work and Wages." Pattullo, a firm believer in state activism, created a "little New Deal" designed to boost the economy by raising the minimum wage and creating public works projects such as dam building. These ideas were largely dependent on federal funding, however, and Ottawa refused to give Pattullo the necessary money to achieve his goals.

In other provinces, governments called upon the federal state to help or enacted programs designed to get governments more involved in the economy. In all of these instances, however, the federal government refused to provide funding, often using the constitutional excuse to do nothing.

New Federal Parties

By the early 1930s, many Canadians realized that the capitalist system was broken and that the inability or unwillingness of the federal government to do anything about the crisis required a new way of doing politics. Clearly, the traditional political parties had no solutions to the problems posed by the Great Depression; political and economic change could only be achieved through new political vehicles. The Great Depression showed many Canadians that neither King's Liberals nor Bennett's Conservatives were willing to do what it took to right the country.

Three groups pushed for radical change during this period. Farmers, especially in the West, opposed the big railway and banking interests from eastern and central Canada. Farmers had created the United Farmers of Alberta and the federal Progressive Party, though both were spent political forces by the early 1930s. Many farmers became more radical in their politics and thought that cooperative ventures such as wheat boards or insurance co-ops, which challenged the dictates of the market, were the best way to run the economy.

Labour groups, such as those led by J.S. Woodsworth (editor of the *Western Labour News* who was thrown in jail during the Winnipeg General Strike), also increasingly saw the capitalist system as against the interests of working people and were turning toward socialism. Finally, intellectuals from central Canada and the East increasingly called for social and economic change. Academics such as McGill's F.R. Scott (who wrote the 1957 poem about King) and Frank Underhill helped to establish the League for Social Reconstruction (LSR) in 1932. The LSR's manifesto called for the "establishment in Canada of a social order in which the basic principle regulating production, distribution and service will be the common good rather than private profit."[7]

The three groups came together at the Depression's height in Regina in 1932 to form a new party. The Co-operative Commonwealth Federation (CCF) was a cooperative, reflecting farmers' wishes for a non-hierarchical and collaborative venture; it was a commonwealth, reflecting a belief that capitalism should be replaced by an economic system that worked for the common good of all the people; and it was a federation, thus bringing together distinct constituencies from across the country with different goals. For instance, though intellectuals back east, such as Scott, were committed to socialism, this aim did not necessarily reflect the wishes of western farmers, who did not think that capitalism should be replaced but rather that its effects should be softened. The new party's platform, the 1933 Regina Manifesto, largely written by socialists such as Scott, included a famous clause calling for capitalism's abolition in Canada.

The CCF scored some early successes, such as winning a 1942 Toronto federal by-election, when teacher Joe Noseworthy defeated a comeback attempt by Conservative Arthur Meighen. In 1943, the Ontario CCF came second in the provincial election. Most important, in 1944 in Saskatchewan, the party won government under the leadership of Tommy Douglas, remaining in power until 1964.

Although the CCF was the most successful new party launched during the Great Depression (it became the New Democratic Party in 1961), other new parties emerged in the 1930s or gained strength because of Canada's economic difficulties. For example, the Reconstruction Party under former Conservative H.H. Stevens also sought to get the state more involved in the economy. Another party that grew popular in this decade was the Communist Party of Canada. Of course, for many, the Communists were seen as a direct revolutionary challenge to the Canadian establishment—and were under constant scrutiny. Their leader Tim Buck was actually imprisoned in the early 1930s and was released to a hero's welcome at a massive rally at Toronto's Maple Leaf Gardens in 1934.

---

7   The full text of the LSR Manifesto can be seen at http://www.alterhistory.altervista.org/Documenti/testiGET.php?titolotesto=SociaCanada.

Federal Government Responses, Round Two

By 1934, Prime Minister Bennett faced mounting pressure to do something. His tariff policies had not improved anything, and unemployment and despair had increased. Moreover, the success of new politicians, policies, and parties, such as the Alberta Social Credit Party and the CCF, made him realize that he faced a political threat. He also faced pressure to do something because of the popularity of the famous "New Deal" measures initiated by US President Franklin Delano Roosevelt (FDR).

Bennett tried to emulate FDR's successful strategy in order to get re-elected and created his own "New Deal" program. He held five radio broadcasts, like FDR's "fireside chats." During these broadcasts, he promised to reform Canadian capitalism through an "interventionist government." This was a far cry from his previous posture and illustrated his decision to change his approach fundamentally.

Bennett's "New Deal" consisted of a number of measures. First, he attempted to reform labour practices, so he promised to introduce a minimum wage and a maximum number of working hours. Second, he tried to reform taxation and banking in the country. He attempted to bring in a progressive income tax, and he created the Bank of Canada in 1935. The central bank would set interest rates, print money, and set exchange rates, giving the government more say over the functioning of the economy. Third, Bennett launched an investigation into the wildly differing prices farmers were getting for their crops, comparing these prices to the amount for which they were sold. Some farmers were selling their grain for $0.50 a pound while elsewhere it was being resold at $2.00 a pound. Fourth, he initiated an unemployment insurance program, national pensions, marketing boards for Canadian products, and public works projects.

However, virtually all of these measures were dismissed by the courts as unconstitutional; although Bennett realized that Ottawa must take a larger role in the economy, the courts prevented him from doing so on jurisdictional grounds. Besides the government's failure to convince the courts of its policies, Bennett's measures were too little, too late, according to many Canadians. During the 1935 election, the new parties created in the wake of the Depression ate away at Conservative support. The CCF, federal SC, and Reconstruction parties combined to take 20 per cent of the vote. King, still Liberal leader, campaigned on the slogan "King or Chaos" and won re-election convincingly.

Rethinking Confederation

All of the demands of provinces and politicians that something must be done about government's role in the economy started to have some impact. Although

King remained reluctant after returning to office to initiate any changes to the way Confederation worked, he was more than happy to strike a royal commission to look into the respective roles of the federal and provincial governments. This way, it seemed as though King was actually doing something while he took as little action as possible.

But the 1940 *Report of the Royal Commission on Dominion-Provincial Relations*, known as the Rowell-Sirois Report, came to some very important conclusions on how the country should function. First, the commission argued that one of the main reasons that the Great Depression had been so difficult on Canadians was that there was a fiscal imbalance between the federal government and the provinces. Although the provinces had the most social responsibilities, such as relief or health care, Ottawa had more taxation revenues. The commission called upon the federal government to collect all the taxes on behalf of the provinces and then give the provinces grants in order to make up their funding shortfalls. Though this did not happen until the Second World War, the report did eventually lead to the notion of equalization—that Ottawa should sometimes distribute money from wealthier provinces to those in difficulty.

Second, the commission argued that Ottawa should take over some provincial responsibilities, particularly unemployment relief, and that the Constitution should be amended to give the federal government control over this relief, making unemployment benefits consistent across the country. A 1940 constitutional amendment created the employment insurance system still in place today.

Finally, the commission advocated the adoption of Keynesian economic policies. English economist John Maynard Keynes argued that state intervention could be used to "prime the economic pump" by creating demand and employment through stimuli such as work projects and social spending. Through deficit spending, a government could make its way out of recession and, once the economy was growing, it could use surpluses to pay off its debts.

King, however, remained reluctant to engage in wholesale state intervention in the economy. In fact, only because of the Second World War did the notion of Keynesianism finally take hold of the government. Indeed, it was really the war, which occasioned a massive growth of the state and of state intervention in the economy, that finally solved the Depression.

Back to Estevan

What happened to the strikers following the Estevan incident? Well, the miners refused to give in, despite the arrest of many strike leaders and the killing of Peter Markunas, Nick Nargan, and Julian Gryshko. In early October of 1931, the company agreed to implement an eight-hour day, increased workers' wages, and provided some relief from company store and company-owned housing policies. These were all significant victories for the strikers, though they did not achieve union recognition for the Mine Workers Union of Canada. Nonetheless, the strike at Estevan stands as an important symbol of worker agency and of the extent to which ordinary people are willing to stand up for their rights, even in times as difficult as the Great Depression. The changes demanded by the workers at Estevan also reflected a demand by Canadians for much deeper and broader change to the economic system, and to the role of government as well. By the start of the Second World War, some of these changes had been achieved.

Further Reading

Campbell, Lara. "We Who Have Wallowed in the Mud of Flanders." *Journal of the Canadian Historical Association* 11, no. 1 (2000): 125–49.

Manley, John. "'Starve, Be Damned!' Communists and Canada's Urban Unemployed, 1929–39." *Canadian Historical Review* 79, no. 3 (September 1998): 466–91. http://dx.doi.org/10.3138/CHR.79.3.466.

McCallum, Todd. "Vancouver Through the Eyes of a Hobo: Experience, Identity, and Value in the Writing of Canada's Depression-Era Tramps," *Labour / Le Travail* 59 (Spring 2007): 43–68.

Owram, Doug. "Economic Thought in the 1930s: The Prelude to Keynesianism." *Canadian Historical Review* 66, no. 3 (September 1985): 344–77. http://dx.doi.org/10.3138/CHR-066-03-02.

Waiser, Bill. *All Hell Can't Stop Us: The On-to-Ottawa Trek and Regina Riot.* Calgary: Fifth House, 2003.

ACTIVE HISTORY: PRIMARY DOCUMENT ANALYSIS, THE REGINA MANIFESTO, 1933

- Examine the text of the Regina Manifesto, which can be found at http://www.socialisthistory.ca/Docs/CCF/ReginaManifesto.htm.

- How does the manifesto reflect the concerns and problems that ordinary Canadians faced during the Great Depression? How did the manifesto reflect the political conflict in the period over the state's role in the economy? What are the most striking features of the manifesto, in your view?

- What political remedies did the manifesto call for? After 1933, which of these demands were eventually put into place? Which ones were not?

TRAGIC TALES
TWO KILLED AS POLICE AND MOUNTIES BREAK UP THE ON-TO-OTTAWA TREK, REGINA, DOMINION DAY (JULY 1), 1935

Militancy in the Face of Depression and Indifference

If the 1925 death of William Davis in Cape Breton reflected the lengths to which companies were willing to go to break up strikes, the events at Estevan in 1931 and at Regina in 1935 illustrated that, despite claiming to fight the Great Depression on behalf of ordinary Canadians, the state remained squarely on the side of employers, often with deadly consequences.

As the Great Depression wore on in the early 1930s, the number of unemployed Canadians reached crisis proportions. R.B. Bennett's solution was to create relief camps where unemployed men could work on infrastructure projects, such as road building, in return for subsistence wages (20 cents a day) and often less than basic accommodations and food. Ottawa put these relief camps, run by the Department of National Defence, in isolated areas in an effort to keep this mass of men far from urban centres. The men in the camps soon began to organize, demanding "work and wages" and creating unions, such as the Relief Camp Workers' Union (RCWU) begun in 1933 in Kamloops, British Columbia. Yet Ottawa refused to recognize these unions or do anything about their grievances.

By 1935, many of the men had had enough. In BC, more than a thousand workers went out on strike, left the camps, and descended on Vancouver. After a two-month protest there, they determined to take their case directly to Ottawa. Their plan was to "ride the rails," to hop on board empty trains heading eastward, picking up other men along the way in an "On-to-Ottawa Trek" that would push the

federal government to do something about the precarious state of the men in these camps. In June 1935, the trekkers left Vancouver and, in a few days, had been joined by hundreds of other men. By the time the On-to-Ottawa Trek reached Regina in mid-June, nearly 3,000 men had gathered together.

As the men picked up more recruits and gained momentum, the federal government was determined to stop the trek. At Regina, Ottawa ordered the trains to stop. Encamped in Regina, the men and the federal government entered into an uneasy standoff, as the two sides traded accusations about the situation. A small group of strikers went to Ottawa to negotiate with the federal government, but the talks broke down, and they soon returned to Regina. Federal representatives then demanded that all the men report to a camp north of the city, after which they would be returned to their homes. With the trains stopped, a number of trekkers attempted to continue on to Ottawa by car and truck, but were turned back by police. With supplies and money running low, the organizers held a public rally in the city's Market Square to raise funds for the men on July 1, 1935.

During this peaceful Dominion Day event (the name was changed to Canada Day in 1982), which was attended by nearly 3,000 people, the RCMP and the Regina police decided to arrest a number of the protest leaders. Unsurprisingly, this provocation resulted in a battle between the men and police, who lobbed teargas, "swung their batons freely" (according to newspaper reports), and fired shots into the unarmed crowd. The strikers fought back with whatever they could, including rocks and sticks. The battle lasted until morning and spilled into the surrounding streets. Two men, striker Dan

McGee and Constable Charles Miller, died during the altercation or afterward of wounds. Hundreds more were injured.

With dozens thrown in jail, the trek stopped in its tracks, and with little chance of having their demands for better wages and work met by the federal government, the strikers returned home, at Ottawa's expense, in passenger trains. Nonetheless, the consequences of the trek and its breakup at Regina were profound. Some men faced charges and jail time, prompting large-scale protests across the country. The Dominion Day events did not help Bennett during the 1935 election, as he was easily defeated by King, who took advantage of the sensational reports to help his campaign. A federal inquiry called after the incident exonerated police, though evidence indicated that they had provoked the riot.

The 1935 On-to-Ottawa Trek also galvanized the labour movement, which achieved significant success during the Second World War as the federal government and many companies, such as those in the automobile industry, finally recognized unions. The state also moved to protect collective bargaining and workers' rights and to legislate better working conditions.

The era of the militant labour movement of the 1930s and of the wartime strikes of the 1940s that achieved so many long-held goals for workers and unions was replaced by a period of stability in the 1950s, as workers and employers both benefited from collective bargaining and a prosperous postwar economy. Yet the events of the On-to-Ottawa Trek, the incident at Estevan, the murder of coalminer William Davis, and the Winnipeg General Strike itself reflect the decades-long battle fought by workers for their rights in this period—and the determination of governments and employers to deny these rights.

ELEVEN CANADIAN SOLDIERS, MURDERED BY THE NAZIS, FRANCE, 1944
CANADA'S WAR?

Just a day after the famous June 6, 1944, D-Day invasion of France during the Second World War, the North Nova Scotia Highlanders, often referred to as Novies, and the Fusiliers de Sherbrooke, two Canadian regiments who had landed on the beaches of Normandy, were making good progress inland, encountering little resistance.

The Canadian column soon found itself on its way toward the small French village of Buron. Just down the road from the Canadians, Kurt Meyer, the commander of the 25th SS-Panzergrenadier Regiment, sat in the bell tower of the nearby Abbaye d'Ardenne (Ardenne Abbey) with a pair of field glasses. Hardly believing his eyes, he watched the Canadian armoured column emerge, oblivious to the presence of about half an entire German tank (Panzer) division, dug in on either side of the road, the tanks positioned in a V formation with only their turrets visible. Behind the Panzers, on higher ground, were batteries of anti-tank guns. The Canadians were essentially walking into the heart of the German defences, and were in no way prepared for what came next.

Meyer ordered his tanks to hold their fire until the entire column was in view. When the attack began, the Canadian tanks were blown to pieces as the terrified crews bailed out and the infantry scattered. The German troops swarmed after the Canadians before they could fall back and regroup, and soon Canadian prisoners were pouring into the orchards, fields, and farm buildings that surrounded the abbey.

Meyer had received intelligence reports of German prisoners shot by Canadians on Juno Beach (where the Canadians had landed on D-Day), so his troops had been told that they should neither take prisoners nor allow themselves to be captured. During the next 24 hours, French civilians living and working around the Abbaye d'Ardenne were the shocked eyewitnesses to the murders of the Canadian soldiers that had been captured. Most were shot after a short period of questioning. In one incident, at about noon on June 8, a conscripted Polish dispatch rider listened in horror as Meyer ordered the execution of a group of North Nova Scotia Highlanders, who were taken one by one out into the abbey garden and shot. All told, Meyer and members of the German 12th SS Panzer Division were ultimately charged in a war crimes trial for the deaths of over 40 Canadian soldiers in the days following the D-Day landings: 23 near the villages of Buron and Authie on June 7, 11 on the same day at Meyer's headquarters at the Abbaye d'Ardenne, and 7 on the next day, also at the abbey. War records show that 20 Canadian POWs were executed in the abbey grounds.

These Canadians were killed fighting a war for civilization. Their sacrifices truly were something that we can point to as having made a difference. How did these men come to die in such circumstances? What consequences did Meyer face for his actions?

Causes of the Second World War

In many ways, the Second World War was a continuation of the First World War. The second war stemmed from a number of causes, many related to continuing German aspirations to dominate Europe and to the consequences of the Great War. The German loss in the First World War and the ensuing terms of the Treaty of Versailles had crippled the German economy. By the 1920s, runaway inflation and severe economic hardship in Germany had resulted in considerable German bitterness toward both the treaty and Germany's loss in 1918.

This feeling was not helped by the rampant protectionism of the 1930s, which had contributed to the Great Depression. As world trade ground to a halt, the absence of countries' trade with each other meant that there were fewer economic linkages that might have prevented armed conflict. In Germany, the fallout from the Versailles Treaty and the Great Depression generated immense political and economic turmoil in this period, which, in turn, created political instability and a power vacuum.

Fascism was another cause of the war. Adolf Hitler and the National Socialist or Nazi party took advantage of instability, uncertainty, and hardship, and called for a strong Germany to re-emerge from the "humiliation" of the First World War. Hitler denounced the Treaty of Versailles and called for German re-armament. Moreover, the Nazis blamed racial minorities, such as the Jews, for the plight of ordinary Germans. With the German government constantly teetering on the brink of dissolution, Hitler gained control of the German government by 1933.

After taking power, Hitler embarked on an economic and military rebuilding program that re-established the German army, retook Germany territory previously demilitarized by the Allies, and enacted racial laws discriminating against Jews in Germany. Hitler also embarked on a territorial acquisition campaign, calling for a "Greater Germany" that included all German-speakers in a "Third Reich" (after the earlier Holy Roman and German empires). This new empire, he claimed, would last for 1,000 years. In 1938, Germany took over Austria and also annexed the Sudetenland, the German-speaking part of Czechoslovakia.

These territorial acquisitions were met by the British and French policy of appeasement: giving way to Hitler in order to keep the peace. Politicians had a misguided hope that Hitler was not actually keen on another war, given the horrors of the Great War. They were wrong. This failure of international diplomacy, of the appeasement of Hitler, reached its height in 1938 when British Prime Minister Neville Chamberlain declared that the agreements he had reached after meeting with Hitler had achieved "peace for our time."[1] Mackenzie King, re-elected Canadian prime minister in 1935, was also in this appeasement camp. He thought not only that the Great War's horrors should never be repeated but also that another European engagement could tear apart Canada's fragile national unity.

Appeasement policies also exacerbated the League of Nations' ineffectiveness. Created in 1919, the league was designed to ensure that another Great War did not occur, but it was ineffectual and weak. The United States had not joined, and most countries did not wish to be bound by international bodies and ignored the league's recommendations.

In any event, the appeasers' hopes that Hitler's territorial ambitions would end with his takeover of Czechoslovakia were misguided. In September of 1939, Hitler invaded Poland, setting in motion a scenario similar to that of 1914. In response to the German invasion of Poland, both France and Britain declared war on Germany, just two days after the September 1 invasion. The world was once again at war.

King, "Limited Liability," and the "Phony War"

Britain's declaration of war on Germany created a serious difficulty for Canada and King: was Canada automatically obliged to declare war as well? King, who remembered well the atmosphere after war was declared in 1914, understood the intensity of English-Canadian demands to help the mother country again.

---

1   For the transcript of Neville Chamberlain's "Peace for Our Time" speech (September 30, 1938), see *Britannia Historical Documents*, http://www.britannia.com/history/docs/peacetime.html.

At the same time, he understood that many French Canadians would feel exactly as they had during the Great War, as did many others across the country who were against conscription. Ultimately, however, King knew that Canada had to join Britain in the war.

But cautious King wanted to make sure that Canadians would decide, that Canada would not seem to be automatically joining Britain in war, as it had in 1914. Thus, in the first week of September, King went on radio and stated that "Parliament will decide" whether or not Canada should go to war. The House of Commons did meet, and it held a series of votes on war measures, but it was King's cabinet that ultimately issued a formal declaration of war on Germany on September 10, 1939.

King also wanted to be as cautious as possible in the conduct of the war, especially regarding the level of Canada's involvement. Most important, he wanted to ensure that the issue of conscription did not reappear. On September 8, 1939, he announced the following:

> The present government believes that conscription of men for overseas service will not be a necessary or effective step. No such measure will be introduced by the present administration. We have full faith in the readiness of Canadian men and women to put forward every effort in their power to defend free institutions, and in particular to resist aggression on the part of a tyrannical regime which aims at the domination of the world by force.[2]

Instead, King developed the notion of a "limited liability" war. "Limited liability" meant, in King's view, that Canada would provide as much financial and material support to Britain as it could. Doing so would also have the effect of rebuilding the Canadian economy from the ravages of the Depression. It also meant that Canada would boost its navy and its air force and build up its army, but primarily for home defence as only volunteer soldiers were expected to serve overseas.

The centrepiece of limited liability was the British Commonwealth Air Training Plan (BCATP). The BCATP, designed to take advantage of Canada's open spaces and its desire to provide supplies such as planes, was an immense pilot-training program. The plan was a success, and, eventually, over 130,000 flyers from Canada, Britain, and other Allied countries were trained in Canada at a cost of more than $1.6 billion, a huge chunk of Canada's war expenditures.

King's limited liability policy made sense in the first part of the war: after Hitler overran Poland, the conflict settled into the "phony war" phase. Essentially,

---

2   Quoted in J.L. Granatstein, *Canada's War: The Politics of the Mackenzie King Government, 1939–45* (Toronto: Oxford University Press, 1975), 16.

nothing happened for more than half a year. After conquering Poland, the Germans did not move on France and Belgium immediately. For many around the world, it seemed that the war had become a non-event.

Of course, many criticized King's policy, "phony war" or not. In Ontario, King was assailed by Mitchell Hepburn, the Liberal premier, who passed a resolution in the Ontario legislature criticizing Ottawa for not doing enough. Hepburn, an onion farmer elected in 1934, took an activist approach to government that appealed to Ontarians adversely affected by the Depression. As an activist, he was displeased with King's "do little" approach toward the war. Adding fuel to policy differences were personality clashes: the two men disliked each other immensely. Though both were Liberals from Ontario, they could not have been more different. "Mitch" was a heavy-drinking ladies' man, a man of action; King was a teetotaller (non-drinker), deeply religious, and incredibly cautious.

At the same time, King was attacked in Quebec for even joining the war by Union Nationale Premier Maurice Duplessis. Duplessis, an extremely conservative leader elected in 1936, was a strong clerico-nationalist, believing that the Roman Catholic Church had a role in provincial affairs, especially in the arena of education and moral regulation. Duplessis challenged King by claiming that Ottawa would impose conscription, a policy despised in Quebec. Quebec protests against conscription's possibility began as early as 1939.

In response, King silenced Duplessis and Hepburn by essentially beating them at the ballot box. During the 1939 Quebec provincial election, King sent his Quebec lieutenant, Ernest Lapointe, to pledge that there would be no overseas conscription, especially if Duplessis was defeated. The plan was effective as the provincial Liberals won. In response to Hepburn, King called a snap federal election, a political master stroke. Basically the election was a referendum on King's policy of "limited liability," which the Liberals won convincingly in March 1940, taking 181 out of 245 seats, including 61 of 65 in Quebec. Thus, by the spring of 1940, King seemed to have matters under control. His chief antagonists, Hepburn and Duplessis, had been silenced. His policy of "limited liability" seemed to be keeping Canada out of any major conflict that might put pressure on the country's national unity.

But, in the spring of 1940, the "phony war" came to a stunning and demoralizing end. In May, Germany invaded France. Unleashing their thunderous blitzkrieg, which overwhelmed the French and British forces, within weeks the Germans had captured the Netherlands, Luxembourg, and Belgium, were threatening Paris, and had chased British and other retreating forces to the French coast. These troops were able to evacuate only with the help of thousands of small British boats. The "Miracle of Dunkirk" rescued much of the British army but left behind all of its equipment and material. It was a devastating defeat.

It quickly dawned on King and many Canadians that France's surrender and Britain's defeat in Europe meant that Canada was now Britain's ranking ally.

Because the United States remained isolationist, Canada would now be expected to bear a greater burden of the war effort. The policy of "limited liability" was effectively dead. King knew a new approach to mobilization was necessary, and he immediately enacted a huge munitions and equipment building plan led by Munitions Minister C.D. Howe, soon known as the "Minister of Everything." King also passed the National Resources Mobilization Act (NRMA), which organized the war effort and enacted conscription, but for home defence only. All eligible Canadian men were registered, but only volunteers who wished to go overseas did so. The NRMA conscripts who stayed home were called "zombies," after the Hollywood movie monsters, the living dead of the soldiering class. There was little outcry against this policy in 1940 because many thought that Canada might actually be invaded if Britain fell.

With the fall of France in June, Canada would now take on a major part in the war, if, that is, Britain actually survived the German assault.

Canadians at War

The period from the fall of France in June 1940 until December of 1941 was one of the darkest in Canadian history, as Britain faced its gravest threat in modern times. During the air war called the Battle of Britain, London was bombed mercilessly, and it looked as though the German invasion and takeover of Britain was imminent. Canadians participated in the Battle of Britain, too, flying Hawker Hurricanes or Spitfires or manning anti-aircraft battalions. The Royal Air Force's repelling of the German Luftwaffe, or air force, was one of the war's great battles, and one of its most vicious. Relentless German bombing of London and other British cities was designed to sap the will of the British people and prepare the groundwork for an invasion force. London was literally bombed to rubble, with thousands of civilian casualties.

In the skies over Britain, thousands of pilots, some of them Canadian, battled relentlessly to stop the bombing. As one Canadian pilot recalled, "This was no joust bound by the rules of chivalry. I had never witnessed such persistent savagery. They were out to kill us by any means possible."[3] Of course, in the end, the Royal Air Force (RAF) was victorious, preventing the Germans from launching a final assault on the island.

As part of the air war, thousands of Canadians also served in the RAF's Bomber Command, launching air raids against German targets after 1940. More than anything, the German blitz of London and the Allied bombing attacks on

---

3   As quoted in J.L. Granatstein and Desmond Morton, *A Nation Forged in Fire: Canadians and the Second World War, 1939–1945* (Toronto: Lester & Orpen Dennys, 1989), 108.

Germany reflected the totality that war had become. This total war was very different than the First World War, in which civilian populations were not directly targeted. Bombing missions that attacked German cities such as Berlin, Frankfurt, or Hamburg faced incredibly high casualty rates, inflicted massive civilian casualties, and have sparked historical debate about whether the attacks were justified or ultimately helped defeat Germany. Fewer than one in three bomber crews survived a 30-operation tour, and almost 10,000 Canadians died while serving in Bomber Command.

Meanwhile, thousands of British children and women were evacuated to Canada in case the island was invaded. Of course, the British survived the aerial attacks, but in the summer of 1940 this survival was not assured. As Winston Churchill famously remarked of Britain's fighter pilots in 1940, "Never in the field of human conflict was so much owed by so many to so few."[4] With the British surviving the German assault, when Hitler invaded Russia in June 1941, the Union of Soviet Socialist Republics (USSR), or Soviet Union, came into the war on the Allied side.

The Canadian army's early participation in the war was an unhappy experience. In 1941, Canadian troops defending Hong Kong, then a British possession, surrendered to the Japanese, who quickly overwhelmed the colony on Christmas Day, 1941. The Japanese had already attacked the American naval base at Pearl Harbor, Hawaii, prompting the United States to join the war on the Allied side. Of the close to 2,000 Canadians defending Hong Kong, almost 300 were killed, about 500 wounded, and the rest taken prisoner. The Canadian soldiers who surrendered suffered immensely as Japanese prisoners of war for many years; approximately 264 of them died as POWs. The Canadian surrender was a political bombshell that rocked King's government and sparked parliamentary inquiries into why the Canadians were so easily defeated.

Another major Canadian setback occurred at Dieppe, a coastal French town. In August 1942, parts of the 2nd Canadian Infantry Division attempted to land at the beach in an effort to test the German defences. But the Germans were far too well entrenched. Of the approximately 5,000 troops that went ashore, over 900 were killed and nearly 2,000 were taken prisoner. The operation was a total disaster. Canadian tanks ran aground on the pebbled beaches, their equipment failed, and their tactics were utterly useless against the German fortifications and counterattack.

The raid's only saving grace was that it gave the Allies a clear idea of what tactics and equipment they should use when the final invasion of France took place. To this day, some Canadian historians feel that the Canadian forces were used in this attack as a sacrificial lamb, as an effort to mollify the Soviets, whose

---

4   Speech in the British House of Commons, August 20, 1940.

leader, Stalin, was calling for some kind of western front to be opened. In the summer of 1942, the Soviets, then allies of the British and Americans, had suffered immense casualties because of the German invasion. Many historians also think that the Canadians were wholly unprepared for such an attack and that they were thus needlessly sacrificed. Of course, on the home front, Dieppe was initially reported as a huge success, despite the reality of defeat.

Canadians also participated in the Battle of the Atlantic. The task of ferrying supplies and material to the British war effort was incredibly important, and the Canadian navy was a significant part of that effort. As German U-boats, or submarines, did their best to sink the supplies that were so crucial to keeping Britain in the war during the dark years of 1940 and 1941, Allied navies did their best to get as many ships across the Atlantic. The cat and mouse game in the early years often went to the Germans, and thousands of Canadian seamen lost their lives.

For example, in September 1941, in one convoy of 64 ships heading across the Atlantic, German U-boats sank 16 of the ships. Overall, by most measures German subs sank almost 2,000 naval and merchant marine ships during the Battle of the Atlantic. Needless to say, this was a large loss of life. But, by the end of the war, with new technologies such as sonar and the better use of airplanes, the Allies were able to get their shipping across far more effectively, and Canadian ships shared in the sinking of approximately 30 enemy submarines.

Canadians got into the thick of the war in late 1943 with the Italian campaign. Unlike in the First World War, Italy joined the Germans and Japanese, or the Axis powers, during the Second World War. Italian dictator Benito Mussolini was a strong ally of Hitler. In the Allied invasion of Sicily and the eventual capture of Italy, Canadians saw much action as they moved northward from the island of Sicily up the Italian peninsula.

Though much of the drive was relatively easy, the Canadians did encounter significant opposition when they ran into German lines south of Rome. At both Ortona and Cassino, Canadians faced determined German defenders, and the battles were harsh. One CBC reporter described the fighting: "The Germans were demons; the Canadians were possessed by demons. The more murderous the battle, the harder both sides fought."[5] One Canadian solder remarked after the battle that "Everything before Ortona was a nursery tale."[6] Rome was finally captured in June of 1944. Eventually, Allied soldiers, Canadians included, defeated the German and Italian armies in Italy and liberated the country, but not without thousands of casualties.

---

5   Matthew Halton, quoted in A.E. Powley, *Broadcast from the Front: Canadian Radio Overseas in the Second World War* (Toronto: Hakkert, 1975), 61.

6   Granatstein and Morton, *A Nation Forged in Fire*, 144.

Figure 11.1 *Canadians in Battle: Forward Observation Post of "B" Battery, 1st Field Regiment, Royal Canadian Artillery, Near Potenza, Italy, September 24, 1943. Photograph by Lieutenant Alex M. Stirton*

Library and Archives Canada, 3260954

June of 1944 also marked the beginning of the D-Day invasion of France. This was the largest invasion in history, and it marked a real change in the war. Now the British, American, and Canadian forces were working together to liberate France and Europe from the Nazi regime. On June 6, 1944, thousands of Canadians landed at Juno Beach, one of the five beaches targeted by the Allies in Normandy, on the northern coast of France. The D-Day invasion was successful, and, by the end of June, the Allies had a strong foothold in France, into which thousands of soldiers and millions of tons of equipment and material poured. Of course, the price of that invasion was high. There were approximately 9,000 Allied casualties that day, including 1,074 Canadians, of whom 359 were killed; there were thousands of German casualties as well.

From that point on, the Canadians took part in a number of engagements across Europe as the Allied armies moved to liberate the continent. The Canadian First Army liberated parts of France (including Dieppe, to the joy of many Canadian soldiers) and Belgium. The Canadians also liberated the Netherlands, which held a special significance for both countries. The Dutch royal family had fled to Canada from the Netherlands after the Nazis invaded in 1940. In 1943, Dutch Princess Margriet was born in the Ottawa Civic Hospital, her mother Queen Juliana's room in the maternity ward temporarily declared as not being part of Canada, so the princess would be born in international territory and derive her citizenship only from her mother. Since Princess Margriet's birth and Canada's part in the liberation of the Netherlands, the Dutch have sent a gift of tulip bulbs every year as a gesture of thanks; these tulips are planted and bloom on Parliament Hill and throughout Ottawa.

Another Conscription Crisis

While Canadians battled in Europe, at home the conscription question began to be raised again. In 1940, King had passed the NRMA, which required conscription for home defence only. Initially, most Canadians agreed that there should not be conscription. Even Conservative leader R.J. Manion, who replaced R.B. Bennett in 1938, stated in 1939 that the Conservatives did not believe in conscription. Of course, this stance did not sit well with many in the party.

Most particularly, it did not sit well with Arthur Meighen. Meighen, the Conservative justice minister during 1917, had instituted conscription and passed all the legislation allowing the Union Government to ensure victory during the 1917 "khaki" election. He had succeeded Robert Borden as prime minister in 1920, lost to King in the 1921 election, formed the government again briefly in 1926, and played the role of King's political nemesis during the 1920s. In 1941, Meighen unexpectedly returned to the helm of the Conservative Party and called for conscription for overseas service.

Meighen's reappearance was not the only threat over conscription that King faced. His own minister of defence, J.L. Ralston, had complained that the country needed to enforce conscription for overseas service as the only fair solution for those who were dying in the war. King's Quebec lieutenant, Ernest Lapointe, had died in 1941, leaving no strong anti-conscription counterweight in cabinet to those now calling for the policy to be implemented.

Faced with these threats, King was torn over what to do. Instead of taking decisive action to enforce conscription, King decided to hold a plebiscite, or referendum, on the question. This was a classic King delaying tactic, and, in April 1942, a nationwide vote was held on whether the government should be "released from its promise" of only sending volunteers to overseas service. To release the government from its pledge meant that the NRMA men, the zombies, could be forced to fight on the front.

The results of the plebiscite were predictable. In Quebec, 72.9 per cent voted no; every other province voted yes, for an overall 66 per cent in favour. In Ontario, for example, the vote was over 80 per cent in favour of "releasing the government" from its pledge. These results put King in a difficult situation: if he instituted conscription, it threatened to break the country in two, as had nearly happened in 1917. Not only that, but he would lose his main power base—Quebec. If he did not institute conscription, however, he would face the wrath of the rest of Canada, which had voted overwhelmingly for the policy—or at least thought they had.

In response, King pulled a fast one. The incident shows King at his political best (some would say his slippery best). Instead of immediately enacting conscription, in 1942, he put forward Bill 80, which simply deleted the NRMA sections stating that conscripts could not be used for overseas service. But, in King's view, deletion of these clauses did not mean that he would actually institute overseas conscription. It meant that the government had been released from its promise not to impose that kind of conscription. In one of the most famous turns of phrase, King announced that Bill 80 would mean "Not necessarily conscription, but conscription if necessary."[7]

Obviously, this position infuriated many who felt that King was being disingenuous at best and totally dishonest at worst. King faced much criticism both inside and outside the government for his refusal to enact conscription immediately. Minister of Defence J.L. Ralston felt betrayed by King's clever manoeuvre and offered his resignation. But King did not accept it, saying that Ralston was too important to the war effort. Ralston stayed on, but the incident would play a role as the drama over conscription continued to unfold.

With Bill 80, King seemed to have dodged the conscription bullet. King's position had been further eased somewhat by the surprising defeat earlier in the year of Meighen in a by-election in Toronto. Meighen had been agitating for conscription outright yet lost to CCF candidate Joe Noseworthy, taking the wind out of the pro-conscriptionist sails. Again, King had been somewhat lucky.

Despite this respite, conscription remained on the front burner. By 1944, the invasion of Italy, D-Day, and the fight to liberate Europe had taken their toll on the Canadian forces. By then, many were again calling for conscription, saying that King should enforce Bill 80 and relocate NRMA conscripts to frontline action. In September 1944, Ralston had gone to Europe to inspect the troops. What he

---

7   Dominion of Canada, *Official Report of Debates, House of Commons*, 19th Parliament, 3rd session, vol. 4 (July 7, 1942): 4011. Available from the Library of Parliament at http://parl. canadiana.ca/view/oop.debates_HOC1903.

found shocked him: Canadian units were woefully undermanned, and morale was low because of the difficulties of the war and lack of support. The Canadian forces had taken many casualties, and troops were simply not being replenished. Ralston returned, determined to force King to put conscription in place.

In Ottawa, King and Ralston faced off over conscription. In cabinet, Ralston made the case that King had held a vote on conscription in 1942 and must now enact it. King, always the tricky politician, was not so easily swayed: he knew that conscription could destroy the country. In the middle of their meeting, King pulled out the letter of resignation that Ralston had given him in 1942, and which King had not then accepted. Now, two years later, he accepted the resignation! Ralston was shocked, as were most of the rest of the cabinet, and the former minister of defence quietly rose, shook hands with King and some in cabinet, and left without saying a word. King had gotten the better of Ralston in this incident.

King replaced Ralston with Andrew McNaughton, a Canadian veteran of the First World War who had recently commanded the First Canadian Infantry Division. Understanding that the Canadian army needed more manpower but reluctant to enforce conscription, King hoped that McNaughton could convince some of the 68,000 NRMA zombies to join the forces overseas. But McNaughton was unsuccessful. His hand finally forced, in late 1944, King reluctantly agreed to release the NRMA men for overseas service: just 16,000 were released for overseas service, but only 13,000 were actually sent. Of these, about 2,500 actually reached the front lines, and 69 were killed in action. This was a fraction of the total of army dead: 23,000. The Canadian forces also lost approximately 2,000 people in the navy (and thousands more in the merchant marine) and over 17,000 in the air force.

By the time NRMA conscripts reached the front, however, the war was quickly coming to a close. King had again gotten lucky. Although many in Quebec were incensed at his enactment of conscription, he had largely avoided the shattering consequences of the policy, consequences that the country had suffered through in 1917. In a protest vote, Maurice Duplessis was returned to power in 1944, but King did not face too much of a political backlash in Quebec. The fact that he was spared is no doubt attributable to his obvious determination to avoid the policy of conscription at almost all costs.

Allied Victory, King's Victory

It became clear in early 1945 that the Allies were on their way to victory. In the Soviet Union, in perhaps the most important battle of the war, Stalingrad had turned the fortunes of war against the Axis powers, as the Soviets held off the Germans, who were soon in retreat. Second, American efforts were having an immense impact, both in Europe and in the Pacific; these marked the dawn of the American empire. Eventually, Hitler was defeated, and Canadians celebrated "Victory in Europe Day" (VE Day) for the first time in May of 1945.

However, Japan was still fighting in the Pacific. In the summer of 1945, the United States dropped two atomic weapons on the Japanese cities of Hiroshima and Nagasaki. Shortly after the bombing of these two cities, the final end of the war came in August of 1945, six years after it had begun. It was the costliest war in history, with at least 50 million people killed and whole countries destroyed.

The war was also a great political victory for King. He had weathered the conscription crisis, largely without recreating the deep divisions of 1917. The country remained relatively strong and united. And King had also cemented himself as a competent and capable wartime leader, who had managed to build Canada's place in the world and claim a rightful stake in the Allied victory—this despite King's prewar denial of Jewish refugees into Canada, his controversial decisions around conscription, and his government's treatment of Japanese Canadians in BC.

King's victory was further cemented in the election results of 1945. Although the Liberals won a much smaller majority (just 125 out of 245 seats with 53 of 65 in Quebec), they did manage to stay in power. This win compared favourably with the fate of wartime leader Winston Churchill in Great Britain, where the Conservative titan was defeated at the polls.

All in all, the Canadian contribution to the war had been immense. Over one million Canadians had served full time in the armed forces; out of this number, 45,000 women signed on to serve in the Canadian military, some in the Canadian Women's Army Corps (CWACS). By the end of the war, they earned only four-fifths of their male counterparts' pay rates at similar ranks. By the war's end, Canada had a massive army, air force, and navy, and Canada had distinguished itself on a number of fronts in the war.

Meyer's Fate

In the two months after he ordered the execution of the Canadians in the Abbaye d'Ardenne, Kurt Meyer's division was nearly annihilated, as the Canadians, British, and Americans pressed into France. He was captured by Belgian partisans and, in September 1945, handed over to the Americans.

In December 1945, Meyer was tried for war crimes and found guilty of "inciting and counselling" his troops to deny quarter to Allied troops and "responsible for the killing of prisoners of war" in the deaths of the prisoners shot in the abbey's garden. Sentenced to death by the trial judge, he was reprieved by a Canadian general who determined that a death sentence was too harsh a penalty for Meyer's crime. Meyer's sentence was commuted to life imprisonment. He finally served only nine years, partly at Dorchester Penitentiary in New Brunswick and partly at a British military prison in Germany. He returned to civilian life in Germany in 1954, after which he wrote a bestselling memoir and eventually became a beer salesman. He died in 1961, and his funeral was attended by thousands of Germans.

Meyer's story was one that fascinated, repelled, and angered Canadians, from his trial to his imprisonment and eventual release. Meyer himself was an extremely polarizing figure. He clearly was an excellent soldier and a German hero for his many exploits in various campaigns during the war; yet his actions, or at least those of his troops, at the Abbaye d'Ardenne were horrific and dishonourable. During his trial and thereafter he was, at times, remorseful, yet, at other times, he claimed the innocence of his troops. Because of the murders and the publicity surrounding his trial (the first major Canadian war crimes trial), Meyer became a household name in Canada. His eventual release and his return to Germany infuriated many Canadians, who saw no justice in the case. To this day, Meyer remains a controversial figure in Canada; in Germany, he is remembered as a war hero.

Was justice served in the case of Kurt Meyer?

Further Reading

Balzer, Timothy. "'In Case the Raid Is Unsuccessful': Selling Dieppe to Canadians." *Canadian Historical Review* 87, no. 2 (September 2006): 409–30.

Caccia, Ivana. *Managing the Canadian Mosaic in Wartime: Shaping Citizenship Policy, 1939–1945.* Montreal: McGill-Queen's University Press, 2010.

Fahrni, Magda. "The Romance of Reunion: Montreal, 1944–9." *Journal of the Canadian Historical Association* 9 (1998): 187–208.

Keshen, Jeffrey A. *Saints, Sinners, and Soldiers: Canada's Second World War.* Vancouver: UBC Press, 2007.

Kikkert, Peter. "Kurt Meyer and Canadian Memory." *Canadian Military History* 21, no. 2 (Spring 2012): 33–44.

Lackenbauer, Whitney P., and Chris M.V. Madsen. *Kurt Meyer on Trial: A Documentary Record.* Kingston: Canadian Defence Academy Press, 2007.

Ward, W. Peter. "British Columbia and the Japanese Evacuation." *Canadian Historical Review* 57, no. 3 (September 1976): 289–308. http://dx.doi.org/10.3138/CHR-057-03-02.

ACTIVE HISTORY: ORAL HISTORY AND ITS CHALLENGES

- Visit the website of the Canadian Memory Project, at http://www.thememoryproject.com/. Examine the site's collections, including the images, and pay particular attention to the audio testimonials of Canadian Second World War veterans.

- After you study a few of these testimonials closely, what insights can you gain about the experiences of these men and women during the war? What is most striking or most interesting to you in the testimonials?

- What are the benefits of using such sources? What are the challenges? How do oral histories differ from other kinds of sources, such as diaries, newspapers, government records, or other text-based primary sources?

PART THREE

POSTWAR CANADA— PEACEABLE, PROSPEROUS, YET DEADLY

Canada's image as an oasis of placidity largely stems from its emergence as a prosperous and peaceful "middle power" in the post-1945 world. And, to a large degree, Canada's peacefulness is obviously true: compared to many nations in the world, Canada has been blessed with a relatively safe, sometimes boring, and mainly un-newsworthy existence. This vision of Canada is certainly true for outside observers, who see the country as a safe haven, one that has attracted millions of immigrants from war-torn, impoverished, and unstable countries around the globe for decades.

And yet, if one digs a little deeper, scratches the surface of Canada a little harder, violent death is still very present. Thankfully, the scale of this death is relatively minor in scope, though it remains nonetheless tragic, always sad, and painfully symbolic. On a host of social, political, cultural, and economic issues, the deaths that have marked postwar Canada—the many murders, executions, assassinations, and suicides—are profoundly important as indicators of change, of grievance, of conflict, and of ongoing debate. Violent and public, death still stalks the land and its peoples, and it remains a powerful indicator of the sometimes stark, harsh, and brutal realities of an otherwise peaceable kingdom.

MURDEROUS MOMENT
JOHN DICK, MURDERED, HAMILTON, 1946

Wars at Home

As Canadians returned to peacetime, many expected that an end to war would bring domestic bliss; Canadians were homeward bound, tired of decades of depression and war. Less than a year after the war was declared officially over, however, Canadians were shocked by one of the most notorious murder cases in Canadian history. The "torso case," as it came to be known, quickly shattered the image of tranquil domesticity that Canadians had imagined for themselves. Behind closed doors, the reality of a postwar life of wedded bliss was not always as it seemed.

In March 1946, a group of young boys were playing on the Niagara Escarpment in Hamilton, Ontario. The escarpment is a hilly landmass that borders and partially surrounds the city. On this spring day, one of the boys thought he spotted the carcass of a pig partially buried on the hill. When he and his friends surrounded the body, they were horrified to discover that, instead of a dead pig, they had found the headless, armless, and legless torso of a man.

Police determined that the torso was all that remained of John Dick, a conductor for the Hamilton Street Railway. Dick's beautiful wife, 26-year-old Evelyn, quickly came under suspicion. The couple had separated only a few months after their October 1945 wedding, following allegations of Evelyn's infidelity. When questioned, Evelyn claimed that a man whom she described as an "Italian hit man" had recently appeared at her door, saying that he was going to "get John" for supposedly cheating with his wife. A few days later, it was discovered that Evelyn had borrowed a neighbour's car and returned it with bloodstains in the back seat; Evelyn claimed that she had cut herself, that the

blood was hers, and that she knew nothing of John's death.

Understandably, Evelyn's trial was one of the most salacious and scandalous in Canadian history. The press coverage was intense and even drew interest from the United States; hundreds of people lined up every day at the Hamilton courthouse to get seats to the trial. As the trial proceeded, across Hamilton a schoolyard song quickly spread:

You cut off his legs . . .
You cut off his arms . . .
You cut off his head . . .
How could you Mrs. Dick?
How could you Mrs. Dick?

Raised by an abusive, drunken father, who had his own difficulties with the law, and by an equally abusive mother, Evelyn grew into an ambitious social climber, and she was apparently quite manipulative herself. By the time she married John, thinking he could provide for her, she had already had two children with other men. One baby had been stillborn.

As her murder trial was still unfolding, the police had cause to search the Dick home. They came upon another grisly finding. In the upstairs attic, sealed in a suitcase of concrete, were the remains of Evelyn's infant son. The discovery made Dick's case even more notorious, and speculation was rife over not just John's murder but the murder of the child. Could Evelyn have really done such a terrifying act? Perhaps she was taking the fall for her father, who had his own violent tendencies?

At trial, Evelyn was found guilty and sentenced to death. Because of some procedural problems with evidence, she was able to get a new trial. In the end, famous lawyer J.J. Robinette was able to overturn her conviction for John's murder, but not for the slaying of baby Peter. Evelyn Dick served 11 years in prison for the heinous crime.

Evelyn Dick was released from Kingston Penitentiary in 1958. The head of the National Parole Board, Alex Edmison, believed that, despite the crimes she was convicted of committing, she deserved a fresh start. No one knows what happened to her, as she disappeared from public view. Author Brian Vallée, who followed her story, claimed in his 2001 book *Torso Murder: The Untold Story of Evelyn Dick* that she married a wealthy man and moved to Western Canada. Likely, she lived many decades under an assumed name, her past hidden from those who knew her as someone else, but Canadians remained shocked and fascinated by the case, decades after the trials. Since the murders, there have been numerous books, films, and documentaries on the case.

The gruesome story of the "torso" murder and the case against Evelyn Dick shockingly reminded Canadians that, despite their emerging pretentions of a suburban existence, evil could lurk behind every white-picket fence.

CHAPTER TWELVE

DEATH BY CAR: 2,921 CANADIANS KILLED IN MOTOR VEHICLE ACCIDENTS, 1953

CARS, CONSUMPTION, AND POSTWAR CANADIAN SOCIETY

Just about everybody drives. For most ordinary Canadians, getting a driver's licence is something of a rite of passage, a coming of age. And even if she or he doesn't drive, the average Canadian has probably spent a fair bit of his or her life sitting in a car. Perhaps a few of us have even been in a car accident.

Tragically, a leading cause of death today for Canadians, especially for young people, is the motor vehicle accident. Thousands of Canadians are killed in car crashes every year. Perhaps surprisingly, in the early post–Second World War period, Canadians were killed in car accidents at an alarmingly higher rate than they are today. In fact, more Canadians were killed in an average year in the 1950s than in the 2000s.

Let's take a typical year in the 1950s. In 1953, 2,921 Canadians were killed in car accidents. Canada's population at the time was eight million. (More than 50 years later, in 2009, the population of Canada had nearly quadrupled to 34 million, yet the total number of Canadians killed in car accidents had actually *decreased* to 2,209). Car accidents were so bad that by the mid-1960s, 5,000 Canadians a year were being killed on the roads. It's horrifying to think about, but, in the three decades after 1945, more Canadians died in road accidents than were killed in the First World War.

The people who died in these car accidents weren't murdered, but they were killed. Was someone or something to blame for all this carnage on the roads? At the time, automakers and governments largely blamed these deaths upon human error, though cars were often too powerful, lacked simple features such as seat belts and crash-proof glass, and were generally designed with styling ahead of safety. In an effort to distract Canadians, car makers and politicians focused upon driver education, which stressed the "manliness" of the safe vehicle operator. This attitude was in keeping with the gendered ethos of the period. Safety features and less powerful automobiles could have cut the number of road casualties, but this type of regulation and awareness was still emerging and did not become central to Canadians' car concerns until the end of the 1960s.

The deaths of over 100,000 people killed on Canadian roads between 1945 and 1975 tell us two important things about Canadian society at this time. First, it points to the incredible growth of car culture in society and the willingness of Canadians to tolerate car-related death in order to keep this car culture. Canadians loved their cars and wouldn't give them up, no matter the number of deaths. Cars, consumerism, and suburbs are directly linked to these deaths, yet often it is difficult for us to see this connection.

Second, it lets us see into *the nature* of this new postwar suburban ideal, one built around cars, consumerism, and suburbanization. The (North) American Dream that we are very familiar with became the new norm. This ideal, this image—one of family, the "family car," traditional gender roles, prosperity, security, and a home in the suburbs—is burned into our collective memory as a standard image of the era. It was, by and large, a profoundly conservative period, when traditional gender roles became very rigid, a time in which any deviation from this ideal (largely unrealistic for many people) was seen as abnormal. But the reality is that it was also an age that belied the image. Like the tragic number of deaths on the road, persistent poverty, conflict over the nature of work and family, and insecurity about the direction of the development of Canadian society challenged the image of a safe, middle-class, and suburban existence.

Baby Boom: Population Growth and Family in the 1950s and 1960s

The number of deaths on Canadian roads was in no small part a consequence of the amazing growth in population in the 1950s and 1960s. Between 1941 and 1962 Canada's population increased from 11.5 million to 18.5 million, an incredible 60 per cent. Two main factors fuelled this population growth.

On the one hand, there was the "baby boom." Canadians had babies, and more babies, and more babies after the war. In the immediate post-1945 period, a number of factors drove this fertility growth: veterans returning from the war, couples who had put off family during the Great Depression and the Second World War, newfound economic security (as we shall see in a moment), and a desire to return to a sense of rootedness after years of disruption. For all of these reasons, the mid-1940s to mid-1960s saw a huge increase in family fertility. In 1945 Canadians had 300,000 babies; in 1947, 372,000 babies; and in 1952,

400,000 babies. After that, the number of babies being born annually in Canada did not drop below 400,000 until 1966.

This immense baby boom had a huge impact on Canadian society. First, Canada became a very child-centred world; if you did not have kids, you were considered "strange" or "abnormal." Having so many children in Canadian homes dramatically changed outlooks on housing and schooling and our notions of childhood—in ways that are familiar to those who reached adulthood in the twentieth century. Parenting, child activities, and child-centred books became hugely popular in this period. From Dr. Spock's parenting books to Dr. Seuss's children's books, child-focused products became a central feature of life for a huge number of Canadians.

Second, the baby boom obviously resulted in a focus on the family. Family became a mantra of the 1950s. With so many children, so many young families, there was a return to religious values, and church attendance increased. There was a new emphasis on so-called family values. This more family-centred and traditional ideal can be seen in the styles and conformity of the 1950s, made familiar through movies and television, from *Leave It to Beaver* to *Father Knows Best*. These sentimentalized representations of the family had a huge impact upon gender roles. The image of the nuclear family—that is, of a father and mother with children, with women at home as housewives and mothers while fathers worked—became ensconced as the norm in the public imagination.

Women became "homeward bound," a return to domesticity that marked a shift away from the gender-bending changes of the Second World War; the "bomb girls" and "Rosie the Riveter" of the war were no more. In the 1950s, women and men were expected to fulfill well-defined roles with little flexibility. The power of this family-focused and child-centred image cannot be underestimated. The incredible stress on the importance of achieving a traditional family and fulfilling prescribed gender roles eventually resulted in a generational backlash in the 1960s.

The other major factor driving population growth was an immigration boom. Between 1946 and 1971, more than 3.5 million immigrants came to Canada. At first, there was a trickle of war brides (mostly British women who had married Canadian soldiers stationed in Great Britain during the war) and of displaced persons, called "DPs" (essentially refugees from war-torn Europe). But the real immigration boom started around 1951. Unlike the depression-ravaged 1930s, during which the average immigration was about 16,000 people a year, the 1950s saw an average annual immigration of close to 155,000! In fact, during the 1950s and 1960s, annual numbers rivalled those of the early Laurier period (except for 1961–62, where numbers dipped owing to a slowdown in the economy).

Much of this immigration was driven by the needs of the economy, but Canadian policymakers were still worried about Canada's "cultural character" in the postwar period. In 1947, Mackenzie King, who was prime minister until 1948, stated that although Canada would continue to seek immigrants to increase population, these numbers would be related to the "absorptive capacity" of the economy.[1]

This was code that Canada would continue to be selective about whom the country let in. Preference was still given to immigrants from Western Europe and the British Commonwealth, so quite a few British, Dutch, and German immigrants came to Canada in this period. The Canadian immigration policy was still race based, and still discriminatory. Of course, there were some immigrants that Canada desired to meet specific labour-market needs. For example, beginning in the 1950s, many West Indian women were admitted for domestic service, but this concession was seen as exceptional, as these immigrants were considered the only ones "suitable" for this kind of work.

Regardless of policy preferences, many new immigrants in this period were from central and southern Europe, primarily from countries such as Greece, Portugal, and Italy. For example, by the late 1950s, Italians made up one-fifth of immigrants, up from one-twentieth in the late 1940s. And, though British immigrants were still a significant group, there was a relative decline of new Canadians from Britain. Obviously, the impact of these immigrants was not just on population growth. The newcomers changed the texture and makeup of the country dramatically. They tended to settle in urban centres in concentrated areas. For example, Italians settled in Toronto in a corridor running from the west to the north of the city, in College Street West (since renamed "Little Italy"), St. Clair West, and later Downsview and, even later, Woodbridge. Here they built a rich community life with shops, restaurants, newspapers, churches, and radio stations.

Again, these immigrant and urban communities clash with the notion of the "ideal family" in the postwar period, which was largely white, English speaking, and suburban. But it is important to point out now that population growth in this period did not simply reflect the long-held images attached to the 1950s.

Economic Boom and Consumerism

Immense population growth was one of the key factors that fuelled the postwar economic boom, which effectively lasted, aside from a few dips, until the 1970s. This was the longest period of economic growth in North American history. The economic boom was helped along by a number of other elements: the economic security provided by the welfare state and Keynesian policies such as the "baby bonus"; pent up consumer demand generated by years of financial insecurity during the Depression and by wartime saving, skimping, and being denied consumer goods (Canadians also had millions of dollars in savings from their wartime work); and the low interest rates during the postwar period, which allowed for easy borrowing and helped to facilitate an expanding economy. Finally, another

---

1   Paul R. Magocsi, "Immigration Policy," *Encyclopedia of Canada's Peoples* (Toronto: University of Toronto Press, 1999), 706.

factor that played a key role in this sustained economic boom was what has been called the postwar labour compromise.

During the 1930s and 1940s, organized labour had become an important aspect of the industrial landscape in Canada. After some bitter battles, unions had achieved recognition in key industries such as steel and automobile manufacturing. After the war, business and government leaders wondered whether labour organizations would become more radical and push for more socialistic solutions to the problems of capitalism—a direction that politicians and employers had witnessed in the 1930s. However, this did not happen. In this conservative era, organized labour, led by the powerful United Auto Workers (UAW), instead turned away from the confrontational tactics of the 1940s and embraced compromise. Higher wages and economic security led to labour peace, by and large, and union membership grew dramatically to encompass nearly one-third of Canadian workers in the 1950s.

As a result, wages increased and the economy grew spectacularly. Overall, the size of the Canadian economy grew from $11.8 billion in 1945 to $38.3 billion by 1960. The workforce increased too, as there was growth in manufacturing, service industries, and construction. Of course, though Canadians lagged somewhat behind their American counterparts, the period was undoubtedly prosperous for the average Canadian. For example, average income doubled between 1946 and the early 1970s.

Ultimately, the booming economy and labour peace signified a massive redistribution of wealth to blue- and white-collar workers and created a new middle class in both Canada and the United States. The key aspect of this new class was not only the growth of its wealth, which was immense, but the similarity of its members' consumption and lifestyle. Along with their matching appetites and tastes in housing, their consumption of items such as cars, TVs, and appliances came to define members of this class and generation more so than at other points in history. This newfound consumerism is something that we, too, can understand; today, in some ways, we exist more as consumers than as citizens.

The most obvious and desired consumer item, and the one that came to define the North American ideal in the 1950s, was the automobile. In the years after the war, Canadians bought cars on an unprecedented scale. In 1941, there was 1 car for every 10 Canadians. By 1971, there was 1 car for every 2.4 Canadians. Put a different way, 36 per cent of households had a car in 1941, 50 per cent had one in 1954, and 78 per cent had one in 1971. In fact, between 1945 and 1973, the Canadian population increased 83 per cent, yet the number of cars increased 577 per cent! As the Canadian Automobile Association proudly declared in 1954, "the modern car is a part of the Canadian way of life with Canadians convinced that owning a motor vehicle is a basic right."[2] Many Canadians would probably agree with that statement.

---

2 "Minister of Finance Asked by C.A.A. to Reduce Federal Excise Taxes on New Cars, Parts, Tires," *Canadian Motorist* (March 1954): 53.

The second great consumer item of this era was, of course, the television. Like the automobile, it is difficult to imagine a world without television. But, until the 1950s, television was an exotic item. During that decade, however, TV became increasingly accessible. In 1952, a TV cost $400, which was about 20 per cent of the average annual income. By 1956, a TV cost under $200. As a result, by the mid-1950s, a majority of southern Ontario families had televisions, and a majority of people on the Prairies had TV by the late 1950s. Along with cars and TVs, Canadians snapped up a host of consumer goods, from kitchen and household appliances to recreational vehicles to children's toys such as Barbies, hula hoops, and Davy Crockett hats. Canadian consumerism, just like love of cars, was a shared North American experience.

All of these goods would be kept in the spanking new homes that came to define the Canadian landscape in the 1950s, as the consumer and demographic booms of the period came together in suburban development. The car was essential in the creation of the suburban boom. It allowed space and distance to be

Figure 12.1 *Suburban Dreams: York Downs Drive, Downsview Subdivision, 1950s*

Source: City of Toronto Archives, Fonds 1257, Series 1057, Item 82. Reprinted by permission of the City of Toronto Archives

covered in short periods, so people could live outside of and separate from the city. One also needed a car to transport young and growing families. At the same time, one of the most visible aspects of Canada's newfound economic wealth could be seen in the area of housing.

Nothing conjures the image of the 1950s in popular culture better than a picture of suburban bungalows and happy families. In 1948, only about a third of Canadians could afford a home; by 1961, homes were affordable to about 60 per cent of Canadians. It helped, too, that the federal government encouraged home ownership through the Canadian Mortgage and Housing Corporation (CMHC). The CMHC was created in 1946 to guarantee mortgages for house buyers. The government also allowed banks into the mortgage industry for the first time, which further helped to spur suburban construction.

The desire and need for housing outside of the city that was created by all these people and all their cars meant the emergence of large corporate developers. Large-scale development replaced the small-scale nature of home building in Canada that had been the norm. For example, in the Toronto area, no firm built as many as 100 homes in 1955. Yet by 1970, 79 per cent of dwelling units were built by companies that constructed over 100 homes. The turning point for large-scale development was the suburb of Don Mills in Toronto, opened in 1953 as a single, corporate project. Don Mills really became the prototype of subsequent corporate suburbs wherein all the commercial buildings, schools, and houses were constructed by a single developer. It was also a turning point in the design of neighbourhoods: for the first time, streets took on curves (in an effort to break up the monotony of subdivisions) instead of a grid pattern.

Changing shopping patterns were another distinguishing factor of suburban living. After 1955, the suburbs developed their own commercial geography. For instance, fast-food restaurants, especially franchises that catered to cars with drive-ins and large parking lots, emerged across Canada in the late 1950s. By the 1960s, there were over 25 fast-food restaurant chains operating in Canada, most US owned or inspired. The first Canadian chain, Harvey's, started in Richmond Hill, Ontario, in 1959, and the early 1960s witnessed the creation of today's well-known and ubiquitous donut shops. In 1961, Dunkin' Donuts and Mister Donut opened, and, a year later, that exemplar of Canadian suburbanism and culture, Tim Horton's, was started in Scarborough, Ontario, although the first franchise began in Hamilton, Ontario, in 1964. The first Canadian McDonald's opened in Richmond, BC, in 1967.

Another example of this unique suburban shopping experience can be seen in the development of malls in the period. Strip malls and indoor malls were almost non-existent in the early 1950s but increased in number and significance after 1955. Initially, malls were fairly small, often one or two strips of stores, and the stores were usually accessed from the outdoors. Malls accounted for less than

2 per cent of retail sales in 1956 but had reached about 15 per cent by 1973. In the 1960s, huge indoor malls such as Yorkdale Shopping Center in Toronto, Fairview Mall in St. Catharines, the Capilano Mall in Vancouver, and Place Bourassa in Montreal were designed to reach out and draw customers from miles away. These places had huge parking lots and were often located near highways. Yorkdale, for instance, was the first really successful mega-mall precisely because it was located adjacent to the new Highway 401.

Highways, the site of so many fatalities in the 1950s and 1960s, were another essential element of the landscape of the period. The construction of roads became a central plank of governments, which tried to meet the demand for highways created by the swelling number of cars and suburban growth. In 1939, all municipalities in Canada spent $18.7 million on roads. By 1953, governments spent $105 million on road construction. The Ontario government built highways such as the Gardiner Expressway (1955–66), the Don Valley Parkway (1961–66), and the 401, which was completed from Windsor to the Quebec border in 1964. The federal government helped to finance the completion of the Trans-Canada Highway across the country, which opened officially in 1962. Highway construction did not just connect the suburb to the city; it also created a huge boom into northern recreational areas. By 1971, painlessly negotiated highways and well-designed cars meant that Calgarians could easily drive to Banff and Lake Louise, Montrealers and Ottawans to the Eastern Townships and the Laurentians, and Torontonians to Muskoka and the Kawarthas. These less-populated areas became the recreational hinterlands of the big cities.

Myths and Realities

At the centre of suburban car culture was the notion of the traditional family of the 1950s, one that enjoyed domestic bliss, preserved strong and "traditional" gender roles within a "perfect" white-picket-fence nuclear family, and emphasized consumerism and conformity. These traditional gender roles did not include the reality of homosexuality, working women, or Canadians whose ethnicity was other than the norm—visible minorities and new immigrants, for example.

The Canadian reality clashed with this 1950s' ideal. For instance, nearly a fifth of women were in the workforce in this period, which questions the notion of the "stay at home" mother. There was a reality of women at work, but the ideal was very difficult to overcome, even if the growth of women at work increased dramatically during this period. In 1941, married women equalled 12.7 per cent of all females in paid employment, but, by 1961, they made up 49.8 per cent of women at work. Though women worked, they still faced discrimination. Women's average incomes were slightly more than half of those of men during this period, and women were regularly fired if they became pregnant.

At the same time, the huge numbers of recent immigrants in the 1950s reflected a quickly changing Canada, one that was much more ethnically, linguistically, and racially diverse. These new arrivals, who mostly gravitated to cities such as Halifax, Montreal, Toronto, and Vancouver, did not easily conform to any suburban ideal. Nor did Canada's aboriginal population, whose existence seemed a world away from the strip malls and conspicuous consumption of some North Americanized dream.

Moreover, not everyone was thrilled with the suburban development that had come to personify the "ideal" family situation. Many experts and elite observers bemoaned the standardization of housing, which they saw as symbolizing the standardization of life: "We found the suburbs were just one big blob of conformity," wrote one suburban "escapee" in *Maclean's* magazine in 1956, "there was such an aggressive, calculated spirit of friendliness, it was almost nauseating."[3]

Another criticism of 1950s' life was that its conformity with US tastes was an attack on a distinctly Canadian way of life, especially in terms of the culture. The 1951 Royal Commission on National Development in the Arts, Letters and Sciences (the Massey Commission) argued for more government support of Canadian culture. This commission also expressed elitist fears regarding the effects of mass culture on the population, wherein many Canadian elites feared Americanization and mass culture.

Another perhaps more obvious reality of this period was that, for all its emphasis on prosperity, wealth was unevenly distributed, and there remained many areas of the country where economic hardship persisted. Despite the dreams of ordinary Canadians and the rhetoric of marketers, the 1950s' ideal was limited by class. Some unionized blue-collar workers did well economically, such as autoworkers in places such as Windsor, Oakville, and Oshawa, but unions represented only about one third of the workforce at their postwar peak. Moreover, the auto industry was basically a southern Ontario phenomenon.

Across the country, levels of income and employment and, therefore, consumption varied. Thus, many Canadians remained poor in the midst of this growth. Some rural and isolated farming and fishing communities remained in terrible poverty throughout this period. In some regions, rural electrification was not achieved until the 1950s! At the same time, governments moved to clear "slums" in cities and, usually, to provide better housing, homes that fit the developing car culture and society's emphasis on middle-class suburban living. Africville, a largely poor black area in Halifax that was bulldozed as part of a public "renewal" project in the 1960s, is a controversial example of this.

Finally, despite all the supposed economic security and domestic bliss, this was a period defined by fear. Not the fear caused by the carnage on the roads: no, Canadians were quite willing to accept the risks that came along with mass

---

3   H. Garner, "You Can Take the Suburbs, I Don't Want Them," *Maclean's* 60, no. 30 (November 10, 1956): 71–75.

automobility. Fear came in the form of Cold War dread over Communist threats (both real and perceived) and atomic annihilation. Accusations that one was a Communist were far more damaging than any real fear of car-culture death. By the mid-1950s, Canadians had replaced the fears of the wartime and of the Great Depression with a new type of ideological fear.

Further Reading

Dummitt, Christopher. "Finding a Place for Father: Selling the Barbeque in Postwar Canada." *Journal of the Canadian Historical Association* 9, no. 1 (1998): 209–23. http://dx.doi.org/10.7202/030498ar.

Harris, Richard. *Creeping Conformity: How Canada Became Suburban, 1900–1960.* Toronto: University of Toronto Press, 2004.

Parr, Joy. "What Makes Washday Less Blue? Gender, Nation and Technology Choice in Postwar Canada." *Technology and Culture* 38, no. 1 (January 1997): 153–86. http://dx.doi.org/10.2307/3106787.

Penfold, Steve. "'Are We to Go Literally to the Hot Dogs?' Parking Lots, Drive-ins, and the Critique of Progress in Toronto's Suburbs, 1965–1975." *Urban History Review / Revue d'histoire urbaine* 33, no. 1 (2004): 8–23. http://dx.doi.org/10.7202/1015671ar.

Stevens, Peter A. "Cars and Cottages: The Automotive Transformation of Ontario's Summer Home Tradition." *Ontario History* 100 (Spring 2008): 26–56.

Strong-Boag, Veronica. "Home Dreams: Women and the Suburban Experiment in Canada, 1945–60." *Canadian Historical Review* 72, no. 4 (December 1991): 471–504. http://dx.doi.org/10.3138/CHR-072-04-03.

ACTIVE HISTORY: QUESTIONS TO CONSIDER

1. How have gender roles, both male and female, been shaped by suburbanization? How have technology, domestic chores, and work shaped postwar notions of traditional gender roles?

2. What factors accelerated Canada's suburbanization after 1945? What role did the state play in shaping the form of suburbanization achieved after the war, and how did that form differ from the one evident before 1939, if at all?

3. Consumerism and suburbanization seem to go hand in hand. How did patterns of consumption change after the Second World War?

4. Was Canada's form of suburbanization thoroughly American, or was it in any way unique from that which developed all across North America in this period?

5. Clearly, the suburban ideal fell short for many Canadians. How did the unevenness of postwar prosperity affect different groups of Canadians in this period?

MURDEROUS MOMENT
KING CAR KILLS THE STREET RAILWAY IN CANADA, CA. 1955

Cars Win the War on Transit

Despite the carnage on the roads that cars caused, there is no question that the postwar suburban era was a golden age for the automobile. Yet it also marked a death knell for the electric street railways that had dominated urban and suburban transit in the period up to the Second World War. In the late 1940s and 1950s, cities and towns across the country willingly gave themselves over almost entirely to the automobile. Electric street railways, a central feature of Canadian cities since the nineteenth century and an engine for urban and suburban growth, were no match for the "modernity" of the car, especially in a newly prosperous postwar Canada. As millions of Canadians purchased cars, moved to suburbs, and drove on brand new highways, the car's ascendance over the surface thoroughfares of the nation was seemingly irresistible. City planners and politicians, more concerned with road building for cars and buses, killed off their public streetcar systems in favour of infrastructure for private cars.

All across the country, and often with the enthusiastic support of citizens, municipalities tore up street railway tracks to make way for the car. The London, Ontario, street railway, begun in 1873, introduced electric streetcars in 1895, but it had already discontinued this service by 1940. After the war, the greatest demise of streetcars occurred. Victoria terminated its electric streetcar service in 1948, as did St. John's; Halifax in 1949; Calgary in 1950; Hamilton, Saskatoon, and Edmonton in 1951; and Montreal and Ottawa in 1959. Smaller cities, such as St. Catharines and Sudbury, Ontario, Nelson, British Columbia, also discontinued their streetcar services by 1950.

Only in Toronto did streetcar service survive. But, even there, it was a close call; by 1966, the city's two busiest streetcar lines were replaced by subways and the Toronto Transit Commission was committed to getting rid of the rest of the city's massive system. Officials thought that the demise of streetcar systems across North America would make it difficult to find the necessary machinery and parts. Eventually, a grassroots campaign to save the streetcars was successful, but this was a rare exception in a world that saw streetcars as an anachronism despite their low costs, low environmental impact, and high ridership.

As street railways were torn down, governments poured millions into building up highways and roads. Many Canadians welcomed the end of streetcars as a sign of progress, but others were saddened by their demise. More than any other event, the decimation of the electric street railways symbolized the victory of King Car over the Canadian landscape.

Winnipeg provides perhaps the best example of the impact of the car. The greatest Canadian boomtown of the nineteenth-century wheat economy, Winnipeg experienced incredible growth between the 1880s and the 1920s. Its first electric street railway commenced service in 1891, and, by the time of the Winnipeg General Strike in 1919, the city's system was extensive. So central was the streetcar to the city's civic life that, during the strike, the flipping of streetcars was a political act so heavy with symbolism that it sparked the events of "Bloody Saturday." Before and after the Winnipeg General Strike, busy main routes, such as Portage Avenue, made the Winnipeg system one of the most heavily used in the country.

The postwar "progress" and prosperity represented by the car brought about the

Figure 12.2 *A Melancholy Moment: Winnipeg's Last Streetcar, 1955*

Archives of Manitoba, N7588

end of the streetcars. In the 1950s, Winnipeg tore up its streetcar tracks, and the last streetcar made its final run in 1955. In the 1960s and 1970s, the city redeveloped its downtown and the main intersection of Portage and Main almost entirely to meet the needs of cars.

With the end of streetcars, the vibrant urban life that had characterized downtown Winnipeg slowly eroded as the city's suburbs flourished.

Cars became the preferred mode of transportation, and fewer and fewer people came downtown. When they did, the cityscape was now marked by parking lots and parking garages, and storefront shopping was quietly and slowly disappearing.

For many, the death of the streetcar was seen as a sign of progress, for others, a lament. But there was no doubt that the streetcar's demise had reshaped Canada's cityscapes in favour of the car.

CHAPTER THIRTEEN

HERBERT NORMAN, SUICIDE, CAIRO, EGYPT, 1957
COLD WAR DIPLOMACY, REPRESSION, AND RELATIONS WITH THE UNITED STATES

Perhaps it should not be surprising that Herbert Norman's life parallels, in so many ways, that of Canada's diplomatic evolution. He was, after all, a diplomat of the first class and a man whose educational, personal, and professional experiences intersected with and were affected by many of the most important international events of his time. Tragically, his death, a dramatic suicide that sparked headlines and international furore, is also a symbol of Canada's quickly evolving relations with the rest of the world, and especially with the United States, in a period marked by internationalism and Cold War conflict.

From Britain to America and Wartime Experiences

Egerton Herbert Norman's early life reflected Canada's shifting alliances and allegiances. Prior to the Second World War, Canada's international relations were changing. Although Canadians themselves remained loyal to Britain and its institutions, Canada's ties to the mother country were slowly loosening, and Canadians also grew increasingly attracted to the United States, especially its popular culture.

Norman's life reflected these changes, though with a dash of internationalism, too. Norman's parents were Methodist Christian missionaries who travelled the world spreading their Christian faith. Norman was born in 1909 in Japan while his parents were on a mission. As a result, he grew up in that country and spoke Japanese perfectly from an early age, one of the few

Westerners to do so. In his late teens, Norman came back to 1920s' Canada, enrolling at the University of Toronto.

An excellent student, Norman went to England to continue his studies at Cambridge University. Cambridge in the 1930s was a vibrant intellectual atmosphere, a place where debate and new ideas abounded. After all, the Great Depression had shaken Western democracies to their core and called into question the capitalist system. Like many other students at Cambridge in this period, Norman questioned capitalism and explored alternative approaches to economic governance.

From there, it was on to Harvard in the United States, where Norman earned his PhD in Japanese history. Going to the United States for education was something that more and more Canadians were starting to do; as the links to Great Britain loosened (and the opportunities of the United States beckoned), Canadians increasingly saw themselves as North Americans as opposed to British subjects.

After finishing his degree, he joined the growing Canadian civil service as a diplomat. Unsurprisingly, given his facility with Japanese, he was quickly posted to Japan in 1940 and was in Japan when the attack on the American military installation at Pearl Harbor brought the United States into the Second World War.

Norman's time in Japan was challenging. When he arrived in Japan, Canada was not at war with the Japanese, and Norman played a key role in keeping diplomatic channels between the West and Japan open during this difficult time. But when Japan attacked the United States in December 1941, Canada joined in declaring war against Japan. As a foreign diplomat of a country at war with Japan, he was interned by the Japanese government, but, eventually, he was sent back to Canada.

Skilled at diplomacy and languages, Norman was indispensable to the Allies, especially to the Americans after the United States took control of Japan in 1945. From there, Norman became a major player on the diplomatic scene. He acted as an advisor to Douglas MacArthur, the US general who was tasked with leading the Allied occupation of Japan following its defeat. And, after 1946, Norman returned to Tokyo to act as the head of the Canadian Mission to Occupied Japan.

Postwar Internationalism

Norman's high-ranking position as a key player on the international scene following the war reflected Canada's far different standing on the world stage after the Second World War than before it. This change was not surprising, as the Canadian military and economic wartime contributions had been tremendous. The Canadian military had performed very well and was a serious force to be reckoned with. The economy had produced billions in food and supplies for Allied countries, primarily Britain. Canadians, for example, won a place in 1943 on the important Combined Food Board created by the Allies.

Figure 13.1 *Herbert Norman's Body Returned to Canada by UN Plane, 1957*

Reprinted by permission of Topham Picturepoint, Torstar Syndication Services

Different, too, was that postwar Canada was an incredibly wealthy country, in both absolute and relative terms when compared to almost every other country in the world. Unlike most of Europe and Asia, Canada, like the United States, had emerged relatively unscathed from the war. Great Britain, a prewar economic power, had been bombed relentlessly. Factories, railways, bridges, dams, fields, and the entire infrastructure of most economies were destroyed while Canada's had been built up tremendously. Britain was economically destitute after the war, dependent on Canadian and American help.

Mackenzie King, who had dominated Canada's foreign policy, was also out of office by 1948. King still wielded considerable influence, but his vision of an isolationist Canada staying out of any foreign entanglements and keeping a low profile on the world stage was effectively dead. King understood this, and his successor, Quebec Liberal Louis St-Laurent, reflected the new engaged and international approach.

Finally, the Canadian position in the world was affected by the strong Canadian civil service. Canadian diplomats and civil servants working in the government and around the globe developed a reputation as being among the finest in the world. People like Norman, Hume Wrong, Escott Reid, and Lester B. Pearson all had an impact on the development of the postwar world.

As a result of these changes, Canada's international position was somewhat unique. Canada was not a major power, but not a minor player, either; it was a "middle power." At the root of Canada's middle-power status lay the "functional principle." The concept was devised by Norman's colleague, Hume Wrong, in 1942. It argued that a country's responsibilities and voice in decision making should be commensurate to its contribution. So, because Canada had provided so much food for the Allies during wartime, Canada should have a voice on the Combined Food Board. The same was true for other areas of Canadian contribution and expertise, such as nuclear energy and aviation.

Canadians also played an important role in creating new international institutions. The war's end created a new ethos in international relations, "internationalism," one opposed to prewar isolationism. At its core, internationalism stemmed from the belief that isolationism—the old League of Nations' breakdown and protectionism—had contributed to the Great Depression and the war. Postwar politicians, especially Americans, were at the forefront of this movement, at least initially.

Canadians pushed this movement, as well, and had their own reasons for supporting internationalism. The British Empire's end meant that Canada could no longer balance the American social, economic, and political pull against that of the UK, the "mother country." Many Canadian were concerned that, without Britain as a counterweight to the United States, Canada would be swallowed up by the giant to the south. In response, Canadians became active participants in building multilateral organizations that epitomized internationalism.

There were three main streams to postwar internationalism: political, economic, and military. Chief among the political multilateral institutions was the United Nations (UN). Even before war's end, Allied countries had congregated at San Francisco in 1945 to develop a new international organization designed to avoid repeating the horrors of the two world wars. Though the UN was largely the creation of the "great powers," Canadians played an important role. Diplomat Lester B. Pearson, who became prime minister in 1963, attended the San Francisco meeting. He epitomized the civil servant of this "golden age" of Canadian diplomacy, and has often been called an "architect" of the UN. Pearson was elected president of the UN General Assembly in 1952.

A second major stream of postwar internationalism was international economic organization. In 1944 and 1945, the United States and a number of countries, including Canada, created new agencies intended to avoid the prewar problems of protectionism and trade barriers. The International Monetary Fund (1945) and the World Bank (1944) were designed both to provide stability for the world's financial markets (as opposed to its trade system) by providing funds for countries under financial strain and to regulate fiscal policies, especially for developing countries.

Another significant institution was the General Agreement on Tariffs and Trade (GATT), which was meant to ensure that countries would work to reduce trade barriers and agree to rules to support these efforts. Canadians, dependent upon trade for their economic prosperity, became leaders at the GATT rounds of tariff negotiations. Dana Wilgress, a former Canadian deputy trade minister, was the GATT's first chairman. Wilgress personified Canadians' efforts at multilateral trade liberalization, just as Pearson came to represent Canada's place at the UN and Herbert Norman to signify Canada's key role in international diplomacy.

Cold War Complications and Communist Red Scares

All of these new postwar international organizations came under severe strain almost immediately because of the growing animosity between the United States and the Soviet Union (USSR), formerly wartime allies and the postwar world's only two superpowers. The United States was the West's greatest economic, cultural, and military power, whose system was based on free markets and democracy. The US government had poured billions into reconstructing Western Europe after the war to keep countries such as Italy and Greece from becoming Communist.

On the other side stood the Soviets, whose system was based on Karl Marx's Communism, which espoused state ownership for all aspects of the economy. After 1945, the Eastern European countries the Soviets had liberated during the war had become Communist, and also Soviet allies. A series of events illustrated that the two countries and their respective allies faced each other in a Cold War battle over ideology, technology, military might, and even way of life.

The first significant incident that exposed the Cold War rift occurred in Canada. In 1945 Igor Gouzenko, a clerk in the Soviet embassy in Ottawa, defected with documents that proved an extensive Soviet spy ring aimed at discovering military and technological secrets existed in Canada, the United States, and Great Britain.

However, Canadian civil authorities, shocked that their Soviet wartime ally could be part of such a scheme, initially refused to believe him, and it took Gouzenko 40 hours to find someone interested in his story.

Gouzenko's revelations caused a diplomatic earthquake. Government investigations uncovered the spy network. In Canada, 16 were charged and 10 convicted of espionage, including Montreal Communist MP Fred Rose. The UK government discovered that some of its citizens were implicated as well. Kim Philby, the British intelligence officer who handled the case, was later exposed as a double agent. He eventually escaped to the Soviet Union in 1963, living out his days as a Russian colonel. Philby had been at Cambridge in the 1930s, at the same time as Herbert Norman.

A second important event ushering in the Cold War was the victory in 1949 of the Communists in China. The "loss" of China was a major blow to the United States and its allies and generated the belief that, if China could "fall," any country was susceptible to Communist dogma. A third event was the explosion of a Soviet atomic bomb in a test in 1949. Now, the United States, the United Kingdom, and Canada were not the only countries with access to nuclear power or nuclear weapons. With the Soviets controlling their own bomb, many in the West grew fearful of the Soviet threat.

These events confirmed the Western powers' earlier decision to create a military alliance outside of the UN—a third element of postwar internationalism—to counter the Soviet threat. Again, Canadians were at the forefront in developing this multilateral institution. Canadian diplomat Escott Reid first argued during a speech at the 1947 Couchiching Conference in Ontario that "the peoples of the Western world want an international security organization with teeth . . . they do not need to amend the United Nations Charter in order to create such an organization. . . . They can create a regional security organization to which any state willing to accept the obligations of membership could belong."[1]

But creating such an organization was no easy thing. By 1949, the United States was threatening to relapse into isolationism, and Canadian diplomats were fearful that, without US support, any alliance would be useless. However, owing to the negotiating skills of Canadian diplomats Norman Robertson and Hume Wrong, talks led to the 1949 North Atlantic Treaty Organization (NATO), a collective security agreement: if one member nation were attacked, all member nations would respond.

Most Western European democracies joined, and, at Canada's insistence, freer trade and cultural exchange were mentioned. Yet NATO was primarily a military pact, a kind of UN-without-the-Soviets agreement, designed to counter the Russian threat in Europe and elsewhere. By 1951, Canada had troops in Europe as

---

1   J.L. Granatstein, *Canadian Foreign Policy Since 1945: Middle Power or Satellite?* (Toronto: Copp Clark, 1973), 55.

part of its NATO obligations, and King's notion that Parliament would decide when to commit soldiers, or that Canada could stay out of foreign engagements, was dead forever.

As a result of all these Cold War events, a Red Scare spread in the United States and Canada in the late 1940s and the 1950s. This is what ensnared Herbert Norman. In the United States, anti-Communist "witch hunts" were conducted by Joseph McCarthy, a Wisconsin senator who claimed to have lists of Soviet spies at work in the government and Hollywood. Hollywood was particularly targeted because of the popularity of movies, which were seen as able to carry propaganda. McCarthy also received information from Federal Bureau of Investigation (FBI) head J. Edgar Hoover. Hundreds of Americans were accused of spying for the Soviets: some were discredited, but many were "blacklisted" (denied employment) or lost their jobs for little cause. Along with Hollywood, McCarthy attacked "subversive" books and suspected Communist sympathizers in government agencies and even in the military.

Americans were not the only ones conducting witch hunts, however. Canada had its own share of junior McCarthys. As in the United States, the state police apparatus, the RCMP, played a key role in the ferreting out of alleged Communists in government. The RCMP worked with the FBI to track down suspected Communists. What emerged was a national insecurity state. According to many, these actions were justified: Canadians were shocked by the Gouzenko affair. The government expanded the RCMP security service to respond to public fears and, as well, to American concerns.

Primarily, this domestic intelligence involved investigating the Communist Party of Canada (CPC), which the RCMP had been doing since the party's founding in 1921. But, during the Great Depression, the CPC was very popular; for example, it held a massive rally at Toronto's Maple Leaf Gardens in 1934. Then, during the war, the Communist Soviet Union had been allied to Canada. However, with the onset of the Cold War, the CPC had again quickly fallen under suspicion. Yet the CPC did not have access to sensitive material and was not in a position to lead a revolution. Persecuting Reds, however, was good politics, as it was being done so effectively in the United States.

Along with investigating the CPC and Communists in government, the RCMP attempted to track down homosexuals holding positions of power, who were susceptible to Soviet blackmail, according to the Mounties. Taking its lead from a US Senate report, the federal government attempted to identify and exclude homosexuals from the civil service, the RCMP, and the military. To this end, the RCMP developed and used a so-called fruit machine, meant to measure biological responses to homoerotic pornography. Although the "fruit machine" never made it beyond the testing stage, by the 1960s, the RCMP had amassed 9,000 files on "suspect" Canadians, only 3,000 of whom were federal public employees.

Herbert Norman became one of those suspected of being a Communist. Although he was a rising star, some in the US security apparatus thought that he was a member of the Communist Party and that, during his time in England, he had become part of a large Communist spy network. Norman himself admitted that he had been interested in Communist ideas in the 1930s, but he felt these accusations were preposterous. In 1951, after Norman had been exonerated by a Canadian inquiry, the US government refused to pass along information to him, citing him as a security threat. Norman was made ambassador to New Zealand, in an effort to get him out of the way and appease the Americans.

But the rumours persisted. In the 1950s, McCarthyism in the United States was rampant and was affecting relations between Canada and her closest neighbour.

Norman, Canada, and the United States: Best Friends, and Enemies?

That Herbert Norman would be caught up in the web of Communist accusations reflects the perils of Canada's increasingly close relationship to the United States. During and after the war, the two countries had emerged with a newfound sense of partnership, one strengthened by the relative decline of the British imperial presence in Canadian considerations. The 1940 Ogdensburg Agreement created the Permanent Joint Board on Defence (PJBD), a pact between Mackenzie King and US President Franklin Roosevelt ensuring US support for Canada if the United Kingdom fell to the Nazis. The Hyde Park Declaration of 1941 continentalized North America for wartime production and supply and allowed Canada's participation in the US-British Lend-Lease agreement, thereby ensuring Canada's economic standing by allowing Britain to use borrowed US dollars to purchase goods from Canada.

After the war, the two countries had worked together on multilateral organizations, had fought in the 1950–53 Korean War to push back communists in that country, and had signed a series of military and economic agreements such as the 1957 North American Air Defence Agreement (NORAD) and the 1958 Defence Production Sharing Agreement (DPSA). This closeness held many advantages. The United States was the world's greatest economic power and biggest market, and Canada's proximity offered incredible economic, consumer, technological, and social benefits.

At the same time, this closeness also held out challenges. How could Canada retain its identity in the face of such an overwhelming cultural influence? Did being so closely tied to the United States threaten Canada's independence in economic, diplomatic, military, and political affairs? Was Canada just trading in one empire for another? Many Canadians worried about US control of the Canadian economy and about the closeness of the two countries' military and security establishment.

This close relationship had tragic consequences for Herbert Norman. In 1956, just a few years after the US government's renewed accusations, Norman was made ambassador to Egypt. He was sent there by his good friend Canadian External Affairs Minister Lester Pearson, who was trying to broker a cease-fire during the Suez Crisis. When Egypt took control of the French- and British-controlled Suez Canal, UK, French, and Israeli troops attacked, sparking an international crisis. Pearson formulated a peacekeeping plan that averted greater conflict, and, because of this plan, he was awarded the 1957 Nobel Peace Prize.

But during the tense weeks of the Crisis, accusations again surfaced from a US congressional subcommittee that Norman was a Communist. The only accusation that would have been worse, in that climate, was that he was a homosexual. Despite Pearson's strident protest to the US government that the accusations were unfounded, Norman was devastated. Hounded for years by an American security establishment that was bent on proving him a Communist, Herbert Norman could not take it anymore. On April 4, 1957, he climbed to the top of the Wadi el Nil Building in Cairo (one of the city's tallest buildings at the time), where the Swedish Embassy was located, and leaped to his death.

Norman left two suicide notes. They were written to his brother and sister:

Dear Howie:

I am overwhelmed by circumstances & have lived under illusions too long. I realize that Christianity is the only true way. Forgive me because things are not as bad as they appear. God knows they are terrible enough—But I have never betrayed my oath of secrecy—But guilt by association as now developed has crushed me. I have prayed God's forgiveness if it is not too late.

Love
Herbert

Dear Howie & Gwen:

You have been much in my thoughts. It is too complicated to explain in a note—Irene someday will discuss it with you—I am completely innocent but a victim to forces bent on my destruction—no I haven't a persecution complex.

I dearly love you both and your family God bless you and save you from any troubled or tragic mishap—one in the family is enough—you must have faith in my complete innocence—despite the filth of slander and speculation that will appear. My Christian faith—never strong enough I fear, has helped to sustain me in these last days. This letter includes in its embrace you and all the youngsters—I write to Grace too—Irene is an angel help her.

Love—warmest love—
Herbert[2]

The reaction to Norman's death was immediate and sharp. Canadians, and some Americans, were outraged at this tragedy. Pearson, who had defended Norman for years against the charges, was devastated to lose a friend and colleague. In his memoirs, he wrote that when he learned of the suicide, "My feelings never reached a lower point in my public career."[3] Many blamed an American security establishment that had gone overboard. Some felt that, despite a detailed 1951 RCMP investigation that had cleared Norman, there might be merit to these accusations and that, because Canada was America's Cold War partner, they needed to be addressed. To this day, there is still debate over the issue. In fact, it was not until 1991 that a government report fully cleared Herbert Norman of accusations that he was a Communist spy. Though there was never any direct confrontation between Canada and the Soviet Union during the long Cold War, it still claimed its victims. Ironically, Canada's close relations with the United States had more to do with Herbert Norman's death than any Cold War confrontation with the Soviets.

Further Reading

Churchill, David S. "An Ambiguous Welcome: Vietnam Draft Resistance, the Canadian State, and Cold War Containment." *Social History / Histoire Sociale* 37, no. 73 (2004): 1–26.

Hewitt, Steve. "'Information Believed True': RCMP Security Intelligence Activities on Canadian University Campuses and the Controversy Surrounding Them, 1961–71." *Canadian Historical Review* 81, no. 2 (June 2000): 191–229. http://dx.doi.org/10.3138/CHR.81.2.191.

Preston, Andrew. "Balancing War and Peace: Canadian Foreign Policy and the Vietnam War, 1961–1965." *Diplomatic History* 27, no. 1 (January 2003): 73–111. http://dx.doi.org/10.1111/1467-7709.00340.

Robinson, Daniel J., and David Kimmel. "The Queer Career of Homosexual Security Vetting in Cold War Canada." *Canadian Historical Review* 75, no. 3 (1994): 319–45. http://dx.doi.org/10.3138/CHR-075-03-01.

Whitaker, Reg. "Spies Who Might Have Been: Canada and the Myth of Cold War Counterintelligence." *Intelligence and National Security* 12, no. 4 (1997): 25–43. http://dx.doi.org/10.1080/02684529708432447.

---

2   The suicide notes can be found at the website *Death of a Diplomat: Herbert Norman and the Cold War*, at http://www.canadianmysteries.ca/sites/norman/murderbyslander/5576en.html.

3   Lester B. Pearson, *Memoirs* (London: V. Gollancz, 1973–1975), 3: 171.

ACTIVE HISTORY: UNDERSTANDING
THE CANADA–US RELATIONSHIP

During the Second World War and in the immediate postwar period, Canada became very close with the United States politically and economically and also culturally and socially, especially as the country's relationship with the United Kingdom faded. Indeed, by the 1950s, many people argued that Canada and the United States shared a "special relationship," a consequence of the two countries' close geography, their wartime cooperation, and their similar development as consumer societies within the context of the Cold War.

Even today, many Canadians think of their country's relationship with the United States as "special." Though, for Americans, this attitude is much less true today than it was in the 1950s. Instead, many Americans might consider as special their country's relationship with the United Kingdom or even Israel. At times in the last few decades, Americans have probably also seen the United States as having had a special relationship with Japan, Vietnam, or even Iraq. But probably not Canada.

Still, in the past, many Canadian observers and many average Canadians did think of the relationship between Canada and its closest neighbour as special. By the 1950s and 1960s, the word was often used by leaders of the two countries in describing the relationship. In 1947 Prime Minister Louis St-Laurent declared, "It is not customary in this country for us to think in terms of having a policy in regard to the United States. Like farmers whose lands have a common concession line, we think of ourselves as settling, from day to day, questions that arise between us, without dignifying the process by the word 'policy.'"[4]

In 1961, John F. Kennedy made this famous declaration in the Canadian House of Commons: "Geography has made us neighbours. History has made us friends. Economics has made us partners. And necessity has made us allies. Those whom nature hath so joined together, let no man put asunder. What unites us is far greater than what divides us."[5]

Prime Minister Lester Pearson responded in 1963: "By reason of geography alone, Canada and the United States are inevitably and inescapably in a special position in relation to each other. The special features of the physical relationship between our two countries are reinforced by other special ties which have developed and have brought us so close together in so many ways."[6]

By the 1960s, the "special relationship" rhetoric was a well-established cliché, reinforced by the sometimes very easy-going and productive relationship that existed between the two countries' leaders, for example, the close relations between St-Laurent and President Dwight Eisenhower in the 1950s and between Lester Pearson and Kennedy in the early 1960s.

Yet the period was marked by conflict as well as cooperation, which probably better describes the nature of the US–Canada relationship. Just consider the countries' interactions on the issue of nuclear weapons. In the 1950s, the United States expected that Canada, as an ally, would have nuclear weapons in its arsenal. But John Diefenbaker and the Conservatives were against the Canadian military having nuclear weapons. At the time, there was a great outcry against nuclear weapons. Because of this anti-nuclear feeling, Diefenbaker delayed deploying nuclear arms for Canada's forces, arguing that it was possible to do so in the event of war. So, instead of having nuclear arms in their US-supplied missiles, the Canadian soldiers replaced them with sandbags.

This infuriated the Americans and particularly Kennedy, who thought that the Canadians were shirking their duty. It also infuriated many Canadians,

---

4   "The Foundations of Canadian Policy in World Affairs," a speech delivered at the University of Toronto by Louis St-Laurent, January 13, 1947. Transcript can be found at Library and Archives Canada, Manuscript Group 30 E 144, A.D.P. Heeney Papers, Vol. 3, Canada–US Relations, 1960–1970.

5   Quoted in Peter C. Newman, *Renegade in Power: The Diefenbaker Years* (Toronto: McClelland and Stewart, 1973), 265.

6   Lester B. Pearson, "Moving Forward Together [from a speech at a meeting of Pilgrims of the United States, New York City, November 6, 1963]," *The Atlantic Community Quarterly* (Winter 1963): 495–500, see page 500.

who argued that Diefenbaker was not meeting NATO and NORAD commitments and that Canada should accept nuclear arms. This serious issue was a major cause of conflict between the two countries.

Diefenbaker's military differences with the United States, and particularly with Kennedy, came to a head during the 1962 Cuban Missile Crisis, the greatest showdown between the United States and the Soviets during the Cold War. In October 1962, US spy planes discovered the construction of nuclear missile sites on Cuba, being built by the Russians. Kennedy "quarantined" Cuba to prevent Soviet ships from landing on the island to complete the missile sites, and he placed US forces on high alert in preparation for an invasion. People really thought that a war was imminent. Because Canada was part of NORAD, and thus part of the North American defence systems being threatened by the Cuban missile sites, Americans expected Canada to be part of this high alert.

Instead, Diefenbaker delayed for three days, fearful that a Canadian alert would be "provocative" and escalate a terrible situation between the United States and the Soviets. Diefenbaker pushed for the United Nations to play a role and openly challenged whether the US state of alert was required. It was a direct challenge to Kennedy and American policy on Cuba. However, unknown to Diefenbaker and explicitly against his wishes, Canadian forces went on alert anyway; they were following NATO and NORAD protocol. When he found out afterwards, he was furious.

Eventually, the conflict was avoided when the Soviets agreed to remove the missiles in exchange for a US pledge not to invade Cuba and removal of US nuclear missiles from Turkey. Though the crisis was averted, the US administration had lost all trust in Diefenbaker and claimed that Canada did not really fulfill its requirements as a NORAD ally.

Diefenbaker remained unrepentant. In his memoirs he wrote, "We were to be accused by our critics of defaulting on our NORAD commitments. Nothing of the kind! It was the Kennedy government that rendered our joint arrangements ineffective. We were not a satellite state at the beck and call of an imperial master."[7]

Another famous conflict came over Vietnam in 1965. After being divided into two countries following the Second World War, in the late 1950s and early 1960s, the Communist North Vietnam began to attack the pro-US South Vietnam, with the help of an insurgency called the Vietcong. The United States propped up South Vietnam and refused to allow elections.

Starting in 1964, the American presence escalated, from "advising" to bombing to ground fighting, which US President Lyndon B. Johnson hoped would force North Vietnam to negotiate a truce. By the time the war ended in 1975 (South Vietnam fell after the US forces left), at least 2 million Vietnamese civilians had died and some 1.1 million combatants from North Vietnam. Almost 60,000 Americans were dead or missing.

Lester Pearson, who became prime minister in 1963, disagreed with Johnson's intention to "bomb North Vietnam to the conference table." The Canadians tried for a month to sway the White House, but this was unsuccessful. In April 1965, Pearson spoke at Temple University in Philadelphia, criticizing American strategy and violating protocol. Johnson later grabbed Pearson by the lapels and yelled at him for the Temple speech.

Yet despite these conflicts, significant cooperation also occurred, and things were nonetheless accomplished. In 1961, Diefenbaker signed the Columbia River Treaty, allowing for the building of dams and power generation along the international Columbia River. The treaty was ratified in 1964. The two countries were also both strong supporters of the General Agreement on Tariffs and Trade (GATT) and worked hard to lower international trade barriers and toward freer trade in the postwar period, especially in the 1960s. Another significant trade accomplishment was the 1965 Canada–US Auto Pact (the Canada-United States Automotive Products Agreement).

So, although many observers of the Canadian-American relationship in the postwar period might see it as being a special one, that relationship is better understood as one marked by ongoing conflict—and cooperation. This dynamic, too, explains why, during the difficulties over Herbert Norman, the two countries remained close allies, and friends.

---

7   John Diefenbaker, *One Canada: The Tumultuous Years, 1962–1967* (Toronto: MacMillan, 1977), 82.

MURDEROUS MOMENT
MARGUERITE "MADAME LE CORBEAU" PITRE, CONSPIRATOR IN THE 1949 CANADIAN PACIFIC FLIGHT 108 BOMBING, LAST WOMAN EXECUTED IN CANADA, MONTREAL, 1953

Modern Terrorism Comes to Canada

Marguerite Pitre has the distinction of being both the first and the last.

Hers was the first attack on a Canadian airliner, and it occurred at the dawn of commercial aircraft travel. As Canadians embraced their cars in the late 1940s and 1950s, another transportation revolution was going on: air travel was becoming as accessible, affordable, and commonplace as train travel had been for generations. In 1937, government-owned Trans-Canada Airlines was created, followed by privately owned Canadian Pacific Airlines in 1942. Both airlines served a number of domestic and international routes, and the number of Canadian passengers flown by airlines jumped from just above 800,000 in 1946 to over 2.8 million in 1953. In the 1960s, jets further revolutionized air travel, and, by 1966, the number of commercial passengers per year surpassed 9 million.

But in 1949, air travel was still relatively rare, and it was not uncommon for travellers to take out life insurance policies before embarking on a flight. This is what Albert Guay did for his wife, Rita, who was booked on a Canadian Pacific Airlines flight from Montreal to Baie-Comeau, northeast of Quebec City. Rita was aware that Albert had taken out the $10,000 policy on her, and she understood, given the uncertainty of early air travel. What Rita did not know was that Albert had also conspired to plant a bomb on board the plane, that he intended to kill her on the flight—and everyone else, in an effort to cover up the crime.

Albert had begun an affair with a young waitress. Trapped in his marriage—divorce was difficult if not impossible before the 1960s in conservative and Catholic Quebec—Albert had been facilitated in his affair by Marguerite Pitre, who rented a room to the two lovers. Pitre had also played a role in planting the bomb aboard the plane, a bomb built by her clockmaker brother Généreux Ruest.

On September 9, 1949, the plot worked almost perfectly for Guay. Twenty-three people, including Guay's wife and four crew members, were killed as the Douglass DC-3 aircraft blew up. But because of a slight delay in taking off, the plane's debris did not disappear into the St. Lawrence River as Guay had intended, but fell on land, providing the police with evidence of the bombing.

Soon, the police had tracked down Guay and Pitre's clock-making brother—and quickly unravelled the plot. Pitre, overcome by guilt, attempted to commit suicide. In hospital, she blurted out details of the conspiracy. When Pitre testified against Guay, always maintaining that she was an innocent who thought the package was a statue, Guay was quickly convicted. But before he was hanged, Guay turned on Pitre and Ruest, fingering them as key accomplices. Guay's last words before being executed foreshadowed the celebrity culture that permeates society today: "*Au moins, je meurs célèbre* [At least I die famous]."[8]

At her own sensational trial, covered by news media from across the continent, Pitre

---

8   Shirlee Smith Matheson, *Amazing Flights and Flyers* (Calgary: Frontenac House, 2010), 131.

continued to maintain her innocence despite the overwhelming evidence against her. Reporters took to calling her Madame le Corbeau—Madame Raven—because of the black clothing she always wore. Pitre's brother was hanged in 1951; she was convicted the same year and faced execution. On January 9, 1953, escorted by two nuns to the gallows, Pitre was hanged, the last of only 13 women to be executed in Canadian history. Pitre's execution illustrated the growing rarity of female executions, and executions in general, in postwar Canada.

The bombing of Flight 108 was not the first attack on a commercial aircraft, but it was the first in Canada and the most horrific mass murder to that time. In the still early days of air travel, it was a shocking act, which, nonetheless, reflected air travel's growing commonality. The intense coverage of the case also reflected the bombing's unprecedented nature, and the cross-border media scrutiny illustrated the growing closeness of Canadian and American culture and the ongoing emergence of media celebrity. Tragically, the incident sparked a copycat bombing and served as an inspiration for generations of bombers, including some in Canada who attacked defenceless airline jets and their passengers for their own political (and in the case of Guay, personal) motives.

CHAPTER FOURTEEN

RONALD TURPIN AND ARTHUR LUCAS, EXECUTED, TORONTO, 1962

THE DEATH PENALTY, DIEFENBAKER, PEARSON, AND SOCIAL CHANGE IN POSTWAR CANADA

The last two executions in Canadian history stemmed from thoroughly violent affairs. The first was the case of Ronald Turpin: On February 12, 1962, Turpin held up a Toronto Red Rooster restaurant, stealing $632.84. During his escape, he was pulled over by Metropolitan Toronto police officer Frederick Nash, ostensibly because Turpin's car had a broken taillight. Turpin, already wanted for a previous run-in with the law, was not going to be taken without a fight. He fatally shot Officer Nash in the chest, and then tried to make a run for it in Nash's police cruiser. But Turpin was quickly apprehended by police. Convicted of the murder of Constable Nash, Turpin was sentenced to die by hanging. Turpin appealed his case all the way to the Supreme Court of Canada, but his appeal was unanimously dismissed.

Also awaiting execution was Arthur Lucas, an American originally from Georgia. In November 1961, Lucas had travelled to Toronto from Detroit and killed Theland Carter, a drug dealer from Detroit who had made the underworld mistake of acting as a police informant. During Lucas' hit on Carter, Lucas also killed Carolyn Ann Newman, allegedly a prostitute who lived with Carter. Lucas, called a "professional hit man" during his trial, returned to Detroit after the killing, but was arrested the next day, extradited to Canada, and put on trial in Toronto, where he was convicted.

Both men were sentenced to hang on December 11, at 12:02 A.M., 1962. At the time, the government in power was that of Progressive Conservative John Diefenbaker. Diefenbaker was a lawyer. He had always been a strong believer in individual rights, but, as a conservative, he also believed that the law should take its course and that the full penalty of the law should be followed. Yet in the early 1960s, many Canadians were coming to see the death penalty as a barbaric form of state-sanctioned murder.

Since the time of John A. Macdonald, the federal cabinet and the prime minister had the power to commute executions (i.e., to change this punishment to one less severe). In December of 1962, the federal cabinet met to discuss the possibility of granting the two men clemency. Lucas's and Turpin's fates set off a firestorm of debate about the death penalty. Across the country, people argued and discussed the merits of capital punishment and whether these two men deserved to

Figure 14.1 *Ronald Turpin*

Reprinted by permission of the Toronto Star

die at the hands of the state for the crimes they had committed. The question of the death penalty was only one of many issues that reflected a period of intense social and political change in Canada.

Despite the pleas and protests of thousands of Canadians, Diefenbaker decided that the two men should hang. Diefenbaker was the last prime minister to approve an execution, and his decision marked the end of a long, gruesome era in Canadian criminal punishment. These would be the last of over 700 executions in Canada since 1867, including, of course, Patrick Whelan, Elizabeth Workman, Louis Riel, Wandering Spirit, and Filumena Lassandro. Diefenbaker's successors in office, Liberals Lester Pearson and Pierre Trudeau, effectively ended the practice.

Figure 14.2 *Arthur Lucas (right)*

On December 10, at Toronto's Don Jail, just hours before their execution, the two men ate the same last meal: steak, potatoes, vegetables, and pie. The meal was served on paper plates. That night, Lucas told the Salvation Army chaplain assigned to the two men, Cyril Everitt, "We is lucky . . . if we were on the street, I could be killed by a car and I wouldn't be ready to meet my maker." Both men could hear the protest going on 180 metres outside their cells, where protestors held signs that read "Public murder." As they walked toward the execution chamber, Turpin and Lucas were told they'd likely be the last people to hang in Canada. Turpin answered, "Some consolation."[1]

At 12:02 AM on December 11, 1962, Turpin and Lucas were taken to the execution chamber and hanged. The men were buried side by side in Toronto. No tombstone or plaque marked their graves.

Shortly before he died in 1986, Everitt told a reporter he had kept a secret about the execution for 24 years. The chaplain said Lucas's head was "nearly torn right off." The hangman had miscalculated the convict's weight. It was a barbaric endnote to a grisly story.

Social Changes: Diefenbaker and Pearson

The sharp debate over the 1962 executions of Turpin and Lucas was a microcosm of a broader conflict over social and political change that was fought from the 1950s to the 1960s. On one level, the death penalty debate represented the bitterness and battles between the two main leaders of the period, John Diefenbaker and Lester B. Pearson. Though from the same generation, the two men reflected a sea change in Canadian attitudes toward a host of social, political, and cultural policies. The two men fought four brutal election campaigns against one another, and their personal and political feuds reflected a wider battle over how postwar Canada should evolve. Diefenbaker, the last prime minister to allow an execution in Canada, represented an older, British, and socially and economically conservative vision of Canada.

Diefenbaker's rise was intimately tied to the long Liberal reign that had seen the "government party" in power from 1935 to 1957. In a period of consensus and conservatism, Mackenzie King's successor, Louis St-Laurent, reflected Liberal caution in terms of domestic policies. A successful Quebec City corporate lawyer, St-Laurent joined King's government in 1942 and in 1948, already 68 years old, became prime minister.

Liberal spin doctors portrayed him as "Uncle Louis," in an effort to keep people from noticing how old he was, and this portrayal suited the times. St-Laurent's era was largely uncontroversial and reflected a continuation of a model of slowly

---

1   Quoted in Robert J. Hoshowsky, *The Last to Die: Ronald Turpin, Arthur Lucas, and the End of Capital Punishment in Canada* (Toronto: Dundurn Press, 2007), 174–78.

building Canada. During his administration, Newfoundland entered Confederation in 1949, the Trans-Canada Highway was begun in 1949 (completed 1962), and the St. Lawrence Seaway project was begun in 1954. The Liberals also cautiously expanded government programs, such as creating the Canada Council in 1957, expanding old age pensions, and establishing the first provincial equalization payments, called for since the 1930s.

Eventually, despite economic prosperity, the long Liberal era ended for a number of reasons. First, the Liberals were old and tired. By the time they wheeled out St-Laurent for the 1957 election, he was 75 years old. More important, the government itself was old. The Liberals had not really renewed themselves with new ideas or new blood, and seemed to be content to offer the same old ideas, management, and people to the electorate.

Second, the Liberals had become arrogant. Their seemingly never-ending grip on power made them feel impervious to criticism, an arrogance personified by C.D. Howe. As the Second World War "Minister of Everything," Howe had been incredibly successful in mobilizing the Canadian economy, and had become very powerful along the way. But when the 1950–53 Korean War ended, people began to wonder why Howe still needed the 1951 Defence Production Act, granting him continued sweeping powers over economic development. These powers extended to the controversial decision to build a gas pipeline from Alberta to Ontario, which Howe uncaringly rammed through Parliament in 1956.

Third, the country was obviously in the mood for change. Unlike the sleepy Liberals, the new Progressive Conservative leader, John Diefenbaker, came out of the Prairies like a storm. He was a populist, a genuine man of the people, and contrasted with the seemingly very much older, distant, and technocratic St-Laurent.

"Dief the Chief" was a criminal lawyer from Saskatchewan, and a case study in political perseverance. He had lost elections in 1925, 1926, 1929, 1933, and 1938 for MP, legislative member, provincial party leader, and even mayor before finally being elected to the Commons in 1940. In 1956, after having already lost it twice, he finally won the leadership of the Progressive Conservative Party.

As a Westerner and descendant of German immigrants, Dief always considered himself an outsider. He was ardently nationalist and a strong believer in civil liberties. He had defended many accused individuals and knew how easy it was for rights to be trampled on. This outsider status was one of the reasons that he was such an effective campaigner: his style was so different from the laid-back one of St-Laurent. During the 1957 election campaign, Dief became famous across the land for his passionate and electric speaking style, and for his ability to connect with people.

For all of these reasons, Dief stormed onto the political stage in 1957, beating the Liberals, who simply couldn't believe they had lost. After getting a minority, Dief went back to the polls a year later and won the largest majority in Canadian history to that time. Dief came to power on a "One Canada" campaign that stressed the "Northern vision" of the country, which would build "roads to resources." Much of this domestic agenda, however, was unrealized.

Nevertheless, Diefenbaker introduced a number of important measures. Coming from Saskatchewan, he was particularly concerned about rural Canada and farmers. Thus, his government's 1961 Agricultural Rehabilitation and Development Act helped many farmers across Canada. He also found a new market in China for Canadian wheat, a policy that differentiated Canada's approach toward Communist China from that of the United States, which refused to trade with the Communists.

Reflecting his populist colours, Dief ensured that minorities and women were better represented in government. He appointed the first female federal cabinet minister, Ellen Fairclough, in 1957. He also appointed Canada's first aboriginal senator, James Gladstone, in 1958, and passed legislation in 1960 to have the franchise (the vote) extended to all First Nations people. Probably his proudest moment, in terms of civil liberties, was the passage of the 1960 Canadian Bill of Rights; though not enacted as part of the BNA Act, it laid down a guideline for Canadian rights that was finally enshrined in the Constitution Act of 1982.

But Dief's most memorable moments came on the international stage. Dief wanted to re-establish Canada's connection to Great Britain. He announced a plan to divert 15 per cent of exports to the United Kingdom, which was a surprise for both Canadian and British policymakers who had not been consulted on this shift. Also, it was an incredibly difficult thing to do, and it did not work, as legislating trade patterns had become increasingly more difficult in a more open world economy.

Diefenbaker also championed human rights outside of Canada. He supported the independence of many non-white Commonwealth countries in a period when Britain was shedding its colonial empire. His position was extremely helpful in smoothing this transition as countries such as Ghana (1957), Nigeria (1960), and Kenya (1963) all declared their independence. Diefenbaker was also an early critic of the racist apartheid regime in South Africa. His anti-apartheid statement in 1961 at the Commonwealth meeting contributed to the withdrawal of South Africa's request to be re-admitted to the Commonwealth.

Diefenbaker's most important activities on the international stage were with the United States. Dief had a contradictory and complex relationship with the United States, as all Canadian prime ministers do. Although he understood the importance of the US relationship to Canada and took steps to build it, such as creating the North American Air Defence Treaty (NORAD) in 1958, he also allowed personal difficulties and his anti-Americanism to cause problems for the country and himself. He clashed sharply with US President John F. Kennedy over Cuba and on whether Canada should have nuclear arms. Conflicted over the issue, the Diefenbaker government's handling of nuclear arms contributed to the downfall of the Tories and an election.

The Liberal win in 1963 was not resounding, but for a party that had come to see itself as the natural governing party of Canada, the return to power was gratifying. Liberal leader Lester B. "Mike" Pearson had enjoyed a very successful career as a civil servant and diplomat before entering electoral politics to become Canada's external affairs minister in 1948. In 1956, he brokered a peace deal between the opposing sides during the Suez Crisis, gaining him worldwide fame and a Nobel Peace Prize in 1957.

Pearson and the Liberals promised a much more activist state than Diefenbaker. They wanted to expand the role of government to build the welfare state and to reshape some of Canada's most important symbols. Although they were in a minority position, the Pearson Liberals passed a number of lasting and important social policy programs, including the 1964 Canada Student Loans Program that granted millions of dollars to help students attend university, the Canada Pension Plan (CPP) in 1965, and the 1966 Canada Assistance Plan (CAP) providing grants for child care, mothers allowances, health care for the needy, and financial support for welfare administration.

Perhaps most important, the Liberals worked to build on the ideas of Tommy Douglas and the New Democratic Party (NDP), and they successfully created and implemented the national medicare system. This universal health insurance program, delivered through provincial plans, came into force in 1968. Programs such as the Canada Pension Plan and medicare reshaped Canadians' relationship with their government, and they remain a foundation of Canadian social welfare into the twenty-first century.

The Flag Debate

The Pearson Liberals also committed to building symbols of Canadian nationhood. Pearson successfully oversaw Canada's centennial celebrations in 1967, including the wildly popular Expo 67 world's fair in Montreal as well as a host of national programs, from infrastructure projects that helped to build hockey rinks to cultural events. The Pearson government also created a national honours program, the Order of Canada, designed to recognize exceptional Canadians and their accomplishments.

Most contentiously, Pearson launched a campaign to design a new Canadian flag. Since the First World War, Canada had used the Red Ensign, a red flag with the Canadian coat of arms on one side and the British Union Jack in the top left corner. Pearson, who had spent a life in international diplomacy, thought that Canada needed a distinctive symbol, one that differed substantially from those of so many other British colonies. He also thought a distinctive Canadian flag would help French–English relations, as francophone Canadians might prefer a flag that had no reminders of Canada's colonial past.

When Pearson introduced the idea of a new flag at a Canadian Legion event in Winnipeg in May 1964, he was jeered and howled down by an angry group of veterans and created a storm of protest in Parliament and across the country.

Though Pearson himself was a veteran of the First World War (as was Diefenbaker), he did not share the views of many Canadians, who felt offended by the notion of changing a flag that Canadians had fought under during both World Wars.

Diefenbaker, leader of the Opposition at this point, led the charge against Pearson's idea of changing the flag: "Flags cannot be imposed, the sacred symbols of a people's hopes and aspirations, by the simple, capricious, personal choice of a Prime Minister of Canada."[2] He compared the new flag to a beer bottle label and issued a battle cry in Parliament, essentially declaring that he would fight to the bitter end to ensure that the flag would not be passed.

In 1964, Pearson appointed Liberal MP John Matheson to chair a special parliamentary committee to bring a proposal to Parliament. The committee proposed a flag of a single red maple leaf on a white background with two red banners on either side. The proposal did not, of course, settle the matter. After a parliamentary debate that lasted nearly six months, the government invoked closure to end debate and forced members of Parliament to vote on

Figure 14.3 *Flag Design Proposal by Group of Seven Member A. Y. Jackson, 1964*

Library and Archives Canada, 2908007

2   CBC, "Diefenbaker's Flag Crusade, 1964," *CBC Archives*, https://www.youtube.com/watch?v=6wmk6fvcJDA.

December 15, 1964: 163 voted for the Maple Leaf flag, 73 were opposed, and 23 abstained. Tellingly, no MP from Quebec voted against the new flag. Just before the vote, Diefenbaker admonished Pearson, "You have done more to divide Canada than any other Prime Minister."[3]

On February 15, 1965, the red maple leaf flew for the first time as Canada's official flag, and, despite some lingering opposition, an issue that had plagued governments for generations had been finally resolved. The flag, called the Maple Leaf, quickly became a powerful Canadian symbol, showing how much Canada had changed in a single generation. Diefenbaker, however, would go to his grave defending the old flag. When he died in 1979 and his body was laid in state in the Parliament buildings, draped over his casket was the Red Ensign, strategically placed over the partially showing Maple Leaf.

The Death Penalty

Let's finish off where we started: the last executions in Canada. Between 1957 and 1963, John Diefenbaker's government commuted 52 of 66 death sentences. That, combined with increasing public protests, indicated that the end of the death penalty was near. Change had come to Canada, in a very fundamental way. After the executions of Ronald Turpin and Arthur Lucas, Pearson put a moratorium on the death penalty. In 1968, Pierre Trudeau succeeded Pearson, and, with Trudeau's ascendance, it seemed that the decisions of Diefenbaker and his cabinet on executions were from a different age. Trudeau, like Pearson and most in the Liberal Party, was against the death penalty. So, although it remained on the books, there were no more executions in Canada.

By the 1970s, a number of high-profile cases had shown that, in some instances, innocent people would have been executed had the death penalty that was still on the books been applied. In the 1970s and 1980s, people such as Donald Marshall Jr., Guy Paul Morin, and David Milgaard were wrongfully convicted of murder and, eventually, released from prison. All of them could have been executed if Canada had practiced the death penalty.

One such prominent case was that of Steven Truscott. In 1959, 14-year-old Truscott was charged and convicted of the murder and rape of 12-year-old Lynne Harper. Truscott was the last person seen with Harper before her body was discovered; she had been strangled with her blouse. Tried as an adult, Truscott was scheduled to be executed in December 1959, but the execution was postponed. The case brought international attention and outrage against the death penalty. Eventually, Truscott's sentence was commuted to life, and he was ultimately let go on parole.

---

3   Philip Buckner, *Canada and the End of Empire* (Vancouver: UBC Press, 2005), 241.

By the early 2000s, new interest from the media led to a reopening of the case. Following the exhumation of Harper's body, no new forensic evidence was discovered, but other "new evidence" did come to light. After a new hearing, Truscott had his conviction overturned in 2007, though he was not declared innocent. In 2008, the Ontario government paid him $6.5 million in compensation. His name was finally cleared. The Truscott case changed the views of many Canadians about the death penalty, and added to the protests against capital punishment.

Finally, in 1976, the Liberal government outlawed the death penalty. This policy was a major issue for Canadians, and put Canada more in line with Europe and other developed nations, most of which had abolished capital punishment. By abolishing the death penalty, Canada put its laws at variance from those of the United States, where the death penalty still exists in a number of states, a reflection of the different forms of federalism in each country. In Canada, criminal law is a federal matter, making national decisions on death penalty legislation final. In the United States, criminal law is a state jurisdiction, which explains why more than half of all states still have the death penalty.

The end of the death penalty was, ultimately, a major indicator of social change in Canada. Like the flag, it represented a shift from an older British nation to a more progressive social democratic state. Not all Canadians were happy with this change. For Ronald Turpin and Arthur Lucas, the change was too little too late—"Some consolation" indeed.

Further Reading

Bryden, P.E. "The Liberal Party and the Achievement of National Healthcare." *Canadian Bulletin of Medical History* 26, no. 2 (2009): 315–32.

Canada. Library and Archives. "Capital Case: Ronald Turpin." *Cabinet Conclusions*, December 1962, http://www.bac-lac.gc.ca/eng/discover/politics-government/cabinet-conclusions/Pages/cabinet-conclusions.aspx.

Champion, C.P. "A Very British Coup: Canadianism, Quebec, and Ethnicity in the Flag Debate, 1964–1965." *Journal of Canadian Studies / Revue d'études canadiennes* 40, no. 3 (Fall 2006): 68–99.

Darbyson, Nicki. "'Sadists and Softies': Gender and the Abolition of the Death Penalty in Canada: A Case Study of Steven Truscott, 1959–1976." *Ontario History* 103, no. 1 (2011): 1–22.

Thompson, Andrew S. "Uneasy Abolitionists: Canada, the Death Penalty, and the Importance of International Norms, 1962–2005." *Journal of Canadian Studies / Revue d'études canadiennes* 42, no. 3 (Fall 2008): 172–92.

Toth, Lenora. "Ready, Aye, Ready—or Not? Diefenbaker's Response to the Cuban Missile Crisis." *Saskatchewan History* 64, no. 2 (Fall/Winter 2012): 34–52.

ACTIVE HISTORY: PRIMARY DOCUMENT ANALYSIS—CABINET DOCUMENTS

- Visit the Cabinet Conclusions at the website http://www.bac-lac.gc.ca/eng/discover/politics-government/cabinet-conclusions/Pages/cabinet-conclusions.aspx. The site covers the period from 1944 until the mid-1970s, and the documents are easily searchable by keyword and date. Make sure to read the introduction to understand the scope and background of the documents.

- Search for instances when capital cases were discussed. How many can you find? How often are capital cases discussed by cabinet?

- What factors played in the cabinet deliberations over whether someone should be granted clemency or not? What role did the prime minister, as the chair of cabinet, play in these decisions?

- Can you find instances when the broader issue of the death penalty itself was debated or discussed in cabinet? What insights can you gain about the debate over capital punishment from reading these documents?

TRAGIC TALES
"TO KILL THE INDIAN IN THE CHILD"— CHARLIE WENJACK, DIED IN 1966, AS DID OVER 3,000 ABORIGINAL CHILDREN WHILE IN INDIAN RESIDENTIAL SCHOOLS, 1870S–1990S

A National Crime

Tragically, Charlie Wenjack's story is not unusual. Over the course of more than a century, thousands of young aboriginal children ran away from the Indian residential school system. They ran away from an institutional effort, maintained by the federal government and major churches, designed to eradicate their culture and language, an educational system that was brutal even by the harsh standards of the day.

It was a system that barely hid other terrors behind neat rows of desks and uniformed children: abuse, violence, starvation, disease, and death. Nearly 150,000 aboriginal children were forced to attend residential schools by a government committed to assimilating First Nations, Métis, and Inuit peoples, and by churches committed to Christianizing and "civilizing" these children, no matter the cost. Many students suffered physical, psychological, and sexual abuse; thousands of others were struck ill by a host of diseases, especially tuberculosis, and by a lack of nutrition. In the 1940s and 1950s, Canadian officials knowingly and willingly conducted nutritional experiments on starving aboriginal school children. Altogether, at least 3,000 aboriginal children died while in residential schools.

When Charlie Wenjack ran away from the Cecilia Jeffrey School residence in Kenora, Ontario, in 1966, he likely did not know the stories of thousands of other children who had resisted and challenged their treatment at these schools. Tragically, many of them perished in the process.

Duncan Sticks, who was eight years old, died running away from the school at Williams Lake, British Columbia, in 1902. Four boys, two aged eight and two aged nine, ran away from the Lejac School also in British Columbia in 1937; their frozen bodies were found huddled together in an embrace barely a kilometre from their homes. In 1941, three young boys ran away from St. Anne's School in Fort Albany, Ontario, and disappeared; their bodies were never found. In 1959, brothers Rocky and Joseph Commanda ran away from the Mohawk Indian Residential School in Brantford, Ontario. The next day Rocky was caught and returned, but 13-year-old Joseph was hit and killed by a train near Toronto's Sunnyside Station as he ran from police.

Charlie Wenjack was only 12 years old, and he was desperate to return to his family, who lived near the Hudson's Bay post on the Marten Falls Reserve on the Albany River in northern Ontario, hundreds of kilometres away from Kenora. Days after he ran away from the school, Charlie's body was found near railway tracks. Dressed only in a thin layer of clothing, Charlie possessed nothing but a sealed jar of matches. He had died of exposure, and had likely hoped that a passing train would have been able to take him home. Instead, his body was shipped home, accompanied by his sisters, who had also been students. No explanation or investigation of his death was even attempted.

In his 2008 national apology for the Indian residential schools, Prime Minister Stephen Harper stated that the policy's purpose was, "as it was infamously said, 'to kill the Indian in the child.'" Harper told First Nations peoples that "Canada sincerely apologizes and asks the forgiveness of the Aboriginal peoples of this country for failing them so profoundly." He also pledged to create an "Indian Residential Truth and Reconciliation Commission" (established in 2007) to educate Canadians and help forge a new relationship between aboriginal peoples and other Canadians. In Harper's words, "Years of work by survivors, communities, and Aboriginal organizations culminated in an agreement that gives us a new beginning and an opportunity to move forward together in partnership."[4]

As Canadians grapple with the scope of the tragedy of residential schools, a policy one historian has called "a national crime," they must recognize that this horrible chapter in Canadian history is as relevant today as it was when the first school opened in the 1800s—or

when Charlie Wenjack ran away in 1966. Despite the rationalizations of an earlier era that these policies were meant to "help" aboriginals, despite the fact that "some former students have spoken positively about their experiences at residential schools," as Harper said in his apology, and despite the fact that the last school was closed in 1996, the legacy of the Indian residential schools is as much a matter of national importance in the twenty-first century as it was a national disgrace in the nineteenth and twentieth centuries.

Indeed, only by truly attempting to embrace our past can we understand it, and hope to begin a process of healing, of justice, and of truth and reconciliation. It is the least Canadians can do for Charlie Wenjack and the thousands of other Indian residential school children who suffered because of this national crime.

---

4   The full apology can be seen at Aboriginal Affairs and Northern Development Canada, "Statement of Apology," *Indian Residential Schools*, https://www.aadnc-aandc.gc.ca/eng/1100100015644/1100100015649.

CHAPTER FIFTEEN

PIERRE LAPORTE, ASSASSINATED, MONTREAL, OCTOBER 1970
QUEBEC, THE QUIET REVOLUTION, AND THE FLQ

In October of 1970, Canada faced its own terrorist crisis. Members of the Front de libération du Québec (FLQ), militant Quebec separatists, had been active since the 1960s. But, in October 1970, they provoked a national crisis. First, in early October, one group or cell of the FLQ kidnapped James Cross, the British trade commissioner in Quebec.

Then, on October 10, 1970, another cell of the FLQ kidnapped Pierre Laporte. Laporte, the provincial minister of labour, was the Quebec government's second most powerful person. He had been playing football on his front lawn with his nephew when two men pulled up in a car and forced him into a vehicle at gunpoint.

Within days, the crisis escalated. The kidnappers released a letter from Laporte to his wife: "My love, I am well, in good health, and I had a good night. I insist so that you and the children will take things in such a way that you will not endanger your health. I think of you constantly, and this helps me bear it all. The important thing is that the authorities stir themselves. My love to you all. Pierre"[1]

Unless the kidnappers' political demands were met, including releasing some of their captured colleagues and reading their manifesto over the airwaves, Laporte would be killed. In a dramatic response, the federal government of Pierre Trudeau declared that a state of "apprehended insurrection" existed in Quebec. At four AM on October 16, ostensibly at the request of Quebec Premier Robert Bourassa

---

1   The text of the letter (translated from French), and other documents related to the October Crisis, can be seen at http://faculty.marianopolis.edu/c.belanger/quebechistory/docs/october/index.htm.

and Montreal Mayor Jean Drapeau, Trudeau invoked the War Measures Act to fight the FLQ and the supposed insurrection.

The War Measures Act, as its title suggests, was meant for wartime: all Canadians' civil liberties were suspended in an effort to destroy the FLQ. This meant that anyone could get thrown in jail without actually being charged with anything, and for no apparent reason. The War Measures Act also meant that the army was called in to take control of the situation. For the first time in Canadian history troops were being used during peacetime. After October 15, 1970, Canadian army troops poured onto the streets of Montreal, Ottawa, and Quebec City. It was truly a shocking sight.

But Trudeau's efforts to save Laporte failed. On October 17, the bloodstained body of Pierre Laporte was discovered in the trunk of a car parked near the Montreal Airport. Laporte had been strangled with the chain of a religious medal that he often wore around his neck. Laporte was the first political assassination in Canada since Thomas D'Arcy McGee, almost exactly one hundred years earlier.

How and why did this happen? The murder of Laporte and the October Crisis set off a shockwave across Canada. Canadians were astounded that such events could take place in their country. The kidnappings, the War Measures Act, and the discovery of Laporte's body forever changed Canadians' views of themselves, their country, and their government.

The October Crisis meant for many the end of innocence for Canada. The 1960s were a period of uprisings, revolutions, and student revolts all across the globe, and, though Canada had been touched by these events, there had been

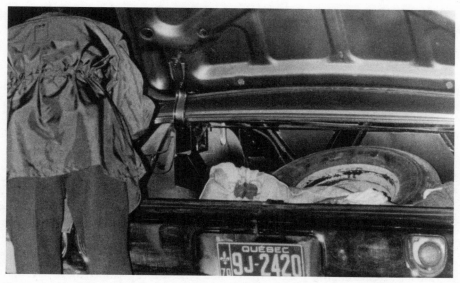

Figure 15.1 *Pierre Laporte's Body Is Found in the Trunk of a Car at the Montreal Airport, 1970*

little bloodshed. But Laporte's assassination made Canadians realize that the idea of their country as a safe oasis in a sea of violence no longer existed. For many Canadians, his murder meant that modern terrorism had truly come to Canada.

To understand the shock of Laporte's murder, we need to understand the broader context of a province experiencing a profound transformation, and demanding further change. Not just FLQ terrorists, but millions of ordinary Quebecers demanded political and economic change, and a new understanding and relationship between themselves and their governments in Quebec *and* Ottawa. This "Quiet Revolution" saw Quebec transformed from a rural, corrupt, and religious province, to a modern, secular, nationalistic, and progressive province. The death of Laporte—the October Crisis itself—was a very loud and shocking moment in this transformation—a moment when the revolution was no longer quiet.

Great Darkness and the Quiet Revolution

Quebec's history before the 1960s is often referred to as *la grand noirceur*, or the great darkness. The name reflects the view that Quebec was held back in its own dark ages, a period when the population was dominated by the church, was economically and socially behind the rest of North America, and suffered from an oppressive and corrupt political regime.

Before 1960, the province was dominated by the Quebec Catholic Church and its philosophy of clerico-nationalism, a nationalistic battle against urbanization, industrialization, and modernity meant to protect Quebec from the insidious influences of Protestantism, the English, and the temptations of the modern world. The "mission" of Quebec's French leaders was *la survivance*: merely insuring the survival of a reproductive, rural, and religious province.

Large families were the norm (birth control was strictly forbidden); Catholic rituals around birth, baptism, confirmation, marriage, and death were the main rhythms of life; and the Catholic Church ran the school system and all social services in the province, save for those designed for the English minority, which had its own system. Outside of Montreal, the economy was underdeveloped and rural, based on resource extraction and small farms. English was the language of business, and English companies dominated the economic landscape.

Because the language of business was English, unilingual francophones were largely shut out of high-paying jobs. They were literally the labourers of the province while English speakers were the foremen and bosses. In 1954, francophones, who made up 80 per cent of Quebec's population, had just 25 per cent of its wealth. Work and pay inequality based on language in Quebec amounted to outright discrimination. Even the commercial face of Montreal, the second largest French-speaking city in the world, was English.

The conservative, rural, and Catholic nature of the province was reinforced and exploited by Maurice Duplessis, known to his followers as "*le Chef*," who dominated provincial politics from the 1930s to the 1950s. His party, the Union Nationale, was very conservative and isolationist, staunchly anti-union, pro big business, and largely corrupt.

The death of Duplessis in 1959 played a significant role in setting off the Quiet Revolution, though a number of brewing social and economic factors had already laid the foundation for the dramatic transformation of the province. Though urbanization had been occurring since the nineteenth century, it accelerated rapidly in the twentieth. Along with urbanization came a significant decline in birth rates. The introduction of the birth control pill and new attitudes toward the role of women meant that Quebec's birth rate went from among the highest in the world to among the lowest by the 1980s.

Modernization, which sped the decline of the Catholic Church and its power, was also helped along by technology. The television age came to Quebec in the 1950s, and television opened the eyes of many to the outside world, which wasn't as evil as it had been portrayed by the clergy. Shows like *Point de mire*, hosted by popular reporter and future premier René Lévesque, brought world events into Quebecers' homes.

Lévesque was among a new breed of Quebecers who had gone to study or work abroad and who questioned why Quebec was so conservative, politically corrupt, and dominated by the church. Lawyer and future prime minister Pierre Trudeau, although educated at a Catholic school, had gone to university in Boston, Paris, and London. In journals and newspapers such as *Cité Libre* and *Le Devoir*, Trudeau and many of Quebec's francophone intelligentsia began criticizing the Duplessis government and the Catholic Church for their conservatism, arguing that unless Quebec society were modernized and democratized, Québécois culture would stagnate and die.

Artists also challenged the dictates of the Duplessis era. Abstract painter Paul-Émile Borduas defied Quebec's church-dominated art scene and criticized the government. Borduas, along with other artists such as Jean Paul Riopelle, formed the Montreal Automatiste movement. The Automatistes 1948 manifesto, the *Refus global*, or "total refusal," attacked church and government oppression and is considered one of the most important documents in creating modern Quebec.

Along with all these dramatic social and cultural changes, economic changes affected Quebec. The 1950s and 1960s were economic boom times for Canada; unemployment was low, incomes rose, and most Canadians prospered. Though big business did well in Quebec, it seemed that the boom was leaving ordinary Quebecers behind. The emerging, university-educated, francophone middle class became frustrated by the lack of opportunity. For them, the solution was to use the provincial state to advance the interests of Quebecers.

Many of these groups—intellectuals, unions, and the middle class—came together to help Jean Lesage's Liberal Party oust the Union Nationale in 1960. A charismatic, capable administrator, Lesage had been a Liberal minister in the federal government and then became leader of the Liberal Party of Quebec in 1958. Lesage's 1960 victory marked a sea change in Quebec. Building upon recent social and economic changes and on the demands of the new political class, the Quebec Liberals' plan was to use the state to modernize the province to the benefit of French-speaking Quebecers. With an ambitious agenda, between 1960 and 1966, the Liberals transformed the Quebec government and had an impact on nearly every facet of Quebec society.

Lesage largely secularized the educational system. In 1964, the Liberals created a provincial ministry of education for the first time, and Paul Gérin-Lajoie served as the first minister of education. Although it remained organized along Catholic and Protestant lines, the new ministry built schools, hired teachers, created the curriculum, wrote textbooks, and established standards across the province. The government also created the CEGEP college system in 1967 and the Université du Québec system in 1968, with campuses across the province in places such as Trois-Rivières, Rimouski, and Montreal.

In social services, the province took over from the church and effectively established a welfare state in Quebec. The government took over the operation of hospitals, welfare, and support services and began drafting the Quebec Pension Plan in 1963. With the changes to the educational system and the social services in the province, the Catholic Church soon began withdrawing from its dominant public role, and the province became much more secularized.

In the economy, the role of the state was extended dramatically. Here, the aim was to provide French speakers with job opportunities and managerial positions, which they had been denied in the English-dominated corporate world. Quebec established provincially owned corporations in iron and steel, mining, forestry, and petroleum to take advantage of the province's natural resources. A new labour code was adopted in 1964 making it easier for people to unionize and allowing for powerful unions. The government also created a lending bank, given the English-dominated banking system that prevailed; even the Bank of Montreal was an English-speaking institution.

But perhaps the most important economic step taken by the Lesage Liberals was the nationalization of hydroelectric companies in Quebec. This policy was so important that the Liberals called an election on the issue in 1962. During this campaign their famous slogan, "*maître chez nous*," or "masters in our own house," was used to great effect to win the election. The Quebec government's takeover of the hydro companies was spearheaded by René Lévesque, who had joined the provincial Liberal Party. A giant Hydro-Québec became the centrepiece of the Quiet Revolution, as it now employed French managers and engineers, advanced made-in-Quebec technologies, championed Quebec development, and funded the modernization of the province.

Of course, all these dramatic changes did not go unchallenged. For some, the Liberals were doing far too much, far too fast. After all, Quebec was a deeply conservative society, and Lesage was asking much of the province by instituting these dramatic changes. In 1966, the Union Nationale, led by new leader Daniel Johnson and backed by many corporations, rallied to narrowly defeat Lesage. Obviously, the Liberals' political defeat did not mean the end of the Quiet Revolution: the Union Nationale did not really rescind any of the major legislative changes that the Liberals had enacted and, in fact, continued the changes, such as the creation of the university system in 1968.

Others, however, were convinced that no matter what Quebecers did to modernize their province, Quebec would always be held back by its status as a province within Canada.

Nationalism, Separatism, and Terrorism

The transformations of the Quiet Revolution in Quebec created a new nationalism in the province. With the end of the church's influence and Quebec's modernization, this new nationalism was rooted in the state and in the distinctiveness of the Quebec experience, now largely based on language. The new nationalists agreed that Québécois society must be progressive and dynamic, but some differed on the way to get there. Lesage thought that a strong Quebec within Canada could allow Quebecers to flourish.

The new nationalism provoked a response from the federal government. As prime minister from 1963 to 1968, Pearson was the first Canadian leader to address Quebec's new nationalism. A long-time diplomat, Pearson believed that Quebec's aspirations could be accommodated through cooperation, one that reflected a willingness to accept Quebec's distinctiveness within the federation quietly. For example, in 1966, Quebec created its own separate pension plan, which still exists.

More important, in 1963 Pearson appointed the Royal Commission on Bilingualism and Biculturalism. The commission, known as the "Bi and Bi Commission," issued a preliminary report in 1965, which found that French speakers were discriminated against in the federal government and made less money in Quebec. It also recognized that changes needed to be made to make the country more responsive to the French fact.

Pearson's accommodation had its limits, though. In 1967, French President Charles de Gaulle visited Quebec for Canada's centennial. With delusions of grandeur and a notion of returning as a conquering hero, he gave a famous speech from Montreal's city hall, declaring *"Vive le Québec libre!"*—which set off a huge celebration in Montreal and galvanized the nascent separatist movement in the province. Pearson sternly asked the French president to leave following his speech.

Despite Pearson's efforts, René Lévesque and others came to view Ottawa as the English-Canadian government that had no business in the province's affairs. Moreover, they saw their minority status within Canada as untenable and claimed that history had proved they would always get the short end of the stick. They pointed to the two conscription crises, the school battles across the country, and the Riel affair as evidence that, as long as Quebec was the only French-speaking province, the rest of Canada would always get its way. Eventually, Lévesque left the Liberals and created the separatist Parti Québécois in 1968, and took power in Quebec in November 1976.

Others viewed the changing demograpy of the province as a reason for it to go its own way. With the end of the high birth rate amongst francophones, the "revenge of the cradle," some forecast the end of French speakers in Quebec within a generation or two. At the same time, there was an awakening in Quebec to the decolonization movements around the world. Many other former colonies of Great Britain and France, such as Nigeria and Kenya, gained independence peacefully; others, such as Algeria, won independence from France only after a long and brutal revolt. Some saw Quebec, a former colony of France and a former conquered colony of England, as another one of these colonial states that needed to gain its independence.

In the early 1960s, a few Quebecers were inspired by Algeria's successful independence movement, one based on forcing the issue through violence. Dividing into "cells" soon after its beginning in 1963, the FLQ began bombing colonial symbols, including statues of James Wolfe, the 18th century English conqueror of Quebec, and of Queen Victoria. Mailboxes, which in the 1960s still bore the symbols of Canada's British royal heritage, were also targeted by the FLQ.

All told, between 1963 and 1970 the FLQ carried out over 200 attacks on statues, buildings, railway tracks, armouries, banks, barracks, English radio stations and anything else that they saw as impeding the creation of an independent Quebec. The FLQ bombing campaign caused at least six deaths and hundreds of injuries. For instance, a huge bomb that exploded at the Montreal Stock Exchange in 1969 caused injuries to 27 people.

During this period, a sense of terror pervaded the province, punctuated at times by horrifying FLQ communiqués, such as this one:

> [T]hose who betray the workers and the Quebec nation—will fear for their lives and they will be right. For the FLQ will kill. . . . Have you ever seen a bus full of the English blow up? Have you ever seen an English library burning? . . . Have you ever seen a Protestant church burning? . . . Be sure you soon will![2]

---

2   Quoted from *La victoire* (Official organ of the FLQ), No. 3, March 1969 in Gerard Pelletier, *The October Crisis* (Toronto: McClelland and Stewart, 1971), 224.

By the end of the 1960s, however, many in the FLQ were becoming increasingly frustrated. Twenty-three members of their organization were in prison, charged or convicted with various crimes. An intensified bombing campaign launched after 1968 did not seem to be having an effect.

Moreover, during the provincial election of 1970, Lévesque's separatist Parti Québécois had been soundly defeated by the federalist Liberal Party of Robert Bourassa. FLQ members believed that they could not wait for the peaceful political separation of Canada and that action had to be taken. In October of 1970, the FLQ cells began the most chilling phase of their revolutionary attacks. They began to kidnap people.

Not-So-Quiet Revolution: October Crisis and Reaction

On October 5, 1970, the FLQ's Libération cell kidnapped James Cross, British trade commissioner in Quebec, demanding the release of the FLQ prisoners. Five days later, the Chénier cell, named after a hero of the Rebellion of 1837, kidnapped Laporte, one of the leading members of the Quebec government and a friend of Pierre Trudeau's. On October 11, a day after Laporte's abduction, the kidnappers released a letter from Laporte to his good friend, Quebec Premier Robert Bourassa:

> My dear Robert,
> I feel like I am writing the most important letter I have ever written. For the time being, I am in perfect health, and I am treated well, even courteously. In short, the power to decide over my life is in your hands. . . . I had two brothers, both are now dead. I remain alone as the head of a large family. . . . My departure would create for them irreparable grief. . . . You have the power of life and death over me, I depend on you and I thank you for it.
> Best regards,
> Pierre Laporte.[3]

The next day, the kidnappers released Laporte's letter to his wife. These letters significantly increased the pressure on the government to agree to the kidnappers' demands. For the next two days, Quebec was paralyzed by fear as negotiations between the FLQ and the government continued through the media. Meanwhile, rumours swirled about the kidnap victims, about new cells of the FLQ springing into action (another cell was named after Louis Riel), about new death threats, and about dozens of bomb threats all over the province.

---

3   See "Documents on the October Crisis," *Quebec History* [website from Marianopolis College], http://faculty.marianopolis.edu/c.belanger/quebechistory/docs/october/laporte1.htm.

At the same time, many supported the aims of the FLQ, if not their means. On October 15, at a huge rally held at a hockey arena, nearly 3,000 people, mostly students, listened to speeches in support of the FLQ. At the end of one speech, the huge crowd broke into chants of "FLQ! FLQ! FLQ!" The rest of the country was mesmerized by these events, as many Canadians were terrified by the notion that an uprising might actually be occurring in Quebec.

Faced with the gravest situation for a Canadian government in decades, on October 16, Trudeau invoked the War Measures Act. Within hours, troops descended on Montreal and Ottawa, and over 400 people were arrested, including members of the separatist Parti Québécois, union leaders, and even entertainers and writers in the province. In a matter of days, nearly 2,000 police raids were conducted.

Across the country, incidents of censorship arose as police confiscated newspapers that published the FLQ manifesto or criticized the use of the War Measures Act. These measures were applied particularly to student newspapers. At the University of Guelph, copies of the student newspaper that contained the manifesto were confiscated by police, though no charges were laid.

Reaction to the War Measures Act was dramatic, and divisive. NDP leader Tommy Douglas felt that using such a harsh law was a wild overreaction to the situation in Quebec and that no type of emergency or crisis was worth taking away Canadians' basic rights. Douglas was attacked in the press by many who saw his position as unrealistic.

Other politicians in Canada supported the use of the War Measures Act. Ontario premier John Robarts claimed that the actions of the FLQ meant that Canada was at war, and he was solidly behind invoking the War Measures Act. Overall, most Canadians and Quebecers supported Trudeau's move. A December 1970 poll found that 88 per cent of Canadians felt that the government's decision was correct, or that the government wasn't being tough enough. In Quebec, 86 per cent of the population felt that way.

Of course, as we know, following the invocation of the War Measures Act, Laporte was killed. On October 20, Trudeau and Bourassa attended the funeral of Laporte. Although his wife had wanted a small private ceremony, it turned out to be a huge state event that generated sympathy across the country for Laporte's family.

In the weeks after the funeral, police ascertained the identities of the FLQ kidnappers who had murdered Laporte and were still holding Cross. On November 2, the federal and Quebec governments offered a reward of $150,000 for information leading to the arrest of the kidnappers. The government also enacted the Public Order (Temporary Measures) Act, which brought the application of the War Measures Act to an end and replaced the original regulations issued under that act with new ones. These new regulations effectively maintained the same status as the War Measures Act, though they were not as extensive in granting the state such sweeping powers. Trudeau had always maintained the government would replace the War Measures Act as soon as possible.

On December 3, the police discovered where the FLQ's Libération cell had been hiding Cross in Montreal. After being surrounded and facing certain capture, the FLQ kidnappers negotiated Cross's release in exchange for safe passage to Cuba. Amazingly, in a scene more dramatic than any Hollywood movie, the kidnappers drove to the Montreal airport to take a plane to Cuba. They were surrounded and escorted by dozens of police cars and motorcycles, their sirens wailing as they drove through the closed off streets to the airport. After they arrived safely in Cuba, Cross was released from the Canadian pavilion at the Expo 67 world fair, which had been declared Cuban territory temporarily. He was an FLQ hostage for 59 days.

Just over three weeks later, on December 28, the murderers of Pierre Laporte were captured after being surrounded at a farmhouse just southeast of Montreal. By the end of 1970, with no new bombings or kidnappings, and with over 400 people having been arrested and virtually all of them released, it seemed that the FLQ was no longer in operation. On January 4, 1971, the last soldiers left Quebec. The October Crisis was over.

The Legacy of October 1970

Pierre Laporte's assassination and the October Crisis itself had a far-reaching impact. Legally, the War Measures Act was ultimately replaced with an Emergencies Act (1988), allowing the government far more flexibility in dealing with crises that might occur. This legal change was a response to the criticism the government faced in suspending civil liberties during the crisis.

Second, and perhaps most obviously, domestic terrorism in the name of Quebec separatism does not exist. Since October 1970, there has been no serious terrorist attack in favour of Quebec separatism. Thankfully, Quebec and Canada avoided the fate of other separatist efforts: Spain, Sri Lanka, and a host of other countries around the world experienced long-standing campaigns of violence after the 1970s.

Now, whether this renouncing of violence was because Quebecers turned away from the FLQ after the murder of Laporte or because the imposition of the War Measures Act was so effective in breaking the terrorist organization is not entirely clear. In the years after the October Crisis, many felt that Trudeau's actions had saved the country and that, by imposing the War Measures Act, he had prevented the never-ending cycle of violence that is apparent in so many other countries.

Others feel that the continuing separatist movement today in Quebec is, in fact, another legacy of the October Crisis. Some argue that the invocation of the War Measures Act actually benefited the separatists. After all, with violent separatism totally discredited with the murder of Laporte, the argument could be made that Quebecers reacted to the suspension of civil liberties by becoming more supportive of peaceful political separatism.

In the long run, maybe Trudeau's actions actually helped the separatist Parti Québécois. The Parti Québécois eventually did gain electoral victory in 1976, but they have never been able to win a referendum in support of separation.

It is important to remember that, in some ways, the fight of the FLQ for a separate Quebec is not over. The separatist Parti Québécois remains a force in Quebec politics, and there have been two referendums on this issue; during the 1995 Quebec referendum, the separatist side came extremely close to winning.

If the separatists do manage to win, it will be in some ways a victory for the FLQ. Not for their tactics, obviously, which most of them denounced years ago, but clearly for the idea that Quebec should be its own country. In that way, the FLQ's aims are still very much with us, even if the FLQ is not.

Further Reading

Aivalis, Christo. "In the Name of Liberalism: Pierre Trudeau, Organized Labour, and the Canadian Social Democratic Left, 1949–1959." *Canadian Historical Review* 94, no. 2 (June 2013): 263–88. http://dx.doi. org/10.3138/chr.1498.

Behiels, Michael. *Prelude to Quebec's Quiet Revolution: Liberalism vs Neo-Nationalism, 1945–60.* Montreal: McGill-Queen's University Press, 1985.

Clément, Dominique. "The October Crisis of 1970: Human Rights Abuses under the War Measures Act." *Journal of Canadian Studies / Revue d'études canadiennes* 42, no. 2 (Spring 2008): 160–86.

Falardeau, Pierre. *Octobre.* Ottawa: ACPAV Inc. and National Film Board of Canada, 1994.

Lévesque, René. "For an Independent Quebec." *Foreign Affairs* 54, no. 4 (July 1976): 734–45. http://dx.doi.org/10.2307/20039610.

Mills, Sean. *The Empire Within: Postcolonial Thought and Political Activism in Sixties Montreal.* Montreal: McGill-Queen's University Press, 2010.

Vacante, Jeffery. "The Posthumous Lives of René Lévesque." *Journal of Canadian Studies / Revue d'études canadiennes* 45, no. 2 (Spring 2011): 5–30.

ACTIVE HISTORY: PRIMARY DOCUMENT ANALYSIS, THE FLQ MANIFESTO

Examine the FLQ Manifesto below and consider the following questions:

1. Can you identify the FLQ's main grievances? Who are their chief targets, and why?

2. Is there a particular political philosophy at work here? What are the FLQ's views on the economy and politics?

3. What insights can you gain into the FLQ's willingness to use violence to achieve their aims by reading this manifesto?

4. What insights can you gain about Quebec society at the time by reading the manifesto?

5. Compare and contrast the FLQ Manifesto to Lévesque's "For an Independent Quebec," cited above.

FLQ Manifesto, Read on-air on Radio-Canada (CBC), Oct. 8, 1970, as a Condition for the Release of Kidnapped British Trade Official James Cross

The people in the Front de libération du Québec are neither Messiahs nor modern-day Robin Hoods. They are a group of Quebec workers who have decided to do everything they can to assure that the people of Quebec take their destiny into their own hands, once and for all.

The Front de libération du Québec wants total independence for Quebeckers; it wants to see them united in a free society, a society purged for good of its gang of rapacious sharks, the big bosses who dish out patronage and their henchmen, who have turned Quebec into a private preserve of cheap labour and unscrupulous exploitation.

The Front de libération du Québec is not an aggressive movement, but a response to the aggression organized by high finance through its puppets, the federal and provincial governments (the Brinks farce, Bill 69, the electoral map, the so-called "social progress" [sic] tax, the Power Corporation, medical insurance—for the doctors, the guys at Lapalme . . .)

The Front de libération du Québec finances itself—through voluntary [sic] taxes levied on the enterprises that exploit the workers (banks, finance companies, etc.). . . .

Once, we believed it worthwhile to channel our energy and our impatience, in the apt words of René Lévesque, into the Parti Québécois, but the Liberal victory shows that what is called democracy in Quebec has always been, and still is, nothing but the "democracy" of the rich. In this sense the victory of the Liberal party is in fact nothing but the victory of the Simard-Cotroni election-fixers. Consequently, we wash our hands of the British parliamentary system; the Front de libération du Québec will never let itself be distracted by the electoral crumbs that the Anglo-Saxon capitalists toss into the Quebec barnyard every four years. Many Quebeckers have realized the truth and are ready to take action. In the coming year Bourassa is going to get what's coming to him: 100,000 revolutionary workers, armed and organized!

. . . .

We've had enough of a Canadian federalism which penalizes the dairy farmers of Quebec to satisfy the requirements of the Anglo-Saxons of the Commonwealth; which keeps the honest taxi drivers of Montreal in a state of semi-slavery by shamefully protecting the exclusive monopoly of the nauseating Murray Hill, and its owner—the murderer Charles Hershorn and his son Paul who, the night of October 7, repeatedly tore a .22 rifle out of the hands of his employees to fire on the taxi drivers and thereby mortally wounded Corporal Dumas, killed as a demonstrator. Canadian federalism pursues a reckless import policy, thereby throwing out of work the people who earn low wages in the textile and shoe industries, the most downtrodden people in Quebec, and all to line the pockets of a handful of filthy "money-makers" in Cadillacs. We are fed up with a federalism which classes the Quebec nation among the ethnic minorities of Canada.

We, and more and more Quebeckers too, have had it with a government of pussy-footers who perform a hundred and one tricks to charm the American millionaires, begging them to come and invest in Quebec, the Beautiful Province where thousands of square miles of forests full of game and of lakes full of fish are the exclusive property of these all-powerful lords of the twentieth century. We are sick of a government in the hands of a hypocrite like Bourassa who depends on Brinks armoured trucks, an authentic symbol of the foreign occupation of Quebec, to keep the poor Quebec "natives" fearful of that poverty and unemployment to which we are so accustomed.

We are fed up with the taxes we pay that Ottawa's agent in Quebec would give to the English-speaking bosses as an "incentive" for them to speak French, to negotiate in French. Repeat after me: "Cheap labour is *main-d'oeuvre à bon marché* in French."

We have had enough of promises of work and of prosperity, when in fact we will always be the diligent servants and bootlickers of the big shots, as long as there is a Westmount, a Town of Mount Royal, a Hampstead, an Outremont, all these veritable fortresses of the high finance of St. James Street and Wall Street; we will be slaves until Quebeckers, all of us, have used every means, including dynamite and guns, to drive out these big bosses of the economy and of politics, who will stoop to any action however base, the better to screw us.

We live in a society of terrorized slaves, terrorized by the big bosses, Steinberg, Clark, Bronfman, Smith, Neopole, Timmins, Geoffrion, J.L. Lévesque, Hershorn, Thompson, Nesbitt, Desmarais, Kierans (next to these, Rémi Popol the Nightstick, Drapeau the Dog, the Simards' Simple Simon and Trudeau the Pansy are peanuts!).

We are terrorized by the Roman Capitalist Church, though this is less and less true today (who owns the square where the Stock Exchange was built?); terrorized by the payments owing to Household Finance, by the advertising of the grand masters of consumption, Eaton's, Simpson's, Morgan's, Steinberg's, General Motors—terrorized by those exclusive clubs of science and culture, the universities, and by their boss-directors Gaudry and Dorais, and by the vice-boss Robert Shaw.

There are more and more of us who know and suffer under this terrorist society, and the day is coming when all the Westmounts of Quebec will disappear from the map.

Workers in industry, in mines and in the forests! Workers in the service industries, teachers, students and unemployed! Take what belongs to you, your jobs, your determination and your freedom. And you, the workers at General Electric, you make your factories run; you are the only ones able to produce; without you, General Electric is nothing!

Workers of Quebec, begin from this day forward to take back what is yours; take yourselves what belongs to you. Only you know your factories, your machines, your hotels, your universities, your unions; do not wait for some organization to produce a miracle.

Make your revolution yourselves in your neighbourhoods, in your places of work. If you don't do it yourselves, other usurpers, technocrats or someone else, will replace the handful of cigar-smokers we know today and everything will have to be done all over again. Only you are capable of building a free society.

We must struggle not individually but together, till victory is obtained, with every means at our disposal, like the Patriots of 1897–1898 (those whom Our Holy Mother Church hastened to excommunicate, the better to sell out to British interests).

In the four corners of Quebec, may those who have been disdainfully called lousy Frenchmen and alcoholics begin a vigorous battle against those who have muzzled liberty and justice; may they put out of commission all the professional holdup artists and swindlers: bankers, businessmen, judges and corrupt political wheeler-dealers. . . .

We are Quebec workers and we are prepared to go all the way. With the help of the entire population, we want to replace this society of slaves by a free society, operating by itself and for itself, a society open on the world. Our struggle can only be victorious. A people that has awakened cannot long be kept in misery and contempt.

Long live Free Quebec!

Long live our comrades the political prisoners!

Long live the Quebec Revolution!

Long live the *Front de libération du Québec!*

Source: "The FLQ Manifesto" in Marcel Rioux, *Quebec in Question* (Toronto: James Lorimer, 1971), translated by James Boake.

☞ MURDEROUS MOMENT ☜
VICTIMS, POLICE, POLITICIANS, AND TERRORISTS: WHAT HAPPENED AFTER THE OCTOBER CRISIS?

Unexpected Endings to Canada's Greatest Terrorist Crisis

What happened to the key actors during and after the October Crisis? Their fates are fascinating.

James Cross, held captive by the FLQ for 59 days, returned to the United Kingdom where he was made a Companion of the Order of St. Michael and St. George (CMG) in 1971, and continued to work in the British government until his retirement.

During the October Crisis, the police rounded up hundreds of innocent people and threw them in jail with little reason. Of the 468 people arrested, 408 were released without being charged, and only 2 faced sentencing. Students, professors, journalists, artists, activists, and members of the Parti Québécois, who did not sympathize with the FLQ, were thrown in jail in 1970. In the 1970s and 1980s, it became something of a badge of honour among many nationalist and separatist Quebecers to have been detained by the police.

In the years after the October Crisis, an investigation into the events discovered that police and the RCMP had not only infiltrated the FLQ but had actually engaged in crimes during the course of their intelligence duties, including stealing Parti Québécois documents and dynamiting and burning down barns outside of Montreal in their undercover actions against the FLQ.

As the report of the "Keable Commission" noted, by the early 1970s, the anti-terrorist unit of the Montreal police so completely controlled the FLQ that "in 1972, we [the police] were the FLQ."[4] In 1984, Canadian intelligence duties were assigned to a separate intelligence agency, named the Canadian Security Intelligence Service, or CSIS. Canada's current spy agency was created as a direct result of the October Crisis.

All three politicians who are identified with the imposition of the War Measures Act had something to gain politically in this period, and all were affected by the Crisis. Quebec Premier Robert Bourassa was trying to pass health-care legislation through the Quebec legislature the very night that the War Measures Act was invoked. Welcoming such draconian legislation to defeat the terrorists certainly detracted from any unwanted criticism of this controversial health-care legislation. Eventually, Bourassa was defeated (in 1976), but he rather miraculously returned to become premier again in 1985.

Then there is the case of Montreal Mayor Jean Drapeau. During the October Crisis, Drapeau was in the middle of an election campaign. At one point during the crisis, Drapeau actually accused his opponents of sympathizing with the FLQ, even though they had nothing to do with the terrorists. Moreover, after the War Measures Act was imposed, a number of his opponents and their campaign workers were actually carted off to jail. Not surprisingly, on October 25, the day of the election, Drapeau won with an amazing 92 per cent of the vote. Despite the massive cost overruns of the 1976 Olympics, Drapeau remained mayor until 1986.

---

4   The Keable Commission, appointed by the Parti Québécois government, was officially known as the Commission d'enquête sur des opérations policières en territoire québécois. The quotation is taken from David C. Rapoport, *Inside Terrorist Organizations*, 2nd ed. (London: Frank Cass, 2001), 85.

Pierre Trudeau was determined to fight the separatists, both the terrorists and the separatist Parti Québécois. Trudeau and separatist leader René Lévesque had known each other for years—and had fought for years over the question of whether Quebec was better off inside or outside of Canada. Although Lévesque totally denounced the terrorist attacks, he did state that the government should negotiate, and he called the 23 FLQ terrorists in jail "political prisoners."[5] This was something that Trudeau attacked him for implicitly. Lévesque would become Quebec premier in 1976, retiring in 1985 without achieving his dream of Quebec independence. Trudeau was reduced to a minority in the 1972 election, but remained as prime minister, save for a short Progressive Conservative interregnum in 1979–80, until he retired in 1984.

As to the FLQ members, their fates may surprise you. Many of them did serve prison time for their activities during the October Crisis. The FLQ terrorists that kidnapped Cross eventually tired of their time in Cuba, and returned to Quebec in the late 1970s to face justice. The longest sentence handed down for the kidnapping was two years. The FLQ members who kidnapped and killed Labour Minister Pierre Laporte also served time in jail. They claimed that Laporte had accidentally hung himself with his religious necklace while trying to escape. The longest prison term served by those convicted in Laporte's death was 13 years.

So what happened to them?

Jacques Rose, a member of the group that killed Laporte, ran a home renovation company in the province with another former member of the FLQ.

Paul Rose, his brother and another member of the cell that murdered Pierre Laporte, became a university professor in Rimouski, a small town in Quebec's Gaspé peninsula, teaching political science.

Jacques Lanctôt, who was one of James Cross's kidnappers, served two years in prison, and, after his release, set up a publishing company and did some journalism, including as an online news columnist.

Serge Demers, who co-founded the FLQ and was convicted of armed robbery and planting bombs, was named chief of staff to Quebec's minister of employment in 1996 during the separatist government of Lucien Bouchard.

Jacques Cossette-Trudel, after his return from Cuba, served two years for the Cross kidnapping and then became a successful filmmaker.

Richard Therrien, who was convicted for hiding the FLQ terrorists who kidnapped and murdered Laporte, was named a Quebec provincial court judge in 1996. When his FLQ past was discovered, he was kicked off the bench, a decision he fought all the way to the Supreme Court of Canada. He lost.

Fascinating, indeed.

---

5   John English, *Just Watch Me: The Life of Pierre Elliott Trudeau, 1968–2000* (Toronto: Vintage Canada, 2007), 100.

CHAPTER SIXTEEN

ROCHDALE COLLEGE'S CINDY LEI COMMITS SUICIDE, TORONTO, 1975

THE COUNTERCULTURE AND THE SIXTIES REVOLUTIONARY MOMENT IN CANADA

In a way, the suicide of Cindy Lei was not just the tragic death of a young woman; it also represented the end of an era, though perhaps not the end of that era's ideals—the counterculture dream of the Sixties. That's because Cindy Lei was a Rochdalian, a person who lived in Rochdale College, the alternative, 18-story student-run residence and educational experiment in downtown Toronto, adjacent to the beating heart of the Canadian counterculture movement, Yorkville. Founded in 1968, Rochdale became an epicentre of the Sixties ethos, and a living example of the counterculture at work. A cooperative educational experiment, Rochdale reflected a wider desire for societal change and a generational demand by the baby boomers for a revolution that touched upon politics, music, sex, gender, and rights.

The dream could be seen in the work of Rochdale College's Peter Almasy, also known as Zipp. Zipp was the creator of the cartoon strip "Acidman," in which an eponymous cartoon hippie described what would happen if he were to become prime minister of Canada:

> The age of consent will be lowered to 12 years, birth control pills
> will be given to all females age 12 or over, hallucinogenic drugs will
> be government inspected and sold in drug stores, pornography will
> be legalized, churches will pay taxes, jails will close down and crimi-
> nals will be treated in hospitals, underground papers will receive gov-
> ernment grants—pass the joint—all cities will be required to open at

least one public beach for nude bathing, the police will be disarmed, homosexuality will be legalized, welfare and unemployment insurance will be increased, discrimination on any grounds will be punished, gambling, abortion and prostitution will be legalized and taxable, censorship will be permitted, sex education will start in kindergarten, students will govern schools and universities . . . yes, it will indeed be a just society.[1]

Though this could be seen as a facetious bit of drug-induced comedy, there was no mistaking the underlying tone and demands of Acidman's goals, a liberalization of attitudes toward sex, drugs, and behaviour, and a direct rebuke of established norms and expectations for men, women, and youth. Indeed, despite the seemingly extreme nature of Acidman's agenda, many of these changes have come to pass, or have partially done so.

When Cindy Lei committed suicide in 1975, though, it seemed as if the counterculture's dreams were dead. She had already been evicted, along with all the other Rochdalians, from the residence adjacent to the University of Toronto. Lei, one of 800 people who lived at Rochdale during its heyday, took her own life after an overdose of sleeping pills. Depressed that the experiment at Rochdale had ended in a haze of drugs, gangs, and a police eviction, many mourned Lei's death, seeing the end of Rochdale as the end of the counterculture; but, surprisingly, despite the seeming demise of Rochdale and the counterculture itself, much of the ethos of the Sixties lived on.

The Sexual Revolution and Trudeau's "Just Society"

Among the greatest legacies of the Sixties were the sexual revolution and the dramatic changes in North American attitudes toward sex, gender, and the role of women. When contrasted to the repressive and unrealistic attitudes toward sex and gender roles in the immediate postwar period and the 1950s, the 1960s truly marked a sexual revolution. It is important to remember that the notions of womanhood in the 1950s were based on traditional gender roles that emphasized being a good wife and mother. Womanhood was to be defined by the housewife, who was primarily a husband's helpmate, a doting mother, and a consumer. The suburban image of a fictional television character such as June Cleaver from the show *Leave It to Beaver* was considered something of an ideal.

---

1   David Sharpe, *Rochdale, the Runaway College* (Toronto: House of Anansi, 1987), 176.

This ideal was very difficult to achieve, and somewhat unrealistic. The notion of "traditional gender roles" for women became even more unrealistic during the 1960s, when many women broke from that idea. By the 1960s, there were dramatic changes in women's employment, birth control, abortion, and sexuality; expectations about women also altered dramatically in this period. Many of these issues will be discussed in more detail in Chapter 19, which examines the changing role of women in the postwar period.

Another key element of the sexual revolution was homosexuality. Now, in the repressive society of the 1950s Canadians were, like their American counterparts, largely "homeward bound," the idea that families (and especially women) should return to a life of "normalcy" following the war by returning home, with fathers and men at the head of the household. With so much emphasis on traditional gender roles and families, anything else was considered abnormal, perverted; homosexuals were relegated to the periphery of society, and homosexuality itself was a criminal act.

By the mid-to-late Sixties, gay rights became a key element of the sexual revolution. In challenging the 1950s' ethos, many gays and lesbians took their cue from the protests of the decade to demand the end of discrimination and harassment. In this as in so many issues related to the 1960s, Canadians were affected by events in the United States. In New York City, the 1969 police raids on the Stonewall Inn, a popular gay bar in Greenwich Village, led to one of the first efforts to resist this type of discrimination. The Stonewall riots became a key starting point for the modern gay rights movement.

In Canada, a gay rights movement also began in the 1960s and advanced throughout the 1970s. We can see this in three cases. The first is the case of George Klippert, which really brought the issue of the rights of homosexuals into the spotlight in the late 1960s. Klippert was a mechanic from the Northwest Territories. In 1965, Klippert had been questioned by police during an arson investigation. Although the police did not think he had anything to do with the arson, during the questioning, Klippert admitted that he had had consensual sexual relations with men.

Because homosexual acts were still considered a crime, he was subsequently charged with "gross indecency" (sexual relations that were considered abnormal) and "buggery" (sex between men). However, Klippert fought back. He took his case all the way to the Supreme Court. But he lost. In 1967, the Supreme Court dismissed his appeal, and Klippert was even deemed a "dangerous offender," which meant that he could be kept in jail indefinitely. Nonetheless, the case generated public outcry. It was becoming clear that many people felt that what was done between consenting adults in private was their own business, even if they might not agree with homosexual acts. As we shall see in a moment, there was a move afoot to change the legal landscape, in part owing to the Klippert case.

A second incident, which in part stemmed from the Klippert case and was also a result of the Stonewall movement, was the first gay rights march in Canada. This march occurred in 1971 in Ottawa, where gays demanded recognition and rights.

Finally, Canada's own "Stonewall" moment did not really come until 1981. In a police action code-named "Operation Soap," Toronto police raided a number of bathhouses in the gay district (traditionally the area around Church and Wellesley streets, just east of Yonge Street) of the city. Two hundred and eighty-six men were charged with a host of crimes, and the incident provoked protests and clashes with the police and led to large demonstrations. Operation Soap was the largest mass arrest in Canada since the October Crisis. The raids resulted in such a backlash that the next night more than 4,000 people marched in protest against the action. Many others formed associations, demanded police respond to the issue, and asked their politicians to protect them. Things had changed in Canada to a large degree from the cloistered 1950s. Eventually, the police had to state that they respected the rights of gay men, and their privacy, and the incident proved to be a major step in gay rights in Canada.

There had been impetus toward gay rights before the bathhouse raids in Canada, however. Pierre Trudeau, elected prime minister in 1968 on the platform of making Canada "a just society," had made a number of famous changes to the Criminal Code in 1969, which led to a host of reforms ensuring that the sexual revolution was well established. Trudeau had been a Quebec lawyer who had fought for individual rights and against the Duplessis regime, and he had helped to usher in the Quiet Revolution. As part of his concern with individual rights and his progressive approach to social matters, Trudeau had famously maintained, "There's no place for the state in the bedrooms of the nation." He set out to modernize Canada's laws toward matters relating to sexuality, marriage, and divorce. He decriminalized birth control; he reformed the law surrounding abortion, allowing it if approved by a hospital medical committee as necessary to preserve the pregnant woman's life or health (however, abortion on demand was still a crime, and it was difficult to get such an abortion); and he established fairly uniform divorce procedures across Canada. Trudeau also decriminalized homosexuality.

Part of the reason Trudeau put these new laws into place was because of the demands being made by women and by gays—and because of certain cases that showed how things were seemingly unfair, such as the Klippert case. Though Trudeau's new laws marked a dramatic change, many of these issues are still debated today. Nonetheless, Trudeau played a role in the sexual revolution in Canada. His commitment to individual rights eventually came to be fully expressed in the 1982 Charter of Rights and Freedoms.

The Counterculture, Youth, Universities, and Rochdale College

All of these events fed into and were part of the underlying changes that helped to create the counterculture of the period. A number of underlying factors also help to explain the emergence of the counterculture: the wave of baby-boom demographic change meant a massive number of young people, many of whom were in university; the wealth of these young people, especially in terms of their disposable income, leisure time, and financial ability to attend university; and the 1950s' conservatism to which the counterculture was a generational reaction.

Of course, not all of Canada was taking part in this counterculture. Cindy Lei and her compatriots at Rochdale were not the norm, and, though the counterculture was a major factor in North American and Canadian society, it was not the only thing going on. After all, at the height of the counterculture, 1967, Canada was celebrating Expo 67, which had little to do with the counterculture movement. Indeed, at the top of the Canadian music charts that year was Bobby Gimby's "Ca-na-da," a song to celebrate Expo and Canada's centennial. It was a huge hit, selling over 300,000 copies.

So what was the counterculture? It was one of the most important elements of the Sixties and remains one of the most memorable images and cultural touchstones of the period. Its nature can be seen through a number of important developments.

First, and very significantly, music played an important role in the creation of the counterculture in Canada. Folk and rock musicians challenged musical traditions and sang about new approaches to thinking about and experiencing society. Canadians became leaders in the folk music revival, and artists such as Joni Mitchell, Neil Young, and Sylvia and Ian Tyson became famous as folk singers. The genre became so popular that the Mariposa Folk Festival, founded in Orillia, Ontario, in 1961, became a huge annual event and a centre point of the counterculture in Canada, with thousands of music fans from across the country and the United States attending.

Rock music also became a key ingredient of the counterculture. This genre challenged preconceived notions of what made up "civility." Rock was infused with a spirit of "sticking it to the man," an anti-establishment attitude found in bands such as the Rolling Stones or The Guess Who, the most popular Canadian act at the time. The signature moment was probably the 1969 Woodstock music festival in upstate New York. Billed as "3 days of peace & music," the festival was something of a capstone for the counterculture for both Americans and Canadians.[2] Since it was right across the border, many Canadians attended the event, which attracted over 100,000 people (though perhaps four times as many claim that they were there). It featured artists such as Jimi Hendrix, Janis Joplin,

---

2   See the original Woodstock poster at http://www.woodstockstory.com/woodstockposters.html.

the Grateful Dead, Crosby, Stills, Nash & Young, and Jefferson Airplane. It was an expression, a real moment of that decade and that generation.

Second, drug use was another element of the counterculture. Drugs were a staple of the scene from the Beatniks to the psychedelic excesses of the Woodstock festival. Drug use became popular and accessible for many Canadians as a way to "turn on, tune in, drop out,"[3] as another way to experience the mood of the period but also to get away from the sadness that marked the Sixties, especially that brought on because of the war in Vietnam. Indeed, the drug culture had a harsher side. Like alcoholism, drug addiction became a major societal issue, and drug use was really caught between notions of criminality and health; its place is still debated in Canadian society today.

A third element of the counterculture was sex. In the 1960s, the advent of the contraceptive pill made sex seemingly risk free. "Free love," as this idea was referred to, became an aspect of the Sixties counterculture that reflected perhaps the most prominent reaction to the repressive 1950s. Whereas the 1950s had seen no discussion of sex at all (on television, couples slept in separate twin beds), in the 1960s, sex seemed to be everywhere.

Much of the spirit of the counterculture came together in Yorkville. Yorkville, an area in Toronto now known more for luxury goods, became an epicentre of the counterculture in English-speaking Canada, as were areas in Vancouver and Montreal. It was here that Joni Mitchell got her start, that the coffee and drug houses flourished, and that the idea of the counterculture really came into prominence. It was here that a person like Cindy Lei found herself, and found others like herself, in Rochdale College.

Indeed, the counterculture found a ready home in the booming universities. The growth in population and suburban centres in the 1950s required a commensurate growth in institutions to support the people in these new communities. Chief among these institutions was the educational system. As a result of this postwar boom, there was a massive building of public and high schools in the 1950s all across the country. In Ontario, for example, the government created the college system beginning in the early 1960s; it included institutions such as Sir Sanford Fleming in Peterborough, Humber in suburban Etobicoke, and Fanshawe in London, all founded in 1967. These colleges were designed to provide training for practical or technical skills.

New universities were also created in this period. Institutions such as Trent (1964), York (1959), Calgary (1966), and Simon Fraser (1965) sprang up in Canadian cities and in Canadian suburbs. There was also an expansion of old schools as well. The University of Toronto grew and established satellite campuses. In many booming universities across the country, the counterculture flourished.

---

3   This phrase was popularized by the psychologist and psychedelic drug advocate Timothy Leary in 1966–67.

Figure 16.1 *Rochdale College*

York University Archives, Clara Thomas Archives and Special Collections, Toronto Telegram fonds, ASC05296

The greatest example of the counterculture's connection to university life was Rochdale College. Founded in 1968 as a "free school" at the University of Toronto, Rochdale provided space for about 800 students in a giant building on Bloor Street that was meant to alleviate the university's student housing shortage. As an academic experiment, Rochdale College had no classes and no curriculum but simple discussion groups led by students or anyone who wished to lead a course that focused on "free learning," for all kinds of people, not just traditional university students. Rochdale was completely student run and quickly became a hippie haven, given its location adjacent to Yorkville. Many in the university and in the wider community were ambivalent about the Rochdale "experiment," whose degree requirements reflected the anti-establishment, free-thinking vibe of the era:

> Tuition for the B.A. granting course is $25.00. Course length is 24 hours, and the degree will be awarded on answering of a skill testing question. Tuition for the M.A. is $50.00. During this course, the length of which will be determined by the student, the student will be required to answer a skill testing question of his choice. For a Ph.D. the tuition is $100.00 and there will be no questions asked.
>
> We are also offering Non-Degrees at comparable rates. A Non-Ph.D. is $25.00. Course duration is your choice; requirements are simple, we ask

that you say something. A Non-M.A. is $50.00 for which we require you
to say something logical. A Non-B.A. will cost you $100.00; you will be
required to say something useful.[4]

At the same time, the college provided all kinds of alternative classes and
approaches, from pottery to music to a radio station. Rochdalians established
day cares, publishing houses, and theatre groups, and, though the emphasis was
on student self-learning and free thinking, the radical optimism of the college led
to a number of lasting contributions to the city's educational and cultural landscape. Cindy Lei, for instance, was not just a student at Rochdale; she also helped
to organize and run all the dance and drama workshops and classes. She also
was an active member of the college's student-run organization and leadership.

Clearly, Rochdale College's approach was different from the traditional university curriculum, both then and now.

Protest, Vietnam, and Radicalism

Protest was another significant element of the counterculture. Civil rights for
American blacks was the first great protest movement of the decade. It was a
great injustice. The postwar rhetoric of democracy or of human rights (especially
in light of the Nazi atrocities) rang hollow in an America where racial discrimination and outright violence toward blacks were commonplace. By the late 1950s
and early 1960s, a number of movements had emerged to challenge the "Jim
Crow" laws of the South that disenfranchised blacks from voting and maintained
a harsh segregation. Leaders such as Rosa Parks and Martin Luther King Jr. led
campaigns against segregated bus systems, lunch counters, and schools. Eventually, these early struggles culminated in the massive 1963 March on Washington
and convinced presidents John F. Kennedy and Lyndon B. Johnson that civil and
voting rights must be extended to blacks; laws passed in the mid-1960s were
major steps forward in this fight.

Blacks faced their own challenges in Canada, where there was still widespread
racism and in some places outright discrimination. For instance, there is the case
of Africville, a small black community in north-end Halifax that had existed since
the 1800s, comprised of about 500 residents. In the mid-1960s the government
decided to "relocate" its residents in the interests of urban renewal, a decision
made without consulting the people of Africville. Between 1964 and 1967 the
provincial government basically expropriated and bulldozed the whole community. Civil rights for blacks were not just an American issue.

---

4   Taken from the Rochdale College degree application; to see this and other documents and
     images related to Rochdale, visit https://files.nyu.edu/spores01/public/rochdale.html.

Civil rights were also an issue for Quebecers. In fact, many Quebecers saw themselves as facing many of the same challenges that blacks in the United States faced. The FLQ writer Pierre Vallières penned the provocative book *White Niggers of America* to punctuate his feelings on the place of French Canadians in North America. The rights of aboriginals also came to the fore at this time. In the Sixties, civil rights crossed borders and colour lines.

Of course, no issue generated as much protest as America's involvement in Vietnam. Canadians did not take part militarily but were certainly on the domestic frontlines in the battle over US policy in Southeast Asia. The United States propped up a failing South Vietnamese government against attacks from the Communist north and the Vietcong insurrection in its midst. By 1968, the United States had over half a million men in Vietnam, and, by the time US forces had left, 58,000 Americans had died, along with over 2 million Vietnamese.

Canada did not partake in Vietnam, and it accepted American war resisters, also called draft dodgers, who refused to fight in the war for reasons of conscience. Though it is not clear exactly how many resisters came to Canada, the estimate is as high as 50,000. In BC, the war resisters flocked to Vancouver and scattered to islands along the province's coast. In Ontario, many resisters congregated in Yorkville. After the war's end in 1975, quite a few returned to the US in 1977 when President Jimmy Carter offered them amnesty. Estimates are that about 25,000 Americans remained.

Draft dodgers were just one aspect of the Canadian role in Vietnam. As in the United States, those opposed to the war held rallies and protests in Canada. Many of these were led by students, who saw US aggression against the Vietnamese as immoral and unjustifiable. Vancouver, Toronto, and Montreal saw protests against the war. Canadians were not only protesting America's involvement in Vietnam but also condemning Canada's own military supplying of the United States. Many Canadian factories produced technology or vehicles or parts for use in the Vietnamese war. Students were not the only ones protesting Vietnam. Groups such as VOW, the Voice of Women, also protested the war. VOW's Kay Macpherson went to North Vietnam to witness and report upon the destruction and death inflicted by the American bombing campaigns. VOW also assisted in a humanitarian knitting project on behalf of North and South Vietnamese children caught in combat zones. The organization also sponsored a trip of women from North and South Vietnam to Canada, arranging for US peace activists to meet with them on Canadian soil.

Protests against Vietnam easily became protests against the United States itself. Students, academics, and even musicians began to strike an anti-American tone as the war continued and the casualties mounted. From autoworkers to rock bands, many criticized America and the obvious contradictions of American life: on the one hand, America claimed to be the wellspring of democracy and freedom, yet it discriminated against black Americans and bombed foreign countries. It was easy to attack American hypocrisy, and one indication of the level of animosity toward US policy was the success of songs such as the Guess Who's "American Woman," which was explicitly anti-American.

At the same time, many Canadians supported the intervention. The Canadian government avoided joining the fight in Vietnam but did participate in an international group designed to mediate the conflict. But many Canadians joined the US Armed Forces to serve in Vietnam, and over 100 were killed in action. Today, there are Canadian Vietnam veterans associations, and there is a Canadian Vietnam Veterans' Memorial in Windsor. Vietnam illustrated the unrelenting closeness, conflict, and contradictions of the country's relations with the United States.

In some instances during the Sixties, protests took a radical and sometimes violent form. This was not just a North American phenomenon: violent student uprisings in Europe in 1968, especially in Paris, reflected a newfound willingness to use violent protest to challenge the established order. In Canada, Canadians had experienced the violent protests and efforts to actually try to incite revolution of the FLQ.

There was also violence in the United States. Student radicalism was widespread south of the border. At the 1968 Democratic Party's national convention, student radical groups such as the SDS, or Students for a Democratic Society, threatened to hijack the party's proceedings. Many of these protestors ended up in jail. Other student protests took a violent turn because of state responses, which illustrated the unwillingness of the state to tolerate civil disobedience. In Ohio in 1970, for instance, US National Guard troops opened fire on unarmed student protestors at Kent State University, tragically killing four people.

Cindy Lei, the End of Rochdale, and the Legacy of the Sixties

When Cindy Lei joined Rochdale in the late 1960s, she quickly became part of the counterculture scene in the building. Alternative learning was just one aspect of the Rochdale experience; students lived in alternative arrangements (a free love experiment, with multiple partners and communal living) and imbibed at legendary parties that involved copious amounts of drugs and alcohol (and sex as well; notorious call girl Xaviera Hollander allegedly made some appearances at college events). But the college also featured aspects that would be familiar to people today: it had a decidedly environmental bent (students grew their own vegetables) and advocated a cooperative and egalitarian spirit, one embracing non-traditional forms of learning and living.

Eventually, and unfortunately for its residents, Rochdale also descended into a drug den, as some of its floors were essentially controlled by biker gangs. It also became a magnet for some of Toronto's homeless and its drug addicts.

In 1971, the federal government notified Rochdale College of impending fore-closure because of mortgage default. Starting on May 15, 1975, after numerous disputes between the property owners and the college leadership, the police were called in to seize control of the building and evict all the residents. Over the next weeks, dozens of police essentially raided the massive structure, dragged "students" out, and, eventually, welded the doors closed. Ironically, the building itself, which still stands on Bloor Street, was converted to a retirement residence.

Though Rochdale was unceremoniously shut down, the legacy of the Sixties, and much of the counterculture, continues to thrive well into the twenty-first century. Along with advances in terms of sexuality and culture, women's rights, and the success of the anti–Vietnam War movement (which eventually turned the tide against US involvement in the country), there were other advances that came out of the period.

One of these was environmentalism. In 1970, the very first Earth Day was held, a movement that emerged from the counterculture's anti-establishment agenda. The next year, in 1971, a group of Canadians and Americans formed Greenpeace and chartered a boat to protest US nuclear testing in the Alaskan islands. From that point forward, Greenpeace became the leading environmental group in the world, famous for its campaigns against nuclear energy and weapons, whaling, and global warming. Another legacy was the advance in gay rights. Many Roch-dalians are no doubt pleased and amazed that, in twenty-first-century Canada, gay rights have advanced so dramatically and that same sex marriage is legal.

Of course, many battles over the legacy of the Sixties counterculture continue to be fought; despite the advances made by minorities, women, gays, and the environmental movement, abortion rights are still targeted, discrimination against visible minorities and gays still abounds, and Canadians have not yet come to grips with the challenges of climate change, despite their general embrace of environmentalism. The Sixties are, in many ways, still with us.

Further Reading

Anastakis, Dimitry, ed. *The Sixties: Style and Substance*. Montreal: McGill-Queen's University Press, 2008.

Henderson, Stuart. *Making the Scene: Yorkville and Hip Toronto in the 1960s*. Toronto: University of Toronto Press, 2011.

Henderson, Stuart. "Toronto's Hippie Disease: End Days in the Yorkville Scene, August 1968." *Journal of the Canadian Historical Association* 17, no. 1 (2006): 205–34. http://dx.doi.org/10.7202/016108ar.

Mann, Ron, director. *Dream Tower*. Ottawa: National Film Board of Canada, 1994.

Palmer, Bryan. *Canada's 1960s: The Ironies of Identity in a Rebellious Era*. Toronto: University of Toronto Press, 2009.

FIRST PERSON ORAL HISTORY ASSIGNMENT: REMEMBERING THE SIXTIES

Ask your relatives (parents, grandparents, aunts, uncles) or people you know who lived during the 1960s about their experiences in the decade. Write a 3–5 page questionnaire to assess the views of people who lived through the Sixties. Questions might include:

- How old were you during the Sixties? Where did you live at this time?

- How do you think different generations experienced or viewed the Sixties? In other words, how did the "baby boomers" experience the decade differently from their parents?

- What were your experiences during the period? Did you take part in any of the counterculture? If not, what were your views of the counterculture?

- What are your most vivid memories and experiences during the decade?

- What do you think are the legacies of the Sixties? Was the decade a positive influence on society today?

- What were your educational experiences during the decade like, if you were in school at that time?

- What are your favourite musical memories of the decade?

MURDEROUS MOMENT
PAUL JOSEPH CHARTIER, KILLED WHILE ATTEMPTING TO BLOW UP THE HOUSE OF COMMONS, 1966

A Little-Known Attack on Canada's Seat of Government

The 1960s were a period of profound change and dislocation. Social, cultural, and political revolution was in the air, and, in some instances, violence, which often lasted into the 1970s, accompanied these calls for change. From the FLQ in Quebec, to the Weather Underground in the United States, the Red Brigades in Europe, and revolutionary uprisings in South America, the world seemed aflame with militant and sometimes violent demands for change that could not be contained within the established political process. Most of the violence in this period emerged from organizations and movements whose causes were rooted in legitimate grievances; they would say that their violent tactics were necessary, though many would disagree.

In other instances, the violence that erupted in the 1960s (and at other times in Canadian history) had little rhyme or reason. People acting alone have at times sought to use violence as a means of expressing their own personal complaints or problems, as a way to highlight some particular grievance or because they are suffering mental illness.

One such person was Paul Joseph Chartier. Chartier was a trucker originally from just outside Edmonton, Alberta, where his family owned a hotel. By the early 1960s, he had fallen on hard times. Chartier declared bankruptcy in 1960, had a number of incidents within the legal system (including threatening a lawyer with death), and was in the midst of a divorce from his wife. By 1966, he was living in Toronto, working as a security guard, had

become mentally unstable, and had spent some time at the Toronto Psychiatric Hospital.

In May of 1966, Chartier drove to Newmarket, Ontario, where he purchased sticks of dynamite. He then drove to Ottawa, intending to bomb the House of Commons. Despite the recent spate of FLQ bombings in Montreal, Parliament Hill security was still rather lax. Chartier walked into the House of Commons with the dynamite hidden on his person. He went to the public galleries, watched the proceedings below as Prime Minister Lester Pearson and Opposition Leader John Diefenbaker tangled over the latest government issue (at the time, Ottawa was gripped with the Gerda Munsinger scandal, a supposed German spy who had had affairs with two high-profile Canadian politicians). Chartier then went to a third-floor bathroom, where he lit the homemade fuse attached to the sticks of dynamite he was carrying.

At 2:57 PM, Chartier was on his way back to the House of Commons when the crude bomb he had fashioned prematurely detonated as he was leaving the bathroom. The blast tore off his arm and ripped through his torso, immediately killing him. The explosion shook the Centre Block of Parliament Hill, and sent politicians scurrying from the crowded chamber to the site of the blast. Only the heavy wooden bathroom door, which blunted the force of the explosion, prevented greater tragedy. Thirty feet away, the north gallery was packed with schoolchildren at the moment of the blast.

As one witness told reporters, "You couldn't see for smoke. All we could see was a slab blown off the toilet and debris. From what I heard, that guy was all over the place. They were talking of taking him out in a plastic bag."[5] Canadians were shocked by the incident, the first indisputable attack on the House of Commons (the 1916 wartime fire had been ruled an accident, not sabotage).

Before the attack, Chartier had allegedly sent a mail bomb to his estranged wife, then living in BC, and a letter to the *Edmonton Journal*, outlining the reasons for his attack. The letter repeated claims that police discovered in a speech they found when they raided Chartier's apartment in Toronto. He wanted to be president of Canada, decried the high cost of living, and claimed that all the politicians were making Canadians "slaves": "Before I thought of becoming president my first wish was to exterminate as many members as possible. I also knew that this might cost me my life, but then I figured someone might benefit. . . . It's too bad we can't give them a jolt, say 10,000 volts, to remind them of their promises."[6] Chartier also lashed out at the social changes occurring in Canada, attacking lesbians and gays who had in the decade become more visible in society.

The notes he made for his speeches also outlined Chartier's plan to rain the dynamite down upon the prime minister, ministers and MPs in the House of Commons from the visitors' gallery. Only a misjudgement of timing prevented what could have been a horrible terrorist attack upon the heart of Canada's democratic and governmental system. Chartier's actions are a reminder that public violence is nothing new in Canada, especially given that the 1960s themselves were rife with such attacks, both in Canada and around the world. Chartier's death also reminds us that Canada's political institutions and symbols have not been immune to terrorist attacks; long before the bombing of the World Trade Centre in New York City and the Pentagon in Washington, DC, in September of 2001, the House of Commons was a target, and, so was the Quebec National Assembly, in 1984.

---

5   Norman Webster, "MPs Say Explosion Premature, Man's Bomb Meant for Chamber," *Globe and Mail*, May 19, 1966, 1.
6   "Chartier Wanted Presidency with June Marks as His Deputy," *Globe and Mail*, May 21, 1966, 10.

CHAPTER SEVENTEEN

THREE EMPLOYEES OF THE QUEBEC NATIONAL ASSEMBLY, MURDERED, QUEBEC CITY, 1984

THE CONSTITUTIONAL WARS TURN DEADLY

Few Canadians have heard of René Jalbert. But he is a genuine Canadian hero whose incredibly brave act—the kind of thing that happens in movies all the time—rarely happens in real life. That's because movies, especially Hollywood action movies, are often complete fiction (even when portraying historical events), but real life is not.

The Cross of Valour citation that René Jalbert received from the governor general tells the story fairly well. The Cross of Valour is the highest civilian award that can be given to a Canadian. The citation reads:

> In a rare display of cool-headedness and courage, René Jalbert, Sergeant-at-Arms at the Quebec National Assembly, subdued a man who had killed three people and wounded thirteen more on the morning of 8 May 1984. The man had entered a side door of the National Assembly building and immediately opened fire with a sub-machine gun; moments later he climbed the main staircase toward the assembly chamber, known as the Blue Room, shooting repeatedly, and then burst into the chamber. As bullets peppered the wall, Mr. Jalbert entered the Blue Room and with icy calm convinced the man to allow several employees to leave the premises. Then he invited the heavily armed man into his downstairs office, in effect setting himself up as hostage while removing the man from the scene. At extreme personal risk, but with unflinching authority, Mr. Jalbert spent four hours persuading the man to surrender to police. The audacity of this retired Major of the

Royal 22nd Regiment, a Second World War and Korean War veteran, almost certainly prevented a higher death toll.[1]

Think about that for a moment. That is real courage, real bravery, real heroism.

The situation that was thrust upon Jalbert was a consequence, in many ways, of the constitutional wars that raged in Canada in the 1970s and the 1980s, and that even spilled into the 1990s. The incident represents a manifestation of the frustration, conflict, and emotions attached to the battle over the Canadian Constitution and particularly around Quebec's place in Canada. Now, at first glance, it does not seem to have any connection to the constitutional battles in Canada that began in the 1960s and are still going on, but consider the circumstances surrounding the incident.

Although the shooter, Denis Lortie, was a deranged member of the Canadian Armed Forces, he decided to attack the Quebec National Assembly, the seat of government in the province. He specifically stated he was out to destroy the separatist Parti Québécois government. Now, there is absolutely no justification for this kind of action. But given the context of the times, during the very stressful and emotional constitutional battles within Canada, it provides us with one chilling example of when Canada's constitutional war moved from being a battle over politics and ideas to one that involved murder.

As such, the case is in some ways the inverse of the FLQ and their murder of Pierre Laporte. Whereas the FLQ used violence and murder to try to achieve Quebec independence, the man who killed three employees of the Quebec National Assembly used violence and murder to try to end the separatist threat to Canada. Both were wrong, yet the cases serve as interesting starting points from which to discuss these issues. However, to understand these incidents, we need to first comprehend the context and circumstances that could have provoked such an attack.

Canada's Constitutional Status, 1867–1968

Long before the constitutional wars of the 1970s and 1980s and the attack on Quebec's National Assembly, the 1867 British North America Act (BNA Act) laid the background for these disputes. There are five important things about Canada's original constitutional document. First, because Canada was a British colony in 1867, this document was based on British principles. Second, it is a federal Constitution. Third, it provided for a strong central government, with "important powers" of trade, banking, immigration, and criminal law given to the federal government and with the provinces given what were seen as less

---

1   The citation can be found on the Governor General's website for honours, at http://www.gg.ca/honour.aspx?id=99702&t=3&ln=Jalbert.

important issues (e.g., social policy, education, cities, prisons, municipalities, hospitals). Fourth, until the 1970s, the main constitutional battles were over this division of powers, and courts usually favoured the provinces. Finally, the BNA Act did not provide a way to change the Constitution itself—when the BNA Act was created, Canadians never imagined not being a part of the British Empire.

But by the 1920s, Canada wanted to go its own way, and because the British themselves no longer wanted to be responsible for colonies, Canadians were granted control of their own Constitution through the 1931 Statute of Westminster. Now, keep in mind the difference between changing the Constitution and devising a formula to change the Constitution, in other words, an amending formula. At times, Canadians did change their Constitution: in 1940, for instance, Ottawa and the provinces agreed on an unemployment insurance system, so they asked London to change the BNA Act, which the British did.

But agreeing to change in the BNA Act is not the same as agreeing on an actual *process* by which Canadians could change the act. After 1931, if Canadians could figure out the procedures for changing the BNA Act, they could bring it home from the British Parliament. The only problem was, Canadians couldn't decide on a formula to change their Constitution. There were grand federal-provincial constitutional meetings in 1927, 1935, 1950, and 1964 that all failed to come to an agreement on how to change the Constitution.

All these conferences failed because of basic differences among Canadians on the Constitution and *how* it had been created and how it should be changed. Some thought that constitutional change required the agreement of all the provinces because provinces made up the country. Many in Quebec adhered to the "compact theory"; because two founding races (French in Quebec and English in the rest of Canada) had created the Constitution, any changes required Quebec's explicit consent. Others argued that provinces were equal, so neither all provinces' agreement nor the specific agreement of Quebec was needed to change the Constitution. All you needed was a majority.

Obviously, this issue was rooted in history, politics, and power. How the Constitution could be changed was the key issue for the federation. In any event, up to that time, the tradition was that any change to the BNA Act would require the unanimous consent of all the provinces. On the question of an amending formula, many thought the country *had* to have Quebec's consent. But with no agreement on how to change the Constitution, for more than five decades after 1931, Canada's Constitution was, quite literally, just sitting in the British Parliament.

Trudeau's Vision Achieved, 1968–84

By the 1960s, there had been little movement on the Constitution, despite the many changes in Canadian society marked by Quebec's Quiet Revolution, aboriginal Red Power, and the sexual revolution. The best way to understand both the lack of constitutional movement and the changes in Canadian society is to look at Pierre Trudeau and his philosophy.

Like him or hate him, Trudeau remains the central figure in helping to explain the battle over the Constitution. Born in 1919 to a well-to-do family, Trudeau was first elected MP in 1965, became justice minister in 1967, and then prime minister in 1968. Trudeau's core beliefs were well-defined. He was against nationalism, especially the nationalism of the Quebec Union Nationale government, and challenged the dogmas of Quebec Premier Maurice Duplessis. He was in favour of individual rights and against any "special status" for Quebec, which he saw as creating a ghetto. At the same time, he understood that many Quebecers did not feel at home across Canada and that Ottawa did not respond to the needs of French-speaking Canadians, and, thus, he thought that the federal government needed to reflect the French fact in Canada. Finally, Trudeau thought Canada needed to grow up; Canadians needing to go to the United Kingdom to change their Constitution was immature and unacceptable.

Perhaps most important, Trudeau was against the new separatism emerging in Quebec in the 1960s. His greatest fight was against René Lévesque and the separatist Parti Québécois (PQ). Lévesque and Trudeau had a long-standing, competitive personal and political relationship; their fight over Quebec and Canada's fate lasted decades, and both achieved incredible political success.

In 1968, Trudeau was elected on the notion of a "just society." A centrepiece policy was to "bring home" the Constitution with an amending formula and a bill of rights. Trudeau thought this would give Quebecers the same rights in Canada as English-speaking Canadians, defeat separatism, and bring forth a new understanding of the way the country worked based on individual rights but also on collective language rights.

Trudeau passed the Official Languages Act in 1969. Trudeau, who had worked in Ottawa in the late 1940s, saw the civil service's lack of bilingualism as a problem and decided that a quiet revolution for Ottawa was necessary. The act declared both English and French to be official languages and ensured Canadians access to the civil service in their language of choice, resulting in a bilingual federal government. Trudeau emphasized that the act was not intended to make Canadians bilingual but to ensure the bilingual provision of services *for* Canadians, no matter their official language, no matter where they lived.

Trudeau then moved onto the constitutional front. In 1971, he almost succeeded in his quest to bring home the Constitution. After difficult negotiations, all the provinces agreed to the "Victoria Charter," a constitutional deal that created a bill of rights and established a constitutional amending formula. However, at the last moment, Robert Bourassa's Quebec government pulled out, believing that the agreement did not provide enough for Quebec and its distinctiveness. The charter's failure was followed by the dramatic 1976 election of the Parti

Québécois, complicating Trudeau's quest significantly. Led by the charismatic Lévesque, Trudeau's colleague and adversary since the 1950s, the Parti Québécois, Trudeau thought, would never agree to any constitutional change, as Lévesque and the PQ ultimately wished only to leave Confederation.

Would Quebec even stay in the country? After much delay and fighting over strategy, the PQ held a referendum on Quebec's place in Canada on May 20, 1980. Quebec voters were asked to give the government permission to negotiate sovereignty association with Canada—not separation, but a step toward it. The referendum saw "No" and "Yes" sides created to convince Quebecers about the fate of Canada. Here, the battle between Lévesque and Trudeau came to a head. Lévesque appealed to Quebecer's nationalism and pointed to a century of injustices for Quebecers, from Riel's fate to schooling to conscription. Trudeau promised "constitutional renewal" if Quebec voted "non." At the height of the campaign, he made a further pledge during a famous speech:

> I make a solemn declaration to all Canadians in the other provinces, we, the Québec MPs, are laying ourselves on the line, because we are telling Quebecers to vote No and telling you in the other provinces that we will not agree to your interpreting a No vote as an·indication that everything is fine and can remain as it was before.
>
> We want change and we are willing to lay our seats in the House on the line to have change.[2]

But Trudeau did not specify what kind of change he was talking about. Some have since argued that Trudeau was misleading, just as others have argued that the referendum question from the Parti Québécois was also vague and misleading.

At the heart of the debate was the nature of Canadian Confederation and whether Canada would survive; for many Quebecers, the period was difficult and emotional, as they faced off with one another in a personal and political battle. Families and neighbours were torn apart by the increasingly heated conflict as the referendum vote neared. Eventually, when the ballots were counted 60 per cent of the province (and 52 per cent of francophones) had voted "non." Federalism, or at least Trudeau's promise of renewed federalism, had seemingly carried the day.

Now, armed with the defeat of the separatists in the referendum, Trudeau decided to take up his quest again. After the referendum, he stated that he would patriate (bring home) the Constitution unilaterally, without provincial consent if necessary, and that it would include an amending formula and a charter of rights and freedoms.

For many, especially in Quebec, this was not what they thought Trudeau had promised in his famous speech. More important, some other provincial

---

2   Quoted in Peter H. Russell, *Constitutional Odyssey: Can Canadians Become a Sovereign People?* (Toronto: University of Toronto Press, rev. ed., 2004), 109.

governments thought Trudeau was grabbing power for the federal government at their expense, and going ahead without their agreement. Eventually, only New Brunswick and Ontario sided with Ottawa. The remaining provinces (the "Gang of Eight"), which included Quebec, believed that Trudeau could not proceed without provincial consent—and took Trudeau to court over the issue.

In 1981, the Supreme Court of Canada ruled that the federal government must negotiate with the provinces: although it was "legal" for Trudeau to proceed without unanimous consent, it was not the "convention," not how constitutional change had worked in the past. Moreover, the court stated that to patriate the Constitution, Trudeau needed "substantial" provincial agreement, though it never specified what this meant—was a majority or unanimity needed? The Court did not even say that patriation specifically required Quebec's agreement. Implicitly, they were stating that the issue was more political than legal and that Trudeau should work it out with the provinces. Thus, Trudeau was forced to go back to the provinces to negotiate a deal. As a result, a "final round" of talks was held in Ottawa in November 1981. A scene of high drama, the conference had profound consequences. During one of the fast-paced discussions, Trudeau made a pitch to Lévesque in French that patriation should come first while the charter of rights and the amending formula could be decided in a referendum: Lévesque agreed. He had broken with the Gang of Eight. As a consequence of this break, the other premiers became fearful that they would lose on such a referendum (who would vote against a bill of rights?). So, on the night of November 4, Ottawa and the nine other provinces met in their hotel and worked out a deal without consulting Quebec. Quebec's representatives were sleeping on their side of the Ottawa River.

The next morning, Lévesque rejected the deal as a "betrayal"; it has gone down in Quebec nationalist mythology as the "night of the long knives" in which Trudeau and the other provinces conspired to leave Quebec out. Of course, this ignores the fact that Lévesque himself had broken with the Gang of Eight and the question of whether Lévesque would have acceded to *any* constitutional agreement, likely not, as he was a separatist. Lévesque, outwitted and isolated by Trudeau, denounced the agreement and went back to Quebec. The deal agreed to by the nine provinces became Canada's new Constitution Act, which Queen Elizabeth II came to Canada to proclaim on April 17, 1982.

The new Constitution Act contained two important elements. First, it had a Charter of Rights and Freedoms. As a liberal, Trudeau believed in entrenched civil rights for individuals; thus it contained basic freedoms and other unique Canadian features such as protections for collective language and aboriginal rights and non-discrimination clauses for certain groups. Yet the Charter places limits on rights, too, by allowing governments to place "reasonable limits" on freedoms (Section 1).

Also, to assuage provincial fears that the Charter could dramatically reduce elected governments' power, Trudeau reluctantly agreed to a mechanism allowing a legislative override of rights. Legislatures could pass a law that had force "notwithstanding" certain Charter provisions, limited to five years (Section 33). Though legally bound by the new agreement, Quebec immediately "protected" all of its key legislation from the Charter by using the notwithstanding clause in a blanket manner.

Second, the Constitution now contained an amending formula outlining three main ways to change the document: some provisions require unanimity (changing the status of the Queen, the Senate, and a few other major things); others require only the agreement of the particular province affected by changes; but the general provisions for change require 7 of 10 provinces containing 50 per cent of the population. In other words, Quebec had no veto.

Many in Quebec felt betrayed. When the Constitution was proclaimed, some Quebecers wore black armbands and the government lowered flags to half mast. Nonetheless, Quebec is bound by the 1982 changes. No province "signed" the Constitution (though they all voted in favour in their legislatures, save for Quebec). In fact, the only signatures on it are those of Queen Elizabeth, Trudeau, Jean Chrétien, and André Ouellet (all three Canadians who signed it, ironically, are Quebecers). Quebec has used the various functions of the new Constitution, including the Charter and the amending formula, numerous times.

Despite being bound by the 1982 changes, Quebec's refusal to agree formally to the Constitution might have sown the seeds of calamity for Trudeau's constitutional vision.

The Attack on Quebec's National Assembly, 1984

By 1984, the seemingly endless elections, conferences, referendums, and emotion-infused debates about the future of the country had taken their toll. Trudeau had won a Pyrrhic victory, but more than a generation of stressful constitutional wrangling had scarred the psyches of ordinary Canadians. This stress was especially felt by Quebecers, who, continually asked to decide Canada's fate, faced the brunt of the constitutional wars.

Politics had driven some Canadians to violence in the past; most recently, FLQ members had resorted to violence to achieve their aims of an independent Quebec. Denis Lortie was already psychologically unstable, but his mental health issues found a tragic release in the political question of Quebec's place in Canada. Lortie was a corporal in the Canadian Armed Forces, stationed in Carp, Ontario, just outside of Ottawa. Also known as the famous "Diefenbunker," the base was an underground station for government officials in case of a nuclear attack. In May of 1984, Lortie, who was later diagnosed with having an episode of paranoid schizophrenia, left the base, telling his commanding officer that he needed to deal with his marital problems. Instead, he headed to Quebec City.

Once in Quebec City, Lortie posed as an ordinary citizen and took a tour of the National Assembly. The next day, Lortie dressed in combat fatigues and armed himself with two automatic rifles and a handgun. He stopped at a radio station and dropped off a tape, which he said must not be played until an hour after he left. Reporters at the station played it immediately and were horrified to discover Lortie intended to destroy the PQ separatist government.

By the time the station warned police, Lortie was already inside the National Assembly. He killed three people, Camille Lepage, Georges Boyer, and Roger Lefrançois. Two were messengers, another an employee of the electoral commission. He also wounded 13 people before being stopped by René Jalbert. Later, it became clear that Lortie intended to assassinate Premier René Lévesque and kill as many members of his government as possible. Only Lortie's mistaken timing prevented him from appearing in the Blue Room when it was in session.

Lortie's rampage shocked Quebecers and Canadians. His actions were not caused by the constitutional wars, but they symbolically reflected the political turmoil faced by Canadians in this period.

Mulroney's Failures, 1984–95

The attack on Quebec's National Assembly came the same year that Brian Mulroney defeated John Turner, Trudeau's successor, and became prime minister. If Trudeau's story is one of Pyrrhic victory, Mulroney's is about failure, and he plays almost as large a role as Trudeau in the constitutional wars.

Although both men were lawyers from Quebec, they could not have been more different: Trudeau was from wealthy, French-speaking, upper-class Montreal; he was classically trained and educated around the world. Mulroney was from a small Quebec mill town, sang songs for the company bosses, and learned his French in the rough-and-tumble streets. While Trudeau travelled the world, Mulroney lived a rags-to-riches story. He worked his way up to become the quintessential corporate lawyer and president of the Iron Ore Company of Canada, a US-owned branch plant. By the 1980s, the two men knew where each other stood, and when it came to the Constitution, were polar opposites.

Mulroney's 1984 victory came partly because of his constitutional promises. Mulroney argued that Trudeau's changes were not credible because Quebec never agreed to them. He argued that Quebec must have veto power, must be recognized as distinct within Canada, and he campaigned on the promise of bringing "Quebec into the constitution with honour and enthusiasm."[3] In his campaign, Mulroney appealed to Quebec nationalists such as Lucien Bouchard. Mulroney's Laval law

---

3   Speech on August 6, 1984, at Sept-Îles. See "Brian Mulroney," *The Prime Ministers of Canada*, http://www.prime-ministers.ca/mulroney/bio_4.php?context=c.

school friend, Bouchard played a key role in securing Mulroney's victory in Quebec. Mulroney appointed Bouchard Canada's ambassador to France and had even held a wedding reception for Bouchard and his second wife at the prime minister's residence at 24 Sussex Drive. Like many other Quebec nationalists after 1982, Bouchard thought that Trudeau had hurt Quebec and believed that the province should have a distinctive, special place in Canada. This perspective reflected Bouchard's belief in the "compact theory," an idea that appealed to Mulroney, who brought Bouchard onto his campaign.

That Quebec's distinctiveness should be constitutionally recognized directly challenged Trudeau's vision of the country. Trudeau believed adamantly in a strong central government and in provincial equality. Mulroney and Trudeau were deeply divided on Quebec's place in Confederation. Mulroney made two hugely draining and ultimately failed efforts at making his own constitutional amendments.

The first was called the Meech Lake Accord, after a Quebec resort town where Mulroney and the 10 premiers hammered out a new deal. In June 1987, Mulroney announced to the country that, miraculously, all provinces had agreed to a constitutional accord, including Quebec. Mulroney had achieved where Trudeau had failed, and Quebec was now a part of the Constitution. Or so it seemed.

Meech Lake was relatively straightforward. Quebec was recognized as a "distinct society" and was now given a veto over constitutional amendments, as there had been no specific Quebec veto under the 1982 constitutional changes. Provinces were to be given a role in the nomination of Supreme Court judges, the right to "opt out" of new federal programs with full compensation, and a role in immigration, especially important to Quebec.

Meech Lake's passage would mean a significant victory for Mulroney and was a fundamental change from Trudeau's vision of the country. With Meech, instead of a nation of equal provinces, there would be a recognition of Canada's two founding nations, with essentially two sets of rules for the country: one for Quebec, one for the other provinces. The distinct society clause granted Quebec's government the right to "preserve and promote" Quebec's distinct status, yet it was still unclear what "preserve and promote" meant.

Though signed by all 10 premiers and Mulroney, the amendment also had to be *ratified* by all provinces. Under the 1982 Constitution, any amendment of this magnitude died unless passed by all provincial legislatures within three years. This procedure did not seem problematic, as, initially, Canadians were largely in support of Meech.

But criticisms begin to emerge. First, people began to attack the accord on the grounds of "executive federalism," charging that 11 white men in suits were deciding Canada's future: Why were First Nations representatives and women's groups left out? In 1981, women and native groups had lobbied the federal government to change the new Constitution. The Charter had quickly been embraced by Canadians after 1982, and some people felt that it should be not changed without wider consultation with average Canadians. Trudeau had made a Constitution that people *identified with*.

Second, people started to wonder: what, exactly, did "distinct society" mean? After all, many people in the country argued that there were many "distinct societies" in Canada. First Nations, for instance, or Newfoundlanders, or franco-Manitobans, or Acadians could all rightfully claim to be distinct.

In a famous 1987 Senate testimony, Trudeau argued that Meech Lake would render Canada into 10 separate fiefdoms and give the separatists what they wanted. In his penetrating logic, he dismantled the "distinct society" agreement and said it was a short few steps to dismantling the whole country. If that was to be the case, he said, Canadians should let Canada "go with a bang rather than a whimper," such as that contained in Meech.[4]

When Quebec in 1989 used the notwithstanding clause to pass a law restricting English-language rights, criticism of the impending distinct society clause erupted. Protests spread across the country, and some municipalities declared themselves "English only" in response to the move. In Brockville, Ontario, English-only zealots stepped on and set alight a Quebec flag in 1990.

Meanwhile, as tensions escalated during the three-year window allowed to ratify the agreement, governments changed. In New Brunswick in 1987 Liberal Frank McKenna won all 58 seats; initially, he was reluctant to ratify the agreement, but he did so eventually. In Newfoundland in 1989 another Liberal (and supporter of Trudeau), Clyde Wells, was elected. He opposed the agreement and threatened to rescind Newfoundland's previous ratification unless changes were made.

Mulroney faced a crisis. Needing to ensure that Meech was ratified, three weeks before the deadline, he called a first ministers' conference. After a week of intense negotiations, additions to Meech were devised to quell the unhappiness. All 10 premiers again signed the "new" accord, although Wells said that he would consult Newfoundlanders before committing.

In the middle of this crisis, Mulroney gave an interview to the *Globe and Mail*. He brashly stated that he forced the issue by creating this crisis with a plan to resolve it at the conference. As he famously said, "That's the day we're going to roll the dice" on the amendment.[5] This rhetoric infuriated many Canadians, who felt that Mulroney was gambling with their country's future.

Two days after the new agreement was announced, Meech faced new challenges. In Manitoba, aboriginal legislative member Elijah Harper waved an eagle feather and refused the unanimous consent needed for the accord to go to a vote. In Newfoundland, Clyde Wells also refused to bring Meech to a vote.

---

4   Trudeau testifying before the Canadian Senate, March 30, 1988. Quoted in Pierre Elliott Trudeau, *With a Bang, Not a Whimper: Pierre Trudeau Speaks Out*, edited by Donald J. Johnston (Toronto: Stoddart, 1988), 172.

5   Susan Delacourt and Graham Fraser, "Marathon Talks Were All Part of a Plan, PM Says," *Globe and Mail*, June 12, 1990, A1.

Dramatically, as the clock ticked down, Meech missed its June 1990 ratification deadline. Mulroney had failed.

Despite this failure, Mulroney tried again. With Quebec separatism running at an all-time high, another conference was held in Charlottetown in 1992. In response to demands from women, aboriginals, Quebec, and the West, Mulroney hammered out a new deal, the Charlottetown Accord. A hodgepodge, with many clauses vague or left unwritten, Charlottetown was opposed by Trudeau and the western-based Reform Party. The accord failed in a nationwide referendum in late 1992, as six provinces and the Yukon Territory rejected it.

Legacies

As a result of these failures, by 1992 support for separatism in Quebec rose dramatically. Quebec politicians such as Bouchard and Jacques Parizeau exploited the so-called humiliation of the Meech and Charlottetown failures to argue that Quebec would never be given proper status in Canada. Bouchard abandoned his best friend Mulroney and started the Bloc Québécois, a federal party representing Quebec's separatists. Provincially, the Parti Québécois returned to power in 1994, determined to separate from a Canada that had, in its view, rejected it three times (1982, Meech, Charlottetown). The PQ held another referendum in October 1995, with a question that called for separation but also an economic "agreement" with Canada.

This time, Ottawa promised no constitutional changes if Quebec voted "non." An incredibly charismatic Lucien Bouchard, who had lost a leg to flesh-eating disease and fought the campaign wearing a prosthesis and using a cane, led the "Yes" side. The federal response was generally weak, and on October 30, 1995, with a 94 per cent turnout of Quebec voters, 49.4 per cent (and a majority of francophones) said "oui" to separation. The result could have turned on a minuscule 27,000 votes.

Since Mulroney's failures and the 1995 referendum, the threat of separatism has receded, and there has been a long lull in the constitutional wars. Despite a 1998 Supreme Court ruling that made it clear that any future vote required a clear majority in favour of separation, a 2000 federal law that required "clarity" for any future referendum question, and the decline of separatist popularity, the question of Quebec's place in Canada has not been entirely resolved.

And what happened to René Jalbert and Denis Lortie? Jalbert died in 1996 of cancer. Despite his mental state, Lortie was tried for first-degree murder in 1985. Procedural problems resulted in two more trials, but, in 1987, he was found guilty of second-degree murder. Sentenced to life in prison with a 10-year minimum before parole, Lortie was released in 1996 after serving 12 years. He lives in Quebec, and currently works in construction.

Further Reading

Cairns, Alan. *Disruptions: Constitutional Struggles from the Charter to Meech Lake.* Toronto: McClelland & Stewart, 1991.

Hébert, Chantal, with Jean Lapierre. *The Morning After: The Quebec Referendum and the Day That Almost Was.* Toronto: Knopf Canada, 2014.

Litt, Paul. "Trudeaumania: Participatory Democracy in tha Mass-Mediated Nation." *Canadian Historical Review* 89, no. 1 (March 2008): 27–53. http://dx.doi.org/10.3138/chr.89.1.27.

Russell, Peter H. "The End of Mega Constitutional Politics in Canada?" *PS: Political Science & Politics* 26, no. 1 (March 1993): 33–38.

Smith, Miriam. "Political Activism, Litigation and Public Policy: The Charter Revolution and Lesbian and Gay Rights in Canada, 1985–1999." *International Journal of Canadian Studies* 3, no. 1 (2000): 81–109.

Vipond, Robert C. "Whatever Became of the Compact Theory? Meech Lake and the New Politics of Constitutional Amendment in Canada." *Queen's Quarterly* 96, no. 4 (Winter 1989): 793–811.

ACTIVE HISTORY: MEDIA ANALYSIS

- Visit the CBC archives and examine the broadcast news report of the 1984 attack on Quebec's National Assembly, at http://www.cbc.ca/archives/categories/society/crime-justice/general-3/gunman-kills-3-at-quebec-legislature.html.

- How does the report contrast with the citation for René Jalbert quoted previously? What facts are still being developed in the story?

- How do the witness testimonials add to the story and its reporting? Do they make the story more compelling or add significant new information to the story?

- What critiques, if any, can you make about the accuracy or approach of the report? Are there any particular biases evident?

- How useful is this type of broadcast report as a historical source? What are its shortcomings?

CHAPTER EIGHTEEN

"LEAP OF FAITH": BRIAN MULRONEY (AND RONALD REAGAN) KILL THE NATIONAL POLICY, 1989

TRADE POLICY AND POSTWAR ECONOMIC DEVELOPMENT

The National Policy, first envisioned and instituted by John A. Macdonald in the 1870s and 1880s, was Canada's longest economic policy. The idea of tariff protection, of taxes upon imported goods, survived for more than a century and was a bedrock of Canadian economic and political policy. What finally killed the National Policy was a betrayal; Brian Mulroney became prime minister in 1984 promising to protect and defend the National Policy, but eventually he turned against it and killed it. In doing so, Mulroney had help from US President Ronald Reagan.

Another idea, that of free trade (ending tariffs on imported goods, especially from the United States), has been a part of the Canadian discourse for as long as the National Policy existed. Canadians who had grown up with the protectionism of the National Policy loathed and feared the idea of free trade. They believed that willingly surrendering to a free trade agreement with the United States would mean the end of Canada as an independent country. Despite these fears, eventually Canadians chose to take a "leap of faith," and, after an incredibly bitter electoral fight over the issue in 1988, Canada embarked on a future of free trade with the United States.

In the 1980s, when the titanic battle over these two ideas—the National Policy of tariffs versus free trade with the United States—came to a head, Canadians often used life-and-death metaphors to describe this conflict. At stake was no less than the future of Canada. These were not just economic issues: they were political, emotional, and even psychological issues. Indeed, many Canadians felt that killing the National Policy and embracing free trade meant courting a fate worse than the demise of Canada; it meant losing their souls forever to the United States. Were they right?

"The Old Policy": Explaining the National Policy

The National Policy of tariff protection was instituted in 1879. It placed a tax on certain goods coming into Canada, usually around 20 to 35 per cent. This tariff was designed to boost Canadian industry by making foreign-made goods more expensive than Canadian-made products. In some instances, foreign manufacturers got around this tariff wall by building branch plants in Canada. For example, in the early 1900s, Ford Motor Company, though it had a giant factory in Detroit, Michigan, built a Canadian plant right across the river in Windsor, Ontario, to get around the tariff.

Along with a tariff-protected industry, the Canadian economy was based on the export of staples such as wheat, lumber, and minerals to other countries for processing. This dynamic—protected industry and the export of natural products—formed the basis of the Canadian economy for more than a century and became a foundational plank of the party that had originally created the policy, John A. Macdonald's Conservative (later Progressive Conservative) Party. The National Policy largely survived the great economic downturn of the 1880s, changes in government from Conservative to Liberal, the Great Depression, two world wars, and the emergence of a postwar world where protectionism started to be challenged around the globe.

Nonetheless, by the end of the Second World War, the National Policy still existed and was largely responsible in helping to create a diverse, export-oriented economy. Canada produced many manufactured and consumer goods such as cars, planes, telecommunications equipment, and aluminum and household products. At the same time, Canada was one of the world's leading producers of lumber, wheat, minerals, oil and gas, and fish: there was significant primary resource production in the country in areas such as mining and forestry. Much of this extraction was conducted by American-owned companies, which provided the funding for these industries. So, for instance, the first great oil strike at Leduc, Alberta, in 1947, was actually made by an American-owned firm. By the 1950s, American capital had come to dominate Canadian resource and manufacturing industries: over 90 per cent of petroleum and chemical production, over 90 per cent of the auto industry, and over 50 per cent of other heavy manufacturing was dominated by Americans.

Finally, as part of this diverse economy, Canada also had a large and growing service industry sector comprised of banks and other financial and legal services and retail sales of all kinds, including malls and fast-food outlets starting in the 1950s and 1960s. Many women worked in the service sector. Overall, then, the economy was booming, especially in the 1950s, but there were questions on the horizon.

Canada's Twilight? The Idea of Free Trade

Despite the National Policy's foundational place in the Canadian economy and Canadian history, some Canadians, especially those in the Liberal Party, thought that the country would be better off with free trade with the United States. Free trade would mean the removal of protective taxes, throwing the Canadian economy open to competition with American manufacturers as the National Policy tariff wall was dismantled.

In 1891, Liberal leader Wilfrid Laurier fought an election campaign on the basis of free trade with the Americans. Handily defeated by John A. Macdonald, who was fighting in his last election (Macdonald's campaign poster read "The Old Flag, The Old Policy, The Old Leader"), Laurier swore off free trade for a generation. When Laurier again tried to bring in free trade in 1911, he was again defeated, a loss that marked the end of his 15 years as prime minister. Having learned Laurier's painful lesson, Canadian political leaders of all stripes fled in fear from tampering with the National Policy for the next seven decades.

Though the 1950s and 1960s were very good times, by the 1970s, the Canadian economy was in serious trouble. The causes were multiple. First, there was "stagflation." For much of the 1970s, inflation (the yearly increase in the cost of goods) in Canada ran at double digits, often a sign of a booming economy. Yet interest rates and unemployment also remained high, resulting in "stagflation": a stagnant economy, yet still inflation. One cause of inflation was the boost in government program spending in Canada (which increased money in the system); government spending in the United States was high as well, especially because of Vietnam War expenditures.

At the same time, and perhaps more pointedly, there was the 1973 OPEC oil embargo. The Organization of Petroleum Exporting Countries (OPEC) of mostly Arab Middle Eastern states was formed in 1960, but its strength and impact were not felt until 1973, when the Arab members of OPEC imposed an embargo against the United States in retaliation for the US decision to support Israel after the 1973 Arab-Israeli War. As a consequence, oil prices rose dramatically and world supply was cut back. With gas-guzzling automobiles, expanding highways, and mushrooming suburbs, the North American economy was increasingly fuelled by oil. When OPEC turned down the spigot and jacked up the price, the impact was tremendous. The increase in oil prices also spurred inflation in most industrial nations.

Another major issue related to stagflation was government deficits, and thus government debt, during the late 1970s. Government spending became a major political issue as Ottawa used deficit spending to finance regional development and social programs. This annual deficit grew dramatically, and, by 1993, the government spent $42 billion more than it took in, and Canada's total debt was in the hundreds of billions of dollars.

A final economic issue was the emergence of the Rust Belt. The decline of manufacturing in North America and the resurgence of Germany and Japan as serious economic competitors dramatically cut into the North American economy by the late 1970s. A recession from 1979 to 1982 resulted in thousands of layoffs and plant closings in Canada and the United States. A good example of this is the near death of Chrysler in 1980–82. Chrysler was a bloated giant in the 1970s with poor products that did not meet fuel economy regulations. Unable to compete and too slow to change, it required government bailouts to survive. But, in the process, it shed thousands of jobs, from about 200,000 workers to less than 100,000.

In any event, because of stagflation, debts, and the economic malaise represented by the Rust Belt, by the early 1980s, people were thinking about new ways to approach the economy and trade policy in particular. They were also beginning to question the Keynesian political and economic policies of the postwar period. To understand how these economic changes affected the politics of the period, we need to look at the emergence of Brian Mulroney.

"Sacred Trust"? Brian Mulroney, National Policy Killer

At first glance, Brian Mulroney seemed an unlikely candidate to kill the National Policy, one of the oldest policies of the Progressive Conservative Party that he eventually came to lead. Mulroney had a compelling story, having worked his way up from the tough Quebec town of Baie-Comeau to become a lawyer. Making his name fighting corruption in Quebec in the 1970s, he then became president of the US-owned Iron Ore Company of Canada. At the same time, Mulroney was perfectly bilingual, and the party's first Quebec leader in nearly a century.

Mulroney's timing was excellent. By the early 1980s, Canadians were ready for new leadership. There was considerable voter fatigue with the Liberals, who had been in power basically since 1963. John Turner, the Liberal leader who succeeded Trudeau as prime minister, lacked Trudeau's charisma and was saddled with the baggage of the long Liberal reign.

Winning his party's leadership in 1984, Mulroney developed a two-pronged strategy. First, he appealed to Quebecers: as the only federal leader from Quebec, he believed that Trudeau's 1982 changes to the Constitution were flawed and that he would right those wrongs and make Quebecers happy. He also appealed to the West as a stalwart fiscal conservative, willing to roll back the state's role in the economy and solve the problems of the 1970s by cutting back on government spending and programs to get rid of debt and get control of government finances.

But, perhaps most important, Mulroney did *not* say he would get rid of the National Policy or pursue free trade. Instead, Mulroney said he had a "sacred trust" with voters that included a historic respect for the national tariff and John A. Macdonald. As a result of these promises, in 1984, Mulroney won the largest electoral landslide in Canadian history.

If Mulroney did not campaign in 1984 on killing the National Policy and embracing free trade, where did these ideas come from? Mulroney's views were changed by a number of factors. At the time, a new ideological approach to the economy was emerging after the deluge of the late 1970s' economic downturn: neoliberalism (sometimes, confusingly, referred to as neoconservatism). Neoliberalism focused on individual rights, market solutions, deregulation, and an end to state intervention in the economy. Leading advocates of neoliberalism included Milton Friedman and Canadian Harry Johnson, both from the University of Chicago, who argued for the end of barriers to trade and regulation so that market forces could operate without the interference of the state. Policies such as the National Policy, argued Johnson, made the economy inefficient and distorted the market place. This thinking was a direct attack on both protectionism and the ideas of John Maynard Keynes, who supported large-scale state intervention in the economy.

There was also a political component of this neoliberal thought and embrace of free trade. Most prominent among those calling for free trade was US President Ronald Reagan, who made it a central platform of his following his 1980 election win. Reagan, and British Prime Minister Margaret Thatcher, were part of a new conservative wave that embraced free trade as a political platform, that espoused loosening regulation on businesses, and that believed in the primacy of the free market and of the individual in society. In a speech shortly after his election, Reagan called for a free trade area for all of the Americas, an idea that seemed far-fetched and spectacular at the time.

In both the United States and Britain, Reagan and Thatcher won big victories with these neoliberal platforms. Reagan said it was time for a new approach, a "morning in America" that called for a return to self-help and individualism, one that was pro-business, anti-union, and pushed deregulation. Thatcher created an image as a tough "Iron Lady": she attacked coalminers' unions, privatized businesses, and deregulated economic sectors all in an effort to unleash the "efficiencies of market." Mulroney was pro-business too; soon after his election, he told a New York financial audience, "Canada is open for business again."[1]

But Mulroney had a problem. He was leader of the party of John A. Macdonald, so to attack the National Policy was to attack more than a century of Conservative policy and challenge the legacy of the greatest Conservative prime

---

1   December 10, 1984, speech reported in "Mulroney Sells Canada in New York," *Canadian News Facts* 18 (1984): 3175.

minister in Canadian history. Killing the National Policy was akin to a Conservative spitting on John A. Macdonald's grave. Even Mackenzie King and the Liberals had backed off comprehensive free trade with the United States in the 1940s, understanding that whoever killed the National Policy for free trade would be accused of selling out the country.

So what was Mulroney to do? He appealed to Canadians' economic judgment by arguing that growing US protectionism required free trade so that Canadians could ensure themselves access to the biggest market in the world, right next door. Mulroney also argued that international trade treaties such as the General Agreement on Tariffs and Trade (GATT) were not providing Canada with growth opportunities. He made the case that Canada–US trade was much more important in the 1980s than it had been when Laurier or King wanted it—that, these days, Canada must have access to its biggest customer. In Mulroney's view, free trade was a way to fight not only general economic decline but also deficits, and it would restore productivity and efficiency in the economy; if the National Policy were killed off, Canadians would be forced to compete on a continental basis, making them better.

Mulroney also made two other arguments. One was based on the findings of a royal commission that Trudeau had initiated in 1982; the report argued that Canada must take a "leap of faith" and embrace free trade with the United States. Finally, Mulroney needed a dramatic policy gesture to fire up the electorate: the Meech Lake Accord was proving troublesome, and a series of scandals was dragging down his government's popularity while deficits were still high and the economy was still in bad shape. The new policy would re-craft his image, and Mulroney would be seen as a partner in the new North Atlantic conservatism represented by Reagan and Thatcher.

So he went into action. Reagan visited Mulroney in Quebec City on St. Patrick's Day in 1985, where the two held exploratory meetings capped off by a gala event that played up both leaders' Irish roots by having them sing "When Irish Eyes Are Smiling." After the "Shamrock Summit," Mulroney instructed Canadian officials to begin negotiations. American representatives, who understood the significance for Canadians of embarking on such a proposal, nonetheless remained hard bargainers. The Canadian side of the effort was led by Simon Riesman, who had already negotiated the continentalizing auto pact in 1965 (integrating Canada's auto sector into the US industry); Riesman was Canada's most veteran negotiator and himself a pit-bull bargainer. After rounds of acrimonious negotiations, an agreement was reached in 1988.

In the United States, the agreement was met with little interest. In Canada, however, although he was heralded as achieving a major breakthrough for Canadians, Mulroney was forced to contest an election on the agreement. The 1988 free trade election was one of the most emotional, bitter, and galvanizing elections in Canadian history.

The Fights of Their Lives: The 1988 Free Trade Election

The fate of the National Policy, and of its nemesis, free trade, was an incredibly polarizing issue in Canada. There was no middle ground. On one side stood Mulroney, his government, virtually all Canadian business (whose interests lay with their success in the market, not with the nation), the West (with its resource-based economy and hatred of what it saw as Ontario's privileged status under the National Policy), Quebec (nationalists and separatists were both in favour), and even Canadian manufacturers, who wanted guaranteed access to the US market. These groups argued that free trade would boost the economy significantly and that Canadians had nothing to worry about.

On the other side of the battle stood, surprisingly, the Liberal Party, led by John Turner. Fighting against free trade went against the natural Liberal position, but Turner believed not only that it was his duty as leader of the Opposition to fight the agreement but that it was a bad agreement as well. Along with (though not beside) Turner and the Liberals were the NDP, led by the very popular Ed Broadbent; many ordinary Canadians, some in the cultural industries (who believed free trade would wipe out Canada's cultural voice); many in the Atlantic provinces; and Ontario, in particular. Ontario's premier, David Peterson, thought that free trade would hobble Ontario's manufacturing industries, a position supported by many labour unions, too.

Opponents argued it would lead to the end of independence for Canada, to a loss of sovereignty, and that Canadians would become Americans in all but name. They believed that any continentalizing agreement would eventually cripple universal health care, social programs, and culture and that Canadians would be forced to accede to American demands, norms, or policies, or face economic repercussions.

As the election battle began in the hot summer of 1988, the attacks from either side came fast and furious. Canadians talked, argued, discussed, and fought over the National Policy and free trade as though their lives and their futures depended upon the outcome. There were huge advertising campaigns by both sides, airwaves were flooded by messages from all kinds of different groups, and government propaganda came pouring out of Ottawa. All was buttressed by a host of conferences and debates; endless newspaper, radio, and television coverage; and everyday arguments between ordinary Canadians.

At the height of the battle, the leaders had a televised debate. In one of the most heated exchanges in Canadian political history, Turner accused Mulroney of having turned his back on Canadian history and, with a single signature, of wiping out the country. Mulroney, feeling the heat of being called a turncoat, dismissed Turner's accusations. But the damage was done: Turner might have turned his party's fortunes around (before the debate, it looked as though the Liberals would be trounced). The debate made the election too close to call.

Figure 18.1 *Free Trade Battle: "A Little Higher, Ron," Aislin, 1986*

Courtesy of the McCord Museum, M998.48.176

The day of the election interest was huge and voter turnout was good, with three-quarters of Canadians casting their ballots (most elections today see less than two-thirds voter turnout). The titanic debate over the economic future of the country had prompted Canadians to make their voices heard on the issue, and, as the results rolled in that night, Canadians across the country were totally riveted by the election outcome, and its consequences.

When the ballots were counted, Mulroney had killed the National Policy. But the results weren't exactly clear cut. Yes, Mulroney and the Conservatives had won, but it was a qualified victory. Though he gained a majority of parliamentary seats in the country (169 out of 295), Mulroney had won only 43 per cent of the vote. A majority of Canadians had actually voted *against* free trade but had split their vote between the Liberal and NDP parties, who had gained 83 and 43 seats, respectively. Turner had gained almost 32 per cent of the vote while Broadbent had garnered 20 per cent, but, because of the "first past the post" electoral system in Canada, Mulroney had squeaked through the middle to victory.

Two other factors besides the split in the anti–free trade vote had helped Mulroney. The Conservative vote had been concentrated in Quebec and the West, where most free trade supporters lived. At the same time, a massive wave of business spending on the radio and television airwaves in favour of the deal had helped to tilt the balance sufficiently in favour of free trade, even though a majority of Canadians voted against the Conservatives.

Mulroney emerged victorious, and the agreement went into effect following its passage in the US Congress and in the Canadian Parliament. Mulroney's victory was the most significant achievement of his political career; Reagan, on the other hand, quietly signed the agreement into law with little fanfare. The agreement went into existence on January 1, 1989, and has been a significant part of the Canadian economic, social, and political landscape ever since.

Legacies: Canada under Free Trade

What did the 1989 Canada–US Free Trade Agreement (FTA) actually do? It had four main elements. First, it reduced tariff and non-tariff barriers in virtually all areas of goods and services. A number of tariff exceptions remained, however. Canada's "supply-managed sectors," such as the dairy and poultry industries, which are governed by marketing boards, were exempted from the agreement. Similarly, the sugar, dairy, peanuts, and cotton sectors were exempted in the United States.

Second, the agreement established "national treatment," allowing US and Canadian exporters to be treated equally, and "rules of origin" to allow goods from one country to enter the other duty free. Each FTA partner maintained its own external tariffs, which govern goods coming from non-FTA countries. The rules of origin are particularly important in certain sectors: in the auto industry, cars and parts must have 50 per cent North American content (i.e., be made in one of the two countries) for them to enter into the other partner's country duty free. (This figure was increased to 62.5 per cent after Mexico joined the United States and Canada in the 1993 North American Free Trade

Agreement, or NAFTA.) It also gave access to natural resources for companies within the FTA.

Third, it established rules regarding investment and services, such as financial services. One important provision is that the governments of FTA countries cannot treat investor companies from member countries any differently than domestic investors, regardless of which FTA country they decide to invest or set up in. Critics claim this provision creates a "bill of rights" for corporations, allowing them to conduct business even at the expense of environmental or health standards—and that corporate rights supersede national laws.

Finally, the agreement created a dispute resolution mechanism for trade problems between the FTA partners. This was supposed to alleviate trade problems, especially in the lumber industry, though, on this score, the agreement has been less than effective in some instances. In particular, Canada and the United States have had continued problems around softwood lumber, for instance.

What actually happened to the economy under free trade? Since the agreement's implementation in 1989, that trade has grown is unquestionable. Unemployment has, generally, remained stable, even after some serious recessions (in the early 1990s and from 2008–10, for example). The economies of the United States and Canada (and Mexico after 1993) are closer, and trade has definitely increased.

But questions remain. The actual benefits of the FTA regime are harder to ascertain. Has the quality of life of the three NAFTA countries improved since the trade agreements were signed? Although unemployment has remained stable, inequality has increased in terms of both family income and wealth. Many have argued that the true benefits of freer trade have been unevenly distributed to corporations who have taken advantage of the new regime. Further, critics point out that, although there is no question that NAFTA ushered in a massive growth in trade, there has been no corresponding growth in incomes or quality of life for workers and average citizens of the three countries. On a host of issues, there are still trade problems, in sectors such as lumber, beef and dairy, and steel. So, though things have shown some improvement, there is much to be desired from the FTA and NAFTA.

Finally, what is the political legacy of free trade? Though a majority of Canadians voted against it, today, Canadians are generally in favour of free trade, and most recent polls find a majority (and sometimes as many as eight in ten Canadians) support free trade. This is a far cry from the vote in 1988. Nonetheless, though Canadians support the idea of free trade, they do have worries about globalization, US influence, corporate influence, and attacks on social programs such as health care.

On the other hand, free trade has not meant a loss of sovereignty for Canadians. In many ways, Canadian and American social, cultural, and political policies have not converged but have actually diverged since 1989. Examples of sharp political and policy differences abound. On social issues, Canada was far ahead of the United States in accepting gay marriage and loosening restrictions on marijuana use. On political issues, Canada refused to join America's 2003 war in Iraq, despite tremendous pressure to do so, and rejected American entreaties to join the US ballistic missile defence program. Cherished social programs in Canada, such as health care, have not been eroded by free trade, and, if they have faced challenges to their continued existence, Canadian domestic issues, not US pressure, are mostly to blame.

This is not to say that Canada is indifferent or unaffected by happenings in the United States; on the contrary, the United States still remains, on many, many issues, "the sun around which Canada revolves." And, though Canada–US relations may be bad or difficult at times, the integrated economy of North America continues on its path. Despite all the rhetoric around free trade and its implications, and the reality that Canada is very much tied to the United States on economic matters, Canadians are very much in control of their destinies, if they choose to exercise the political will to shape those destinies as they wish.

Further Reading

Anastakis, Dimitry. *Autonomous State: The Struggle for a Canadian Car Industry from* OPEC *to Free Trade.* Toronto: University of Toronto Press, 2013.

Ayres, Jeffrey M. "Political Process and Popular Protest: The Mobilization Against Free Trade in Canada." *American Journal of Economics and Sociology* 55, no. 4 (1996): 473–88. http://dx.doi.org/10.1111/j.1536-7150. 1996.tb02646.x.

Bashevkin, Sylvia. "In the Shadow of Free Trade: Nationalism, Feminism and Identity Politics in Contemporary English Canada." *Journal of Canadian Studies / Revue d'études canadiennes* 35 (Summer 2000): 109–29.

Blake, Raymond. "The Canadian 1988 Election: The Nationalist Posture of Prime Minister Brian Mulroney and the Progressive Conservatives." *Canadian Review of Studies in Nationalism* 30 (2003): 65–82.

High, Stephen. "'I'll Wrap the F*** Flag Around Me': A Nationalist Response to Plant Shutdowns, 1969–1984." *Journal of the Canadian Historical Association* 12, no. 1 (2001): 199–225. http://dx.doi. org/10.7202/031148ar.

Inwood, Gregory J. *Continentalizing Canada: The Politics and Legacy of the Macdonald Royal Commission.* Toronto: University of Toronto Press, 2005.

ACTIVE HISTORY: THE FREE TRADE AGREEMENT DEBATE

- In many ways, the discussion over Canada's decision to join the United States in a free trade agreement is very much still with us. Though the agreement was formalized in 1989, debate still rages as to whether or not it was a good decision.

- Make the case either for or against free trade: Consider the economic, political, social, and cultural implications of continental economic integration. Utilize sources such as:

  o The Department of Foreign Affairs site on free trade, at http://www.international.gc.ca/trade-agreements-accords-commerciaux/agr-acc/us-eu.aspx?lang=eng.

  o The CBC's digital archives on free trade at http://www.cbc.ca/archives/categories/economy-business/trade-agreements/canada-us-free-trade-agreement/topic-canada-us-free-trade-agreement.html.

  o Publications and articles such as those from the Canadian Centre for Policy Alternatives, at https://www.policyalternatives.ca/.

- What are the key issues in this debate? How have things changed since 1989? What have been the benefits and drawbacks of free trade? Can you say, definitively, whether it has been good or bad for Canadians?

MURDEROUS MOMENT
SHIDANE ARONE, MURDERED BY CANADIAN TROOPS, SOMALIA, 1993

Canada's International Soldiers: From Peacekeepers to Pariahs?

Between the 1950s and the 1990s, Canada established a well-earned reputation as one of the world's leading peacekeeping countries. Many have credited Lester B. Pearson with helping to establish this role for Canada during the 1956 Suez Crisis in the Middle East. Canadian Armed Forces personnel have participated in United Nations peacekeeping operations across the globe, in countries such as the Congo, Cyprus, Cambodia, and the former Yugoslavia. Canadians had so imbued in themselves this idea of a "peacekeeping nation" that the notion had seemingly become a cornerstone of Canadian identity. Peacekeeping statues were erected in Ottawa, while peacekeepers appeared on Canadian currency.

Much of that reputation was utterly destroyed by the events of March 1993, in the East African nation of Somalia. In the early 1990s, Somalia was torn by civil war and chaos as warlords essentially took control of the country. UN peacekeepers were dispatched to try to maintain order and distribute food and aid supplies. A multinational US-led peace support operation was also underway. Among those dispatched to the country in 1992 were Canadian soldiers, including the Canadian Airborne Regiment, considered the elite of the Canadian Armed Forces.

The Canadian Forces had established a base near the Somali town of Belet Huen, 300 kilometres from the capital of Mogadishu. On the night of March 16, 16-year-old Shidane Arone was caught trying to sneak into the base, ostensibly for the purpose of stealing something of value that he could sell on the black market. Following his "capture," Canadian forces proceeded to torture and brutalize the young

man. Two soldiers, Master Corporal Clayton Matchee and Private Kyle Brown, bound and beat Arone, pinned his arms behind a wooden stake, sodomized him with a broomstick, and took photos of the torture. Appallingly, more than a dozen Canadian troops were aware of what was transpiring that night, and none did a thing to stop what were clearly wrong, and criminal, activities. By the next morning, Arone was dead.

When the horrifying images of Arone's torture and treatment were revealed to the world, they exposed the reality that Canadian soldiers had already been involved in a number of incidents in Somalia, including the killing of two unarmed civilians. The images and the actions of these Canadian soldiers found echoes in the American soldiers' 2004 Abu Ghraib prison and torture scandal in Iraq.

The Canadian government, facing international condemnation over the incident and an outraged public at home, disbanded the Canadian Airborne Regiment and called a public inquiry. In 1997, the government of Jean Chrétien controversially cut short the inquiry and forced the commission to produce its report. The inquiry's findings were extremely damning of the Canadian Armed Forces, the military leadership, and the culture at National Defence Headquarters in Ottawa that had allowed the "rogue" behaviour in "the Airborne" to flourish and even hindered the Somalia investigation.

One of the soldiers involved, Matchee, attempted to commit suicide by hanging himself but succeeded only in causing himself irreparable brain damage. Private Brown was dishonourably discharged, convicted of manslaughter, and sentenced to a five-year prison term, of which he served a third. Eventually, both men claimed that their actions were spurred by the antimalarial medicines administered to Canadian troops and that they were scapegoats for commanding officers who did nothing to stop the attacks. In 2008, Matchee, whose family had fought the charges against him and claimed he was unfit to stand trial owing to his mental state following his suicide attempt, was released from a mental institution, and the charges against him were dropped.

Reportedly, Arone's last words before he died at the hands of the Canadian soldiers were "Canada, Canada."[2] Despite Canada's terrible record in Somalia, thousands of Somalis have since immigrated to Canada to escape their war-torn country and the political persecution they faced. The murder of Shidane Arone brings into question not only the role of the military in shaping international perceptions of Canada but Canada's broader international role and reputation, race relations, and the continuing affects of immigration upon Canada's national identity.

How differently would all these issues have developed if Shidane Arone had not been killed at the hands of Canadian troops in 1993?

---

2   CBC, "Somalia Affair: Dismissal with Disgrace," *CBC Digital Archives*, http://www.cbc.ca/archives/categories/war-conflict/peacekeeping/the-somalia-affair/dismissal-with-disgrace.html.

CHAPTER NINETEEN

FOURTEEN QUEBEC WOMEN, MURDERED, MONTREAL, DECEMBER 6, 1989

WOMEN IN POSTWAR CANADA AND VIOLENCE

I remember this so well. It was my first year of university. Classes had just ended and exams were beginning. It still haunts me, because I couldn't believe that something like this could happen on a university campus in Canada. I remember seeing it on the news, reading the newspaper headlines, and being completely mortified as I walked across my own campus. It changed me—and changed my understanding of women, of men, and of the nature of violence.

On December 6, 1989, just after 5 PM, a man walked into the engineering school of the University of Montreal, the École Polytechnique. "Poly," as many students referred to the school, was a university just like any other in Canada. It was the end of term, the last week of classes. Brandishing a semi-automatic rifle, the man entered a lecture hall, where two women were giving a presentation. It was the last day of their class. He told all the men to get out. Initially, the students thought it was a joke, but, after he fired a round into the ceiling, the men did as they were told. He then forced the women into a corner, and, after screaming that they were all "feminists," proceeded to kill as many women in the lecture hall as he could. Leaving the classroom, he wandered the halls, screaming "I want the women!" and shooting any female he could find.

These are the 14 victims of that horrible day:

Geneviève Bergeron, 21 years old
Hélène Colgan, 23 years old
Nathalie Croteau, 23 years old
Barbara Daigneault, 22 years old

Anne-Marie Edward, 21 years old

Maud Haviernick, 29 years old

Maryse Laganière, 25 years old

Barbara Klucznik-Widajewicz, 31 years old

Maryse Leclair, 23 years old

Anne-Marie Lemay, 22 years old

Sonia Pelletier, 28 years old

Michèle Richard, 21 years old

Annie St-Arneault, 23 years old

Annie Turcotte, 20 years old

I will not write the name of the murderer. He killed himself. But he left a suicide note in which he blamed feminists for ruining his life and named 19 prominent Quebec women whom he would have targeted if he could. He also praised Denis Lortie, the man who had attacked the Quebec National Assembly in 1984.

This was one of the darkest days in Canadian history. A true act of terrorism, and horror.

For many, the massacre at the École Polytechnique that day came to symbolize violence against women. What was the response?

There were a number of reactions and responses. Some were as simple as the white ribbon campaign started by a group of men in London, Ontario, where I was at university. Canadians also erected memorials across the country to signify their remembrance of these victims and to remind themselves of the horror of that day.

There were political implications as well. In Quebec, the police totally revised their response strategy to such incidents, a revision that was extremely beneficial when another, similar incident, though without the same horrifying results, occurred at Montreal's Dawson College in 2006.

Another political implication was gun control. When the federal Liberals took power in 1993, they passed a far-reaching gun control law, one that included the registration of long rifles, such as the one used by the killer that day. Since then, pro-gun advocates have fought this law. In fact, the Conservative Party pledged to get rid of the gun registry while in opposition, and did so in 2012 upon gaining power, despite the pleas of the parents, brothers, and sisters of some of these shooting victims, who had argued and testified in favour of stricter gun control laws.

Yes, the event was horrible, and it showed the persistence of violence directed at women, simply because they are women. But we need to remember that, though these women were victims of violence, they were also representative of the major strides women have taken in Canadian society in the postwar period. We need to remember that these were young engineers, who happened to be women. The fact that they were women did not prevent them from accessing the opportunity to become engineers.

But it is to our eternal sadness that it was their womanhood, and their success as engineering students, that made them targets.

Women in the Postwar Period

Dramatic changes occurred for women in Canada in the postwar period, particularly in the 1960s. Among the greatest legacies of the Sixties was the sexual revolution that occasioned dramatic changes in North American attitudes toward sex, gender, and the role of women. When contrasted with the repressive and unrealistic attitudes toward sex and gender roles in the immediate postwar period and the 1950s, the new thinking of the 1960s truly marked a sexual revolution.

It is important to remember that 1950s' notions of womanhood were based on traditional gender roles that emphasized being a good wife and mother. Womanhood was to be defined by the housewife, who was primarily a husband's helpmate, a doting mother, a keeper of the home, and a consumer. Of course, that clashed with the reality of women's lives. Many women worked in this period. Twenty-nine per cent of the Canadian workforce in the early 1960s was composed of women. Many women lived in unhappy homes. There was abuse, estrangement, and separation. Many women simply did not fit the ideal of the perfect woman, no matter how much society pressured them to do so.

Often, then, when the real world intruded, women bore the brunt of the conservative ethos of the period. Divorce was something that could not be easily contemplated, and, in order to get a divorce, one had to have eyewitness proof or photographic evidence of adultery. Parliament had to pass a private member's bill to grant a divorce in Quebec and Newfoundland, right up to the 1960s. Birth outside of wedlock was a "family disgrace," and women were often "sent away" to northern towns to have children out of sight; abortions were scandalous, unspoken of, and criminal.

Yet many of these things did happen. But they did so away from watchful eyes, out of the media spotlight, and in back alleys. The reality of so many of these events was pushed into the background, with grave consequences for ordinary people, especially women. It would take another type of revolution to force these issues into the broad light of day.

Second Wave Feminism

Of course, women began to challenge conservative ideals in the 1950s and 1960s. This period marked second-wave feminism, which built upon the first-wave battles over the right to vote in the early part of the century. Where did this movement come from?

To start, a number of Canadian feminists began to call attention to the problems Canadians faced in the postwar period. Some of these women had taken part in the battles over suffrage. Others were new to the cause. These second-wave feminists wrote books and articles, were activists, and also became politically involved.

For instance, there was Thérèse Casgrain. Casgrain was a long-time activist and defender of women's rights in Quebec. In the 1930s and 1940s, she was one of the leaders of the movement to gain Quebec women the provincial vote, achieved in 1940. In the 1950s, she led the Co-operative Commonwealth Federation (CCF) in Quebec, making her the first female leader of a major federal or provincial political party in Canada. In the 1960s, Casgrain founded the Quebec branch of the Voice of Women (VOW), a feminist movement dedicated to world peace. During all this time, she fought for women's rights.

Women politicians were also becoming more prominent, though they remained rare. Ellen Fairclough was the first female federal cabinet minister, appointed in 1957. In the 1960s, Judy LaMarsh became a leading Canadian politician. LaMarsh had a long and accomplished career in public and private life. She had served in the Canadian Women's Army Corps (CWACs) as a sergeant. After leaving the army, she practiced as a lawyer and was a trailblazer and leader in that profession. Finally, after having run successfully for Parliament, she became a minister in Lester Pearson's cabinet. As a cabinet minister in the 1960s, LaMarsh played a leading role in the creation and passage of the Canada Pension Plan and "medicare" legislation.

Notwithstanding these political success stories, there was still discontent with women's place in Canadian society. Grassroots women's organizations, such as the Committee for the Equality of Women in Canada, founded in 1966, argued for some federal response to the status of women in Canada.

A second source that galvanized ordinary women into action was a book explaining something of the unhappiness that women felt. In 1963, *The Feminine Mystique* by Betty Friedan was published. Friedan had sent a questionnaire to other women in her 1942 Smith College (Massachusetts) graduating class and found that many of her classmates indicated a general dissatisfaction with their lives. This finding led Friedan to conduct more detailed research into "the problem that has no name," which she associated with the "feminine mystique," a false notion of femininity that limits women to the roles of wife, mother, and housewife.

Because of this "mystique," women felt unfulfilled in this fabricated role that required them to be financially, intellectually, and emotionally dependent upon their husbands and to find identity and meaning in their lives only through their husbands and children. *The Feminine Mystique* was a publishing success and, more important, gave voice to the challenges facing women at the time. It was read all across North America, including in Canada, by thousands of women.

Third and more important, women also challenged long-held notions about their place by going to university. As we have already discussed, the number of women on campuses grew dramatically. In 1955, there were fewer than 15,000 women on campus. By 1970, there were over 100,000 women enrolled in universities in Canada. This was a major change, one that some people did not accept easily as women began to challenge the male-dominated culture of classrooms and campuses.

This growth meant that women were now slowly breaking the barriers to employment and professions. Of course, they still faced severe limitations in the types of jobs that they could do—and harsh expectations of what a woman's place in society was. But university enrolment is one indicator of the new approaches that women were taking in this period. It is no coincidence that after the 1960s and 1970s, professions such as law and medicine, once totally dominated by men, were opening to women. Indeed, by the beginning of the twenty-first century, women were holding their own in professions that they had once been excluded from. In some years, the majority of graduates in law and medicine are women, and women do well in professions such as dentistry and business administration. One area in particular, however, remains male dominated: engineering.

A fourth reason that explains the strength of second-wave feminism was the battle over reproductive technology and over the laws related to contraception. The pill was introduced in Canada in the early 1960s. Yet birth control was technically still illegal, according to Section 207 of the Criminal Code, which made it a crime to prevent contraception. However, doctors could prescribe the pill for therapeutic purposes, primarily to control women's menstrual cycles.

By 1963, the Canadian Federation of Societies for Population Planning was founded, and, by 1966, the Canadian Medical Association was actively promoting birth control. That year, over 50 million contraceptives were sold in Canada, the first municipally funded birth control clinic opened in Scarborough, Ontario, and people began agitating in earnest for the decriminalization of birth control.

Now the pill is noteworthy for a few things besides giving women the right to control their reproduction. Obviously, it created the possibility of "free love," which the Sixties are well known for. But it also is reflective of a patriarchal society: it placed the onus for avoiding pregnancy almost entirely upon women. Also, the early pill was a hormonal roller coaster, as it took years to perfect the dosage of estrogen "bumps" that prevented ovulation.

A fifth source of the women's movement was the inspiration that women gained from the civil rights battles of the postwar period. Many women saw their inequality in society as being analogous to that of African Americans in the United States or French Canadians in Quebec. They saw fighting for women's equality as a battle for liberation, which tapped into the protest movements of the 1960s. The women's movement generated widespread activism and reaction, and soon governments in the 1960s were asking what could be done to address the growing number of issues raised by women.

The 1970 Royal Commission on the Status of Women

Women's experience of work, family, children, gender roles, and pregnancy were changing rapidly, and, by the mid-1960s, the questions surrounding women's role in Canadian society were such that the government struck a royal commission to study the matter. The Royal Commission on the Status of Women (RCSW) was created in 1967 by the Pearson government. For many, the RCSW was as important as two other significant government investigations into the civil rights questions of the day: the 1963 Royal Commission on Bilingualism and Biculturalism and the 1966 Hawthorn Report that examined the situation of Canada's aboriginal population.

Florence Bird, one of Canada's best-known reporters, was chosen to chair the RCSW. Bird had been a feminist activist and writer for many years, but some feminists questioned whether or not this investigation was actually a real response. Even Bird herself wondered whether the RCSW was just "a political gimmick to allow women to let off steam" and worried "that the final report would be pigeon-holed and forgotten."[1]

The RCSW was serious about its work, however. Nearly 500 briefs were written on the role of women in society and 1,000 letters of opinion and testimony were received on issues such as the political rights of women, women in the workplace, marriage and divorce, and the position of women in criminal law. Indeed, any matter relating to the status of women in Canada could be brought before the RCSW.

The commission reported in 1970. Its recommendations included obvious and necessary ideas, such as that women should be given equal opportunity in all fields of economic, educational, and social endeavour or that women should not face discrimination. These recommendations showed a willingness of the commissioners to recognize the dramatic changes that had been wrought in women's lives, especially in the 1960s. The RCSW's final report also recommended equalizing minimum wage rates between women and men, amending the Unemployment Insurance Act to allow for maternity leave, and amending the Canadian Labour Code to prohibit dismissal or layoff due to pregnancy, which still happened on a regular basis.

Some recommendations of the report were controversial for the time. It recommendations. It recommended a national child-care program (finally created in 2005 by the Paul Martin government only to be cancelled by the Stephen Harper Conservatives when they took power in 2006); that household work should be covered by minimum wage laws and other forms of labour compensation, which essentially constituted a guaranteed annual income (the GAI, which still does not exist); and the changing of divorce laws to make it easier for women to get a divorce and so as to ensure an equitable distribution of the household assets following divorce.

---

1   As quoted in Kimberley Spears, "The Royal Commission on the Status of Women in Canada, 1967–70: Radical Feminism and Its Implications," in Sharon Anne Cook, Lorna R. McLean, Kate O'Rourke, eds., *Framing Our Past: Constructing Canadian Women's History in the Twentieth Century* (Montreal: McGill-Queen's University Press, 2001), 252–56 at 253.

In reaction to the RCSW, women's groups organized to encourage the implementation of the commission's recommendations. The National Action Committee on the Status of Women (NAC), created in 1971, lobbied the government, fought for women's rights, and brought court challenges against laws and legislation that discriminated against women. In the 1970s and 1980s, the NAC became Canada's foremost women's organization, leading the fight to end violence against women and poverty and in favour of women's rights. Another key organization was LEAF, the Women's Legal Education and Action Fund, founded in 1985 following enactment of the Section 15 equality clause of the Charter of Rights and Freedoms. LEAF, supported by leading feminist activists such as Doris Anderson, brought cases to court that ensured the equality rights of women—now a central component of the Charter.

One of the key battles included the then-controversial RCSW recommendation that women should have access to abortion on demand before the 12-week point of their pregnancy. Until that time, abortion was seen as a criminal issue, not an issue of women's reproductive rights or health. As a result, in the 1950s and 1960s, illegal abortions were a leading cause of women being hospitalized, injured, or even dying.

Abortion

Abortion provides an important way of discussing women's changing role and rights in Canada. The abortion recommendation by the RCSW recognized that women's reproductive rights had become a touchstone of the feminist movement in the 1960s. Indeed, the battle over abortion, first seriously broached in the 1960s, remains a controversial issue in our society today.

As has been already mentioned, all abortion before the 1970s was seen as a criminal act and was considered immoral by many Canadians. The first Canadian law making abortions illegal was passed in 1869, and this legislation was tightened by male politicians in 1892 because of fears that white women would stop having children; meanwhile, religious organizations argued that abortion went against God's teachings. But, in the 1960s and 1970s, women saw reproductive rights as the most fundamental rights for women, an idea held not just by feminists but by many women across the country. It was an issue of having control over one's body. Women began to challenge traditional views and laws, and the RCSW's recommendation further galvanized the movement in favour of women's reproductive rights.

Ironically, the leading Canadian voice in favour of access to abortions was a man. Dr. Henry Morgentaler was a Polish-born Jew who had survived the Nazi death camps, come to Canada, and become a physician. Owing in part to his experiences with the Nazi regime (many in his family had been killed), he was a secular humanist and a strong believer in women's rights. This included the right to abortion, so Morgentaler led a decades-long legal and personal battle for abortion rights.

Starting in the 1960s, Morgentaler challenged the Criminal Code provisions that did not allow women free access to abortion; he provided women abortions on demand in clinics in Montreal and Toronto. He was thrown in jail numerous times, and juries often threw out the charges against him. Eventually, in the 1980s, he challenged the Criminal Code provisions regarding abortion under the equality section (Section 7) of the 1982 Charter of Rights and Freedoms.

Finally, in 1988, the law making abortion a crime was struck down by the Supreme Court. However, it is important to note that, although the court struck down the law that categorized abortion as a crime, it did not say that abortion was legal. In fact, it did not say anything about the law besides declaring that the specific sections of the Criminal Code related to abortion violated the Charter, and overturning Morgentaler's conviction. The Supreme Court reasoned that "the structure of the system regulating access to therapeutic abortions is manifestly unfair" so that making abortion illegal violated a woman's right to "security of the person . . . in accordance with the principles of fundamental justice" under the Charter of Rights.[2] There was one attempt in the early 1990s to pass a new law criminalizing abortions that doctors did not deem necessary to preserve women's health, but the bill died in the Senate. Technically, Canada has no law regarding abortion. Nonetheless, the decision was a major victory for second-wave feminists and for women's rights in Canada. But it was not an unambiguous victory; abortion is no longer criminalized, but there is a lack of access in some areas of the country, and some provincial governments refuse to allow private abortion clinics or to fund abortions outside of hospitals as a medically necessary procedure.

This ambiguity around abortion reflects, in many ways, women's current status in Canada. Women have no doubt achieved many of the things that second-wave feminists set out to accomplish. Many of the recommendations of the Royal Commission of the Status of Women were implemented, eventually. But there remains in Canadian society (and around the world) many barriers and challenges for women. Discrimination in the workplace still exists, as do criticisms about women's role in society. Then, of course, there is the persistent issue of violence against women; the massacre in Montreal was only the worst manifestation in Canada.

Will We Remember Them?

Geneviève Bergeron was in her second year at the École Polytechnique. A scholarship student, she played clarinet, sang in a choir, and played basketball and swam.

---

2   *R. v. Morgentaler* (1988), 1 SCR 30, 44 DLR (4th) 385.

Hélène Colgan was in the last year of her mechanical engineering degree and wanted to continue on and do her master's degree. In the months before December 6, she had received three postgrad job offers and was thinking of taking the offer from a company just outside of Toronto.

Nathalie Croteau was also in her last year and about to graduate as a mechanical engineer. At the end of that December, she had planned a two-week vacation in Cancun, Mexico, with her classmate, Hélène Colgan.

Barbara Daigneault expected to graduate by the end of the year. She acted as a teaching assistant in engineering at the Université du Québec à Montréal, where her father was a professor.

Anne-Marie Edward was a chemical engineering student who loved skiing and diving.

Maud Haviernick, a second-year metallurgical engineering student, was an environmental design graduate from the Université du Québec à Montréal.

Barbara Klucznik-Widajewicz, the oldest of the group killed, was a mature student in first-year nursing. She had arrived in Montreal from Poland with her husband only two years earlier.

Maryse Laganière, recently married, was the only non-student killed. She worked in the École Polytechnique's finance department.

Maryse Leclair was in fourth-year metallurgy and was one of the top students in the school. The first victim whose name was known, she was discovered, dead, by her father, Lt. Pierre Leclair of the Montreal police.

Anne-Marie Lemay was a fourth-year mechanical engineering student.

Sonia Pelletier was the top student in her year in mechanical engineering. From the small town of St-Ulric, Quebec, Sonia had five sisters and two brothers. December 10 was to be her graduation day, and she had a job interview lined up for the following week.

Michèle Richard, in her second year of metallurgical engineering, was presenting a paper with Maud Haviernick when she was killed.

Annie St-Arneault, in mechanical engineering, was in her last class before graduation. Annie had a job interview with Alcan Aluminum scheduled for the following day and planned to marry her high-school sweetheart.

Annie Turcotte, the youngest of the women murdered that day, was only 20. Described as gentle and athletic, she enjoying diving and swimming. She chose metallurgical engineering to one day help improve the environment.

We should remember them—for the people who loved them, the things they never accomplished, and the places they could have shaped. How different would the world have been if these women had not been killed?

Further Reading

Campbell, Gail G. "'Are we going to do the most important things?' Senator
    Muriel McQueen Fergusson, Feminist Identities, and the Royal Commission

on the Status of Women." *Acadiensis* 38, no. 2 (Summer/Autumn 2009): 52–77.

Mahon, Rianne. "The Never-Ending Story: The Struggle for Universal Child Care Policy in the 1970s." *Canadian Historical Review* 81, no. 4 (December 2000): 582–622. http://dx.doi.org/10.3138/CHR.81.4.582.

Movement, 1945–1970." *Labor: Studies in Working Class History of the Americas* 5, no. 4 (Winter 2008): 83–106.

Sangster, Joan. "'Queen of the Picket Line': Beauty Contests in the Post–World War II Canadian Labour Movement." *Labour: Studies in Working Class History of the Americas* 5, no. 4 (Winter 2008): 83–106. http://dx.doi.org/10.1215/15476715.2008.029.

Sangster, Joan. "Feminism and the Making of Canadian Working-Class History: Exploring the Past, Present and Future." *Labour / Le Travail* 46 (Fall 2000): 127–65. http://dx.doi.org/10.2307/25149098.

Sethna, Christabelle, and Steve Hewitt. "Clandestine Operations: The Vancouver Women's Caucus, the Abortion Caravan, and the RCMP." *Canadian Historical Review* 90, no. 3 (September 2009): 463–95.

Sethna, Christabelle, Beth Palmer, Katrina Ackerman, and Nancy Janovicek. "Choice, Interrupted: Travel and Inequality of Access to Abortion Services since the 1960s." *Labour / Le Travail* 71 (Spring 2013): 29–48.

Villeneuve, Denis, director. *Polytechnique*. Montreal: Alliance Films, 2009.

TRAGIC TALES
TRACY LATIMER, "MERCY KILLING," SASKATCHEWAN, 1993

The Rights of the Disabled v. "Compassionate Homicide"

The case of Tracy Latimer and her father Robert is as sad as it is tragic and difficult.

Tracy Latimer was born in 1980 with severe cerebral palsy, a condition that causes physical disability. A quadriplegic with the mental capacity of a three-month-old baby, Tracy was in a constant state of extreme pain. Nonetheless, she sometimes smiled and knew happiness. She could not feed herself, could not speak, could not walk, and required full-time care, a challenge for the Latimers, canola and wheat farmers near Wilkie, Saskatchewan, just outside of Saskatoon. In 1993, when she was 12 years old, doctors recommended that Tracy face yet another operation, this time to remove a bone in her thigh. She would have to recover with medication no stronger than regular painkillers owing to her physical inability to handle stronger medicines, which might have rendered her comatose.

Faced with having his daughter suffer another round of horribly painful procedures and with no certainty that they would improve her condition or in any way end the constant pain Tracy undoubtedly endured, Robert Latimer did what many would consider unimaginable. On October 24, 1993, he placed Tracy in his Chevrolet truck parked in the garage, started the vehicle, and attached a hose from the exhaust to the cab, where Tracy sat. Tracy died from the carbon monoxide.

When confronted by police, Latimer eventually admitted his actions. He stated unequivocally that he had killed his daughter to save her from a life of torturous pain and suffering. Latimer believed that this was best for Tracy, and he could not stand to see her face another day in such pain. As he had admitted to police that he had consciously planned the death of his daughter, a premeditated act, Latimer was charged with first-degree murder.

The case prompted a national outcry, one of sorrow, of rage, and of uncertainty. Canadians grappled with the difficult moral dilemma that was Robert Latimer's choice to kill his young daughter. Advocates for the disabled were outraged; Tracy was no farm animal to be put down because she was lame, but a human being, with rights of her own. Those who condemned the act argued that Latimer's actions, if sanctified, opened the door to a world in which the disabled could be targeted or killed out of "mercy"—that asking who "deserved" to be killed, even if the killing were motivated by compassion, crossed a moral, ethical, and legal line. No one, they argued, had the right to kill another human, especially the most vulnerable humans who could not speak for themselves.

Latimer's defenders argued that he had done what only a truly caring father must do, despite the consequences he faced. Tracy's life, they argued, was no life at all, and Latimer's act was one of compassion, not murder. Latimer clearly loved his daughter dearly and sought to end her pain and suffering in the only way he could. Defenders of his actions felt that the justice system had failed him, had brought greater tragedy upon a family already devastated.

A year after Tracy's death, Latimer was convicted of second-degree murder, the Crown prosecutors having reduced the charge. The conviction marked only the beginning of a legal odyssey for Latimer, as the Supreme Court of Canada ordered a new trial when irregularities in the case were discovered. In 1997, Latimer was convicted of second-degree murder again.

This time, however, the jury recommended that Latimer be paroled after only a year, a sharp departure from the standard second-degree sentence, usually 25-years imprisonment with no chance of parole for at least 10 years.

The trial judge had stated that the case was unique and that Latimer's decision to kill his daughter was no cold-blooded murder but the action of a caring and altruistic parent. He sentenced Latimer to less than two years, giving him a "constitutional exemption" from the maximum sentence. The Crown prosecutors disagreed and appealed the ruling. In 1998, the Saskatchewan Court of Appeal reversed the decision and ordered Latimer to serve the full 25-year sentence, with no parole for 10 years. This ruling was upheld by the Supreme Court in 2001, despite Latimer's legal arguments that his sentence was a form of "cruel and unusual punishment" under the Charter of Rights and Freedoms. Having exhausted his legal avenues, Latimer went to prison in 2001.

In 2008, after serving seven years in prison, Robert Latimer was granted temporary day parole from his Victoria, British Columbia, prison to visit his sick mother. By 2010, the National Parole Board granted him full parole, and Latimer returned home to Saskatchewan.

The Latimer case galvanized national attention on the issue of euthanasia and prompted debates and discussion on the question of "mercy killing" and the role of the law, of doctors, of advocacy groups, and of ordinary people in decisions about this issue. More broadly, it reflected an ongoing national discourse about social change and the moral and ethical questions that surround the "right to life."

Canadians did not find easy answers and continue to struggle with these issues. Tracy Latimer remains a symbol of the divisiveness and difficulty surrounding her death—and, unquestionably, of the love, pain, and horrible actions of her father.

CHAPTER TWENTY

DUDLEY GEORGE, MURDERED, IPPERWASH, ONTARIO, 1995
ABORIGINAL RIGHTS AND RESISTANCE IN THE POSTWAR PERIOD

The Incident

What happened at Ipperwash Provincial Park in Ontario in 1995? Why was Dudley George, an unarmed aboriginal protestor demanding the return of native lands, shot by an Ontario Provincial Police (OPP) officer? Who was responsible? Was it because, as some would interpret the events, George was taking part in an illegal occupation of a provincial park by aboriginal groups who had no right to be there? Was this an unfortunate circumstance but one brought on by George and his fellow protestors' illegal activities?

Or was he murdered in cold blood by a government that cared only about the political perception of doing something about the occupation at Ipperwash? Did the officer who shot Dudley George do so because the OPP had allegedly been told by then-Ontario premier Mike Harris "I want the fucking Indians out of the park"?

Or was Dudley George a martyr, and a victim, a symbol of two centuries of ill-treatment and neglect? Did his death represent something broader about the nature of white–aboriginal relations?

There is no question that this was a high-profile murder in Ontario. Let us examine the facts of the incident. In the nineteenth century, the Anishnabek Nation (also known as Chippewa) in the area agreed to share nearly six million hectares of land with European settlers, although they kept a number of areas for themselves, including the area around Stony Point and Ipperwash, on the shores of Lake Huron. Over time, the aboriginals sold off some lots, including a portion to Ontario in a 1927 transaction later described in a court case as having "the odour of moral failure" on the part of the government.[1] That portion became Ipperwash Provincial Park in 1936. In 1942, in the midst of the Second World War, the Canadian army used the War Measures Act to evacuate the aboriginals forcibly from the area and set up a temporary military training camp on part of the Stony Point Reserve. Aboriginals were forced to leave their homes and relocate to another native community, Kettle Creek. Though aboriginal groups protested this vigorously at the time and in the decades that followed, the Canadian government refused to leave the site.

In May 1993, after nearly 40 years of waiting, members of the Kettle and Stony Point First Nation protested by occupying some of the land. The next year, the federal government announced that it wanted to negotiate the return of the Ipperwash camp to the First Nations people. After a confrontation with the Chippewa, the military personnel left the base. Not long after, in September of 1995, a few dozen First Nations members occupied Ipperwash Provincial Park to protect and reclaim a sacred burial ground. The recently elected Progressive Conservative premier, Mike Harris, was determined to end the protest and remove the aboriginal protestors from the park.

On Labour Day weekend, the confrontation escalated as the OPP was called in. During the protest, Anthony (Dudley) George was shot by Ontario Provincial Police Acting Sergeant Kenneth Deane. George died that night.

These are the facts of the case, though this is only a brief overview of this event.

More broadly, the killing of Dudley George is a key event in aboriginal–white relations. The battle over Ipperwash and the killing of Dudley George reflect the deep anger and bitterness of First Nations, Métis, and Inuit peoples at the unjust treatment they have received for centuries at the hands of white society and the government. It also represents a newfound resistance and agency that was being expressed by First Nations groups. With this stand, First Nations were saying that they were not and will not be dependent, as they once might have been, and that they were committed to making Canadians realize this.

To really understand this case and why Dudley George was killed on September 6, 1995, we need to look at the long-standing causes of the conflict between white and aboriginal society, and also at the context of this moment. One thing before continuing: this case interchangeably uses the terms First Nations, aboriginal, indigenous, native, and Indian, thereby reflecting not only the changing use of these terms over time but also the varying practices within scholarly literature. Even "Indian" is used sometimes as a contemporary term.

---

1   Supreme Court of Canada (1995), 24 O.R. (3d) 654 (Gen. Dev.) at 690.

The Causes

By the Second World War, when the federal government took over the Stony Point Reserve, Canada and Ontario's native peoples were in a very difficult position. Many aboriginals experienced some level of dependency upon the federal government. Of course, it had not always been this way; for most of the period after native-white contact, whites had depended upon aboriginals (for technology, for food, for guidance, for trade). Native dependency emerged due to a number of factors.

First, demographically, aboriginal numbers had dwindled. Disease had ravaged native populations. Without many of the natural immunities of whites and facing diseases that were not indigenous to North America, such as small pox, aboriginals faced high mortality rates in the eighteenth and nineteenth centuries. Aboriginals also experienced poor living conditions and generally far lower life expectancies than whites. Sadly, this situation is largely true today, as well. Aboriginal population had stagnated as a result of these challenges. In 1871, First Nations peoples made up just over 100,000 out of about a 3.5 million total population; by 1941 aboriginals were still only less than 150,000, but now out of 11.5 million.

Second, government policy helped to create this dependent relationship. Under the British North America Act of 1867, aboriginals were the responsibility of the federal government. In the period after 1867, the Canadian state practiced a policy of assimilation. Government policymakers believed that the best way to "save" Indians was to assimilate them into the "Canadian way of life." This assimilation policy was called Canadianization.

Canadianization and assimilation were primarily attempted through the Indian Act of 1876. The Indian Act did a number of things. It created a class system within First Nations society, as "status" Indians were aboriginals that did not have the franchise (the vote) and lost their "status" if they decided to take up the vote. It stipulated that aboriginal women who married white men lost their status. It changed native governance, creating a band system that took away native processes and replaced them with the decision-making procedures of white government. It banned First Nations cultural practices such as the potlatch and the sun dance, banned the use of aboriginal languages in state-supported schools, and prohibited the consumption of alcohol on reserves. It restricted movement from reserves (an actual pass system was put in place), and it institutionalized assimilation policy through the creation of Indian residential schools. Finally, government policy toward land through the treaty system basically disenfranchised First Nations of their territory.

A third major factor that helps to explain the dependency and difficult circumstances of First Nations people by the beginning of the twentieth century is technological and economic change. The nineteenth century's industrial revolution, urbanization, and great immigration booms had a severe impact on native–white relations and on the dynamic between the two peoples. With a railway, who needed guides or canoes or pemmican? With the end of the fur trade, who needed trade ties or native trapping expertise? By the mid-twentieth century, native life seemed to be on the wane, and aboriginals seemed to have become increasingly invisible in modern Canadian society, especially in contrast to their visibility in Canadian society in the nineteenth century.

But, at the same time, aboriginals resisted white domination during this period. The First Nations did not give up their outlawed customs; they continued to practice them in secret or in open defiance of the authorities, often at great cost, and maintained their rituals and languages. Many parents refused to allow their children to attend Indian residential schools, and many children themselves, such as Charlie Wenjack, ran away from these schools (see p. 206).

In a collective act of political resistance, they refused enfranchisement: until 1960, when they were granted the vote unconditionally, very few aboriginals decided to take up the vote, illustrating their unwillingness to give up their status as Indians.

Perhaps most important, aboriginal groups started to form organizations to represent themselves, particularly after the Second World War. This was not a coincidence. The active role that aboriginals took during the Second World War galvanized activism and emphasized to aboriginal leaders the hypocritical stance of many Canadians who were willing to fight against Hitler's racial horrors but tolerated racial inequality at home. The war itself provided a particular spark for the Ipperwash incident, as well.

The Context

Let's now turn our attention to the context of the 1990s, during which the Ipperwash incident occurred, a context very much informed by developments in First Nations society and by native–white relations in the post–Second World War period. This postwar period was marked by an awakening for aboriginals, and the road to political awareness and native rights emerged in the 1950s and 1960s for a number of reasons. Native soldiers distinguished themselves in action during the Second World War, as a number of native veterans returned as heroes—though even Stony Point aboriginal veterans who returned from the war found that there was little they could do about the takeover of aboriginal territory in Ipperwash by their own Canadian army. At the same time, many white Canadians were becoming aware, and feeling guilt, about the Canadian treatment of aboriginals, especially in light of the Nazi treatment of racial minorities.

The situation was also shaped by broader events. By the early 1960s, Canadian international efforts to fight against racial inequality rang hollow in the face of Canadians' atrocious treatment of aboriginals at home. Prime Minister John Diefenbaker fought against racial injustice in places such as South Africa, which only further highlighted the terrible conditions of aboriginals in Canada. Aboriginals were also inspired by the growing civil rights movements in the United States and by comparable struggles in Canada. As blacks in the United States sought equality, so did French Canadians and women in Canada. These movements galvanized a whole generation of activists. For native activists, who rightfully saw themselves as the "first" nations of Canada and who had faced a longer history of dispossession and ill-treatment, the time was right to start demanding rights and equal treatment forcefully.

Importantly, we must recognize that, during this postwar awakening, whites were not just "giving" aboriginals rights: aboriginal peoples were demanding, fighting for, and winning rights themselves. They have agency. As a result, "Red Power" emerged in the postwar period, especially in three main areas: politics, land and resources, and increased militancy. All these aspects of aboriginal agency were present at Ipperwash in September 1995.

Context I: Growing Political Power

After the Second World War, aboriginals became increasingly active in the political sphere and pushed for self-government. Political activism had long been a part of aboriginal advocacy, but it was renewed in the postwar period with the appointment of James Gladstone, the first aboriginal senator, in 1958. Though some criticized this move as mere tokenism in that it did not really give aboriginals any new powers, Gladstone's appointment brought a newfound presence for aboriginals and their issues in Canada. By the late 1950s, First Nations exhibited a much broader willingness to mobilize and organize, as is documented by the emergence of modern native groups such as the National Indian Council in 1961.

As a result of this new activism, the government of Lester B. Pearson commissioned a report in 1966 that was officially known as A Survey of the Contemporary Indians of Canada: Economic, Political, Educational Needs and Policies. Unofficially, it was called the "Hawthorn Report" after George Hawthorn, the anthropologist commissioned to conduct the study. The report exposed the harsh realities of native society in Canada, particularly the challenges of poverty facing aboriginals. The report argued that Canadian society had to take a new approach to natives and suggested that aboriginals should have the status of "citizens plus"—namely, having all the rights of Canadian citizens in addition to rights as natives. In part, the recommendations of the Hawthorn Report reflected a push towards a renewal of the idea of participatory democracy, of trying to engage people; it also reflected the necessity of recognizing native identity, in addition to addressing some of the social and economic issues facing aboriginals in Canada.

In the wake of the Hawthorn Report, in 1969 the Liberal government of Pierre Trudeau published the unfortunately titled White Paper, meant to be an action plan for aboriginals and a response to their growing activism. In keeping with Trudeau's belief in the equality of all citizens and his campaign rhetoric about making Canada a "just society," Trudeau and his minister of aboriginal affairs at the time, Jean Chrétien, produced a report that recommended abolishing the Indian Act; aboriginals would give up their status, consequently, and become "equal." Trudeau and Chrétien's belief at the time was that aboriginals, like other groups in society, were seeking equal status under the law. They completely misread and misunderstood the position of native groups, who saw the White Paper as nothing more than another effort at assimilation. Aboriginals did not want just to be "equal" to other Canadians; they wanted recognition, self-government, and their own rights. In a period of Red Power, the Trudeau government's "White Paper" sparked a tremendous reaction by aboriginal groups.

Indeed, First Nations activists and groups were appalled by the government's plans. Activists such as Harold Cardinal expressed his outrage at the White Paper by penning a rejoinder to Trudeau and Chrétien, *The Unjust Society*. A relatively new aboriginal activist group, the National Indian Brotherhood (created in 1968), rejected the Trudeau plan and its idea of "equality," calling it another assimilationist attempt. At a general assembly of this organization in 1982, the Assembly of First Nations (AFN) came into being. The AFN remains the most powerful First Nations group and is an umbrella for all native groups in Canada.

In the 1980s, the AFN's effectiveness and the growing political power of First Nations groups in Canada could be seen in a number of events. During the 1982 fight over the Constitution and the Charter of Rights and Freedoms, the AFN successfully lobbied for significant changes to the Charter that enshrined treaty rights but also ensured a language of self-government for native groups going forward. The effectiveness of aboriginal groups in shaping policy in Ottawa could also be seen in 1985, when the Indian Act was changed so that native women retained their status even if they married non-aboriginals and moved off a reserve. This was a major victory for both native groups and aboriginal women.

Aboriginals' growing political power was also apparent during the constitutional battles of the late 1980s and early 1990s. In 1990, Elijah Harper, an aboriginal member of the Manitoba legislature, refused to allow a vote on the constitutional amendment known as the Meech Lake Accord because it neither dealt with native issues nor advanced self-government, effectively killing the agreement. Aboriginal leaders also played a key role in the 1992 Charlottetown Accord, which also failed in a national referendum. Then, during the 1995 secession referendum in Quebec, the province's Cree made it clear that any Quebec separation could not proceed without the approval of aboriginal groups and, instead, pushed the Canadian government to continue addressing land rights.

All of these issues, as well as the Oka crisis in the summer of 1990, prompted the federal government to launch the seminal Royal Commission on Aboriginal Peoples (RCAP) in 1991. Its massive, 5-volume, 4,000-page report, published in 1996, pointed to new solutions and directions for aboriginal–white relations and suggested a turning away from assimilation or integration as policy. However, many of these recommendations have not been implemented, and advocates for aboriginal rights have accused the government of neglecting and ignoring the RCAP, as well as many other issues in aboriginal–white relations.

Context II: Land Claims and Resource Development

Land claims and resource development comprise the second major theme of postwar aboriginal–white relations. Disputes about both go back to the beginning of the relationship between the Crown (that is, the governmental authority in Canada) and aboriginal tribes. In many ways, the relations that inform conflicts over land and resources predate Canada and are based on the Royal Proclamation of 1763, a key document establishing aboriginal–white legal interactions. Initially, conflicts were about fishing, logging, and hunting rights; but now they also involve resource development from hydro to oil and gas to diamonds. In the case of Ipperwash, the dispute centred on territory expropriated by the federal government and the ownership of ancient aboriginal burial grounds.

Until the 1960s, aboriginals were basically dispossessed of land and their rights over land. In some areas of Canada, especially in the North, aboriginal groups had little to no say over what happened to the very lands upon which they had existed for thousands of years. This situation began to change in the 1970s because of the newfound agency of First Nations groups to assert themselves politically. Three examples illustrate how land and resources issues have changed for aboriginals in Canada.

One key postwar development was the 1976–77 James Bay and Northern Quebec Native Claims Settlement Act between the government (both federal and provincial) and the Cree and the Inuit of northern Quebec. In the lead-up to this landmark event, the Cree and Inuit got a court injunction in 1973 to halt a massive hydroelectric project planned by the provincial government. As a result, the government was forced to negotiate an agreement that addressed the environmental and social impact of the development and that gave affected aboriginal groups direct compensation for use of their land. Following this, the federal government announced that it would settle as many land claims as possible, opening the door to more court cases and settlements.

A second important event was the 1977 Mackenzie Valley Pipeline Inquiry, also known as the Berger Inquiry. In the mid-1970s, aboriginals challenged in the courts the decision to build a pipeline through the Mackenzie Valley in the

Northwest Territories. Judge Thomas Berger was sympathetic to native rights and land claims and actually visited the Mackenzie Valley to assess the potential impact of the pipeline upon native life and the environment. Berger, in his famous report, decided that aboriginals must have some say in the development of the pipeline and that nothing could be built until the various land claims were settled. This was a major step forward for native rights and resource management.

Another important court decision was the 1997 Supreme Court case *Delgamuukw v. British Columbia* (pronounced Del-ga-mook). Here, the Supreme Court recognized aboriginal title, that is, the idea that aboriginal claims over the land that had not been surrendered to the Crown were valid and that any claims needed to be settled between the government and the aboriginal groups and tribes that had title over the territory. The case stemmed from a British Columbia situation wherein an aboriginal group in that province had taken the government to court after fighting for decades (in the case of Delgamuukw, for over 70 years), making the case that they had never given up their land and had never signed any treaties, which meant that governments were required to settle over their territory.

These cases reflected the challenging environment that aboriginals faced and the long-standing grievances that had existed for literally centuries over questions of land and claims. These long-standing grievances in some cases boiled over into open conflict.

Context III: Conflict and Resistance

This is the third major theme of aboriginal–white relations in the twentieth century. The slow move toward the recognition of native rights and claims and the reluctance of many in white society to recognize these claims have led to conflict at times. Many of these high-profile issues and incidents have been about land or about aboriginal groups occupying native land and wanting it returned, such as at Ipperwash.

Militant aboriginal resistance became a powerful tool, especially in the 1960s, with the "awakening" of native groups in the United States such as the American Indian Movement (AIM). AIM was involved in a number of protests against and confrontations with the US federal government in the 1970s; most notably it occupied the town of Wounded Knee in South Dakota in 1973. This type of confrontation also appeared in Canada.

Some conflicts have been about outside influence upon indigenous people's territory. For instance, in the 1970s and 1980s, as part of its commitment to the North Atlantic Treaty Organization (NATO), Canada agreed to let its allies conduct war games on Cree territory, which prompted protests. The aircraft overflights and practice bombing sessions in Labrador had negative effects on the Innu people in that territory by disrupting deer migrations and interfering with Cree society. Innu elders were arrested for blocking runways and protesting the building of air bases in Labrador in 1988.

A number of high profile Canadian incidents have generated international headlines and drawn attention to the plight of aboriginals and the question of rights and resistance. One incident, in Cache Creek, BC, reflected the new impetus toward direct militancy inspired by AIM in the United States. In 1973–74, aboriginals from the Bonaparte Indian Reserve set up a toll for motorists crossing through the reserve on a provincial highway, which they enforced with rifles. David Roberts, a 17-year-old involved in the blockade, was accidentally killed during the incident. The blockade reflected an emergence of Red Power, as the aboriginal protesters wore the AIM insignia.

Perhaps the most famous modern clash between whites and aboriginals in Canada, and one that generated international headlines and scrutiny of Canada's relations with aboriginals, occurred at Oka, Quebec, not far from Montreal, in the hot summer of 1990. Near Kanesatake, a Mohawk reserve in Quebec, developers wanted to extend a golf course on to what was considered sacred native land. Mohawks, outraged at this plan, which they had tried to prevent through the courts, occupied the land in question and set up barricades. The Sûreté du Québec (Quebec's provincial police) were called in, and, after a firefight with Mohawk warriors, one police officer was killed. Soon, the Kanesatake Mohawks were

Figure 20.1 *Aboriginal Protest, Bonaparte Reserve, BC, 1972*

Source: Copyright Glenn Baglo/*Vancouver Sun*. Reprinted by permission of the *Vancouver Sun*

joined by natives from across the country. One group blockaded a key bridge to Montreal. As the crisis escalated, the federal government accepted a request to send in Canadian troops, leading to a tense 78-day standoff. Eventually, the two sides agreed to negotiate. No golf course was built.

In some ways, the events at Oka foreshadowed events at Ipperwash, as did another aboriginal occupation in Gustafsen Lake, BC, in the summer of 1995. It should be noted that Dudley George was the first native land claims protester to be killed by government action in Canada in the twentieth century. These scenes of conflict reflect for many the continuing unwillingness of white society to address native concerns and grievances.

Conclusion

So what happened in the end?

Well, the courts were clear on who was to blame for the actual death of Dudley George. During a criminal trial, Ontario Provincial Police Officer Kenneth Deane was found guilty of criminal negligence causing death. Deane was sentenced to two years and forced to resign; though he protested his innocence and fought in court against the charge, he was unsuccessful in claiming he had simply mistaken a stick that George was holding as a firearm. As the judge told Deane, "I find, sir, that you were not honest in presenting this version of events to the Ontario Provincial Police investigators. You were not honest in presenting this version of events to the Special Investigations Unit of the Province of Ontario. You were not honest in maintaining this ruse before this court."[2] Deane served two years of community service for the crime.

As to the government's role, from 1995 to 2003, the Conservative government refused to allow an inquiry into the events at Ipperwash. When they came to power in 2003, the new Liberal government appointed former Ontario Chief Justice Sidney B. Linden to investigate the incident. The inquiry found that Premier Mike Harris had not directly instructed the OPP to evict the native protesters, but it faulted the government for forcing the issue when the OPP had initially planned a cautious approach with the protestors.

In a twist of fate, former OPP officer Deane was killed in a car accident on his way to testify at the Ipperwash Inquiry in 2006. Eventually, Ipperwash Provincial Park was returned to the Stony band in 2009. This issue was resolved, though at the cost of Dudley George's life, but a wide gulf between white Canadians and aboriginals remains, as both sides strive to come to an a post-colonial understanding and relationship.

---

2   As quoted in Peter Edwards, *One Dead Indian: The Premier, the Police and the Ipperwash Crisis* (Toronto: McClelland & Stewart, 2003), 198.

Further Reading

Anderson, Chris, and Claude Denis. "Urban Natives and the Nation: Before and After the Royal Commission on Aboriginal Peoples." *Canadian Review of Sociology and Anthropology / La revue canadienne de sociologie et d'anthropologie* 40, no. 4 (November 2003): 373–90. http://dx.doi.org/10.1111/j.1755-618X.2003.tb00253.x.

BC Treaty Commission. *A Lay Persons's Guide to Delgamuukw*. http://www.bctreaty.net/files/pdf_documents/delgamuukw.pdf.

Brownlie, Robin Jarvis. "'A better citizen than lots of white men': First Nations Enfranchisement—an Ontario Case Study, 1918–1940." *Canadian Historical Review* 87, no. 1 (March 2006): 29–52.

Edwards, Peter. *One Dead Indian: The Premier, the Police and the Ipperwash Crisis*. Toronto: McClelland & Stewart, 2003.

Miller, J.R. *Skyscrapers Hide the Heavens: A History of Indian–White Relations in Canada*. Toronto: University of Toronto Press, 1989.

Milloy, John. *A National Crime: The Canadian Government and the Residential School System, 1879–1986*. Winnipeg: University of Manitoba Press, 1999.

Obomsawin, Alanis, director. *Kanehsatake: 270 Years of Resistance*. Ottawa: National Film Board of Canada, 1993. http://www.nfb.ca/film/kanehsatake_270_years_of_resistance/.

Ontario. *Report of the Ipperwash Inquiry*. Toronto: Ipperwash Inquiry, 2007. http://www.attorneygeneral.jus.gov.on.ca/inquiries/ipperwash/index.html.

Pulla, Siomonn. "Resisting Regulation: Conservation, Control, and Controversy over Aboriginal Land and Resource Rights in Eastern Canada, 1880–1930." *International Journal of Canadian Studies* 45/46 (2012): 467–94. http://dx.doi.org/10.7202/1009915ar.

ACTIVE HISTORY: FILM REVIEW

- Write a review, in journalistic style, of the Alanis Obomsawin film *Kanehsatake: 270 Years of Resistance*, available at the National Film Board website.

- Comment upon the style and effectiveness of the film. Your review should include some synopsis of the film, in addition to a critique of the film (both positive and negative). How does the film take a particular stand? What are some of its key sources and points of argumentation? What is most effective about the film or least effective?

- How does this film help us to understand both the events in 1990 and the broader story and context of aboriginal–white relations in Canada?

TRAGIC TALES
SUE RODRIGUEZ, DEATH BY ASSISTED SUICIDE, BRITISH COLUMBIA, 1994

One Woman's Fight to End Her Own Life

Euthanasia, bringing about death in order to end pain and suffering, is an issue that reflects a growing shift in Canadian attitudes toward religion, illness, and death in the postwar period. At the same time, suicide has been considered a sin for generations, and major churches hold that any person who commits suicide faces condemnation. As Canada became increasingly secularized in the twentieth century, however, and especially over the last 50 years, Canadians began to come to terms somewhat with assisted suicide. After all, older Canadians in our time often face diseases and physical challenges never experienced by previous generations.

Sue Rodriguez became a symbol of the emerging dilemmas related to euthanasia and suicide in the postwar period. Rodriguez was not old, but, in the early 1990s, she became very ill. Born in Winnipeg and raised in Ontario, Rodriguez moved to British Columbia in the 1980s. In 1991, Rodriguez was diagnosed with amyotrophic lateral sclerosis or ALS, also known as "Lou Gehrig's Disease" after a famous American baseball player who died from the illness. ALS is a debilitating disease that causes its victims a slow and painful degeneration of their motor skills. Faced with the likelihood that she would become increasingly incapable of doing even the simplest of tasks, such as hugging her young son, Rodriguez made the decision to end her own life. In a memoir she wrote that "if I cannot move my own body, I have no life."[3]

Rodriguez, already confined to a wheelchair, launched a fight to be able to kill herself. In the words of her supporters, she wanted to die with dignity. But to do so, she needed assistance. Though morally condemned, suicide itself has not been illegal in Canada since 1972; but *assisting* someone to kill himself or herself was a violation under Section 241(b) of Canada's Criminal Code and was punishable by up to 14 years in prison. Rodriguez, unable to kill herself because of her condition, needed another person's help, which made her act illegal. And if she received assistance from a physician, that doctor would not only face criminal charges but would lose her or his license to practice medicine.

Determined to end her life, Rodriguez challenged Section 241(b) of the Criminal Code by arguing that the law was an infringement of her Charter rights to "life, liberty and security of the person" and to protection against "cruel and unusual punishment" and that it also violated her equality rights. Taking her case all the way to the Supreme Court of Canada, Rodriguez argued that not allowing her to control her own body was an infringement upon her most basic rights. "Whose body is this?" became the question she asked as she fought her legal battle to end her own life.

In 1993, the Supreme Court of Canada decided against Rodriguez, and her case was defeated. In part, the Supreme Court argued, although the law did infringe on her right to do what she wished with her body, society had long maintained a prohibition on aiding suicide, one in keeping with fundamental values that sought to ensure that vulnerable individuals could not

---

3   Lisa Hobbs Binnie, and Sue Rodriguez, *Uncommon Will: The Death and Life of Sue Rodriguez* (Toronto: Macmillan, 1994), 27.

be targeted or persuaded to kill themselves. The court also found that Rodriguez did not face a cruel or unusual punishment, as the state itself was only prohibiting an action in this case and not administering anything. Overall, though four justices thought that Rodriguez could, for varying reasons, have someone assist her suicide, five did not, a further reflection of how divided Canadian society was over this issue.

Undaunted, Rodriguez made arrangements for her own death, in defiance of the law. On February 12, 1994, a date chosen by her, Rodriguez died, though the exact circumstances of her passing remain unknown. The only two people with Rodriguez in her Vancouver Island home were an unnamed physician and NDP Member of Parliament Svend Robinson, himself a long-time advocate of assisted suicide. When Rodriguez died, it was Robinson who informed the coroner and held a nationally televised press conference to draw further attention to the issue. Neither Robinson nor the attending physician faced any charges under the Criminal Code because of the event.

Rodriguez's court battle and death did not end the debate over assisted suicide or discussions about euthanasia and suicide. The case remained highly controversial, sparking impassioned positions both from those who advocate for a "right to die," from those who think protecting the vulnerable from being "assisted" to a death they do not want trumps an individual's "right to die," and from those who think any form of suicide, assisted or not, is morally and ethically unforgiveable. In a 2015 case that received national attention, the Supreme Court of Canada reversed its position and struck down the legislation that prohibited doctor-assisted suicide. Nonetheless, it remains to be seen how Canadians will grapple with a question that will become, sadly, increasingly common, given the diseases and demographic trends of twenty-first century society.

CHAPTER TWENTY-ONE

THE 329 PEOPLE ON AIR INDIA FLIGHT 182, MURDERED OVER THE ATLANTIC OCEAN, 1985

CHALLENGES TO IMMIGRATION AND MULTICULTURALISM IN AN AGE OF TERROR

From the Opening Remarks of the Honourable John C. Major, C.C., Q.C.

On the release of the Report of the Commission of Inquiry into the Investigation of the Bombing of Air India Flight 182, June 17, 2010

The bombing of Air India Flight 182 on June 23, 1985 was an act of terrorism. Three hundred and twenty-nine persons—passengers and crew—died in the North Atlantic off the coast of Ireland. The majority of the passengers were Canadian; one quarter of the victims (82) were under the age of thirteen. Their families still grieve for them here in Canada.

The bomb that blew up Air India Flight 182 was manufactured in Canada as part of a plot that was developed in Canada. The bomb was hidden in luggage that was placed on a Canadian plane in Vancouver and later transferred to Air India 182 in Toronto which stopped in Montreal to pick up additional passengers before it commenced its fatal flight. Another bomb was placed on a Canadian plane in Vancouver, in luggage destined for an Air India flight, and exploded in Narita, Japan, killing two baggage handlers.[1]

---

1   Commission of Inquiry into the Investigation of the Bombing of Air India Flight 182, "Opening Remarks," *Air India Flight 182: A Canadian Tragedy* (Ottawa: Public Works and Government Services Canada, 2010), available at http://epe.lac-bac.gc.ca/100/206/301/pco-bcp/commissions/air_india/2010-07-23/www.majorcomm.ca/en/reports/finalreport/commissioner-remarks.pdf.

* * *

In June of 1985, Sikh extremists put a bomb on board a Boeing 747 Air India flight from Montreal to New Delhi that originated in Toronto. The bomb exploded on June 23 while the plane was over the Atlantic Ocean, just off the coast of Ireland, killing all 329 passengers and crew on board. It was, to that point, the worst single terrorist attack in history until the attacks of September 11, 2001, on the United States.

The Air India Flight 182 bombing was part of a plot by Sikh extremists to provoke and attack India. In the early 1980s, the Indian government had clamped down on their religion and their efforts to create their own country out of the Indian region of the Punjab. Sikhism is a minority religion in India, though it constitutes the majority religion of the Punjab state of India. The Sikh religion dates to the fifteenth century, and some Sikhs have sought independence from India since that country itself achieved independence from Great Britain in 1947.

The Air India disaster prompted decades of investigation that cost over $130 million. Despite this, because of the procedural and administrative problems of the investigation, only one man, Inderjit Singh Reyat, was actually found guilty of the crime, though he was part of a terrorist network operating in Canada that organized the attacks. A number of others who were unquestionably involved went free because of legal challenges and errors in the investigation that left many of the victims' family members horrified at the incompetence of police and investigators.

Though at first blush, this terrorist attack seems only barely linked to Canada, it is, in fact, the worst terrorist attack ever committed by Canadians against Canadians. Indeed, though some Canadians initially thought "foreigners" had perpetrated this act of terror, Canadian Sikhs were responsible. Also, of the 329 people on board that day, nearly 300 were Canadians, most of Indian origin, and most from the Toronto area. These were Canadians who were killed, killed by people who were also from Canada.

From Justice Major's Opening Remarks, June 17, 2010

I stress that this is a Canadian atrocity. For too long the greatest loss of Canadian lives at the hands of terrorists has been somehow relegated outside the Canadian consciousness. For this reason, in December 2007, we released our first report—"The Families Remember"—to chronicle the human toll inflicted by terrorists. The moving testimonials described the unfulfilled potential, the broken dreams, and the loss of great leaders, high achievers, and role models—young and old. All were loved and their families were left to struggle with unimaginable suffering. Their stories are Canadian or have a strong Canadian connection.

But the story of Air India Flight 182 goes beyond the loss of life, as terrible as that is. This was the largest mass murder in Canadian history.

A cascading series of errors contributed to the failure of our police and security forces to prevent this atrocity. The level of error, incompetence, and inattention which took place before the flight was sadly mirrored in many ways for many years, in how authorities, Governments, and institutions dealt with the aftermath of the murder of so many innocents: in the investigation, the legal proceedings, and in providing information, support and comfort to the families.

Initial Reaction and Response to the Incident

The explosion of Air India 182 was a major international incident, and one of the most brutal terrorist attacks in modern history. Of the 329 passengers and crew, 268 were Canadian citizens and 24 were Indian citizens, including 21 in the crew. The remaining victims were from the United Kingdom, the Soviet Union, the United States, Brazil, Argentina, Spain, and Finland.

Strangely, it took the events of September 11, 2001, to make many Canadians realize that this was a Canadian story, that it was, in some people's view, "Canada's 9/11." Indeed, people started to think that it *was* a Canadian story only years after it happened. In fact, in 1985, when the incident occurred, Canadian Prime Minister Brian Mulroney called the president of India to offer his condolences— but not the families of the victims who were Canadian. Not until 2005, 20 years after the incident, did the Canadian government recognize the event by declaring a national day of mourning for the victims.

The disconnect between perceptions of this event as foreign and the fact that it was actually Canadian highlights one of the key questions of postwar Canadian development: who is Canadian, and what does it mean to be a Canadian?

In trying to answer these questions, this chapter addresses three interrelated themes. First, it examines the background, issues, and problems associated with immigration. The second theme concerns the origin, operation, and impact of Canada as a multicultural society and of the Canadian government's official multicultural policy. Finally, the chapter examines some of the challenges to both immigration and multiculturalism that have occurred in the Canadian context, and the broader meanings of these challenges.

All three of these themes are, of course, closely linked to the economy, to ethnicity, and to identity. Moreover, in Canada over the last century, a tension has existed between, on the one hand, immigration and multiculturalism and, on the other, a desire to maintain economic stability and a certain identity. Immigration and multiculturalism have seemed to challenge these desires, but, for the most part, the concern of many that immigration or embracing other cultures would have negative affects has been largely misplaced. Indeed, despite rare events such

Figure 21.1 *A Woman at the Air India Memorial, 2007*

Reprinted by permission of the *Toronto Star*

as the Air India bombing, it is clear that immigration and multiculturalism have had, on balance, far more of a positive impact on both the Canadian bottom line and Canadians' sense of identity than detractors might admit.

Importantly, however, both immigration and multiculturalism have come under severe strain since the 1985 Air India disaster, and especially since the events of the terrorist attacks of September 2001 in the United States. Terrorism and its threat to Canadian society have taken on racial tones in many instances, a circumstance challenging our notion of what it means to be a citizen. The Air India Flight 182 bombing brings all of these strains into sharp contrast.

The Question of Immigration

The majority of the Air India victims and the perpetrators were immigrants to Canada or the children of immigrants. This prompts questions. Did immigration cause this terrorist attack? What are the benefits and drawbacks of immigration? Is there a historic link between immigration and terrorism? Questions such as these go back to the founding of the Canadian state, given that one of the key episodes of Confederation-era Canada was the assassination of immigrant politician Thomas D'Arcy McGee by convicted perpetrator Patrick James Whelan, also an immigrant.

What factors affect immigration to Canada, and how do they relate to the Air India incident?

First, there are economic reasons for immigration. Historically, economics is perhaps the most significant factor affecting immigration to Canada. Most commonly, people emigrate in order to make a better economic life for themselves and their children. For example, a "sojourning" immigrant goes to a country to work temporarily, intending to return to the home country after making economic advancements. Many people came to Canada to work and send back money; some returned home but some stayed and sent for their families. Many immigrants from the Indian subcontinent, Asia, and elsewhere have come to Canada for economic reasons and to improve the economic fortunes of their families.

Second, social factors shape people's decisions on whether to emigrate from a country and, of course, on which destination country to immigrate to. Historically, persecution, whether for religious, political, sexual, or ethnic reasons, has been a leading social factor causing large groups of people to leave a country. In the case of Air India, many Sikhs left India owing to what they felt was religious and political persecution. Another social factor is, of course, family. Family ties often lead to "chain migration," as one family member migrates and then provides a link for the next family member and so on.

A third factor influencing immigration is demographics. In some instances, population pressures force people to move out of their countries. For example, overpopulation in some cities, such as Mumbai or Delhi in India, or even in rural areas such as the Punjab, where farmland is no longer available or too costly, has prompted emigration. The 1840s Potato Famine led to mass Irish emigration to North America, as the island could no longer sustain its population.

Fourth and finally, imperialistic or political factors are at play, at times, as well. Some countries, including Canada, have had policies of conscious colonization or of attracting immigrants. Initially, much of New France's growth in the seventeenth century came after the French government of Louis XIV established a policy of populating the colony. After that, British settlers from the United States populated Canada following the American Revolution. Canadian growth in the nineteenth century was fuelled primarily by emigration from the "mother country," Britain, Western Europe, and Scandinavia.

All of these reasons for immigration can also be viewed as either "push" or "pull" factors, or both. Forcing people out of an area, or drawing them to an area, or both can be at work at the same time. The reasons for emigration and immigration are diverse and overlapping. Of course, at times, some issues loom more largely than others in determining the shape of immigration.

Canadian policy toward immigration has been shaped by these factors, which provide a background for the Air India disaster, as well. There have been three main phases in Canadian immigration policy since Confederation. During the first phase, from the nineteenth century until the 1950s, the demands of labour, on one hand, and considerations of race, on the other, remained the central factors in Canadian immigration policy. During this period, business interests had the most influence in demanding that the government allow workers into the country so employers could obtain cheap labour and keep wages low.

But governments often "closed the door" when political, racial, or demographic concerns were raised. For example, trade unions disliked open-door policies, which hurt their workers, and both British and French Canadians were reluctant to accept "other" groups into Canadian society. One example of this economic versus racial dynamic can be seen in the case of Chinese railway workers. In the period before 1885, businesses such as the Canadian Pacific Railway forced open the door to get the railway built, but, after its completion, government closed the door in response to the racial concerns voiced by British Columbians and other Canadians.

By 1903, the head tax imposed on Chinese immigrants in 1885 was raised to $500, and, by 1923, the Chinese Immigration Act (known today as the Chinese Exclusion Act) was enacted, resulting in little to no official immigration from China, though there was much illegal immigration. Thus, public pressure, especially in Canada's West, pushed government on the "Chinese question" because Chinese immigration no longer had the support of business as the railway was complete.

Another example of the role of race can be seen in the restrictive, raced-based immigration policy Canada retained toward what it considered "undesirables." For instance, in the 1930s, German Jews faced severe persecution that became even harsher after the war began in 1939. Yet, as an anonymous senior Canadian official in Mackenzie King's government stated in a private discussion with journalists, when it came to Jewish immigration to Canada, "None is too many."[2] This statement, uttered in 1945, reflected King's attitude toward Jewish immigration, noted in his diary in 1938, and his political view that such immigration would cause him difficulties in the province of Quebec, where there was deep antipathy toward Jewish immigration.

The post–Second World War period marked a second phase in Canadian immigration policy. The rhetoric employed by the Allies in winning the war and the horrors discovered at the concentration camps of the mass genocide of Jews and others changed attitudes toward race and ethnicity. With humanitarian concerns and democracy newly of significance for Canadian policymakers, the door was slightly opened for immigrants previously considered "undesirable." This policy was only slightly less racist and still used economic factors in determining immigration.

For instance, after the war, Canada did relent and allow some "displaced persons," or DPs, into the country, primarily to keep a good humanitarian record and (again) to avoid a labour shortage. These included people from the Netherlands or from Germany whose homes and livelihoods had been destroyed by the war. Approximately 165,000 displaced persons came to Canada between 1947 and 1953.

Then, in 1951, Canada made agreements to allow minuscule numbers of immigrants from countries previously prevented from sending people, including Asian countries. The quota system allowed 150 Indian, 100 Pakistani, and 50 Sri Lankan immigrants annually. So, although Canada no longer denied entry to "undesirables," the racist structure of the immigration system remained: non-white countries had a quota, which kept Canadian immigration policy still sensitive to racial concerns.

Another example of Canada's race-based immigration policy was the 1952 Immigration Act. Section 61 still empowered government officials to reject immigrants on the basis of nationality, including ethnic background and country of origin. This act maintained the premise that admission to Canada was a privilege rather than a right and that Canadian labour needs should dictate immigration levels. However, one important aspect of the legislation allowed those who did meet the immigration standards to sponsor family members or dependants. Thus, although it did allow some larger scale immigration, and Canada began to accept "previously undesired" groups such as Italians and Greeks (who were coming largely to fill labour demands), the policy still remained race sensitive.

---

2   Irving Abella and Harold Troper, *None Is Too Many: Canada and the Jews of Europe, 1933–1948* (Toronto: University of Toronto Press, 2012).

By the late 1950s, the system was coming under severe criticism. When John Diefenbaker came to power in 1957, he was determined to change immigration policy. Diefenbaker, a strong supporter of individual rights and a descendant of German immigrants, felt strongly about the issue. Diefenbaker's time marked the beginning of the third, much less racist phase, which developed in five steps.

First, in 1962, Diefenbaker's government amended the Immigration Act to end overt discrimination based on race. From then on, Canada would not have quotas based on the origin of a person; immigrants still had to meet economic, health, and legal standards. Though still somewhat restrictive, the system was a step forward in ending the race-based policy that had marked the Canadian approach to immigration for nearly a century.

Second, this non-discriminatory policy was continued by Lester B. Pearson's Liberal government in 1967. The Liberals introduced a new "objective" points system allowing anyone to apply to Canada, regardless of race. The points system established five long-term criteria, including the applicant's personal qualities, education and training, age, skills, and the occupational demand for these skills. Four short-term criteria also helped to satisfy immigration officials of the applicant's suitability to Canada. These included arranged employment, knowledge of English or French, the presence of a relative in Canada, and the general status of Canadian employment opportunities. The nine factors could total a maximum of 100 points, and each independent applicant required 50 points to be accepted into Canada. This 1967 revision remains the basis of Canada's independent immigration system.

Third, along with the sponsorship and points system, Canadians developed a response in the 1960s to the question of refugees. Canada had some experience dealing with the issue of DPs in the 1940s and 1950s, but, by the 1960s, the country was trying to develop a policy that made a distinction between those with economic needs and those forced from a country because of persecution, be it political, religious, or of any other type. As part of this, Canada accepted groups of refugees in the postwar period. Some came as Cold War political refugees. Canada accepted some 37,000 Hungarian refugees fleeing Soviet repression in 1956; and about 12,000 Czechoslovakians came to Canada following their failed revolution in 1968.

Canada signed the United Nations Convention Relating to the Status of Refugees and its 1967 Protocol in 1969. By the 1970s, Canadians accepted numerous refugee groups, including Tibetans and Ugandans, who fled political turmoil in their countries in the early 1970s, and the Vietnamese "Boat People" after 1975. Of course, there is still great debate in Canada about refugees and Canadian refugee policy, as can be seen in the heated discussions over the Chinese refugees who came to BC in boats in the late 1990s.

Fourth, in 1976 Pierre Trudeau's government revised the Immigration Act. It maintained the "points system" and Canada's labour needs as the basis for selecting "independent immigrants," but it placed many categories of immigrants outside of these qualification standards. The act not only advocated a broad basis of selection but established an appeals procedure for those denied entry. Designed to ensure a less race-based, more "fair" immigration system, it still reflected economic needs. For instance, in the 1970s, West Indies women were brought to Canada to fill perceived employment needs in domestic service and nursing.

Fifth and finally, in 1986, Brian Mulroney's government created the entrepreneur class. If an individual wished to come to Canada and invest $250,000, he or she could achieve speedy access to immigration and visas. This step was in part a response to the uncertainty surrounding the handover of Hong Kong by the British to the Chinese in 1997.

Currently, the types of immigration allowed by the Canadian government include independent (points system), including various work programs; family assisted; and refugee (the entrepreneur class was discontinued in 2014). Canada is a nation of immigrants and has accepted, on average, over 200,000 immigrants and refugees a year in the 1990s and 2000s.

From Justice Major's Opening Remarks, June 17, 2010

[T]his Commission believes that there would be great merit in a demonstration of solicitude by the present Government for the families of the victims of the bombing. To this end, we propose the creation of an independent body to "recommend an appropriate ex gratia payment and to oversee its distribution."

The families, in some ways, have often been treated as adversaries, as if they had somehow brought this calamity upon themselves. This goes against the Canadian sense of fairness and propriety. Our report sets out the inherent injustice of what has transpired in terms of the treatment of the families of the victims to date at the hands of previous Governments. The time to right that historical wrong is now.

Multiculturalism in Canada

Immigration in the twentieth century cannot be discussed without addressing the issue of multiculturalism. But multiculturalism itself is a multidimensional and amorphous concept. What exactly is multiculturalism? Let's remember that Canada has always been multicultural. A diversity of First Nations groups existed long before whites ever appeared in North America. In the colonial period, Canada was made up of French, English, Irish, Scottish, and a host of other ethnicities and nationalities. This diversity increased in the nineteenth century, with the great immigration boom of the Laurier period, and again in the post–Second World War period.

Multiculturalism itself exists on different levels: as an official policy, in Canadians' daily existence, and in the past. An official dictionary definition is "the promotion of both cultural differences and social equality as an important aspect of society," though Canadians themselves no doubt have their own experience and definitions of what constitutes multiculturalism.

Of course, different factors help to create Canada as a multicultural society, and multiculturalism has both formal and informal aspects. Factors helping to create a multicultural society include the existence of aboriginal peoples and founding groups, immigration, and cultural communities. Informal aspects of multiculturalism (and ethnicity) include the family, racial and physical traits, language, music, food, and sports. Formal aspects of multiculturalism include ethnic associations, media (e.g., news and broadcast outlets that are language based), education and schools (again, based on language and sometimes religion), businesses (ethnic businesses such as restaurants, law firms, doctors), arts (exhibitions, dance, theatre), and churches, which have a major role in maintaining cultural identity.

What is different about Canada is the emphasis placed on creating laws that maintain the notion that Canada is a multicultural society. "Official multiculturalism" is a central aspect of the ethnic experience in Canada and emerged, starting in the late 1960s, through five important developments.

First, official multiculturalism actually emerged out of the conflict between Canada's French and English. Ukrainian and other groups challenged the Royal Commission on Bilingualism and Biculturalism (established in 1963) and its bicultural definition of Canada and demanded access to the commission. They argued that Canada must recognize more than just "two founding nations," an important moment for non-French and non-English "group rights" in Canada. This broadening appealed to Pierre Trudeau, often considered one of the main instigators of official multiculturalism: multiculturalism challenged the notion of Quebec's special status, encouraged and emphasized individual rights and equality rights, and reflected Canada's bilingual and multicultural reality.

As a result, in 1971, Trudeau's government created an official multiculturalism policy within a bilingual framework. Further, in 1972, Ottawa established a Multiculturalism Directorate within the Department of the Secretary of State; for the first time, there was a minister of state for multiculturalism.

A third step was the 1977 establishment of the Canadian Human Rights Act. This legislation prohibited discrimination on various grounds, including race, national or ethnic origin, colour, religion, or sex. Thus, law protected the concept of equality for all ethnic groups and cultures in Canadian society, and one could not discriminate against visible minorities.

Fourth, perhaps the greatest single recognition of multiculturalism came in 1982 with the enactment of the Canadian Charter of Rights and Freedoms. This document was probably Trudeau's greatest achievement and is foundational for

Canada as a multicultural society. Canada was the first country in the world to enshrine multiculturalism as a constitutional aspect of the country.

A fifth and final step was the 1988 Canadian Multiculturalism Act, passed by Progressive Conservative Brian Mulroney. No legislation existed that explained how multiculturalism actually worked as the law of the land. The 1988 act established the basic principles that multiculturalism is a central feature of Canadian citizenship; that every Canadian has the freedom to choose to enjoy, enhance, or share his or her heritage; and that the federal government has the responsibility to promote multiculturalism throughout its departments and agencies.

Challenges to Immigration and Multiculturalism

Since the 1960s, a number of people have criticized both multiculturalism policy and increased immigration to Canada. These criticisms have been developed by politicians and pundits and by immigrants themselves and became heightened after the Air India disaster and, especially, after 9/11. Some contemporary arguments against immigration are seemingly timeless: they were made in the 1950s and even the 1850s. They include complaints that immigration will "increase unemployment," will result in "a drain on the welfare system," will allow "undeserving refugees into Canada," and will lead to "ethnic conflict." This last point became particularly salient after the Air India disaster.

Many of the arguments against multiculturalism have also been made for decades. Multiculturalism's critics accuse the policy of creating a nation of non-Canadians or of immigrant "special interest groups." They see multiculturalism as fragmenting Canadian society and as placing ethnic groups outside of "the mainstream," or they argue that larger ethnic groups will dominate, getting more power within the multicultural universe and hierarchy. Some critics have pointed to official multiculturalism's creation during the rise of Quebec nationalism as a federalist attempt to undermine Quebec's unique position and an attack on the concept of two founding nations. First Nations groups have also critiqued multiculturalism for its insensitivity in considering aboriginals just another "ethnic group."

Finally, since September 11, a backlash against multiculturalism accuses the policy of being too "permissive" in society, of allowing the kind of "ghettoization" and separation of various cultural groups from Canadian society as a whole—a circumstance that, it is argued, led to the Air India terrorist attacks.

These arguments largely do not hold up to scrutiny. In terms of economic impact and population growth, immigration has been an unquestionable economic boon to Canada; without immigration, Canada's natural growth rate would be negative. Moreover, the benefits of multiculturalism—which brings a diversity of cultures and ideas to Canada, allows Canadians to share cultural experiences, and actually maintains race relations—far outweigh the actions of a few misguided individuals such as the Air India bombers.

Nonetheless, multiculturalism has come under attack especially since the 1980s, punctuated by a few high-profile incidents that reflect the limits of Canadians' tolerance. In 1990, many Canadians were outraged by the accommodation provided to a Sikh in the RCMP, who, after a fight, was allowed to wear a ceremonial turban in place of a traditional Mountie Stetson. More recently, Quebec has grappled with the question of "reasonable accommodation," sparked by concern over the wearing of traditional *burkhas* by female adherents of Islam.

These issues, and the initial confusion surrounding the citizenship of the Air India victims, points to an ongoing question about citizenship and identity in Canada: what does it mean to be Canadian?

Conclusion

Violence, even terror, has been a part of the Canadian landscape since the country's very founding in 1867. Immigration has regularly sparked a backlash against many groups of newly arrived Canadians, especially those of non-white ethnicities or those whose experiences were shaped by particular political or economic circumstances. From the 1840s onwards, many Irish immigrants faced discrimination; during the Fenian Raids, suspected Irish nationalists were profiled. During the First World War, Germans and Italians faced harassment and detention. Japanese Canadians during the Second World War were forcibly removed from their homes and interned across the country. In the 1970s and 1980s, many South Asian immigrants faced discrimination and prejudice. In the 2000s, Middle Eastern Canadians faced suspicion and scrutiny following the 9/11 attacks.

Indeed, despite Canada's immigration record, overall, there have been many instances of exclusion, racism, and discrimination. In the case of the Air India disaster, another kind of discrimination was visited upon the families of the victims; they were rendered invisible by a largely white Canadian society that refused to see them as fellow Canadians and fellow citizens. More than anything, this fact points to the ongoing discussion and debate of what factors constitute Canadian identity and Canadian values—of what it means to be a Canadian. This matter will continue to play a role in the Canadian discourse into the twenty-first century.

Further Reading
Bannerji, Himani. *On the Dark Side of the Nation: Essays on Multiculturalism, Nationalism and Gender.* Toronto: Canadian Scholars' Press, 2000.
Bohaker, Heidi, and Franca Iacovetta. "Making Aboriginal People 'Immigrants Too': A Comparison of Citizenship Programs for Newcomers and Indigenous Peoples in Postwar Canada, 1940s–1960s." *Canadian Historical*

Review 90, no. 3 (September 2009): 427–62. http://dx.doi.org/10.3138/ chr.90.3.427.

Commission of Inquiry into the Investigation of the Bombing of Air India Flight 182. *Air India Flight 182: A Canadian Tragedy*. Ottawa: Public Works and Government Services Canada, 2010. http://epe.lac-bac.gc.ca/ 100/206/301/pco-bcp/commissions/air_india/2010-07-23/www.major comm.ca/en/default.htm.

Iacovetta, Franca. *Gatekeepers: Reshaping Immigrant Lives in Cold War Canada*. Toronto: Between the Lines Press, 2006.

Lee, Carol F. "The Road to Enfranchisement: Chinese and Japanese in British Columbia." *BC Studies* 30 (Summer 1976): 44–76.

Mina, Noula. "Taming and Training Greek 'Peasant Girls' and the Gendered Politics of Whiteness in Postwar Canada: Canadian Bureaucrats and Immigrant Domestics, 1950s–1960s." *Canadian Historical Review* 94, no. 4 (December 2013): 514–39. http://dx.doi.org/10.3138/chr.1177.

Walker, Barrington, ed. *The History of Immigration and Racism in Canada: Essential Readings*. Toronto: Canadian Scholars' Press, 2008.

ACTIVE HISTORY: QUESTIONS TO CONSIDER

1. Examine the 2010 final report of the Commission of Inquiry into the Investigation of the Bombing of Air India Flight 182. Peruse any sections that you think are relevant.

2. What were the inquiry's key findings? How did the previous investigations fail in fulfilling their task?

3. What are, in your view, the benefits of immigration and multiculturalism? What are the challenges? What can the story of Air India Flight 182 tell us about both the benefits and challenges of immigration?

4. How have conceptions of citizenship changed in Canada since the mid-twentieth century? How do citizenship, immigration, and identity coexist in Canada?

TRAGIC TALES
AMANDA TODD AND REHTAEH PARSONS, SUICIDE, 2012 AND 2013

Bullying and the Internet

In the twenty-first century, Canadians have embraced the Internet. Indeed, the Internet has fundamentally transformed so many aspects of life, from commerce to music to travel to education and many things in between. It has truly wrought a communications, information, and technology revolution, akin to those occasioned by the printing press, the telegraph, the automobile, the telephone, or the television in its scope. Young Canadians, in particular, cannot imagine an existence without the always-present online world, one made even more accessible by the proliferation of devices from laptops to smartphones to tablets.

They especially see social media as central. Facebook, Twitter, Instagram, and a host of other social networking tools have allowed Canadians to project their "virtual selves" to huge groups and networks of people, friends and strangers alike. Social media technology has been a wonderful thing for many Canadians, as they have been able to make and maintain friendships, keep in touch with relatives, tell the world important and good news (and sometimes not so good news), and express themselves.

Yet social media and the Internet can have a dark side. Two cases, from opposite sides of the country, show that the Internet has enabled forms of cyberbullying as vicious as it is tragic in its consequences. Both cases involve young women, and both illustrate the perils of social media and of unlimited communication via the Internet more generally.

In 2012, Amanda Todd, a young woman from Port Coquitlam, British Columbia, hanged herself in her family home. In 2007, Todd,

then in seventh grade, had joined a chat room. One of the participants convinced her to expose herself, and naked images of Todd soon surfaced online and were quickly circulated. The images led to four years of harassment and cyberbullying, and, despite twice changing schools, Todd could not leave the incident behind. The harsh treatment persisted, both online and in the real world.

As the bullying continued and her mental and physical health deteriorated, Todd posted an online video to YouTube, "My Story: Struggling, bullying, suicide, self harm," in which she used cue cards to tell her story and the horrible experiences she had faced. The video itself quickly went viral. In the end, it did not help Todd overcome the bullying she faced; just over a month after posting the video, she killed herself. She was 15 years old.

In 2011, Rehtaeh Parsons, a 15-year-old student from Dartmouth, Nova Scotia, went to a party. At the party, Parsons was allegedly raped by four boys. During the incident, a photograph was taken of her that was later circulated online by the alleged perpetrators. The photo led to Parsons's harassment, taunting, and bullying by schoolmates. An investigation of the incident resulted in no charges for sexual assault being laid, despite the photographic evidence (child pornography charges were eventually laid against two of the alleged perpetrators; both pled guilty). In 2013, Parsons could no longer cope with the bullying, and, like Todd, attempted suicide by hanging herself in her parents' home. Four days later, her parents made the tragic and painful decision to take her off life support. She was 17 years old.

Bullying has always existed; it's a problem that communities, educators, and social services have long tried to stop. But the suicides of Todd and Parsons show that bullying still exists despite efforts (as Prime Minister Harper told Canadians in 2013 in reaction to Parsons's death) to start calling bullying by its real name: criminal activity. When bullying is coupled with the Internet, it can take on particularly virulent and, ultimately, tragic forms. New laws criminalizing cyberbullying have been called for, yet legislation is only effective if it is enforced properly and if community values reflect those laws. Though two young women are dead, the justice system has been unable to bring those responsible to account for their actions.

Not surprisingly, given the pervasiveness of our digital culture, the consequences and legacy of the suicides of both these young women can be seen online. Amanda Todd's family created a Facebook page as a memorial and directs people to donate to the Amanda Todd Foundation that raises awareness about online bullying. Similarly, the Parsons family created an "Angel Rehtaeh" memorial page on Facebook. In both instances, the Internet activist group Anonymous ("hactivists") threatened to expose, in the case of Todd, the identity of the person who circulated the pictures and, in the case of Parsons, the identities of the alleged rapists, leaving them open to vigilante justice.

The Internet has created a brave new online world. Though this technology provides a seemingly unlimited potential to change people's lives for the better, it has also provided a new and expanded forum for some of humanity's worst behaviour, such as bullying.

CONCLUSION: CANADA, A NATION OF HOPE

Though death stalked the peaceable kingdom long before the idea of Canada as a nation-state even emerged, it remains a hopeful place. Despite all the conflagrations, clashes, and conflicts, despite all the murders, executions, assassinations, and suicides, Canada remains a magnet for many people around the world. That waves of immigrants continue to come to this country, notwithstanding the oftentimes horrible treatment some of them receive when they arrive, testifies to the enduring attractiveness of Canada. Though a sometimes violent place with a long litany of injustices and brutalities committed against some of its own people, Canada remains, on the global scale, a relatively safe haven and an increasingly open and tolerant society. Canada is, in many ways, indeed a peaceable kingdom.

This is not to say that the country and its peoples do not face challenges in the future, challenges and issues that may themselves, in time, spark new violence. Many of these issues are as old as the country itself, if not older, and many of them are emerging. Be it aboriginal–white relations, French–English relations, gender relations, or matters of class, politics, immigration, or the environment, Canadians continue to grapple with these issues. At times, progress is slow and hard to grasp, given the sometimes brutal actions of institutions, governments, corporations, and of ordinary people toward one another. But, in other instances, the promise of Canada, the hope that it will become, in the words of Thomas D'Arcy McGee, a "new nationality" where people of different religions, languages, and backgrounds prosper together, remains possible.

There are other hopeful signs as well. Despite the violence, there has been cooperation, consultation, and a slow recognition that Canadians need to work together on so many of these issues. Most times, violence is avoided, and Canadians have resolved many of the issues they have faced without resorting to aggression or tragedy.

Thus, while this book is about death, I hope it leaves the reader with a more positive outlook than might be imagined. Though there has been much death in the peaceable kingdom, Canada remains a nation of hope.

INDEX

Aberhart, William "Bible Bill," 142–143
abolitionism, 39
aboriginal peoples and populations.
    See also First Nations; Inuit; Métis
    assimilation, 50, 278, 281, 282
    in Constitution and Charter, 281
    dependency on government, 278–279
    displacement, 276–277, 285
    equal rights, 279–281
    government policy, 277, 278
    land claims and resource development,
        282–283, 284
    law and legislation, 129–130
    native rights (*See* native rights)
    occupation of land, 277
    and politics, 200, 280–282
    population, 278
    race relationships, 279–280
    residential schools, 206–207
    resistance and activism, 276–277, 279–285
        (*See also* Red River, MB, and resistance)
    self-government, 130
    as soldiers, 279
    status system, 278, 279, 281
    treaties, 57
    treatment in North-West Canada, 49–50,
        54, 57–58
    and westward expansion, 23–24, 25, 38
    women, 281
abortion, 270–271
Acadia, minority schooling, 59
Act of Union (1840), 9
Africville, NS, 231
agriculture. *See* farms and farmers
Air India Flight 182, 289–293, 297
air travel, attacks and terrorism, 193–194,
    289–293
airplanes and air raids, in wars, 72, 155–156
Alaska, boundary, 43

Alberta, 120–121, 142–143
alcohol, 39, 120–121, 125
Algonquin Park, ON, 105–106, 108, 111
Almasy, Peter, 224–225
amending formula, for Constitution, 240, 241,
    242–243, 244
American Federation of Labor (AFL),
    94–95, 96
American Indian Movement (AIM), 283
annexationist movement, 10
Anishnabek Nation, 276–277
Anti-Confederation League, 20–21
army (Canadian army), 262–263, 277, 279,
    285. *See also* Great War; Second World
    War
Arone, Shidane, 262–263
art, 110–112, 211
Asians, immigration, 64–65, 295
Assembly of First Nations (AFN), 281
assimilation of aboriginal peoples, 50, 278,
    281, 282
assisted suicide, 287–288
Atlantic provinces, 13, 21, 59, 132.
    See also specific province
atomic bomb, 186, 191–192, 200
automobiles. *See* cars

baby boom, 170–172
Balfour Declaration (1926), 118
baseball, in 1920s, 114–115
Batoche, SK, 48
Battle of Britain, 155
Battle of Duck Lake, 48
Battle of the Atlantic, 157
Bennett, George, 33–34
Bennett, Richard Bedford, 115, 141–142, 145,
    148
Berger, Thomas, and Berger Report, 282–283
Big Bear, 50, 57